D0208045

# DICTIONARY OF THE BLACK THEATRE

# DICTIONARY OF THE BLACK THEATRE

## BROADWAY, OFF-BROADWAY, AND SELECTED HARLEM THEATRE

**Allen Woll**

**Greenwood Press**
Westport, Connecticut • London, England

**Library of Congress Cataloging in Publication Data**

Woll, Allen L.
Dictionary of the Black theatre.

Bibliography: p.
Includes index.
1. Afro-American theater—New York (N.Y.)—Dictionaries. I. Title.
PN2270.A35W64 1983 792'.08996073 82-21090
ISBN 0-313-22561-3 (lib. bdg.)



Library of Congress Catalog Card Number: 82-21090
ISBN: 0-313-22561-3

First published in 1983

Greenwood Press
A division of Congressional Information Service, Inc.
88 Post Road West
Westport, Connecticut 06881

Printed in the United States of America

10 9 8 7 6 5 4 3 2 1

To my parents

# CONTENTS

# PREFACE

Douglas Turner Ward, director of the Negro Ensemble Company, recently admitted the difficulty of defining the concept of "black theatre." He ultimately concluded that the black theatre is "by, about, with, for and related to blacks," but it need not include every one of these characteristics.[1]

Although, at first glance, this may seem an extremely broad definition, it is certainly appropriate when considering the history of black participation in the American theatre in the twentieth century. Most of the plays performed by black actors between 1917 and 1940 were written by white authors. Conversely, black authors have written plays for white casts from Will Marion Cook's *The Southerners* (1904) to Lorraine Hansberry's *The Sign in Sidney Brustein's Window* (1964). Similarly, many plays concerning problems of interest to blacks have been written by whites, and performed by predominantly white casts, such as *Deep Are the Roots* (1945).

*Dictionary of the Black Theatre* adopts Ward's wide-ranging definition of the phenomenon of black theatre. This work includes references to Broadway, Off-Broadway, and selected Harlem plays that are "by, about, with, for and related to blacks," from 1898 to 1981. To be sure, this does not encompass the entire range of black theatre in America.[2] Additional reference works are needed in the future to detail the lengthy and rich history of the Harlem theatre, as well as the important contributions of the regional theatre to the Black Theatre Movement.

Part I of this work documents more than three hundred shows from 1898, the date of the first black musical comedy (*A Trip to Coontown*) to December 1981 (*Dreamgirls*). Following the title of each show, its theatre, opening date, and number of performances are given (n.a.p. indicates that the number is not available). The creative personnel (producer, author, director, composer, and lyricist), the cast credits (with characters portrayed in parentheses), and finally the show's songs follow.[3] Presentations of a group of one-act plays are discussed under the collective title, with individual playlets following. Each entry concludes with a plot summary, a survey of critical comment, and an analysis of the historical context of important shows. Asterisks refer the reader to separate entries on other plays or to biographical entries in Part II.

Since many of the shows of the early part of this century have not left scripts, it is necessary to rely on critical commentary for plot summaries and production details. Unfortunately, this approach entails certain problems. White critics for major newspapers have often been hostile to the aspirations of black theatre artists. While this attitude has been demonstrated throughout the century, it was most evident in the 1920s and the 1960s. In the 1920s, critics rewarded black shows that tended to follow the pattern of the hit musical *Shuffle Along* (1921). Created by blacks, *Shuffle Along* tended to support white images of black behavior and entertainment. Any show that deviated from this model and attempted to create a new image of a black show was often harshly criticized. For example, when *Put and Take* opened three months after *Shuffle Along*, *Variety*'s critic commented: "Colored performers cannot vie with white ones, and colored producers cannot play within an apple's throw of Ziegfeld and try to compete with him. . . . Here the colored folks seem to have set out to show whites that they are just as good as anybody. They may be as good, but they're different, and, in their entertainment they should remain different, distinct, and indigenous."[4] Hence, experimentation was often discouraged, while shows that followed patterns set by the minstrel stage were often viewed favorably.

Similar problems emerged in the late 1960s and early 1970s. As black theatre became politicized and attacked the white establishment, threatened critics reacted in a harsh and hostile fashion. This hostility is particularly evident in the reaction to the early plays of LeRoi Jones, such as *Dutchman* and *The Toilet*.

In order to counteract this bias, black critical commentary is utilized to provide a balanced judgment of the shows described in this dictionary. Nevertheless, theatre audiences rarely made such comparisons, and the comments of white critics almost always dictated the success or failure of plays performed by blacks. Only in the mid-1970s has this dominance been slightly weakened.

Excerpts from newspaper reviews have been selected from opening night notices which typically appear the following day. Magazine reviews usually appear in the weekly edition following the premiere. Therefore, dates for these review excerpts are not given in the text. If an excerpt is from a review or critical commentary that appeared at a later date, the publication information follows the quote in brackets.

Part II of *Dictionary of the Black Theatre* includes biographical entries of major performers, writers, and directors and notes on major organizations that have encouraged the black theatre in New York City in the twentieth century. Several of the essays on major figures have been contributed by guest scholars. The name of the contributor follows each entry.

Following each entry is a listing of credits for all individuals whose complete credits are not mentioned in the text. The credits listing for actors includes all New York City performances which they originated. Replacement roles or understudy parts are not included unless they are of major importance to the individual's career. Similarly, the credits listing for directors includes only New York City performances. Whenever an actor appears in several shows in a particular year, the production date follows *only the last* show in the series. The entry concludes with a listing of suggested references concerning the topic.

*Dictionary of the Black Theatre* contains three appendices: a chronology of shows discussed in the text; a discography of recordings of black shows; and a selected bibliography of studies relating to black theatre history and criticism.

I would like to thank the staffs of the various libraries that were consulted in the preparation of this book. The excellent Theatre Collection of the Free Library of Philadelphia [PFL/TC] provided ample information for this work. The Theatre Collection of the New York Public Library at Lincoln Center [NYPL/TC] and the Museum of the City of New York supplied clippings files and programs for early black musicals and dramas. The Music Collection of the Library of Congress and the Schomburg Center for Research in Black Culture offered scripts and data on several of the shows discussed herein. Finally, the staff of the Rutgers University Library at Camden, New Jersey, graciously assisted me in the search for obscure bits of information. The expertise of all the librarians in these facilities hastened the successful completion of this book.

## NOTES

1. *The New York Times*, August 31, 1980, II, 17.

2. Foreign imports performed by foreign companies, operas, dance performances, and one-man or one-woman shows of a concert nature (for example, *An Evening with Diana Ross* [1976]) are excluded from this text. Revivals of classic plays with black casts, such as *The Cherry Orchard* (1973) and *Mother Courage* (1980), are not included in the first section of this book, but are listed in the actors' or directors' credits in the second part. Revivals of plays with a black theme, such as *Take a Giant Step* (1956) or *Cabin in the Sky* (1964), are noted in discussions of individual plays in the first part of this work.

3. The credits for early black shows are often plagued by erratic spelling. Ada Overton Walker was often listed as Aida; Elizabeth Welsh finished her career as Elisabeth Welch; and Adelaide Hall occasionally appeared as Adalade. I have chosen to list these names as they appeared in the original programs with correct or alternate spellings following in parentheses.

Similar instances may be noted in modern times, as actor Douglas Turner becomes Douglas Turner Ward, the director. Actor Sonny Jim follows suit and becomes J. E. Gaines, the writer. Perhaps the most noteworthy name change among modern black playwrights is the change from LeRoi Jones to Imamu Amiri Baraka. Again, alternate versions of names are provided in parentheses.

4. *Variety*, August 26, 1921, p. 17.

# INTRODUCTION: A BRIEF HISTORY OF THE BLACK THEATRE

Broadway's first introduction to the black theatre came with two musicals in 1898. *A Trip to Coontown* by Bob Cole and Billy Johnson and *Clorindy, the Origin of the Cakewalk* by Will Marion Cook and Paul Laurence Dunbar set the tone for black theatrical performances for the first decade of this century. These musical comedies marked a slight advance over the minstrel shows of an earlier age. While they retained several of the stereotyped notions of black behavior from the minstrel stage, they also began to widen the spectrum of black entertainment. Although accepted cautiously at first, the black musical soon became a Broadway staple. With such presentations as *In Dahomey* (1903), *Abyssinia* (1906), *The Oyster Man*, *The Shoo-Fly Regiment* (1907), and *The Red Moon* (1909), Broadway audiences were introduced to the top black performers of the age: Bob Cole, Bert Williams, George Walker, J. Rosamond Johnson, and Ernest Hogan.

The growing popularity of these black musical productions was halted abruptly by 1910, as death and illness stalked the major talents of these shows. With the deaths of Cole, Walker, and Hogan, the black theatre experienced a major setback. Only Bert Williams remained, but he accepted a Flo Ziegfeld offer to join the ever popular *Follies* as a headliner. Thus, the black theatre remained without its major innovators and organizers as the second decade of the century began.

James Weldon Johnson, a noted lyricist for several early black musicals, called this period "the term of exile" in his classic study of black culture in New York City, *Black Manhattan* (1930). Exile might be too strong a word. Although black theatre virtually vanished from Broadway from 1910 to 1917, it flourished in Harlem with such groups as the Lafayette Players. Here black performers were no longer limited to musical shows (although they remained popular), as they experimented with serious dramas and classic revivals. The budding Harlem theatre gave blacks a greater latitude in performing roles than had been allowed in the earlier decade. Ironically, Broadway audiences began to travel to Harlem to enjoy a form of theatre that was no longer available on the Great White Way. Even Flo Ziegfeld purchased segments of Harlem revues for inclusion in his *Follies* productions.

Black shows returned to Broadway in great numbers after the surprising triumph of *Shuffle Along* (1921) by Eubie Blake, Noble Sissle, Flournoy Miller, and Aubrey Lyles, which ran 504 performances. This fast-paced musical comedy provided several song hits, breathless choreography, and physical comedy which impressed both critics and audiences. Its success legitimized the black musical on Broadway, and a torrent of imitators followed. Some maintained *Shuffle Along*'s high quality (such as *Runnin' Wild* [1923] and *Blackbirds of 1928*), while others attempted to cash in on this new interest in black shows. As these entertainments became increasingly profitable, whites gradually replaced blacks in the creative and financial areas of production. While blacks remained onstage in these revues of the late 1920s, they slowly disappeared from behind the scenes. Nevertheless, these musicals introduced Broadway audiences to some of the major talents of the age—Florence Mills, Bill Robinson, Adelaide Hall, Paul Robeson, Josephine Baker, and Ethel Waters.

The success of the black musical in the 1920s helped to open the door for dramatic plays performed by blacks (but almost always written by whites). These plays usually concerned such themes as poverty and miscegenation, but black superstition and mythology remained of major interest to white playwrights. Several of these shows received favorable notices and major awards, such as *In Abraham's Bosom* (1926), *Porgy* (1927), and *The Green Pastures* (1930). Although these plays by white authors appear racist by modern standards, James Weldon Johnson argued that they served the function of convincing Broadway theatre critics and audiences that blacks could perform dramatic roles with "thoughtful interpretation and intelligent skill." While black writers of musical comedies managed to share in the 1920s boom in black theatre, black dramatists generally missed out. Only Garland Anderson's *Appearances* (1925), Frank Wilson's *Meek Mose* (1928), and Wallace Thurman's *Harlem* (1929) received productions during the 1920s.

Broadway reeled with the Great Depression, and black performers and playwrights suffered far more than whites. Part of the problem stemmed from the refusal of producers to look for new directions for black shows as third-rate imitations of *Shuffle Along* and *The Green Pastures* proliferated. While a few of these productions received favorable reviews, most disappeared within the week. The notable exceptions were the Gershwins' *Porgy and Bess* (1935) and Langston Hughes's *Mulatto* (1935). Hughes's play established a long-run record for a black playwright that would not be broken until 1959 by *A Raisin in the Sun*.

While black playwrights and performers fared poorly in the commercial theatre of the 1930s, many received work with the Federal Theatre Project (FTP). This Works Progress Administration (WPA) effort provided jobs for black actors and playwrights by sponsoring such plays as *Walk Together Chillun*, *Conjur Man Dies*, and *Turpentine* in 1936, and *The Case of Philip*

*Lawrence, Swing It*, and *The Trial of Dr. Beck* in 1937 for brief New York runs. The FTP sponsored black theatre not only in New York, but throughout the rest of the United States as well.

Black theatre (like the rest of the American economy) seemed to revive during the war years. Although a majority of the Broadway shows performed by blacks were still written by whites, Richard Wright received rave reviews for his adaptation (with Paul Green) of his novel *Native Son* in 1941. While Broadway revelled in such musicals as *The Hot Mikado, Swing Mikado, Swingin' the Dream* (1939), *Cabin in the Sky* (1940), and *Carmen Jones* (1944), black dramas flourished in Harlem with the formation of the American Negro Theatre (ANT). The ANT provided experience for writers, actors, directors, stage managers, and the like during the 1940s. Some of its productions received Broadway runs, the most notable being the long-run comedy *Anna Lucasta* in 1944.

The number of shows performed by blacks declined greatly in the post-war era. To a certain extent this phenomenon marked the growing integration of the Broadway theatre, as black performers began to appear in plays and musicals that might have previously had all-white casts. Serious dramas began to tackle the real problems of black life in America. Gone were the mythical fancies of *The Green Pastures*, as new shows (*Deep Are the Roots* [1945], *On Whitman Avenue* [1946], *Set My People Free* [1948], and *Mister Johnson* [1956]) tentatively broached the problems of racism. Black authors contributed to this reevaluation of American life with such works as *Our Lan'* (1947), *Take a Giant Step* (1953), *Trouble in Mind* (1955), and *A Land Beyond the River* (1957).

*A Raisin in the Sun* (1959) marked the culmination of this trend, as well as the beginning of a new era. Lorraine Hansberry's drama of a black family from Chicago that wants to move to the suburbs despite white opposition won the New York Drama Critics Circle Award for Best Play. The critical acclaim and audience acceptance of this long-run hit opened the doors for new black plays of a serious nature.

Black theatre flourished during the 1960s. The acceleration in the civil rights movement during this decade increased the intensity of the political message of plays written by blacks. It was in this atmosphere that the work of LeRoi Jones (Imamu Amiri Baraka) began to pass into the mainstream. The 1960s black theatre also revealed a new interest in black history and culture. The roots of black music were explored in *Black Nativity* (1961), *Tambourines to Glory*, and *Trumpets of the Lord* (1963), while *In White America* (1963) and *A Hand Is on the Gate* (1966) explored the history of race relations in the United States.

New producing organizations encouraged the growth of black theatre in the late 1960s. The Negro Ensemble Company, the New Lafayette Theatre, and the New Federal Theatre, all directed by black artists, sponsored the early works of such talents as Ed Bullins, Charles Fuller, Samm-Art Williams, Phillip Hayes Dean, Ron Milner, and Joseph A. Walker. Joseph Papp's Public Theatre and the American Place Theatre also played a crucial role in developing black creative talent.

The themes of the 1960s tended to move from Off-Broadway to Broadway in the 1970s. As in the 1920s, musical comedies led the way, with audiences welcoming such revues as *Bubbling Brown Sugar* (1976), *Ain't Misbehavin'*, and *Eubie!* (1978). Yet, serious dramas also won critical recognition, such as *The River Niger* (1973), *For Colored Girls Who Have Considered Suicide/When the Rainbow Is Enuf* and *Eden* (1976), and *Home* (1980). It should be noted that these Broadway hits began in the Off-Broadway caldrons of the Negro Ensemble Company, the New Federal Theatre, and the Public Theatre.

Perhaps the major advance of the 1970s was the marked increase in the black audience in New York theatres. One of the ironies of black theatre history is that whites have traditionally composed a majority of the audience. Even as late as the 1920s (when black musicals and dramas flourished on Broadway), many theatres remained segregated, limiting blacks to the balcony or (in the case of *Shuffle Along*) separate sections of the orchestra. As late as the 1960s, producers still tended to ignore the potential of the black theatre audience. In the 1970s, however, such shows as *Ain't Supposed to Die a Natural Death* (1971) and *The Wiz* (1975) actively courted a black audience on Broadway, while the Negro Ensemble Company, the New Federal Theatre, and the New Lafayette Theatre attempted to do the same Off-Broadway and in Harlem.

As the 1980s begin, black theatre has become a vital and accepted part of the New York drama scene. While Lorraine Hansberry's winning of the New York Drama Critics Circle Award provoked surprise and comment, black writers and performers achieved major awards on a regular basis in the 1970s. By 1982, Charles Fuller's Pulitzer Prize for *A Soldier's Play* or the Tony Award sweep for *Dreamgirls* were accepted with an equanimity that would have been unexpected twenty years earlier.

# Part I:
# THE SHOWS

# A

**ABYSSINIA** (Majestic, February 20, 1906, 31 p.). Producers: Bert Williams* and George Walker.* Composer: Will Marion Cook.* Book and lyrics: J. A. Shipp and Alex Rogers.* Directors: "The Authors."

Cast: Bert Williams (Jasmine Jenkins), George Walker (Rastus Johnson), Chas. Moore (Elder Fowler), Lottie Williams (Miss Primly), Hattie McIntosh (Callie Parker), George Catlin (Wong Foo), Maggie Davis (Serena), R. Henri Strange (Menelik), J. A. Shipp (Tegulet), Alex Rogers (Bolasso), J. E. Lightfoot (Zamish), Wm. C. Elkins (Hadji), Clemo Harris (Lion), Annie Ross (Tai Tu), Aida Overton Walker* (Miram).

Songs: Janhoi; Jolly Jungle Boys; Ode to the Sun; Where My Forefathers Died; Twilight at Home Sweet Home; This Is Our Holiday; Marketplace Songs; Rastus Johnson, USA; It's Hard to Find a King Like Me; Answers You Don't Expect to Get; The Man with All the Money in the World; Here It Comes Again; Goodbye Ethiopia.

*Abyssinia* abandoned the comic approach to Africa of Williams's and Walker's earlier show, *In Dahomey** (1903). The Africans of *Abyssinia* were depicted as the representatives of an ancient and praiseworthy culture, while the Americans were the targets of humor. The reviews for *Abyssinia* were generally favorable, with all the critics praising the costumes and the spectacular scenery.

Mistaken identities plague the visit of Rastus Johnson (Walker) and Jasmine Jenkins (Williams) to Abyssinia. Ras is mistaken for a rebel chief, and Jas, trying to protect his friend from the officials, grabs a vase from a market stall. The official then charges Jas with theft and explains that the penalty for such a crime is the loss of the offending hand. This dilemma allows Williams to sing "Here It Comes Again." "It," of course, is the inevitable trouble that always follows the beleaguered Williams. The emperor's daughter reveals the misunderstanding, and Ras and Jas are freed. As they leave, they sing to their newfound friends: "We wish you success, may you ever progress—Ethiopia, good-bye."

**AFRICANA** (Daly, July 11, 1927, 72 p.). Producer, director, and author: Earl Dancer. Composer and lyricist: Donald Heywood.*

Cast: Ethel Waters,* Billy Mills, Henry Winifred, Margaret Beckett, Baby Goins, Mike Riely, Paul Bass, Al Winkins, Ed Pugh, Bobby Goins, Louis Douglas, Edna Barr, Taskiana Four, Eddie and Sunny.

Songs: Hey He, Hi, Ho; Lightning Steps; I'm Coming Virginia (Lyrics by Heywood and Will Marion Cook); I'm Satisfied; See Dan; Show Boat; Old Fashioned Minstrel; Mississippi Flood; A Step a Second; Clorinda; A Few Minutes of Melody; Harlem Breakdown; Banana Maidens; Walter Sings a Song; The Count and the Countess; Africana Stomp.

Ethel Waters, now billed as "the world's greatest colored comedienne," stopped the show nightly in *Africana.* This revue featured songs and comedy routines from Waters's many years on the road. *Variety* commented that "Ethel Waters is the kick of *Africana,*" and praised almost every song she performed, including such hits as "My Special Friend Is in Town," "Dinah," "Shake That Thing," "Take Your Black Bottom Outside," and "I'm Coming Virginia." *Time* followed suit, devoting half its review to Miss Waters's talents: "She uses a typical husky, soft voice to unusual advantage, employs mannerisms frankly and disarmingly Negroid, understands the art of 'living' her songs, so that they take on dramatic quality. In Harlem, she is queen. In Manhattan, she stopped the show."

*Africana,* a summer entry, quickly ran into difficulties as no backers could be found to finance a run during the fall season. After an abortive move to the National Theatre, *Africana* returned to the road and ultimately closed in Saint Louis.

**AFRICANA** (Venice, November 26, 1934, 3 p.). Producer: Perry-Wood. Author, composer and lyricist: Donald Heywood.* Additional lyrics: Abe Tuvim. Director: Peter Morell.

Cast: Jack Carr, Howard Gould, Joseph Byrd, Earl Carter, Olivette Miller, Walter Richardson, Nita Gale, Dan C. Michaels, Barrington Guy, Gretchen Branch.

Songs: Yamboo; Stop Beating Those Drums; No Peace in My Soul; Just a Promise.

Donald Heywood provided several songs for *Africana,** an Ethel Waters* vehicle of 1927, and had experienced some success. He utilized the earlier title again in 1934 for his new show, but there the similarity ended. Billed as a "Congo operetta," *Africana* was an ambitious study of cultural conflict between a traditional African king (Jack Carr) and his British-educated son. *The New York Times* praised Heywood's "good songs," including "Stop Beating Those Drums," "Just a Promise," and "No Peace in My Soul."

Unfortunately, a disastrous opening night irritated the critics and certainly influenced their opinions. As the overture began, a man in evening dress ran down the aisle and attacked the conductor with an iron bar. The audience at first assumed that Almany Dauoda Carmaro was part of the show, but when cast members came to the orchestra leader's aid, the seriousness of the situation was recognized. Carmaro claimed that he had planned *Africana* with Heywood and had received no credit. The judge later gave Carmaro a suspended sentence, but the damage was done as opening night was reduced to chaos. The second act began after 10:30, and many of the seats were empty by that time. As a result, the second *Africana* managed only a brief run.

**AIN'T MISBEHAVIN'** (Longacre, May 9, 1978, 1,604 p.). Producers: Emanuel Azenberg, Dasha Epstein, The Shubert Organization, Jane Gaynor, and Ron Dante. Idea: Murray Horwitz and Richard Maltby, Jr. Composer: Thomas "Fats" Waller.* Director: Richard Maltby, Jr.

Cast: Nell Carter,* Andre De Shields, Armelia McQueen, Ken Page, Charlaine Woodard.

Songs: Ain't Misbehavin' (Fats Waller-Harry Brooks-Andy Razaf*); Lookin' Good But Feelin' Bad (Waller-Lester A. Santly); Honeysuckle Rose (Waller-Razaf); Squeeze Me (Waller-Clarence Williams); Handful of Keys (Waller-Maltby-Horwitz); I've Got a Feeling I'm Falling (Waller-Harry Link-Billy Rose); The Jitterbug Waltz (Waller-Maltby); How Ya Baby (Waller-J. C. Johnson); The Ladies Who Sing with the Band (Waller-George Marion, Jr.); Yacht Club Swing (Waller-Herman Autrey-J. C. Johnson); When the Nylons Bloom Again (Waller-Marion); Cash for Your Trash (Waller-Ed Kirkeby); Off-Time (Waller-Brooks-Razaf); The Joint Is Jumping (Waller-Razaf-Johnson); Lounging at the Waldorf (Waller-Maltby); Keepin' Out of Mischief Now (Waller-Razaf); Find Out What They Like (Waller-Razaf); Black and Blue (Waller-Brooks-Razaf); 'T Ain't Nobody's Biz-ness If I Do (Porter Grainger-Everett Robbins); Spreadin' Rhythm Around (Jimmy McHugh-Ted Koehler); Mean to Me (Roy Turk-Fred Ahlert); Your Feet's Too Big (Ada Benson-Fred Fisher); That Ain't Right (Nat King Cole); Fat and Greasy (Grainger-Charlie Johnson); I'm Gonna Sit Right Down and Write Myself a Letter (Fred Ahlert-Joe Young); Two Sleepy People (Hoagy Carmichael-Frank Loesser); I've Got My Fingers Crossed (McHugh-Koehler); I Can't Give You Anything But Love (McHugh-Dorothy Fields); It's a Sin to Tell a Lie (Billy Mayhew).

*Ain't Misbehavin'*, conceived by Murray Horwitz and Richard Maltby, Jr., brought a cavalcade of Fats Waller songs to Broadway via the Manhattan Theatre Club. The Broadway version won three Tony Awards: "best musical," "best director of a musical" (Richard Maltby), and "best featured actress" (Nell Carter). The success of the show was based on the marvelous Waller music, but also on Maltby, choreographer Arthur Faria, and musical superviser Luther Henderson's attempts to evoke the eras of the 1930s and 1940s. The entire original cast has received great praise and has become involved with a variety of other theatre, film, and television projects. *Ain't Misbehavin'* has endured despite numerous cast changes during its lengthy run. The show helped to spark a revival of interest in Waller's music, and several of his long unavailable recordings have been reissued.

**AIN'T SUPPOSED TO DIE A NATURAL DEATH** (Barrymore, October 20, 1971, 325 p.). Producers: Eugene V. Wolsk, Charles Blackwell, Emanuel Azenberg, and Robert Malina. Book, music and lyrics: Melvin Van Peebles.* Director: Gilbert Moses.*

Cast: Dick Williams,* Gloria Edwards, Ralph Wilcox, Barbara Alston, Joe Fields, Marilyn B. Coleman, Arthur French, Carl Gordon, Madge Wells, Lauren Jones, Clebert Ford, Sati Jamal, Jimmy Hayeson, Toney Brealond, Beatrice Winde, Albert Hall, Garrett Morris, Bill Duke, Minnie Gentry.

Songs: Just Don't Make No Sense; Coolest Place in Town; You Can't Get Up Before Noon Without Being a Square; Come Raising Your Leg on Me; You Gotta Be Holdin' Out Five Dollars on Me; Sera Sera Jim; Catch That on the Corner; The Dozens; Funky Girl on Motherless Broadway; Tenth and Greenwich; Heh Heh Good Mornin' Sunshine; You Ain't No Astronaut; Three Boxes of Longs, Please; Lily Has Done the Zampoughi Every Time I Pulled Her Coattail; I Got the Blood; Salamaggis Birthday; Come on Feet, Do Your Thing; Put a Curse on You.

Melvin Van Peebles, known primarily for his films *Story of a Three-Day Pass*, *Watermelon Man*, and *Sweet Sweetback's Baadasssss Song*, brought two shows to Broadway during the 1971-1972 season. *Ain't Supposed to Die a Natural Death* opened the season, while *Don't Play Us Cheap!** closed it. Van Peebles's musical mosaic of ghetto life received mixed reviews. Clive Barnes professed to represent the views of white audiences: "Whites can only treat *Ain't Supposed to Die a Natural Death* as a journey to a foreign country, and on those terms it has the power to shock and excite. It is by no means a comfortable evening, and many Broadway theatregoers will not understand what it is saying." Clayton Riley, entertainment editor of *The Amsterdam News*, responded to Barnes with a black's view of the new play: "Playwright and composer Melvin Van Peebles has pulled these visions [of black life] together, set their flash to a very beautiful music and placed them onstage . . . in a dazzling theatrical experience." [*The New York Times*, November 7, 1971]

The show limped along as a result of the mixed reviews, but through discount tickets and a concerted effort to woo black audiences, it finally achieved a respectable run. Gilbert Moses received a Drama Desk Award for his direction, and Beatrice Winde received a Theatre World Award for her performance.

**AKOKAWE** (St. Marks, May 19, 1970, 44 p.). Producer: Negro Ensemble Company.* African writings selected by: Afolabi Ajayi. Director: Afolabi Ajayi.

Cast: Andre Womble, Norman Bush, Frances Foster,* Esther Rolle,* Clarice Taylor,* Allie Woods, Afolabi Ajayi, Amandina Lihamba, Paul Makgoba, Ifatumbo Oyebola, Babafemi Akinlana, Louis Espinosa.

*Akokawe* ("Initiation"), a joint effort of the Negro Ensemble Company (NEC) and the Mbari-Mbayo players, provided an evening of African drama, poetry, dance, and song. Selected by Nigerian actor Afolabi Ajayi, the vignettes focused on the conflict between African and European civilization in Act I, and the malaise felt by African expatriates in Act II. While NEC veterans Frances Foster, Esther Rolle, and Clarice Taylor received ample praise, critics took special notice of Tanzanian actress Amandina Lihamba. *Theatre Arts* claimed that "she combines over-all attractiveness with wide-eyed enthusiasm in a manner that rivets audience attention to her."

**ALL GOD'S CHILLUN GOT WINGS** (Provincetown, May 15, 1924, 43 p.). Producer: Provincetown Players. Author: Eugene O'Neill. Director: James Light.

Cast: Paul Robeson* (Jim Harris), Mary Blair (Ella Downey), Lillian Greene (Mrs. Harris), Dora Cole (Hattie), Charles Ellis (Shorty), Frank Wilson* (Joe), James Martin (Mickey), James Meighan (Organ Grinder), William Davis, Virginia Wilson, George Finley, Marvin Myrck, Jimmy Ward (Children).

While Broadway audiences willingly accepted the black musicals of the early 1920s, tempers flared when it was learned that Eugene O'Neill's new play would feature "a Negro . . . in the male part and a white actress . . . opposite." The published version of *All God's Chillun Got Wings*, which appeared in *The American Mercury* prior to the play's opening, also revealed that the interracial couple would kiss onstage. Newspapers condemned the play before it opened, claiming that it "would stir up unfortunate racial feelings." Even Mayor John Hylan of New York City promised an investigation and almost halted the premiere when he refused to license the appearance of black and white children together on the stage. As a result, director James Light read the opening scene of the play to the audience. In this scene, O'Neill explained that "among children race prejudice is not strong."

While critics dismissed the play, Paul Robeson received raves. *The New York Times* commented: "All this Mr. Robeson denotes with admirable directness and dignity—admirable force, too, and even fire. It is a performance that grips attention and tingles in the nerves."

The Circle in the Square revived *All God's Chillun* in 1975 with Robert Christian in the leading role.

**THE AMEN CORNER** (Ethel Barrymore, April 15, 1965, 84 p.). Producer: Mrs. Nat Cole. Author: James Baldwin.* Director: Frank Silvera.

Cast: Beah Richards* (Sister Margaret), Isabell Sanford (Sister Moore), Juanita Moore (Sister Boxer), Frank Silvera (Luke), Cynthia Belgrave (Sister Sally), Toby Russ (Sister Rice), Helen Martin (Sister Douglas), C. P.

Walker (Man), Amentha Dymally (First Woman), Yvette Hawkins (Second Woman), Gertrude Jeannette (Odessa), Whitman Mayo (Brother Boxer), Josie Dotson (Sister Jackson), Art Evans (David).

The success of James Baldwin's third play, *Blues for Mr. Charlie,** in the 1963-1964 season paved the way for the New York premiere of his first dramatic work, *The Amen Corner.* Baldwin wrote the play early in his career after he completed his first novel *Go Tell It on the Mountain.* His agent considered it an "irresponsible act," since Broadway producers were not exactly clamoring "for plays on obscure aspects of Negro life." *The Amen Corner* tells the tale of Sister Margaret Alexander (Beah Richards), a model of purity in her store-front Harlem church. Unfortunately, her husband, an alcoholic jazz musician, and her son refuse to follow in her footsteps. When her long-absent husband returns home to die, Sister Margaret is forced to reevaluate her standards of morality. While she returns to her family, she loses her position in the church.

Baldwin created Sister Margaret as a symbol of black life in America. He explained in his introduction to the play: "In all of this, of course, she loses her old self. . . . Her triumph, which is also, if I may say so, the historical triumph of the Negro people in this country, is that she sees this finally and accepts it, and although she has lost everything, also gains the keys to the kingdom. The kingdom is love, and love is selfless, although only the self can lead one there. She gains herself."

While critics found Baldwin's play somewhat weak, Beah Richards's performance as Sister Margaret received raves. Richards also won a Theatre World Award and topped *Variety*'s Drama Critics Poll for her performance.

**AMERICAN NIGHT CRY** (Actors Studio, March 7, 1974, 12 p.). Producer: The Production Committee of The Actors Studio Inc. Author: Phillip Hayes Dean.* Director: Richard Ward.

**Thunder in the Index**
Cast: Don Blakely, Lenka Peterson, Jean-Pierre Stewart.

**This Bird of Dawning Singeth All Night Long**
Cast: Sylvia Miles, Josephine Premice.

**The Minstrel Boy**
Cast: Don Blakely, Cleo Quitman.

*American Night Cry* provided three one-act plays by Phillip Hayes Dean, author of *The Sty of the Blind Pig** (1971). *Thunder in the Index* is set in a psychiatric ward where a seemingly sane black man (Don Blakely) has been strait-jacketed by a white Jewish doctor (Jean-Pierre Stewart). Yet, it is shortly revealed that the doctor is a mental patient as well. *This Bird of Dawning Singeth All Night Long* features Sylvia Miles as a white prostitute who is confused about her identity. Events become complicated as a black woman (Josephine Premice) arrives late one night and claims that she is the prostitute's sister. *The Minstrel Boy* presents the case of Rainbow Rivers (Blakely), who hangs himself when he hears that his white show business friend is dead. Is he really dead or is this story fabricated by the wife (who is the friend's lover)? These three plays concerning loss of identity disappointed the critics. Mel Gussow of *The New York Times* found the plays "disjointed" and looked "forward to Dean's full-length plays."

**ANDREW.** See THE CORNER.

**ANNA LUCASTA** (Mansfield, August 30, 1944, 957 p.). Producer: John Wildberg. Author: Philip Yordan. Director: Harry Wagstaff Gribble.

Cast: Hilda Simms (Anna), Canada Lee* (Danny), Theodora Smith (Katie), Rosetta LeNoire (Stella), Georgia Burke (Theresa), John Proctor (Stanley), Frederick O'Neal* (Frank), George Randol (Joe), Hubert Henry (Eddie), Alvin Childress (Noah), Alice Childress* (Blanche), Emory Richardson (Officer), John Tate (Lester), Earle Hyman* (Rudolf).

Philip Yordan, author of *Anna Lucasta*, originally wrote a drama of a Polish family's adventures in a small Pennsylvania town. Although many producers liked it, none would option the play. Abram Hill,* founder of the American Negro Theatre,* suggested that the play be rewritten as the story of a black family. Hill and Harry Wagstaff Gribble revised the play, and it received raves in a Harlem try-out. It moved to Broadway with a new emphasis on comedy and became one of the season's biggest hits.

*Anna Lucasta* borrows heavily from *Anna Christie*. Here Anna (Hilda Simms) is a Brooklyn prostitute who returns home to marry a southern hick. This is a favor to her father who will receive $800. When Anna meets her future husband, she quickly grows to love him. An ex-boyfriend (Canada Lee) almost derails the wedding, but love conquers all in the final act.

*Billboard*'s critic praised the entire cast: "The cast is excellent almost without exception. Hilda Simms, who created 'Anna' uptown, makes an auspicious stem bow. She plays with understanding and restraint—a welcome addition to our ranks of younger Negro actresses. Earle Hyman . . . does a job in the difficult role of the young husband. He gets force and drive into what could be a namby-pamby part. Canada Lee, of course, turns in a bang-up job as the . . . sweetheart."

**APPEARANCES** (Frolic, October 13, 1925, 23 p.). Producer: Lester W. Sagar. Author: Garland Anderson.* Director: John Hayden.

Cast: Lionel Monagas* (Carl), Edward Keane (Frank Thompson), Daisy Atherton (Mrs. Thompson), Robert Toms (Fred Kellard), Mildred Wall (Elsie Benton), Hazele Burgess (Louise Thornton), Frank Hatch (Judge Thornton), Doe Doe Green (Rufus), Evelyn Mason (Ella), Joseph Sweeney (Jack Wilson), Clifton Self (Police Officer), Louis Frohoff (Judge

Robinson), William Davidge (Clerk), Leatta Miller (Stenographer), Edwin Hodge (Gerald Saunders), James Cherry (Hiram Matthews), Wilton Lackaye, Jr. (A. A. Andrews).

Garland Anderson's *Appearances* was the first serious drama on Broadway written by a black author. Anderson, a former bellhop in a San Francisco hotel, used his public relations skills to interest top stars of Broadway and Hollywood in his new play. He even gave an autographed copy of his play to President Calvin Coolidge.

During the rehearsals of *Appearances*, two leading ladies (Myrtle Tannehill and Nedda Harrigan) left the show because they discovered "there were going to be three Negroes in the cast." Harrigan denied the charges to *The New York Times*, claiming that she was not leaving because of "race prejudice," but "the production of a play called for so close an association with the other players that she felt she could not be happy under the circumstances." [November 2, 1925] Anderson was reportedly quite hurt by the actions of these actresses.

*Appearances*, an essay on the power of positive thinking, won praise from several critics. In general, they ignored Anderson's optimistic philosophy of life and concentrated on the courtroom drama in the second and third acts of the play. Carl (Lionel Monagas), a black bellhop, is framed by a crooked district attorney and a woman of low morals. She claims that Carl tried to attack her, while Carl insists that she tried to extort money from him. In the second act, Carl, confident that he will triumph, pleads his own case in court. In a gripping finale, the true villains are revealed.

*The New York Times* gave this new show a generally favorable review: "A finely conceived, crudely wrought protest against lynch law is this drama, *Appearances*, which has in it moments of power and a great many moments of ponderousness and stiffness. The fact that it was written by a Negro bellboy, and that it breathes a passionate sincerity, makes it impressive and absorbing." After a brief New York run, the show also enjoyed a modest success in London.

**AT HOME WITH ETHEL WATERS** (Forty-eighth Street, September 22, 1953, 23 p.). Producers: Charles Bowden and Richard Barr. Director: Richard Barr.

Cast: Ethel Waters* with Reginald Beane at the piano.

Despite several favorable reviews, *At Home with Ethel Waters* enjoyed only a brief run. The revue featured the hits of Waters's career, songs from *Plantation Revue*,* *Rhapsody in Black*,* *As Thousands Cheer*, and *Cabin in the Sky*.* Perhaps the spartan nature of the production deterred audiences, as Waters appeared on stage with only her accompanist Reginald Beane. Miles Jefferson, *Phylon*'s critic, wrote of Miss Waters: "The complete composure, the warm assurance and the genuine emotional impact, whether she be living a tragic incident, or dancing a frivolous caper, labelled this artist once more as supreme in her field. The failure of the public to rally to her was one of those mysteries which has been observed too frequently of late on Broadway."

# B

**BALLAD FOR BIMSHIRE** (Mayfair, October 15, 1963, 74 p.). Producers: Ossie Davis,* Bernard Waltzer, and Page Productions. Composer and lyricist: Irving Burgie. Book: Irving Burgie and Loften Mitchell.* Director: Ed Cambridge.

Cast: Ossie Davis (Sir Radio), Frederick O'Neal* (Neddie Boyce), Robert Hooks* (Dennis Thornton), Christine Spencer (Daphne Byfield), Miriam Burton (Iris Boyce), Alyce Webb (Vendor), Ural Wilson (Grafton), Jim Trotman (Spence), Clebert Ford (Howie), Sylvia Moon (Millie), Jimmy Randolph (Johnny Williams), Fran Bennett (Matron), Joe A. Calloway (Arthur Roundville), Lauren Jones (Maude), Hilda Harris (Hilda), Charles Moore (Watchman), Eugene Edwards (Lead Man).

Songs: Ballad for Bimshire; Street Cries; 'Fore Day Noon in the Mornin'; Lately I've Been Feeling So Strange; Deep in My Heart; Have You Got Charm?; Hail Britannia; Welcome Song; Belle Plain; I'm a Dandy; Silver Earring; My Love Will Come By; Chicken's a Popular Bird; Pardon Me, Sir; Yesterday Was Such a Lovely Day; The Master Plan; Chant; Vendor's Song; We Gon' Jump Up.

Broadway visited with *Jamaica** in 1957, and now Off-Broadway returned to the scene with *Ballad for Bimshire.* Irving Burgie (Lord Burgess), the composer of "Jamaica Farewell" and "Island in the Sun," joined forces with Loften Mitchell, author of *A Land Beyond the River*,* to create a musical look at West Indian life. Howard Taubman, writing in *The New York Times*, dismissed the plot as "conventional" and "slow-moving," but said it hardly mattered since the songs and production numbers were "well worth the price of admission." Taubman singled out six songs for praise and gave compliments to virtually the entire cast, especially Ossie Davis, Frederick O'Neal, and Christine Spencer.

**A BALLET BEHIND THE BRIDGE** (St. Marks, March 15, 1972, 39 p.). Producer: Negro Ensemble Company.* Author: Lennox Brown. Director: Douglas Turner Ward.*

Cast: David Downing* (Joseph Drayton), Michele Shay (Vain Woman), Duane Jones (National Guard Commander), Frances Foster* (Mrs. Drayton), Neville Richen (Maraval), David Connell (Borbon), Adolph Caesar* (Laisingh), Stephen Cheng (Achong), Jack Landron (Alcoholic), Gilbert Lewis (Mano Drayton; King), C. David Colson (European King; Mahon), Carolen Ross (European Queen), Howland Chamberlain (Priest), Larry Desmond (Mahal), Esther Rolle* (Shouter Woman), Lauren Jones (African Queen; Prostitute), Norman L. Jacob (Jesus Monkey), Robert Stocking (Head Teacher).

Only Douglas Watt of *The New York Daily News* approved of *A Ballet Behind the Bridge*, a fifth season entry for the Negro Ensemble Company. Lennox Brown, a Trinidadian playwright, examined the contrasting lives of two young men in his native country. Joseph Drayton (David Downing), the college-educated New York-bound youth, provides a stark contrast to his brother Mano Drayton, who has just killed a black doctor, his white wife, and his son. Brown tried to compare the plight of the brothers to the plight of Trinidad throughout its history via flashbacks to mythical black and white kingdoms of the fifteenth century. The critics found these historical analogies weak and repetitious, but admired Brown's ear for dialogue.

**BAMBOOLA** (Royale, June 26, 1929, 34 p.). Producer: Irving Cooper. Music and Lyrics: D. Frank Marcus and Bernard Maltin. Book: D. Frank Marcus. Director: Sam Rose.

Cast: Isabell Washington (Anna Frost), Mercedes Gilbert (Rhodendra Frost), Monte Hawley ('Lije Frost), Hilda Perleno (Sheila Nesbit), Percy Winters (Samson Frost), George Randol (Ludlow Bassom), Ray Giles (Deputy Sheriff), John Mason (Sambo), Dusty Fletcher (Dusty), Billy Andrews (J. Quentin Creech), Billy Cortez (Myrtle Wyms), Brevard Burnett (Tom Gin), Revella Hughes (The Song Bird), Cora Merano (Maid), Ray Giles (Preacher).

Songs: Evenin'; Ace of Spades; Dixie Vagabond; Rub-a-Dub Your Rabbit's Foot; Bamboola; Somebody Like Me; Tailor Made Babies; African Whoopee; Tampico Tune; Song of Harlem; Shoutin' Sinners; Anna; Hot Patootie Wedding Night.

*Bamboola* (or *Bomboola*), billed as "a unique Afro-American musical comedy," was hurt by a July heat wave. Box office receipts dwindled so quickly that the show's leads were forced to accept a $10 weekly wage in place of their usual $100. The chorus members received only $1. The cast and orchestra refused to perform for such wages, and the show promptly closed.

*Bamboola* is the name of the show-within-a-show. Anna (Isabell Washington), "a Dixie vagabond," comes to New York to appear in *Bamboola*. She meets the composer of the show, and they fall in love. Despite some difficulties with an actor who tries to win her hand, Anna marries the composer in the finale, a jazz wedding ("Hot Patootie Wedding Night").

**BANDANA LAND** (Majestic, February 3, 1908, 89 p.). Producer: F. Ray Comstock. Composer: Will Marion Cook.* Book and lyrics: J. A. Shipp and Alex Rogers.* Musical numbers staged by: Aida Overton Walker.*

Cast: Bert Williams* (Skunkton Bowser), George W. Walker* (Bud Jenkins), Alex Rogers (Amos Simmons), Ada Banks (Mandy Lou), Hattie McIntosh (Sophie Simmons), Charles H. Moore (Pete Simmons), Aida Overton Walker (Susie Simmons), Muriel Ringgold (Cynthia), Maggie Davis (Julia Smothers), Bessie Vaughan (Sue Higgins), Ida Day (Babe Brown), Katie Jones (Becky White), Minnie Brown (Angelina Diggs), Mord Allen (Si Springer), James E. Lightfoot (Mr. Wilson), Sterling Rex (Mr. Jones), J. Leubrie Hill (Sandy Turner), Lloyd G. Gibbs (Deacon Sparks), Lavinia Rogers (Sadie Tompkins), Henry Troy (Fred Collins, Jr.).

Songs: Corn Song; Kinky (lyrics: Mord Allen); 'Tain't Gwine to Be No Rain; Exhortation; Any Old Place in Yankee Land Is Good Enough for Me; Red Red Rose; The Sheath Gown in Darktown (J. Leubrie Hill-Mord Allen); In My Old Home (Tom Lemonier-Mord Allen); At Peace with the World (Mord Allen-Bert Williams); Bon Bon Buddie; Salome Dance (Joe Jordan); Southland; The Right Church But the Wrong Pew (Cecil Mack*-Chris Smith).

*Bandana* (or *Bandanna*) *Land* received the most praise of the Williams and Walker shows, with the *Dramatic Mirror* explaining that it was "one of the rare plays that one feels like witnessing a second time." This musical abandoned the African locale of the earlier Williams and Walker shows and switched to a topic closer to home. *Bandana Land* involved Bud Jenkins's (Walker's) attempts to swindle a railway company in a land speculation deal. At the same time, Jenkins hopes to relieve Skunkton Bowser (Williams) of his fortune as well. Jenkins successfully tricks the railway company, but, at the last moment, Bowser realizes Jenkins's foul intentions and outwits him. Every aspect of the show won praise, and it seemed the most joyful Williams and Walker effort. Unfortunately, it was the last.

Early in the run of *Bandana Land*, Walker began to exhibit symptoms of paresis. He began to lisp, stutter, and forget his lines during his performance. He managed to continue the role until February 1909, but by then the ravages of his disease had progressed too far. *Bandana Land* was Walker's last stage appearance.

**THE BAPTISM** (Writers' Stage, May 1, 1964, 3 p.). Producer: Richard Fulton. Author: LeRoi Jones (Imamu Amiri Baraka).* Director: Leo Garen.

Cast: Taylor Mead (Homosexual), Jarrett Spruill (Minister), Russell Turman (The Boy), Beverly Grant (Old Woman), Mark Duffy (Messenger).

Reviews for LeRoi Jones's one-act play, *The Baptism*, were divided. *The New York Post* gave it rave notices, while *The New York Times* dismissed the play. The Boy (Russell Turman) is revealed to be the Son of God in an unusual chapel which features a homosexual in red leotards (Taylor Mead), a violent minister (Jarrett Spruill), and a deceived old woman (Beverly Grant). Even Christ is not able to bring peace to this violent modern world, as The Boy slaughters virtually everyone in the chapel.

**THE BARRIER** (Broadhurst, November 2, 1950, 4 p.). Producers: Michael Myerberg and Joel Spector. Book and lyrics: Langston Hughes.* Composer: Jan Meyerowitz. Director: Doris Humphrey.

Cast: Lawrence Tibbett (Colonel Thomas Norwood), Muriel Rahn (Cora Lewis), Wilton Clary (Bert), Lorenzo Herrera (William), Charlotte Holloman (Sally), Dolores Bowman (Livonia), Reri Grist (Maid), John Diggs (Houseman), Laurence Watson (Sam), Victor Thorley (Talbot), Richard Dennis (Fred Higgins), Robert Tankersley (Plantation Storekeeper), Jesse Jacobs (Undertaker), Stuart Hodes (Assistant to the Undertaker).

Langston Hughes's 1935 play, *Mulatto*,* returned to Broadway in 1950 as an opera with music by Jan Meyerowitz. After successful showings at Columbia University and the University of Michigan, *The Barrier* began an out-of-town try-out in Baltimore. As a result of a booking jam when the show arrived in New York City, *The Barrier* opened without adequate time for rehearsals or an appropriate advertising campaign. This fact, coupled with chilly reviews (George Jean Nathan left after the first act), condemned *The Barrier* to a short run.

Nevertheless, Miles Jefferson, critic for *Phylon*, wrote: "It closed after four performances—a great pity, for despite minor flaws it generated authentic feeling in its indictment against racial intolerance. There were complaints that the music lacked dramatic cogency, but it compared favorably, in this reviewer's opinion, with the music of that overwhelming success on Broadway, *The Consul*, by Gian Carlo Menotti."

**A BEAST'S STORY.** See CITIES IN BEZIQUE.

**BEHOLD! COMETH THE VANDERKELLANS** (De Lys, March 31, 1971, 23 p.). Producer: Woodie King* Associates. Author: William Wellington Mackey.* Director: Edmund Cambridge.

Cast: Graham Brown (Dr. Vanderkellan), Frances Foster* (Mrs. Vanderkellan), Roxie Roker (Desiree Vanderkellan), Carl Byrd (Gregory), Robert Christian (Luiz).

William Wellington Mackey, who had just won a Rockefeller Foundation Grant, presented a domestic drama of the Vanderkellan family. A Vanderkellan has been a president of Holden College for three generations, but now, in the 1960s, students in revolt call for Vanderkellan's (Graham Brown) resignation. As Vanderkellan summons his wife and children to discuss this problem, the focus switches to the family's difficulties. Richard Watts of *The New York Post* compared Mackey's play to the plays of Eugene O'Neill, and found him "a dramatist who deserves attention and respect."

**THE BELIEVERS: THE BLACK EXPERIENCE IN SONG** (Garrick, May 9, 1968, 310 p.). Producers: Jesse DeVore, Harold L. Oram, and Gustav Heningburg. Book: Josephine Jackson and Joseph A. Walker.* Composers and lyricists: Benjamin Carter, Dorothy Dinroe, Josephine Jackson, Anje Ray, Ron Steward, and Joseph A. Walker. Director: Barbara Ann Teer.*

Cast: Voices, Inc.: Benjamin Carter, Jesse DeVore, Dorothy Dinroe, Barry Hemphill, Josephine Jackson, Sylvia Jackson, Shirley McKie, Don Oliver, Anje Ray, Veronica Redd, Ron Steward, James Wright, Joseph A. Walker (Narrator).

Songs: African Sequence; Believers' Chants; Believers' Laments; This Old Ship; Where Shall I Go?; What Shall I Believe in Now?; I Just Got in the City; City Blues; You Never Really Know; Early One Morning Blues; Daily Buzz; Childrens' Games; School Don't Mean a Damn Thing; I'm Gonna Do My Things; Where Do I Go from Here?; Burn This Town; Learn to Love.

*The Believers* was one of the first attempts to chronicle the black experience in America by the use of song and dance. Josephine Jackson and Joseph A. Walker fashioned a libretto that examined black history from its roots in Africa, to the era of American slavery, and to the northward and urban migration of the twentieth century. Song thus became a historical document in the attempt to understand the meaning of black American history. While the critics were divided in their assessment of the evening, John Lahr, of *The New York Free Press*, noted: "The music, in its eloquent, unliterary manner, vaults the boundaries of sociological niches, speaking a special private language. The tribal chants, the slave songs, the blues, the revival, the jazz idiom, the street cries, are all here and beautifully orchestrated. There is more musical and vocal talent on stage than in any show on or off-Broadway."

**BIG CITY BLUES.** See COMPANIONS OF THE FIRE.

**BIG TIME BUCK WHITE** (Village South, December 8, 1968, 124 p.). Producers: Zev Bufman, Ron Rich, and Leonard Grant. Author: Joseph Dolan Tuotti. Director: Dick Williams.*

Cast: Dick Williams (Big Time Buck White), Kirk Kirksey* (Hunter), David Moody (Honey Man), Van Kirksey (Weasel), Arnold Williams (Rubber Man), Ron Rich (Jive).

*Big Time Buck White* originated in Budd Schulberg's Watts Writers'

Workshop in Los Angeles. After a commercial production on the West Coast, it moved virtually intact to Off-Broadway, and garnered raves for its white author Joseph Dolan Tuotti and its black cast. Although emerging in the aftermath of the Watts riots, the play displayed an ironic sense of humor that was greatly admired by the New York critics.

*Big Time Buck White* assumed the form of a political meeting. The first hour concerns the preparation for the meeting, while the remainder concerns the interview with Big Time Buck White (Dick Williams), with questions (both real and planted) coming from the theatre audience. Dick Williams, who also staged the play, was praised for his portrayal of the militant black power leader; Kirk Kirksey, Ron Rich, and David Moody also got rave notices. After the initial Off-Broadway success, the show was remade into a musical (*Buck White*)* to considerably less acclaim.

**BIG WHITE FOG** (Lincoln, October 22, 1940, 64 p.). Producer: The Negro Playwrights Company.* Author: Theodore Ward.* Director: Powell Lindsay.

Cast: Canada Lee* (Victor Mason), Hilda Offley (Ellen Mason), Maude Russell (Juanita Rogers), Eileen Renard (Caroline Mason), Bertram Holmes (Phillip Mason), Louise Jackson (Mrs. Brooks), Kelsey Pharr (Lester), Alma Forrest (Wanda), Roburte Dorce (Percy), Muriel Cook (Claudine Adams), Edward Fraction (Dan Rogers), P. Jay Sidney (Count Strawder), Andrew Walker (Count Cotton), Robert Creighton (Brother Harper), Trixie Smith (Sister Gabrella), Bertha Reubel, Almeina Green (Nurses), Jerry Grebanier (Nathan Piszer), Stanley Prager (Marx), Valerie Black (Caroline), Carl Crawford (Philip), Lionel Monagas* (Police Sergeant), Ted Thurston (Police Lieutenant).

Theodore Ward's *Big White Fog* was produced by the Federal Theatre Project* in Chicago in 1938 for a ten-week run. The Negro Playwrights Company presented a revised version of the play at the Lincoln Theatre in Harlem in 1940.

*Big White Fog* concerns the progressive disillusionment of Victor Mason (Canada Lee) with the Marcus Garvey movement. Mason eventually loses his life savings and his faith in Garvey. He turns to communism as a new solution to the problems of blacks in America, but he is killed by the police when he resists eviction from his apartment. His son Lester later explains that his comrades are a "light in the big white fog."

The notion that America's blacks could be attracted to communism angered the mainstream critics who visited *Big White Fog*. John Mason Brown of *The New York Post* commented: "As it meanders through its heart-breaking materials to reach its final Communist solution, the melodrama seems for all the world like an echo of every playwrighting fault committed in the worst of the scripts presented down at the erstwhile Theatre Union." Nevertheless, Brooks Atkinson, after confessing his aversion to communism, admitted in *The New York Times* that *Big White Fog* "is the best serious play of Negro authorship about race problems that this courier has happened to see. . . . Mr. Ward writes like a professional in the politically conscious genre. What he has to say is hard, bold, and disturbing."

**BILLY NONAME** (Truck and Warehouse, March 2, 1970, 48 p.). Producers: Robert E. Richardson and Joe Davis. Book: William Wellington Mackey.* Composer and lyricist: Johnny Brandon. Director: Lucia Victor.

Cast: Donny Burks (Billy Noname), Hattie Winston* (Dolores), Andrea Saunders (Louisa), Andy Torres (Li'l Nick), Charles Moore (Big Nick), Roger Lawson (Young Billy), Thommie Bush (Young Tiny), Eugene Edwards (Rev. Fisher), Alan Weeks (Tiny Shannon), Eugene Edwards (Mr. Milton), Glory Van Scott (Barbara), Urylee Leonardos (Harriet).

Songs: King Joe; Seduction; Billy Noname; Boychild; A Different Drummer; Look Through the Window; It's Our Time Now; Hello World; At the End of the Day; I Want to Live; Manchild; Color Me White; We're Gonna Turn on Freedom; Mother Earth; Sit In—Wade In; Movin'; The Dream; Black Boy; Burn, Baby Burn; We Make a Promise; Get Your Slice of Cake.

*Billy Noname* opened in the new Truck and Warehouse Theatre on East Fourth Street. This musical, with a libretto by William Wellington Mackey, examines the life of Billy (Don Burks), a young black writer, from the date of Joe Louis's championship bout to the killing of Martin Luther King, Jr. Billy's life is shown to parallel black history during this period. Critics praised the cast, the staging by Lucia Victor, and the "brilliant" choreography by Talley Beatty. Donny Burks also won a Theatre World Award for his performance. Nevertheless, critics panned the book and doomed *Billy Noname* to a brief run.

**BLACK BODY BLUES** (St. Marks, January 19, 1978, 40 p.). Producer: Negro Ensemble Company.* Author: Gus Edwards.* Director: Douglas Turner Ward.*

Cast: Samm-Art Williams* (Arthur), Norman Bush (Andy), Catherine E. Slade (Joyce), Frankie R. Faison (Louis), Douglas Turner Ward (Fletcher).

The Negro Ensemble Company offered two plays by fledgling playwright Gus Edwards in the 1977-1978 season: *The Offering** and *Black Body Blues*. Julius Novick, writing in *The Village Voice*, found that "*Black Body Blues* deals with sensitive matters and does not violate their complexity." The complex matters concern the dilemma of Arthur (Samm-Art Williams), a former boxer and now a servant, and his relationship with his white employer. Arthur is torn between the white world of his employer, who treats him kindly and with respect, and the black world of his brother, a pusher, and his girlfriend, a prostitute. The brother returns late one night and shoots the employer, saying to Arthur, "I put a bullet in your master and I freed you." Arthur, however, doubts this simplistic assessment of the situation. Critics praised both Edwards's efforts as well as the performances of the admirable cast. Samm-Art Williams won plaudits for his "winning" performance.

**BLACK BOY** (Comedy, October 6, 1926, 37 p.). Producer: Horace Liveright. Authors: Jim Tully and Frank Dazey. Director: David Burton.

Cast: Paul Robeson* (Black Boy), Edith Warren [Fredi Washington*] (Irene), Fuller Mellish, Jr. (Shrimp), Edward Redding (Square Deal), Charles Henderson (Mauler), Edward Gargan (Whitey), James Ford (Eddie), Percy Verwayne (Yellow), Robert Collyer (Squint), Henry Troy (Langhorne Dubree), G. O. Taylor (Chauffeur).

*Black Boy* describes the rise of a $10-a-bout sparring partner to the world championship. Black Boy lives high in his new life and begins drinking. He loses a big fight and his friends desert him. Poor, once again, Black Boy becomes a common laborer.

This trite fighting plot provided Paul Robeson with a major role. *The New York Herald Tribune* noted: "Paul Robeson gives a vivid and sentimental account of the rise and fall of a Negro pugilist. . . . He dominates the play by the simpler and surer means of a sheer gianthood of genuineness, native understanding, and deep-voiced likability." Robeson also sang in *Black Boy*, a major trademark of his dramatic roles: "And he so sings that you forgive and forget all else."

Theophilus Lewis, a black drama critic, also praised Robeson but harshly lambasted the play in *The Messenger*: "The way the play is written all the white characters are first cousins of the Devil while the leading colored character is compounded of the holiness of Simon, the Cyrenian . . . and the innocence of Little Eva. To give this blend of airy nothings the appearance of a substantial human being requires nothing less than the touch of histrionic genius and fortunately Robeson has it. . . . His work alone invests the flimsy role with dignity and charm."

**BLACK BROADWAY** (Town Hall, May 4, 1980, 25 p.). Producers: George Wein, Honi Coles, Robert Kimball, and Bobby Short.

Cast: John W. Bubbles,* Nell Carter,* Honi Coles, Charles Cook, Carla Earle, Mercedes Ellington, Leslie Gaines, Terri Griffin, Adelaide Hall,* Gregory Hines,* Bobby Short, Wyetta Turner, Elisabeth Welch,* Edith Wilson.*

*Black Broadway* was one of the many attempts to present the untold tale of the history of the black musical comedy. Unlike its predecessors (*Bubbling Brown Sugar*,* *Ain't Misbehavin'*,* and *Eubie!**), *Black Broadway* returned some of the stars of the black musicals of the 1920s and 1930s to their former glory. Such veterans as John W. Bubbles (Sportin' Life in *Porgy and Bess**), Adelaide Hall (*Blackbirds of 1928**), Elisabeth Welch (*Runnin' Wild**), and

Edith Wilson (*Plantation Revue**) revived the songs that they had made famous. Wilson, incidentally, made her debut on the same Town Hall stage almost sixty years earlier in *Put and Take.** Such contemporary favorites as Bobby Short, Gregory Hines (*Eubie!*), and Nell Carter (*Ain't Misbehavin'*) filled in the historical gaps from the time of Bert Williams* to the present in this highly praised revue.

**BLACK GIRL** (De Lys, June 16, 1971, 234 p.). Producers: Woodie King,* Dick Williams* and the New Federal Theatre.* Author: J. E. Franklin.* Director: Shauneille Perry.*

Cast: Kishasha (Billie Jean), Arthur W. French III (Little Earl), Lorraine Ryder (Sheryl), Gloria Edwards (Norma), Loretta Green (Ruth Ann), Louise Stubbs (Mama Rosie), Minnie Gentry (Mu'Dear), Jimmy Hayeson (Mr. Herbert), Arthur French (Earl), Saundra Sharp (Netta).

*Black Girl*, originally produced by the New Federal Theatre, brought a Drama Desk Award to J. E. Franklin. Her play considered several generations of women in a small Texas ghetto. Seventeen-year-old Billie Jean (Kishasha) wants to be a dancer, but her two half-sisters, Norma (Gloria Edwards) and Ruth Ann (Loretta Green), plot a more conventional existence for her. Similarly, Mama Rosie (Louise Stubbs) offers no help or love to her daughter. Only the grandmother (Minnie Gentry) manages to help her fulfill her dreams. Elenore Lester praised *Black Girl* highly in *The New York Times*: "This is a simple direct play which produces strong vibrations from the convergence of two live themes—growing up female and growing up black." [July 11, 1971]

**BLACK NATIVITY** (Forty-first Street, December 11, 1961, 57 p.). Producers: Michael R. Santangelo, Barbara Griner, and Eric Franck. Author: Langston Hughes.* Director: Vinnette Carroll.*

Cast: Marion Williams and the Stars of Faith, Alex Bradford, Clive Thompson, Cleo Quitman, Carl Ford, Howard Sanders.

Songs: Joy to the World; My Way Is Cloudy; No Room at the Inn; Most Done Travelling; Oh, Jerusalem, in the Morning; Poor Little Jesus; What You Gonna Name Your Baby?; Wasn't That a Mighty Day; Christ Was Born; Go Tell It on the Mountain; Rise Up, Shepherd, and Follow; What Month Was Jesus Borned In?; Sweet Little Jesus Boy; Oh Come All Ye Faithful; If Anybody Asked You Who I Am?; Children, Go Where I Send Thee; Meetin' Here Tonight; Holy Ghost, Don't Leave Me; We Shall Be Changed; The Blood Saved Me; Leak in the Building; Nobody Like the Lord; His Will Be Done; Said I Wasn't Gonna Tell Nobody; Get Away Jordan; Packin' Up; God Be With You.

Langston Hughes's "Christmas Song Play" caused quite a furor before its opening. Two performers who had been contracted under the play's original title ("Wasn't It a Mighty Day") found the new title "offensive" and sacrilegious. They were replaced shortly before the opening, and the show retained its new title. The evening was divided into two parts: "The Child Is Born" (Act I) and "The Word Is Spread" (Act II). Dominating both sections were the performances of Alex Bradford and Marion Williams and the Stars of Faith. Edith Oliver of *The New Yorker* found their gospel singing "just plain glorious," as did the other critics. Despite its short New York City run, *Black Nativity* embarked on an American tour and then visited Spoleto, London, and even New Zealand to triumphant acclaim.

**BLACK PICTURE SHOW** (Vivian Beaumont, January 6, 1975, 41 p.). Producer: Joseph Papp and the New York Shakespeare Festival. Author and director: Bill Gunn.* Composer and lyricist: Sam Waymon.

Cast: Albert Hall (J. D.), Dick Anthony Williams* (Alexander), Graham Brown (Norman), Carol Cole (Rita), Paul-David Richards (Philippe), Linda Miller (Jane), Sam Waymon (Vocalist).

Songs: I'm So Glad; Mose Art; Bird of Paradise; Variation on "Chopin in E Minor"; Memory; Bitch in Heat; Digits; Science Fiction; Vintage '51; Afghanistan; Terminate; and Black Picture Show; I Feel So Good (Waymon-Gunn).

Bill Gunn wrote and directed his own play for the New York Shakespeare Festival. Most critics found the plot obvious and somewhat reminiscent of Odets's plays of the 1930s. The play concerned the selling out of black talent by white producers. Dick Anthony Williams portrays an aging dramatist, and Albert Hall, his son, a prosperous film director. The play opens as the elder playwright is dying, and the son proposes to tell the audience the story of his last day on earth.

Despite the criticism of the theme of the play, most critics praised the writing and the acting. Clive Barnes commented in *The New York Times*: "What is rewarding about the play is the brilliant writing, and, generally speaking, the sure sense Mr. Gunn has for characterization. . . . The Shakespeare Festival usually offers good acting, but this was exceptional by those standards—and could well justify Gunn's decision to direct his own play."

**A BLACK QUARTET** (Tambellini's Gate, July 30, 1969, 111 p.). Producers: Woodie King* Associates.

**Prayer Meeting or the First Militant Minister.** Author: Ben Caldwell.* Director: Irving Vincent.

Cast: Dennis Tate (Burglar), L. Errol Jaye (Minister).

**The Warning—A Theme for Linda.** Author: Ronald Milner.* Director: Woodie King.

Cast: Vikki Summers (Linda), Louise Heath (Nora), Loretta Green (Joan), Jo-Ann Robinson (Paula), L. Errol Jaye (Grandfather), Jimmy

Hayeson (Nasty Old Man), Paul Rodger-Reid (Donald), Minnie Gentry (Grandmother), Joan Pryor (Mother).

**The Gentleman Caller.** Author: Ed Bullins.* Director: Allie Woods.

Cast: Minnie Gentry (The Maid), Dennis Tate (The Gentleman), Sylvia Soares (Madame), Frank Carey (Mr. Mann).

**Great Goodness of Life (A Coon Show).** Author: LeRoi Jones (Imamu Amiri Baraka).* Director: Irving Vincent.

Cast: L. Errol Jaye (Court Royal), Jimmy Hayeson (Attorney Breck), Sam Singleton (Young Man), Frank Carey (Voice of the White Judge), Paul Rodger-Reid (Hood), Anna Maria Horsford (Young Woman), Dennis Tate (Leader).

*A Black Quartet* managed a successful run for a show opening in mid-summer. Critics praised this seemingly diverse collection of four one-act plays, but noted that they were united by their reflection of "a different facet of black agony." The curtain-raiser, *Prayer Meeting*, by Ben Caldwell, provided a chance encounter between a thief and an Uncle Tom preacher. *The Warning—A Theme for Linda*, by Ronald Milner, concerned a three-generation matriarchy and their wariness of men. Bullins's *The Gentleman Caller*, the most elaborately designed of the four plays, provided a symbolic look at race relations as seen in the interaction of mistress and servant. LeRoi Jones closed the evening with *Great Goodness of Life (A Coon Show)*, in which a middle-class black man is accused of harboring a murderer in his house. In order to redeem himself he must execute the murderer, who, he later discovers, is his son. Critics praised the versatile cast, especially L. Errol Jaye and Minnie Gentry, who assumed a wide variety of roles throughout the evening.

**BLACK RHYTHM** (Comedy, December 19, 1936, 6 p.). Producers: Earl Dancer and J. H. Levey. Librettist, composer, and lyricist: Donald Heywood.* Directors: Earl Dancer and Donald Heywood.

Cast: Avon Long* (Rhythm), Jeni LeGon (Jenny), Maude Russell (Laura), William Walker (Mr. Heydon), Alex Lovejoy (Cornbread), Babe Matthews (Babe), Walter Richardson (David Songbird), Franklin Klien (Mr. Feinstein), Joe Byrd (Dusty), Speedy Wilson (Bodidly), Geneva Washington (Eva), Eddie Baer (Slim), John Foss (Eugene), Sammy Gardner (Toby), Sinclair Brooks (Swing), Walder Davis (Ghichi), Clarence Albright (Money), Eddie Matthews (Joe Michaels), Ina Duncan (Wardrobe Sal), Woodrow Wilson (Van Bugg), Barrington Guy (Sonny).

Songs: Truckers' Ball; Bow Down, Sinners; Orchids; Here 'Tis; Black Rhythm; Doin' the Toledo; Emaline.

By 1936, the black revues that had been popular during the previous decade virtually disappeared from Broadway. Donald Heywood and Earl Dancer attempted to revive the genre with *Black Rhythm*, with a cast recruited from

Harlem's nightclubs. Heywood's bad luck continued to plague him, however. (See *Africana* [1934].) As Jeni LeGon began her opening song, someone in the audience threw a stinkbomb at the stage. After the bomb was located, a deodorant was sprayed throughout the orchestra while the show continued. The distracted performers forgot their lines, and, understandably, the premiere was a disaster.

**BLACK SOULS** (Provincetown, March 30, 1932, 13 p.). Producer: William Stahl. Author: Annie Nathan Meyer. Director: James Light.

Cast: Morris McKenney (Andrew Morgan), Rose McClendon* (Phyllis), Juano Hernandez* (David Lewis), Leonia Dawson (Ettie Boy), Carl Crawford (Jamie Boy), Serena Mason (Corrine Thompson), Hayes Pryor (Ulysses Clark), Alven Dexter (Senator Verne), Guerita Donneley (Luella), Sylvester Payne (Junius Augustus), Thomas Coffin Cooke (Governor of the State).

Critics compared Annie Nathan Meyer's *Black Souls* to a lecture. During the first act, characters pondered such questions as "Whose souls are white and whose are black?" Others wondered whether racial equality would be achieved by reform or revolution. Yet, none of these questions was answered in the final two acts of the play. Murder and vengeance eradicated the philosophical concerns of the first act. Nevertheless, Rose McClendon, star of many black dramas of the early 1930s, received major praise, as did co-stars Juano Hernandez and Morris McKenney.

**BLACK SUNLIGHT** (St. Marks, March 19, 1974, 8 p.). Producer: Negro Ensemble Company.* Author: A. I. Davis. Director: Kris Keiser.

Cast: Mary Alice* (MHandi's Wife), Richard Jackson (MHandi), Robert Stocking (Wajji), Gary Bolling (Police Commissioner Kuunsa), Robert Christian (Cabinet Member NKundi).

*Black Sunlight*, a 1973-1974 "season-within-a-season" entry by the Negro Ensemble Company, presents an unflattering view of a mythical African kingdom on the eve of independence. Leader MHandi (Richard Jackson), the new chief head of state, learns that his friend NKundi (Robert Christian) has been plotting against the new government. MHandi refuses to believe this news, but he finally receives convincing proof. NKundi confronts the new leader and explains that he is planning to turn the new nation into a dictatorship. The critics found this reflection of Kwame Nkrumah of interest in the scenes of confrontation between leader and revolutionary, but found the characterization of MHandi somewhat unbelievable.

**THE BLACK TERROR** (Public, November 10, 1971, 180 p.). Producer: Joseph Papp and the New York Shakespeare Festival. Author: Richard Wesley.* Director: Nathan George.

Cast: Earl Sydnor (Radcliffe), Kirk Young (Ahmed), Kain (Keusi), Susan Batson (M'Bahlia), Paul Benjamin (Antar), Don Blakely (Geronimo), Dolores Vanison (Dancer).

*The Black Terror* brought a Drama Desk Award for its author Richard Wesley and star Kain. Critics agreed that this new play was as much a debate as a taut drama. Keusi (Kain), a member of the underground group, the "Black Terror," is given the task of assassinating Police Commissioner Savage with the help of fellow revolutionary M'Bahlia (Susan Batson). The debate focuses on a conflict within the "Black Terror" concerning the means and ends of revolution. Critics generally approved the effort, with Clive Barnes of *The New York Times* praising the "strong and forceful" writing and characterizations.

**BLACK VISIONS** (Public, April 4, 1972, 64 p.). Producer: Joseph Papp and the New York Shakespeare Festival.

**Sister Son/ji.** Author: Sonia Sanchez.* Director: Novella Nelson.*
Cast: Gloria Foster* (Sister Son/ji).

**Players Inn.** Author: Neil Harris. Director: Kris Keiser.
Cast: Juanita Clark (Barmaid), Bill Cobbs (Customer), Berk Costello (Tittylip), Walter Cotton (Johnny), Tommy Lane (Spabby), Hank Frazier (Deadeye), Sylvester Vonner (Numberman), Jeffrey Miller (First Junkie), Jojo Kokayi (Second Junkie), Norman Beim (White Detective), Tucker Smallwood (Black Detective), Lou Rogers III (Drop Man).

**Cop and Blow.** Author: Neil Harris. Director: Kris Keiser.
Cast: Bill Cobbs (Tex), Robert Judd (Nosegut), Barbara Montgomery* (Barmaid), J. A. Preston (Frank), Jojo Kokayi (Knowledge), Berk Costello (Tittylip), Tommy Lane (Zulu), Tucker Smallwood (Hitman), Sylvester Vonner (Policeman), Frank Bara (First White Detective), Rick Petrucelli (Second White Detective), John Henry Redwood (Black Detective).

**Gettin' It Together.** Author: Richard Wesley.* Director: Kris Keiser.
Cast: Morgan Freeman* (Nate), Beverly Todd (Coretta), Lou Rogers III (Radio D.J.).

*Black Visions* consisted of four one-act plays by three playwrights: Sonia Sanchez, Neil Harris, and Richard Wesley. *Sister Son/ji* opened the evening with a monologue of a woman looking back at her past. While critics praised Gloria Foster's performance ("Gloria is the Glory," said Walter Kerr), Clive Barnes, argued in *The New York Times* that "it never became theatre." Neil Harris's *Players Inn* and *Cop and Blow* presented two glimpses of life in a Harlem bar. Richard Wesley, whose recent *The Black Terror** had received excellent reviews, finished the evening with *Gettin' It Together.* This "simple, brief drama about recognizable people" presented the plight of a man and woman who could not live with (or without) each other.

**BLACKBERRIES OF 1932** (Liberty, April 4, 1932, 24 p.). Producers: Max Rudnick and Ben Bernard. Book: Eddie Green.* Composer and lyricist: Donald Heywood* and Tom Peluso. Director: Ben Bernard.

Cast: Eddie Green, Tim Moore,* Mantan Moreland,* Dewey Markham, Gertrude Saunders, Jackie Mabley, Alice Harris, Dusaye Brown, Sammy Paige, Johnny Long, John Dickens, Thelma Meers, Harold Norton.

Songs: The Answer Is No; Blackberries; Brown Sugar; First Thing in the Morning; Harlem Mania; Love Me More—Love Me Less (Peluso-Ben Bernard).

*Blackberries of 1932* was producer Max Rudnick's attempt to copy Lew Leslie's successful *Blackbirds of 1928*.* Writer Eddie Green and songwriters Donald Heywood and Tom Peluso provided several hours of entertainment for *Blackberries*. The show remained virtually unedited, and the first act on opening night ended after 11:00! Rudnick described *Blackberries* as a "dancical revue presented to you as you expect to see it." This, according to many critics, was the major problem of *Blackberries*. It followed the standard formula of the black musical revues and brought nothing new to the genre. Although Tim Moore, Mantan Moreland, Eddie Green, Johnny Long, and Dewey Markham received praise for their comic performances, *Blackberries of 1932* closed within the month.

**BLACKBIRDS OF 1928** (Liberty, May 9, 1928, 518 p.). Producer and Director: Lew Leslie. Music: Jimmy McHugh. Lyrics: Dorothy Fields.

Cast: Adelaide Hall,* Bill Robinson,* Aida Ward, Tim Moore,* Ruth Johnson, Crawford Jackson, Marjorie Hubbard, Blue McAllister, Lloyd Mitchell, Eloise Uggams, Billy Cortez, George Cooper, Mamie Savoy, Mantan Moreland,* Elizabeth [Elisabeth] Welch,* Harry Lucas, Willard McLean, Baby Banks, Philip Patterson, Earl Tucker.

Songs: Shuffle Your Feet; Dixie; Diga Diga Do; I Can't Give You Anything But Love; Bandanna Babies; Magnolia's Wedding Day; Porgy; Doin' the New Low Down; I Must Have That Man; Here Comes My Blackbird.

Lew Leslie, a former actor, began to specialize in black revues with *Plantation Revue** in 1922. He produced similar shows in London and Paris, as well as in his Fifty-seventh Street nightclub, *Les Ambassadeurs*. He envisioned Florence Mills* as the star of Broadway's *Blackbirds*, but her untimely death led to the casting of Adelaide Hall. Bill "Bojangles" Robinson, recruited from the vaudeville stage, was brought in as a last-minute cast replacement. Although he forgot several lines on opening night, *Variety* noted that "all was forgiven" when he began a chorus of "I Can't Give You Anything But Love." This song, by Jimmy McHugh and Dorothy Fields, quickly became the show's hit. Originally designed as a tribute to Charles Lindbergh ("I Can't Give You Anything But Love, Lindy") in *Harry Delmar's Revels*, the song was slightly revised and interpolated into *Blackbirds*.

Although Leslie's shows featured the top black talents of the day, he rarely hired black songwriters for his shows. "Whites," he explained in an interview, "understand the colored man better than he does himself." Nevertheless, there has been speculation that Fats Waller* sold the rights to "I Can't Give You Anything But Love" to McHugh, but this possibility has not been confirmed.

*Blackbirds of 1928* became the longest running black musical of the 1920s. Leslie attempted to repeat his success with new versions of "Blackbirds," but none received the acclaim of the 1928 show.

**(LEW LESLIE'S) BLACKBIRDS OF 1930** (Royale, October 22, 1930, 57 p.). Producer and director: Lew Leslie. Book: Flournoy Miller* and Al Richards. Composer: Eubie Blake.* Lyricist: Andy Razaf.*

Cast: Ethel Waters,* Flournoy Miller, Mantan Moreland,* Neeka Shaw, Jimmy Baskette, Mercia Marquiz, Broadway Jones, Minto Cato, Crawford Jackson, Blue McAllister, the Berry Brothers, and Cecil Mack's* Blackbird Choir.

Songs: Roll Jordan; Cabin Door; Memories of You; Mozambique; You're Lucky to Me; My Handyman Ain't Handy No More; Take a Trip to Harlem; We're the Berries; That Lindy Hop; Dianna Lee; Green Pastures (Lyrics by Will Morrissey and Andy Razaf); Papa-De-Da-Da (Spencer Williams, Clarence Todd, and Clarence Williams).

Lew Leslie continually tried to duplicate the success of *Blackbirds of 1928*,* but, despite considerable talent, the new editions failed to survive during the depression years. The 1930 version, billed as "Glorifying the American Negro," teamed Ethel Waters and Flournoy Miller as the leads, while Eubie Blake and Andy Razaf provided the songs. Critics praised the entire enterprise, although some resented the 11:45 curtain on opening night.

The show proved a bonanza for Eubie Blake. He received $250 weekly for conducting the *Blackbirds* orchestra, but he earned considerably more from royalties for his hit-studded score, as many songs became standards. Ethel Waters's version of "You're Lucky to Me" and Minto Cato's rendition of "Memories of You" stopped the show. Razaf's sentimental lyrics for these songs provided a sharp contrast with "My Handyman Ain't Handy No More," which was laden with classic double entendres.

Despite the praise from the critics, *Blackbirds of 1930* perished at the box office. Ethel Waters recalled the show in her autobiography, *His Eye Is on the Sparrow:* "*Blackbirds* opened . . . right next to the flea circus. Our show was a flop, and the fleas outdrew us at every performance. The Depression came and made our business worse. But it didn't dent the take of the flea circus at all. It reminded me of the old . . . joke about the flea circus that became so prosperous that each flea was given his own private dog."

**BLACKBIRDS OF 1933** (Apollo, December 2, 1933, 25 p.). Producer: Sepia Guild Players, Inc. and Lew Leslie. Book: Nat N. Dorfman, Mann Holiner, and Lew Leslie. Director: Lew Leslie.

Cast: Bill Robinson* (Guest Star), Edith Wilson,* Eddie Hunter,* John Mason, Lionel Monagas,* Speedy Smith, Slappy Wallace, Brady Jackson, James Thomas Boxwill, Henry Williams, Worthy and Thompson, Kathryn Perry, Blue McAllister, Mary Mathews, Cecil Mack's Choir.

Songs: I'm Walkin' the Chalk Line; I Just Couldn't Take It Baby; Your Mother's Son-in-Law, Doin' the Shim Sham (Alberta Nichols-Mann Holiner); A Hundred Years from Today; Tappin' the Barrel; Victim of the Voodoo Drums; Let Me Be Born Again; What—No Dixie? (Victor Young-Joseph Young and Ned Washington).

The third edition of *Blackbirds* failed to impress the critics. The skits, mainly parodies of current Broadway shows and films, were dismissed as "unfunny" and "almost embarrassing." Similarly, the songs by Alberta Nichols and Mann Holiner, which had saved *Rhapsody in Black*,* also escaped notice.

Only one fact managed to save *Blackbirds of 1933* from mediocrity. Bill Robinson, billed as a "guest star" in two second act appearances, almost made the critics forget the show's problems. Brooks Atkinson of *The New York Times* devoted his entire review to Robinson's genius: "Without wasting energy or time or directing attention to anything except his virtuoso feet, he devotes himself to tap dancing, which is a form of physical exercise he has translated into magic."

**(LEW LESLIE'S) BLACKBIRDS OF 1939** (Hudson, February 11, 1939, 9 p.). Producer, author, and director: Lew Leslie.

Cast: Lena Horne,* Hamtree Harrington, Tim Moore,* Dewey "Pigmeat" Markham, Beryl Clarke, Joyce Beasley, Kate Hall, Lavinia Williams, Dorothy Sachs, Vic Mizzy, Rosalie King, Mitchell Parish, Atta Blake, Laurene Hines, Mickey Jones, Rosetta Crawford, Louisa Howard, Norma Miller, Edith Ross, Lorenza Robertson, Charles Welch, Bobby Evans, Al Bledger, Taps Miller, Frank Riley, Louis Haber, Irving Taylor, Sammy Fain, Norman McConney, Jerry Laws, William Downes, Robert Clarke, Coleman Hill, George Greenridge, Ralph Brown, Joe Byrd, J. Rosamond Johnson's* Choir.

Songs: Thursday (Dorothy Sachs-Louis Haber); Name It and It's Yours; You're So Indifferent (Sammy Fain-Mitchell Parish-Abner Silver); I Did It for the Red, White, and Blue; Dixie Isn't Dixie Anymore (Rube Bloom-Johnny Mercer).

The short-lived *Blackbirds of 1939* ("A Harlem Rhapsody") proved to be

Lew Leslie's last attempt to duplicate the success of his 1928 edition. Despite the omnipresence of Mr. Leslie both backstage and in the orchestra pit, the show lingered only a week. Nevertheless, Leslie, the impresario who propelled Florence Mills,* Bill Robinson,* Ethel Waters,* and Adelaide Hall* to fame, managed to discover another future star. Leslie plucked young Lena Horne from the Cotton Club chorus in 1936 and groomed her for Broadway stardom. Critics greeted Horne's performance favorably, but commented that there was room for improvement. Brooks Atkinson's observations in *The New York Times* were typical: "Among those present is a radiantly beautiful sepia girl, Lena Horne, who sings 'Thursday' and 'You're So Indifferent' in attractive style, and who will be a winner when she has proper direction."

**THE BLACKS** (St. Marks, May 4, 1961, 1,408 p.). Producers: Sidney Bernstein, George Edgar, and Andre Gregory. Author: Jean Genet. Translator: Bernard Frechtman. Director: Gene Frankel.

Cast: Roscoe Lee Browne* (Archibald Wellington), James Earl Jones* (Deodatus Village), Cynthia Belgrave (Adelaide Bobo), Louis Gossett* (Edgar Alas Newport News), Ethel Ayler (Augustus Snow), Helen Martin (Felicity Trollop Pardon), Cicely Tyson* (Stephanie Virtue Diop), Godfrey Cambridge (Diouf), Lex Monson (Missionary), Raymond St. Jacques (Judge), Jay J. Riley (Governor), Maya Angelou Make (Queen), Charles Gordone* (Valet), Charles Campbell (Drummer).

The success of Jean Genet's *The Blacks* helped to spark the boom in black theatre Off-Broadway during the 1960s. *The New York Times*' Howard Taubman declared *The Blacks* "an event": "As theatre it combines the excitement of originality with the simplicity of ritual. As language it whispers with tenderness and roars with passion. As an exploration into the heart of the Negro it moves from anger to aspiration." Genet's analysis of class, color, and colonialism takes the form of a play-within-a-play. Blacks in white masks portray the colonial masters, while the remaining characters portray the common people of a mythical country.

*The Blacks* provided opportunities for black actors who had languished in Broadway productions of the 1950s to shine anew. Howard Taubman noted: "The craftsmen and artists who have contributed to this interpretation deserve their meed of credit. So do the actors, who bring vibrancy and intensity to their performances. Read the names of all in the cast with respect, and remember with special warmth Roscoe Lee Browne, James Earl Jones, Cynthia Belgrave, Ethel Ayler, Helen Martin, Cicely Tyson and Godfrey M. Cambridge."

**LES BLANCS** (Longacre, November 15, 1970, 40 p.). Producer: Konrad Matthaei. Author: Lorraine Hansberry.* Director: John Berry.

Cast: James Earl Jones* (Tshembe Matoseh), Earle Hyman* (Abioseh Matoseh), Cameron Mitchell (Charlie Morris), Marie Andrews (Dr. Marta

Gotterling), Charles Moore (Warrior), Joan Derby (Witch Doctor), Dennis Tate (First African), George Fairley (Second African), Gregory Beyer (African Child), Clebert Ford (Peter), William Ware (Third African), Humbert Allen Astredo (Dr. Willy Dekoven), Ralph Purdum (Maj. Rice), Garry Mitchell (First Soldier), Gwyllum Evans (Second Soldier), Lili Darvas (Madame Neilsen), Harold Scott (Eric).

*Les Blancs*, Lorraine Hansberry's final work, was adapted for the stage by her husband Robert Nemiroff. Although unfinished before Hansberry's death, *Les Blancs* still managed to bring raves from the critics. Walter Kerr commented in *The New York Times*: "Virtually all of *Les Blancs* is there on stage, vivid, singing, intellectually alive, and what is there is mature work, ready to stand without apology alongside the completed work of our best craftsmen."

James Earl Jones received a Drama Desk Award for his performance as Tshembe, an African educated in Europe and America. He returns home a day after his father's funeral and swiftly discovers that he is caught between cultures. His father, a tribal chieftain, represents the ways of the past, while black freedom fighters seem to represent the wave of the future. Yet, Tshembe views his country's options with the eyes of a Western-educated intellectual. Clayton Riley, writing in *The New York Times*, found James Earl Jones's performance "magnificent": "Whether poised on the edge of some towering rage or consumed by some strange mixture of grief and guarded humor, he builds a performance that penetrates the soul of the viewer with its precision and formidable, self-renewing power. No moment of the play is unaffected by his presence." [November 29, 1970]

**THE BLOOD KNOT** (Cricket, March 1, 1964, 240 p.). Producers: Sidney Bernstein and Lucille Lortel. Author: Athol Fugard. Director: John Berry.

Cast: James Earl Jones* (Zachariah Pieterson), J. D. Cannon (Morris Pieterson).

*The Blood Knot*, by white South African playwright Athol Fugard, provided an excellent vehicle for the talents of James Earl Jones. The "blood knot" is between two brothers, sons of the same mother, but one is black and the other is white. Fugard's play strips away the brotherly feelings and reveals the tensions underneath in this metaphorical look at South African life. *The New York Times* praised stars Cannon and Jones for giving *The Blood Knot* "the brilliant performance it deserves": "Jones plays Zachariah with a rare grasp of his slow simplicity with its warmth and shyness, and he brings tension and fury to the bitter, explosive scenes."

**THE BLUE BOY IN BLACK** (Masque, April 30, 1963, 23 p.). Producer and director: Ashley Feinstein. Author: Edmund White.

Cast: Cicely Tyson* (Joan), Billy Dee Williams* (Robert), John Hillerman (Jim Lawland), Alice Drummond (Isabel Lawland), Lois Zetter (Mother), Stan Watt (John), Anthony Redfern (Visitor).

Despite a brief run, *The Blue Boy in Black* allowed critics to take note of Cicely Tyson and Billy Dee Williams. Joan (Tyson), the maid in a wealthy household, uses her feminine wiles to snag the man of the house, but is unable to attract the man she loves (Williams). Her world collapses, and she retreats into a fantasy world built around Gainsborough's *Blue Boy*. While Tyson received critical praise, reaction to the play was mixed. *Theatre Arts* noted: "It is clear that Mr. White can write crisp and searching dialogue; he has an original and true sense of humor." *The New Yorker*, however, disagreed: "Mr. White cannot handle smoothly enough its switches in style from satire to straight comedy to fantasy to serious drama."

**BLUE HOLIDAY** (Belasco, May 21, 1945, 8 p.). Producers: Irvin Shapiro and Doris Cole. Director: Joe Hack.

Cast: Ethel Waters,* Josh White,* Mary Lou Williams, Timmie Rogers, Josephine Premice, Willie Bryant, Muriel Gaines, Lillian Fitzgerald, Lavinia Williams, Talley Beatty, Mildred Smith, Evelyn Ellis,* The Three Poms, The Chocolateers, the Hall Johnson* Choir, the Katherine Dunham* Dancers.

Songs: I Want to Give It All to the Stage; Blue Holiday; That's Where My Heart Will Be; Sleep Time Lullaby (Al Moritz); Free and Equal Blues (E. Y. Harburg-Earl Robinson); The House I Live In (Robinson-Lewis Allen); Evil-Hearted Man (Traditional); Hard Time Blues (Josh White-Warren Cuney); Yours Is My Heart Alone (Franz Lehar); Duke Ellington Medley (includes: Mood Indigo; Sophisticated Lady; Solitude).

*Blue Holiday* was generally dismissed as a "variety show," which might have been suitable for nightclubs but not for Broadway. While several parts of the show received praise, Wolcott Gibbs of *The New Yorker* found the whole "familiar and repetitive." Ethel Waters provided the main draw with a medley of her song hits and a reprise of a scene from *Mamba's Daughters*.* Josh White received the best reviews for his performance of such songs as "Hard Times Blues," "Evil-Hearted Man," "The House I Live In," and "Free and Equal Blues."

**BLUES FOR MR. CHARLIE** (ANTA, April 23, 1964, 148 p.). Producer: Actors Studio Inc. Author: James Baldwin.* Director: Burgess Meredith.

Cast: Al Freeman, Jr.* (Richard Henry), Diana Sands* (Juanita), Rosetta LeNoire (Mother Henry), Pat Hingle (Parnell), Rip Torn (Lyle Britten), Clyde Williams (Arthur), Frankie Brown (Disc Jockey), Percy Rodriguez (Rev. Meridian Henry), Wayne Grice (Tom), Otis Young (Ken), Lincoln Kilpatrick (Pete), David Baldwin (Lorenzo), Ann Wedgeworth (Jo Britten), John McCurry (Papa D), Pat Randall (Hazel), Patricia Quinn

(Susan), Ralph Waite (Ralph), Joe Don Baker (Ellis), Ann Hennessey (Lillian), Bill Moor (Rev. Phelps), Pat Corley (Stenographer), Dick Bradford (The State), Otis Young (Counsel for the Bereaved), Grachan Moncur III (Trombonist).

Prior to the opening of *Blues for Mr. Charlie*, James Baldwin explained: "I'm not concerned with the success or failure of this play. I want to shock the people; I want to wake them up; I want to make them think; I want to trick them into an experience I think is important." *The New York Times* found that Baldwin succeeded in his aims. Howard Taubman wrote: "Baldwin has written a play with fires of fury in its belly, tears of anguish in its eyes and a roar of protest in its throat . . . *Blues for Mr. Charlie* is a summons to arms in this generation's burning cause—the establishment in this country of the Negro's full manhood, with all the perquisites of that simple and lofty station."

Although Baldwin's play has the structure of a courtroom drama, the plot weaves between present and past, reality and illusion, and thought and action. During the trial of the southern storekeeper for the murder of a black pastor's son, characters remove themselves from the action and speak their true feelings on the plight of blacks in America to the audience. Al Freeman, Jr., as the pastor's son, Percy Rodriguez, Rosetta LeNoire, and Diana Sands received critical praise for their performances.

**BOESMAN AND LENA** (Circle in the Square, June 22, 1970, 205 p.). Producers: Theodore Mann, Paul Libin, and John Berry. Author: Athol Fugard. Director: John Berry.

Cast: James Earl Jones* (Boesman), Ruby Dee* (Lena), Zakes Mokae (Old African).

Athol Fugard, the South African playwright, was unable to attend the premiere of *Boesman and Lena* because he was denied a passport by his government. The play received rave reviews on its New York opening, and cast members James Earl Jones and Ruby Dee won honors for their portrayal of the title characters. Dee, according to Clive Barnes of *The New York Times*, gave one of the finest performances he had ever seen, and she won both Obie and Drama Desk Awards for her efforts. The play concerns the dehumanization of Boesman and Lena by South African life. Living on the fringes of society, they are constantly on the move in their search for survival. Boesman beats Lena, but she remains with him. Lena befriends an elderly African (Zakes Mokae), but Boesman eventually kills him, and the couple continues their trek.

**BOHIKEE CREEK** (Stage 73, April 28, 1966, 30 p.). Producers: Patrick Baldauff, Frank Boone, and Gillian Crowe. Author: Robert Unger. Director: Donald Moreland.

Cast: James Earl Jones* (Arnie; Bo), Moses Gunn* (Able; Coke), Richard

Havens (Folk Singer), Georgia Burke (Aunty Mom), Wayne Grice (Tinch), Dennis Tate (Halfbeak), Billie Allen (Reba), Julius Harris (Harold).

Robert Unger's *Bohikee Creek* provides four vignettes of life on the banks of a South Carolina river that winds to the ocean. Stanley Kauffman, writing in *The New York Times*, praised the director (Donald Moreland) and the cast (especially Moses Gunn and Georgia Burke), but had harsh words for the playwright: "His plays are executed with moderate competence. But, they show small originality and virtually no sense of personal style." The second interlude, a conflict between a Nigerian exchange student (Wayne Grice) and his Carolinian schoolmate (Dennis Tate) was selected as the best piece of the evening by several critics.

**BOTTOMLAND** (Princess, June 27, 1927, 21 p.). Producer, composer, and librettist: Clarence Williams. Directors: Aaron Gates and Clarence Williams.

Cast: Eva Taylor (May Mandy Lee), Clarence Williams (Piano), Sara Martin (Mammy Lee), James A. Lillard (Pappy Lee), Louis Cole (Jimmy), Katherine Henderson (Tough Tilly), Slim Henderson (Joshua), John Mason (The Dumb Waiter), Charles Doyle (Henry Henpeck), Nuggie Johnson (Shiftless Sam), Raymond Campbell (Skinny), Edward Farrow (Rastus), Olive Otiz (Sally), Willie Porter (Mammy Chloe), Emanuel Weston (Kid Slick), Edwin Tonde (Policeman Doolittle), Craddock and Shadney (Specialty).

Songs: Steamboat Days (lyrics: Clarence Williams); Shootin' the Pistol (lyrics: Chris Smith); Bottomland (lyrics: Jo Trent); You're the Only One (lyrics: Ken Gray); Come on Home (Donald Heywood); Dancing Girl (lyrics: Spencer Williams); Any Time (Joe Jordan); When I March with April in May (lyrics: Spencer Williams).

Clarence Williams explained the evolution of his new musical comedy as follows: "Complying to the thousands of requests from radio friends to see and hear the Clarence Williams Trio in person, I have written a musical comedy in three acts with special music, entitled *Bottomland.* Eva Taylor and Sara Martin, the world's foremost Okeh recording artists, have been engaged as co-stars."

Although critics praised the evening's music and dance, they lamented the fact that such talented performers were trapped by such a weak book. The plot, which *Billboard* claimed "would hardly do credit to a child," concerns May Mandy Lee (Eva Taylor) "a happy, but ambitious" southern woman. She receives letters from her friend Sally about the joys of New York City, and she resolves to follow her north. When May arrives, she discovers that Sally has become an alcoholic who sings in a second-rate nightclub. The club then provides the setting for the Clarence Williams musical numbers. "Shootin' the Pistol" and the title song received the most praise from the critics.

**BRAIN SWEAT** (Longacre, April 4, 1934, 5 p.). Producers: James Montgomery and Henry R. Stern. Author: John Charles Brownell. Director: Robert Ober.

Cast: Billy Higgins (Henry Washington), Rose McClendon* (Carrie Washington), Barrington Guy (Charlie Washington), A. B. Comathiere* (Rev. Elisha Tatum), Pearl Wright (Angie Johnson), Dick Campbell (Jake Johnson), Viola Dean (Lucy), Marie Young (Laura), Andrew Tribble (Flatfoot Molly), E. J. Blunkall (Mr. Covington).

John Charles Brownell, author of *The Nut Farm* (1929) and *Her Majesty, the Widow* (1934), designed a white view of black life in a short-lived 1934 comedy, *Brain Sweat.* Henry Washington (Billy Higgins) discovers a pamphlet which tells him to use his mental powers to the fullest. He decides to quit his job and "think" for two years. Henry's wife tires of his laziness and wishes he would drown himself. When she finds his hat on the river bank, she gives him a grand funeral. It turns out that Henry is actually in Memphis, where he has put his "brain sweat" to good use and become a success.

The critics found this comedy amiable at best, but had praise for the performances. *The New York Times* noted that "Rose McClendon, as the long-suffering Mrs. Washington, plays with all the delicacy of a sensitive artist; she has a presence and a grace that are wholly admirable." Billy Higgins, who had been seen in *Hot Chocolates** and vaudeville, gave a remarkable performance in the leading role. Robert Garland of the *World-Telegram* found that he "draws a character that is replete with a disarming and twinkling sort of fun."

**BROTHERHOOD** (St. Marks, March 10, 1970, 64 p.). Producer: Negro Ensemble Company.* Author and director: Douglas Turner Ward.*

Cast: William Jay (James Johnson), Frances Foster* (Luann Johnson), Tom Rosqui (Tom Jason), Tiffany Hendry (Ruth Jason).

The ironically titled *Brotherhood* appeared as a one-act curtain-raiser for the 1970 revival of Douglas Turner Ward's *Day of Absence.** Ward's satire provides a fantastic encounter between a white couple (the Jasons) and a black couple (the Johnsons). The white couple's living room is mostly hidden from the audience and the Johnsons as well, as white sheets and blankets cover statuary, a painting, and furniture. After a "marvelous" evening, the Jasons remove the covers and reveal "a staggering profusion of diverse artifacts of Niggerphobia." The painting is revealed as a mural depicting the bloody slaughter of blacks in America. Accompanying this ritual is a recording of "Ol' Black Joe."

**BROWN BUDDIES** (Liberty, October 7, 1930, 111 p.). Producer: Not designated. Book: Carl Rickman. Composer: Joe Jordan.* Lyricist: Millard Thomas. Director: Ralph Rose.

Cast: Bill Robinson* (Sam Wilson), Adelaide Hall* (Betty Lou Johnson), Shelton Brooks* (Deacon Siccamore), John Mason (Spider Bruce), Thomas Moseley (Mathews), "Little Ferdie" Lewis (Hamfat), Ada Brown (Mammy Johnson), Alma Smith (Jessie Watkins), Andrew Tribble (George Brown), Putney Dandridge (Ukelele Kid), Walter Brogsdale (Bill Jones), Maurice Ellis (Pete Jackson), Ethel Jackson (Mabel), Nancy Sharpe (A Woman), Sam Jones (A Policeman), Hank Smith (Trumpeter), Wm. E. Fountaine (Pugh), Joseph Willis (Houston Charlie), James Lillard (Captain Andrews), Carroll Tate (Medical Officer), Edgar Brown (Orderly), Red and Struggy (Privates Red and Struggy), Thomas Wye (YMCA Man), Archie Toms (Corporal).

Songs: Gettin' Off; Brown Buddies; Sugar Cane; My Blue Melody; Carry On; I Lost Everything Losing You; Sweetie Mine. Additional songs by other composers: Give Me a Man Like That (George A. Little-Art Sizemore); When a Black Man's Blue (Little-Sizemore-Ed G. Nelson); Missouria (Nat Reed); I Hate Myself for Falling in Love with You (Abner Silver-Dave Oppenheim); Happy (Reed-Bob Joffe); Don't Leave Your Little Blackbird Blue (Jordan-Porter Grainger-Shelton Brooks); Darky Rhythm (Peter Tinturin-Joe Young); Dance Away Your Sins (J. C. Johnson); Betty Lou (Jordan-J. Rosamond Johnson).

*Brown Buddies* reunited the stars of *Blackbirds of 1928*,* Bill Robinson and Adelaide Hall, and reaffirmed their unique talents. Bill Robinson again dazzled the critics with his dancing. Richard Lockridge, critic for *The Sun*, explained: "He croons with his feet and laughs with them and watches them as they do things which apparently surprise him as much as they do the rest of us, and please him, if possible, even more." Even though he performed with his arm in a sling (he was accidentally shot by a policeman in Pittsburgh), the critic for *Time* still found Robinson's "peerless hoofing and broad smile worth anyone's three dollars." The critics also praised Adelaide Hall's "luxuriant voice."

The plot of *Brown Buddies* assumed a surprisingly serious tone. The "Brown Buddies" are a troupe of black soldiers from East Saint Louis who travel to France during World War I. The scenery shows a devastated land marked by shell holes and withered trees. During the second act, the show brightens considerably as Bill Robinson, accompanied by Red and Struggy, perform an extended dance routine for a USO show. Everyone returns safely to Saint Louis on the day before Prohibition becomes law, thus allowing an energetic song-and-dance number for the finale.

**BROWN SUGAR** (Biltmore, December 2, 1937, 4 p.). Producer and director: George Abbott. Author: Bernie Angus.

Cast: Christola Williams (Rosalinda), Juan Hernandez* (Sam), Beulah E. Edmonds (Louella), Richard Huey (Bartender), T. Burton Smith (Tom Warfield), John T. L. Bunn (Trot), Martin de C. Slade (Lonny), Ira Johnson (Charlie), Kathryn Lavall (Ruby), Alvin Childress (Slim), Richard McMyers (Sylvester), Paul Johnson (Tar), Eric Burroughs (Musken), Ruby Elzy (Sarah), Bertram Holmes (Jeb), Julian Miles (Officer Leroy), Jimmy Waters (Man), Haven Johnson (Rosco), Canada Lee* (Henry), Georgette Harvey* (Lily May), Butterfly McQueen (Lucille), William Tinney (Walter), Allen Tinney (George), Beth Dixon (Stella), Irene Hill (Cleo), John Shellie (Pete Malley), Ernest Rowan (First Mate), George W. Smith (Officer Kent), George Fitzpatrick (O'Hara), Fred Wallace (McQuade).

John Mason Brown of *The New York Post* found *Brown Sugar* a "mediocre Harlem script." Mrs. Bernadine Angus's second play of the season claimed to be a "paean of uptown Manhattan," but critics thought it was just the opposite. Christola Williams starred as a black woman who murders a white man and then attempts to put the blame on another, Sam Jackson (Juan Hernandez). Louella (Beulah E. Edmonds), Sam's wife, helps him evade the police and escape on a tramp steamer. The real murderer is discovered, and Louella hopes for happier days to come.

Brown found the cast "excellent": "Juan Hernandez, Christola Williams, Beulah Edmonds, and Georgette Harvey are capable players. They cannot be blamed if they are forced to hide their lights under the bushel basket of Mrs. Angus's bad playwrighting."

**THE BROWNSVILLE RAID** (St. Marks, December 5, 1976, 112 p.). Producer: Negro Ensemble Company.* Author: Charles Fuller.* Director: Israel Hicks.

Cast: Douglas Turner Ward* (Sgt. Maj. Mingo Saunders), Samm-Art Williams* (Cpl. Clifford Adair), Adolph Caesar* (Pvt. John Holliman), Charles Weldon (Pvt. James Newton), Reyno (Pvt. Dorsey Willis), Bill Cobbs (Pvt. Reuben Collins), Arthur French (Cpl. Boyd Conjers), Lawrence Keith (Captain), Wayne Elbert (Pvt. Richard Johnson), Ethel Ayler (Dolly Saunders), Charles Brown (Orderly), Robert Fitzsimmons (Mayor Combs), Owen Hughes (Theodore Roosevelt), Graham Brown (Emmett Scott), William Mooney (Maj. Blocker), Frank Hamilton (Gen. Garlin), Sam Finch (Sentry).

Charles Fuller's *The Brownsville Raid* revealed a little known incident of black American history. A black regiment of the army was sent to Brownsville in 1906, where the townsfolk did everything possible to rid themselves of the new residents. One night, a group of men (allegedly the soldiers) shot up the town and killed a Mexican. The evidence against the soldiers appeared sparse, and it seemed that the townspeople staged the incident to frame the soldiers. The ruse was successful, and the soldiers were dishonorably discharged without a hearing. Theodore Roosevelt delayed the discharge until after the election, so that blacks might not be dissuaded from voting for the Republican party.

Critics praised Fuller's "fairness" and "truthfulness" in dealing with these historical events. While Clive Barnes of *The New York Times* hesitated to single out any individual for praise since this was a "team show," he lauded the performances of Douglas Turner Ward, Adolph Caesar, Arthur French, Graham Brown, and William Mooney.

**BUBBLING BROWN SUGAR** (ANTA, March 2, 1976, 766 p.). Producers: J. Lloyd Grant, Richard Bell, Robert M. Cooper, Ashton Springer, and Moe Septee. Book: Loften Mitchell.* New songs: Danny Holgate, Emme Kemp, and Lillian Lopez. Director: Robert M. Cooper.

Cast: Avon Long* (John Sage; Rusty), Josephine Premice (Irene Paige), Vivian Reed (Marsha; Young Irene), Joseph Attles (Checkers; Dusty), Ethel Beatty (Ella), Barry Preston (Charlie; Count), Lonnie McNeil (Skip; Young Checkers), Vernon Washington (Bill; Time Man; Bumpy; Emcee), Newton Winters (Ray; Young Sage), Carolyn Bird (Carolyn; Gospel Lady; Female Nightclub Singer), Alton Lathrop (Gene; Gospel Lady's Son), Dyann Robinson (Helen), Charlise Harris (Laura), Anthony Whitehouse (Tony; Waiter; Dutch), Chip Garnett (Jim; Male Nightclub Singer), Barbara Rubenstein (Judy; Dutch's Girl).

Songs: Harlem '70 (Holgate); Bubbling Brown Sugar (Holgate-Lopez-Kemp); That's What Harlem Is To Me (Andy Razaf*); Harlem Sweet Harlem (Holgate-Kemp); Nobody (Alex Rogers*-Bert Williams*); Goin' Back in Time (Holgate-Kemp-Lopez); Some of These Days (Shelton Brooks*); Moving Uptown (Holgate-Mitchell); I'm Gonna Tell God All My Troubles; His Eye Is on the Sparrow; Swing Low, Sweet Chariot; Sweet Georgia Brown (Maceo Pinkard); Honeysuckle Rose (Fats Waller*-Razaf); Stormy Monday Blues (Earl "Fatha" Hines); Rosetta (Hines); Sophisticated Lady (Duke Ellington*-Mitchell Parish-Irving Mills); In Honeysuckle Time (Eubie Blake*-Noble Sissle); Solitude (Ellington-Eddie De Lange-Mills); C'mon Up to Jive Time (Holgate-Kemp-Lopez); Stompin' at the Savoy (Benny Goodman-Chick Webb-Edgar Sampson-Razaf); Take the 'A' Train (Duke Ellington-Billy Strayhorn); Harlem Time (Holgate-Kemp-Lopez); Love Will Find a Way (Blake-Sissle); Dutch's Song (Kemp); Brown Gal (A. Long-Lil Armstrong); Pray for the Lights to Go Out (Renton Tunnan-Will Skidmore); I Got It Bad and That Ain't Good (Ellington-Paul Francis Webster); Harlem Makes Me Feel (Kemp); Jim, Jam, Jumpin' Jive (Cab Calloway); There'll Be Some Changes Made (Billy Higgins-W. Benton Overstreet); God Bless the Child (Billie Holiday-Arthur Herzog, Jr.); It Don't Mean a Thing (Ellington-Mills).

*Bubbling Brown Sugar* was the first musical revue to explore the history of black music on Broadway and in Harlem. It would be followed by others —*Ain't Misbehavin'** and *Eubie!**—in an attempt to fill a missing chapter in black musical history. This revival of the music of Blake, Ellington,

Waller, and several others won the attention of Broadway audiences, if not the critics. Veterans Avon Long, Joseph Attles, and Josephine Premice provided memories of past shows, while such newcomers as Vivian Reed and Chip Garnett (both Theatre World Award winners) gave the show a contemporary razzle-dazzle. Billy Wilson, the choreographer, received praise for his uncanny revival of historical dance favorites. After a long Broadway run, *Bubbling Brown Sugar* also found success in a London production.

**BUCK WHITE** (George Abbott, December 2, 1969, 7 p.). Producer: Zev Bufman and High John Productions. Book and score: Oscar Brown, Jr. Directors: Oscar Brown, Jr., and Jean Pace.

Cast: Muhammad Ali (Buck White), Herschell Burton (Hunter), David Moody (Honey Man), Ted Ross (Weasel), Charles Weldon (Rubber Band), Don Rich (Jive), Eugene Smith (Whitey), Don Sutherland (Black Man).

Songs: Honey Man Song; Money, Money, Money; Nobody Does My Thing; Step Across That Line; H. N. I. C.; Beautiful Allelujah Days; Tap the Plate; Big Time Buck White Chant; Better Far; We Came in Chains; Black Balloons; Look at Them; Mighty Whitey; Get Down.

While *Big Time Buck White** enjoyed favorable reviews and a 124-performance Off-Broadway run, the musical version, *Buck White*, faded within the week. The highlight of the new show was the appearance of Muhammad Ali (Cassius Clay) in the title role. The critics found his performance adequate, but the rewritten play lacked the power of the original. While the Oscar Brown songs were received favorably, few had a chance to hear them during the show's brief run.

**BUT NEVER JAM TODAY** (Longacre, July 31, 1979, 8 p.). Producers: Arch Nadler, Anita MacShane, and the Urban Arts Theatre. Book: Vinnette Carroll* and Bob Larimer. Composers: Bert Keyes and Bob Larimer. Lyricist: Bob Larimer. Director: Vinnette Carroll.

Cast: Marilynn Winbush (Alice), Cleavant Derricks (Caterpillar; Cook; Tweedledee; Seven of Spades), Lynne Thigpen (Persona Non Grata), Lynne Clifton-Allen (Black Queen), Jeffrey Anderson-Gunter (White Rabbit; Cheshire Cat; Mock Turtle), Reginald Vel Johnson (Duchess; Humpty-Dumpty; King of Hearts), Jai Oscar St. John (Mad Hatter; Tweedledum; Two of Spades), Sheila Ellis (March Hare; Five of Spades; Cook), Celestine DeSaussure (Dormouse; Cook), Charlene Harris (White Queen; Queen of Hearts).

Songs: Curiouser and Curiouser; Twinkle, Twinkle Little Star; Long Live the Queen; A Real Life Lullabye; The More I See People; My Little Room; But Never Jam Today; They; Riding for a Fall; All the Same to Me; I've Got My Orders; God Could Give Me Anything; I Like to Win; And They All Call the Hatter Mad; Jumping from Rock to Rock.

Vinnette Carroll had hoped to produce a Broadway musical version of Lewis Carroll's *Alice in Wonderland* for several years. In 1978, her new version of *Alice* (originally a workshop production for the Urban Arts Corps), with music by Micki Grant,* closed in Philadelphia. This lavish musical (from the producers of *Annie*) had a lackluster look which diminished the pleasure of the songs and choreography. *Alice* was reworked into *But Never Jam Today*, with only Cleavant Derricks and Jeffrey Anderson-Gunter remaining from the original production. Unfortunately, this renewed effort was to little avail, and Carroll's new production faded after only eight performances.

# C

**CABIN IN THE SKY** (Martin Beck, October 25, 1940, 156 p.). Producers: Albert Lewis and Vinton Freedly. Book: Lynn Root. Composer: Vernon Duke. Lyricist: John La Touche. Directors: George Balanchine and Albert Lewis.

Cast: Ethel Waters* (Petunia Jackson), Dooley Wilson* (Little Joe Jackson), Katherine Dunham* (Georgia Brown), Rex Ingram* (Lucifer, Jr.), Todd Duncan* (The Lawd's General), Louis Sharp (Dr. Jones), J. Rosamond Johnson* (Brother Green), Georgia Burke (Lily), Milton Williams (Fleetfoot), J. Louis Johnson (John Henry), Al Moore (Dude), Earl Sydnor, Earl Edwards, Maurice Ellis (Henchmen), Al Stokes (Devil's Messenger), Wilson Bradley (Messenger Boy), Dick Campbell (Domino Johnson), and the Katherine Dunham Dancers.

Songs: The General's Song; Pay Heed; Taking a Chance on Love (additional lyrics: Ted Fetter); Cabin in the Sky; Do What You Wanna Do; My Old Virginia Home on the River Nile; Love Me Tomorrow; Love Turned the Light Out; Honey in the Honeycomb; Savannah.

*Cabin in the Sky* in some ways seemed a 1940s version of *The Green Pastures*.* Although Vernon Duke, George Balanchine, and Boris Aronson traveled to Virginia to discover the "general atmosphere" of black life, they produced yet another white version of black mythology.

Both "the Lawd's General" and Lucifer, Jr., fight for the soul of Little Joe (Dooley Wilson). The Lawd gives the errant Joe six months to redeem himself, but Satan plants every temptation in his path. Joe's flesh is weak, and he succumbs to the charms of Georgia Brown (Katherine Dunham). Yet, Little Joe's wife, Petunia (Ethel Waters) intervenes at the last moment and saves him from perdition.

The remarkable performances saved the musical from parody. Brooks Atkinson of *The New York Times* gave Ethel Waters a rave review: "As for Little Joe's wife, she is played by Ethel Waters, one of our great show people, with force and frankness that are completely overwhelming. Miss Waters is a thorough actress. She can act with her mouth, eyes, hands, arms—in fact, with her whole body. Her acting has the pliant rhythm of a dance."

Metro-Goldwyn-Mayer filmed *Cabin in the Sky* in 1943 with Ethel Waters, Eddie "Rochester" Anderson, and Lena Horne* in leading roles. An Off-Broadway revival in 1964 featured Rosetta LeNoire, Tony Middleton, and Ketty Lester.

**CARIB SONG** (Adelphi, September 27, 1945, 36 p.). Producer: George Stanton. Composer: Baldwin Bergersen. Librettist and lyricist: William Archibald. Directors: Katherine Dunham and Mary Hunter.

Cast: Katherine Dunham* (Woman), Avon Long* (Fisherman), Harriet Jackson (Singer), Mable Sanford Lewis (Fat Woman), Mercedes Gilbert (Tall Woman), William Franklin (The Husband), Elsie Benjamin (Fishwoman), La Rosa Estrada (Shango Priest), Tommy Gomez (Boy Possessed by a Snake), Vanoye Aikens (Leader of the Shango Dancers).

Songs: Go Sit By the Body; This Woman; Water Movin' Slow; Basket, Make a Basket; Woman Is a Rascal; A Girl She Can't Remain; Market Song; Sleep, Baby, Don't Cry; Today I Is So Happy; Can't Stop the Sea; You Know, Oh Lord; Go Down to the River; Oh, Lonely One.

After Katherine Dunham's triumph as Georgia Brown in *Cabin in the Sky*,* she returned to Broadway in William Archibald's musical of West Indian life. As a corn planter's beautiful wife, she runs off with the village fisherman. When she becomes pregnant, her husband murders her. While critics praised the score, the scenery, and the choreography, they complained that there was "very little play." Nevertheless, Dunham, Avon Long, and William Franklin won praise for their performances.

**CARIBBEAN CARNIVAL** (International, December 5, 1947, 11 p.). Producer: Adolph Thenstead. Composer and lyricist: Samuel L. Manning and Adolph Thenstead. Directors: Samuel L. Manning and John Hirshman.

Cast: Pearl Primus, Josephine Premice, Claude Marchant, Sam Manning, Pamela Ward, Billie Allen, Alex Young, Eloise Hill, Smith Kids, Trio Cubana, Peggy Watson, Duke of Iron, Curtis James, Fred Thomas, Padjet Fredericks, Dorothy Graham.

*Caribbean Carnival*, billed as "the first calypso musical ever presented," featured the talent, music, and dances of the West Indies. After several name changes, from *Calypso* to *Bongo*, *Caribbean Carnival* reached Broadway as a revue featuring Pearl Primus, Josephine Premice, and

Claude Marchant. While the music and choreography received praise, most critics missed the skillful hand of a director who could trim this "overlong" musical to a manageable length. As a result, *Caribbean Carnival* lasted for only a brief time on Broadway.

**CARMEN JONES** (Broadway, December 2, 1943, 502 p.). Producer: Billy Rose. Libretto and lyrics: Oscar Hammerstein II. Music: Georges Bizet. Directors: Hassard Short and Charles Friedman.

Cast: Muriel Smith (Carmen), Luther Saxon (Joe), Carlotta Franzell (Cindy Lou), Napoleon Reed (Corporal Morrell), Robert Clarke (Foreman), Jack Carr (Sergeant Brown), Sibol Cain (Sally), Edward Roche (T-Bone), William Jones (Tough Kid), Cozy Cole (Drummer), Melvin Howard (Bartender), Edward Christopher (Waiter), June Hawkins (Frankie), Jessica Russell (Myrt), Edward Lee Tyler (Rum), Dick Montgomery (Dink), Glenn Bryant (Husky Miller), P. Jay Sidney (Mr. Higgins), Fredye Marshall (Miss Higgins), Alford Pierre (Photographer), Urylee Leonardos, Ethel White (Card Players), Ruth Crumpton (Dancing Girl), William Dillard (Poncho), Sheldon B. Hoskins, Randolph Sawyer (Dancing Boxers), Melvin Howard (Bullet Head), Tony Fleming Jr. (Referee).

Songs: Lif' 'Em Up and Put 'Em down; Honey Gal o' Mine; Good Luck; Dat's Love; You Talk Just Like My Maw; Carmen Jones Is Goin' to Jail; Dere's a Cafe on de Corner; Beat Out Dat Rhythm on a Drum; Stan' Up and Fight; Whizzin' Away Along de Track; Dis Flower; If You Would Only Come Away; De Cards Don't Lie; Dat Ol' Boy; Poncho de Panther from Brazil; My Joe; Get Yer Program for de Big Fight; Dat's Our Man.

*Carmen Jones* transferred Bizet's *Carmen* from the world of opera to Broadway, as it became an all-black musical of contemporary life. Don José became Joe, an army corporal, the toreador Escamillo, a prize fighter, and Carmen, a worker in a parachute factory during World War II. Nevertheless, the basic context of *Carmen* remained intact.

Oscar Hammerstein II, the lyricist, and producer Billy Rose entrusted John Hammond, Jr., with the casting of the show. The noted jazz music expert assembled a cast of unknowns for the show. Muriel Smith, who played Carmen Jones, worked in a photographic laboratory to finance her music studies when Hammond discovered her.

Both music and drama critics received the new show favorably. Howard Barnes, critic for *The New York Times*, wrote: "The theater has taken over opera in *Carmen Jones*, and the result is wonderful to behold and hear. The new Billy Rose production is a triumphant demonstration that showmanship is as important as musical facility in an operatic presentation."

After a brief tour, *Carmen Jones* returned to Broadway on May 2, 1945, and April 7, 1946, for limited runs. A May 31, 1956, revival again featured

Muriel Smith in the title role. She, however, was replaced in the 1954 film version by Dorothy Dandridge.

**CARRY ME BACK TO MORNINGSIDE HEIGHTS** (John Golden, February 27, 1968, 7 p.). Producer: Saint Subber and Harold Loeb. Author: Robert Alan Aurthur. Director: Sidney Poitier.*

Cast: Louis Gossett* (Willie Nurse), Cicely Tyson* (Myrna Jessup), Johnny Brown (Henry Hardy), David Steinberg (Seymour Levin), Diane Ladd (Alma Sue Bates).

*Carry Me Back to Morningside Heights*, a comedy about white guilt during the civil rights movement, was dismissed by all the critics. The comedy is noteworthy only because it marked Sidney Poitier's debut as a Broadway director, and it featured interesting performances by Louis Gossett, Cicely Tyson, and Johnny Brown.

**THE CASE OF PHILIP LAWRENCE** (Lafayette, June 7, 1937, 55 p.). Producer: Negro Theatre Unit of the Federal Theatre Project* of the Works Progress Administration. Author: George MacEntee. Director: J. A. Smith.*

Cast: Maurice Ellis (Phil Lawrence), Frauline Alford (Nancy), Thomas Moseley (Chick Turner), William Brown (Half Pint), Louis Sharp (Heavy Head), Milton Lacey (Jim), Gerald De La Fontaine (Racy Green), Alberta Perkins (Martha "Mom" Robbins), Estelle Hemsley (Mrs. Jenkins), Dorothy Paul (Sue Wilkins), Frances Smith (Blues Singer), Clarence Brown (Accordian Player), Robert Veritch (Dreamy Duke), Eleanor Scher (Marian), Bebe Townsend (Cigarette Girl), Mabel Thorne (Matron), Sidney Easton, Walter Duke (Bodyguards), Bertram Miller (Prosecuting Attorney), George Nixon (Defense Attorney), Fritz Weller (Judge), James Williams, Edward J. Fleischer (Detectives), William Melville (College Professor), J. Louis Johnson (Reverend Stowe), Steve Horn, Pat McCullough (Guards), Wanda Macey, Bertram Holmes, Shirley Macey (Children).

This presentation of the Negro Unit of the Federal Theatre Project pleased most of the critics, with several calling it a "Harlem *Broadway*," a reference to the smash 1926 play. *The Case of Philip Lawrence* considers a contemporary theme. Lawrence (Maurice Ellis), a college-educated athlete, is a brilliant young man, but is unable to find any job but a redcap after he graduates. The early part of the play concerns his embitterment, but then, as *Variety* noted, the play turns to "melodrama." Lawrence is framed in the murder of Dreamy Dale, a noted politician, when the actual murderer, Chick Turner (Thomas Moseley), thrusts a gun in Lawrence's hand. At the last moment, Nancy (Frauline Alford), Lawrence's girlfriend, appears and reveals the truth. *Variety* dissented from the generally favorable reviews, noting that the author failed to deal with "the genuine social problem" revealed in Act I of *The Case of Philip Lawrence*.

**CEREMONIES IN DARK OLD MEN** (St. Marks, February 4, 1969, 40 p.). Producer: Negro Ensemble Company.* Author: Lonne Elder III.* Director: Edmund Cambridge.

Cast: Douglas Turner [Ward]* (Mr. Russell B. Parker), Arthur French (Mr. William Jenkins), William Jay (Theopolis Parker), David Downing* (Bobby Parker), Rosalind Cash* (Adele Parker), Samual Blue, Jr. (Blue Haven), Judyann Jonsson (Young Girl).

*Ceremonies in Dark Old Men* won a Drama Desk Award for author Lonne Elder III, as well as continued praise for the Negro Ensemble Company, which was then entering its second season. Clive Barnes of *The New York Times* compared the play to O'Casey's *Juno and the Paycock* for "its mood, poised between comedy and tragedy." The play concerns Russell B. Parker (Douglas Turner Ward), a former vaudeville hoofer and now a Harlem barbershop owner, and his struggle to remain honest in a difficult world. Critics exulted in the rich performances. Barnes found that Ward "had a tragic range and power, with just the right undercurrent the author demanded." He also praised William Jay as Parker's older brother, and Rosalind Cash as his sister, but felt that singling out actors did an injustice to the others in this "marvelous" ensemble company.

*Ceremonies in Dark Old Men* moved to the Pocket Theatre (April 28, 1969) to continue its run with a different cast. Richard Ward appeared as Russell Parker, Billy Dee Williams* as Theopolis Parker, and Bette Howard as Adele. This version ran 320 performances.

**CHANGE YOUR LUCK** (George M. Cohan, June 6, 1930, 17 p.). Producer: Cleon Throckmorton. Composer and lyricist: J. C. Johnson.* Book: Garland Howard. Director: Cleon Throckmorton.

Cast: Cora La Redd (Bandana Babe Peppers), Alberta Hunter (Mary Jane), Hamtree Harrington (Ebenezer Smart), Leigh Whipper* (Evergreen Peppers), Alex Lovejoy (Big Bill), Jimmy Thomas (Cateye), Garland Howard (Hot Stuff Jackson), Alberta Perkins (Malindy), Sam Cross (Profit Jones), Speedy Smith (Skybo Snowball), Sterling Grant (Romeo Green), Neeka Shaw (Josephine Peppers), Chick McKenney (Diamond Joe), Mable Grant (Mathilda), Millie Holmes (Passionate Sadie), Emma Maitland (Rat Row Sadie), Aurelia Wheeldin (Tack Annie), Dorothy Embrie, Mary Mason, Lillian Cowan (Sisters of Mercy), Henry Davis (Henry), James Davis (James), Van Jackson (Van), Bertha Roe (Ansy), Gertie Chambers (Gertie), Sammy Van (Charleston Sam), Louie Simms (Shake a Hip), Buster Bowie (Shake a Leg), J. Lewis Johnson (Captain Jones), and S. W. Warren, Chas. Gill, Billy Cole, and C. P. Wade (The Four Flash Devils).

Songs: Sweet Little Baby o' Mine; Can't Be Bothered Now; Ain't Puttin' Out Nothin'; Religion in My Feet; You Should Know; Wasting Away; Walk Together Children; Honesty; Mr. Mummy Man; My Regular Man; I'm

Honest; We're Here; Open That Door; Change Your Luck; Percolatin'; Travellin'; What Have I Done?; Rhythm Feet.

*Change Your Luck* featured an "enervating and pointless" book concerning the attempts of Hamtree Harrington to avoid the Prohibition agents. Fortunately, according to several critics, the libretto was virtually jettisoned by the second act, thus allowing a continual flow of song and dance. *Change Your Luck* even resorted to a female boxing match as did *Messin' Around** during the previous year, with Emma Maitland and Aurelia Wheeldin once again returning to battle for the championship.

**CHARLIE WAS HERE AND NOW HE'S GONE** (Eastside, June 6, 1971, 17 p.). Producers: Art James, Carl Sawyer, and Ted Rado. Author: Dennis Turner. Director: Jerry Adler.

Cast: Joe Morton (Charlie), Robert Guillaume* (Allen), Rosalind Cash* (Carla), Philip Williamson (Young Charlie), Robert LuPone (Sailor), Jerome Anello (First Mover), Norman Thomas Marshall (Second Mover), David Friedman (Scott).

In *Charlie Was Here and Now He's Gone*, Charlie (Joe Morton) changes from a sensitive ghetto youngster to a dope addict. Allan (Robert Guillaume), the local pusher, uses Charlie to stage a kidnapping of a rich Princeton youth. Most critics dismissed the play as a "crime melodrama," which the *Village Voice* thought might be appropriate for a "taut hour or so of television." Nevertheless, critics praised the performances of Morton, Guillaume, and Rosalind Cash, as a prostitute. As a result of the generally dismal reviews, *Charlie* lingered only seventeen performances.

**THE CHIP WOMAN'S FORTUNE** (Frazee, May 7, 1923, 16 p.). Producer: Ethiopian Art Theatre and Raymond F. O'Neil. Director: Raymond F. O'Neil.

**The Chip Woman's Fortune.** Author: Willis Richardson.*

Cast: Evelyn Preer (Liza), Sidney Kirkpatrick (Silas), Marion Taylor (Emma), Laura Bowman (Aunt Nancy), Solomon Bruce (Jim), Arthur Ray (A Man).

**Salome.** Author: Oscar Wilde.

Cast: Evelyn Preer (Salome), Sidney Kirkpatrick (Herod), Laura Bowman (Herodias), Arthur Ray (Young Syrian), Lionel Monagas* (Page of Herodias), Lewis Alexander (First Soldier), Coy Applewhite (Second Soldier), Charles Olden (Cappadocian), Solomon Bruce (Jokanaan), Charles Olden (First Jew), George Jackson (Second Jew), Walter White (Third Jew), Arthur Thompson (Tigellinus), Marion Taylor (Slave of Herodias).

**A Comedy of Errors.** Author: William Shakespeare.

Cast: Evelyn Preer (Adriana), Lionel Monagas (Antipholus of Ephesus),

Barrington Guy (Antipholus of Syracuse), Charles Olden (Dromio), Arthur T. Ray (Solinus), Sidney Kirkpatrick (Aegeon), Solomon Bruce (Balthazar), Nathaniel Guy (Angelo), Lewis Alexander (First Merchant), Le Roy Bingham (Second Merchant), Arthur T. Ray (Pinch), Laura Bowman (Aemili), Edna Morton (Luciana), Marion Taylor (A Courtesan), Coy Applewhite (Officer).

Raymond F. O'Neil, a Cleveland director, brought the Ethiopian Art Theatre to Broadway with the assistance of backers Julius Rosenwald (president of Sears-Roebuck) and Joseph Schaffner (of Hart, Schaffner, and Marx). O'Neil's goal was to show the diversity of his cast's talents in a "jazzed version" of Shakespeare's *A Comedy of Errors*, a controversial Oscar Wilde play, *Salome*, and a one-act comedy by black dramatist Willis Richardson.

*The Chip Woman's Fortune* received the most praise from the critics. *The New York Times* found it an "unaffected and wholly convincing transcript of everyday character. . . . Willis Richardson has limned half a dozen characters candidly, sympathetically, truly." The Chip Woman lives in Silas's home, where she cares for her landlord's invalid wife. When Silas loses his job, he fears he will lose his beloved Victrola to the bank. When Silas asks the Chip Woman for help, she hesitates because she has been saving money for her son who is in jail. The son returns and the Chip Woman discovers she has enough money to help her son and Silas. As the curtain descends, all are dancing to ragtime music on the Victrola.

*Salome* and *A Comedy of Errors* received harsh treatment from the critics. Perhaps, as James Weldon Johnson suggested in *Black Manhattan*, critics were unwilling to accept blacks in roles normally played by whites. The reviews hurt the box office, and the company departed for an appearance at the Lafayette Theatre in Harlem.

**THE CHOCOLATE DANDIES** (Colonial, September 1, 1924, 96 p.). Producer: B. C. Whitney. Book: Noble Sissle* and Lew Payton. Composer: Eubie Blake.* Lyricist: Noble Sissle. Directors: Noble Sissle, Eubie Blake, and Julian Mitchell.

Cast: Eubie Blake (At the Piano), Noble Sissle (Dobby Hicks), Lottie Gee (Angeline Brown), Lew Payton (Mose Washington), Josephine Baker (That Comedy Chorus Girl; A Deserted Female), Amanda Randolph (Mandy Green), Gwendolyn Feaster (Sammy), Addison Carey (Black Joe Jr.), J. Mardo Brown (Struttin' Drum Major), W. A. Hann (Bill Splevins), William Grundy (Hez Brown), Inez Clough (Mrs. Hez Brown), Elizabeth [Elisabeth] Welsh* [Welch] (Jessie Johnson), Valaida Snow (Manda), Fred Jennings (Uncle Eph), Ivan H. Browning (Dan Jackson), Ferdie Robinson (Shorty), Russell Smith (Johnnie Wise), Johnny Hudgins (Joe Dolks), Lee J. Randall (Silas Green), George Jones, Jr. (Bookmaker), Charlie Davis (Snappy), Curtis Carpentier (Jockey), John Alexander and Chic Fisher (Jump Steady),

Richard Cooper (Cashier), Percy Colston (Bookkeeper), Claude Lawson (Draft Clerk), Mildred Smallwood (Mischief), Lloyd Keyes (Attorney).

Songs: Mammy's Choc'late Cullud Chile; Have a Good Time, Everybody; That Charleston Dance; The Slave of Love; I'll Find My Love in D-I-X-I-E; Bandanaland; The Sons of Old Black Joe; Jassamine Lane; Dumb Luck; Jump Steady; Breakin' 'Em Down; Jockey's Life for Mine; Dixie Moon; Land of Dancin' Pickaninnies; Thinking of Me; All the Wrongs You've Done Me; Manda; Take Down Dis Letter; Chocolate Dandies.

Sissle and Blake's follow-up to *Shuffle Along** began as *In Bamville* on the road. By the time it reached New York, it became *The Chocolate Dandies*. The new show lacked several *Shuffle Along* veterans, as George White lured away Miller,* Lyles,* and others to appear in *Runnin' Wild*,* but it had several virtues. *The Chocolate Dandies* was considerably more lavish than its predecessor, as the costumes and sets received considerable praise. A highlight of the show even featured three live horses in a simulated race. The songs were "catchy," with "Dixie Moon," "Slave of Love," and "Bandanaland" selected as the show's hits. Virtually every cast member received kind words from the critics. While most reviewers praised Sissle, Blake, Johnny Hudgins, and Lew Payton, some called attention to a former cast-replacement from *Shuffle Along*, Josephine Baker. Baker, billed as "That Comedy Chorus Girl," wowed the audience with her imitation of silent screen star Ben Turpin. She would later abandon these slapstick comic routines on her road to international stardom.

To a certain extent, the opulence of *The Chocolate Dandies* became its major problem. Because of its large cast and high production costs, it experienced only six profitable weeks during its run. Thus, although several critics rated the show as equal to or better than *Shuffle Along*, *The Chocolate Dandies* was not able to run as long as the earlier, and much less expensive, show.

**CITIES IN BEZIQUE** (Public, January 4, 1969, 67 p.). Producer: Joseph Papp and the New York Shakespeare Festival. Author: Adrienne Kennedy.* Director: Gerald Freedman.

**The Owl Answers**

Cast: Moses Gunn* (Goddam Father), Cynthia Belgrave (Bastard's Black Mother), Joan Harris (Clara Passmore), Henry Baker (White Bird), Paul Benjamin (Negro Man), Tony Thomas (Shakespeare), Joseph Walker (Chaucer), Clee Burtonya (William the Conqueror).

**A Beast's Story**

Cast: Moses Gunn (Man Beast), Amanda Ambrose (Woman), Cynthia Belgrave (Woman Beast), Tony Thomas (Human).

Gerald Freedman, director of *Cities in Bezique*, commented: "Adrienne

Kennedy is a poet of the theatre. She does not deal in story, character, and event as a playwright. She deals in image, metaphor, essence, and layers of consciousness.'' Thus, when Clara Passmore (Joan Harris) finds that Shakespeare, William the Conqueror, and Anne Boleyn have entered her subway car, both critics and members of the audience discover that Kennedy's *The Owl Answers* will not resemble traditional theatrical structures. In this play images predominate over plot, as in the companion piece, *A Beast's Story.*

Critics were divided in their assessment of Kennedy's new play. Clive Barnes of *The New York Times* felt that ''this is an evening that no one interested in the development of the new theatre should easily forgo.'' Walter Kerr disagreed in the same newspaper, ''If these plays don't work—and I don't think they do—it is because we are always left outside of them, counting fragments that never quite fuse.'' [January 19, 1969] Nevertheless, critics applauded the efforts of cast members Moses Gunn and Joan Harris.

**CLARA'S OLE MAN.** See THE ELECTRONIC NIGGER AND OTHERS.

**CLORINDY.** See COOK, WILL MARION.

**COCKFIGHT** (American Place, October 7, 1977, 28 p.). Producer: American Place Theater. Author: Elaine Jackson. Director: Woodie King, Jr.*

Cast: Mary Alice* (Reba), Morgan Freeman* (Sampson), Charles Brown (Carl), Gylan Kain (Jesse), Cynthia McPherson (Claudia).

Elaine Jackson's *Cockfight*, presented by the American Place Theatre, examined the relationships of black men and women in American society. Several critics found the piece ''didactic,'' and Richard Eder of *The New York Times* argued that Ntozake Shange had covered similar ground ''with far more wit and grace'' in *For Colored Girls** (1976). Nevertheless, Edith Oliver of *The New Yorker* found that Jackson ''has quite a satiric ear and the makings of a humorist.''

*Cockfight* originated in Frank Silvera's Writers' Workshop in Harlem in 1976. The play takes place on a chicken farm on the outskirts of San Francisco, where Reba (Mary Alice) and Jesse (Gylan Kain) have been living for several years. Reba is demanding and ambitious, while Jesse still wonders about his future. Will he be a writer, or, perhaps, a country-and-western singer? Jesse slowly drifts apart from Reba during the course of the evening. While most critics viewed the play unfavorably, several had kind words for Gylan Kain and Mary Alice in the leading roles.

**COMIN' UPTOWN** (Winter Garden, December 20, 1979, 45 p.). Producers: Ridgely Bullock, Albert W. Selden, and Columbia Pictures. Book: Philip Rose and Peter Udell. Composer: Garry Sherman. Lyricist: Peter Udell. Director: Philip Rose.

Cast: Gregory Hines* (Scrooge), Tiger Haynes (Marley), John Russell (Bob Cratchit; Deacon), Larry Marshall (Tenant's Representative; Christmas Past), Saundra McClain (Recreation Center Director; Christmas Present), Robert Jackson (Minister; Christmas Future), Loretta Devine (Mary), Duane Davis (Young Scrooge), Vernal Polson (His Assistant), Ned Wright (Rev. Byrd), Esther Marrow (Gospel Singer), Virginia McKinzie (Mrs. Cratchit; Deacon's Wife), Shirley Black-Brown, Allison R. Manson (Cratchit Daughters), Carol Lynn Maillard (Martha Cratchit), Kevin Babb (Tiny Tim).

Songs: Christmas Is Comin' Uptown; Somebody's Got to Be the Heavy; Now I Lay Me Down to Sleep; Get Your Act Together; What Better Time for Love; It Won't Be Long; What I'm Gonna Do for You; Get Down, Brother, Get Down; Sing a Christmas Song; Have I Finally Found My Heart?; Nobody Really Do; Goin', Gone; One Way Ticket to Hell; Born Again.

*Comin' Uptown* reunited many of the white creative talents from *Purlie** (1970) and *Raisin** (1973) to provide a black version of Dickens's *A Christmas Carol* set in Harlem. The choice of Harlem may have seemed unusual, but director and co-author Philip Rose explained: "The story is about the rebirth of a man. With all the grimness of parts of Harlem, families go on raising children, getting them an education, struggling. The Cratchit family in both stories is a lower-middle-class family trying to get ahead." [*The New York Times*, November 27, 1979] Despite this refurbishing of Dickens, *Comin' Uptown* barely managed to linger past the Christmas holidays. The only praise went to Gregory Hines (who had recently won a Tony nomination for *Eubie!**) for his performance as Scrooge.

**COMPANIONS OF THE FIRE/BIG CITY BLUES (A TRILOGY)** (St. Marks, February 7, 1980, 22 p.). Producer: Negro Ensemble Company.* Director: Horacena J. Taylor.

**Companions of the Fire.** Author: Ali Wadud.
Cast: Charles Brown (Man), Barbara Montgomery* (Woman).

**Big City Blues (A Trilogy).** Author: Roy J. Kuljian.
Cast: Samm-Art Williams* ("Jackhammer Man"), Chuck Patterson ("Revival"), Frances Foster* ("Goodbye Mrs. Potts").

Critics found that this double bill revealed the impressive talents of the performers of the Negro Ensemble Company. Since both *Companions of the Fire* and *Big City Blues* were extremely weak vehicles, the actors were forced to carry the evening on their own shoulders. Mel Gussow of *The New York Times* surmised that "these articulate actors could have improvised more interesting scenes." *Companions of the Fire* by Ali Wadud features a chance encounter between a slightly deranged Harlem orator who dresses like a general (Charles Brown) and a prostitute who is a compulsive eater

(Barbara Montgomery). *Big City Blues* presents three vignettes of life in Los Angeles. Most critics favored Samm-Art Williams's portrayal of a blue collar worker who feels he is being controlled by a machine, his jack-hammer.

**CONJUR MAN DIES** (Lafayette, March 11, 1936, 24 p.). Producer: Negro Theatre Unit of the Federal Theatre Project* of the Works Progress Administration. Author: Rudolph Fisher.* Directors: Augustus Smith* and Joe Losey.

Cast: Lionel Monagas* (Dr. John Archer), William Brown (Bubber Brown), Irving Ellis (Jinx Jenkins), Dooley Wilson* (Perry Dart), Estelle Hemsley (Aramintha Snead), Dorothy Paul (Martha Crouch), Paul Johnson (Hanks), Jay Mondaaye (Brady), Louis Sharp (Samuel Crouch), Phil Thomas (Smitty), Walter Brogsdale (Brooks), Bertram Miller (Dr. Miller), Emanuel Middleton (Small), Jacqueline Martin (Landlady), Percy Verwayne (Spider Webb), Wardell Saunders (Doty Hicks), Francis Smith (Entertainer), Julian Costello (Tynes), Fritz Weller (M'Gana Frimbo), Walter Duke (Man on the Stoop), Mozelle Holmes (Girl).

Rudolph Fisher dramatized his 1932 novel *The Conjur-Man Dies: A Mystery Tale of Dark Harlem* for the stage, but he died in 1934 before the play was produced. Thus, when critics complained about the clumsiness of the script, it should be remembered that Fisher was unable to revise it before the 1936 production, a task completed by Arna Bontemps and Countee Cullen. Nevertheless, several critics admired this Federal Theatre Project production. Robert Garland of the *World-Telegram* found it "confusing," yet "as directed by Augustus Smith and Joe Losey, his associate; as back-grounded by Manuel Eastman's imaginative settings; as acted with contagious gusto by a cast of Negro actors, *Conjur-Man Dies* has a way with it. Neither comedy, tragedy, nor good mystery melodrama, it is something of all three." All critics noted that the audience loved the play, stopping the performance with continual laughter and applause.

The Conjur Man of the title seemingly appears as a corpse as the play begins. Dr. John Archer (Lionel Monagas) and Detective Dart (Dooley Wilson) are called in to discover the murderer. Complicating the investigation is the strange reappearance of Frimbo, the conjur man, in Act II. This complicates the action, as the detectives now have to find the identity of the original corpse. The murderer then eliminates the resurrected Frimbo, and the detectives discover the jealous undertaker is at fault. The plot machinations allow for fascinating visits to a variety of Harlem locales which give the play some of its most humorous scenes.

**CONTRIBUTIONS** (Tambellini's Gate, March 9, 1970, 16 p.). Producers: Jonathan Burrows, Ruthe Feldman, and Ken Gaston. Author: Ted Shine. Director: Moses Gunn.*

**Shoes**

Cast: Donald Griffith (Travis), Charles Grant (Ronald), Jim Jones (Marshall), Joe Attles (Mr. Mack), Stanley Greene (Mr. Wisely).

**Plantation**

Cast: Claudia McNeil* (Martha), Stanley Greene (Roscoe), Leonard Elliott (Bishop), Jay Garner (Papa Joe Vesquelle), Yvonne Sherwell (Mrs. Vesquelle).

**Contribution**

Cast: Claudia McNeil (Mrs. Grace Love), Donald Griffith (Eugene Love), Louise Stubbs (Katy Jones).

Critics took note of Ted Shine's *Contribution* the previous season in the Negro Ensemble Company's* *An Evening of One Acts.* *Contribution* then became the centerpiece of three Shine one-actors at the Tambellini's Gate Theatre in early 1970. *Contribution*, a comic tale of a maid's unique revenge in a southern town, still dominated the evening, with a "splendid" performance by Claudia McNeil. *Plantation* features the dilemma of a bigoted white New Orleans millionaire who discovers that his first child is black. *Shoes* concerns the debate between a high school youth and an old friend: Should his $150 wages be spent for college or a new pair of alligator shoes? Clive Barnes of *The New York Times* praised the entire evening: "Mr. Shine's theme is of rapidly changing black attitudes, and the gap between the old and new black generations. . . . He is an interesting newcomer who writes from the heart with a brash and bitter humor."

**THE COOL WORLD** (Eugene O'Neill, February 22, 1960, 2 p.). Producer: Lester Osterman. Authors: Warren Miller and Robert Rossen. Director: Robert Rossen.

Cast: Billy Dee Williams* (Duke Custis), P. Jay Sidney (Hurst), Raymond Saint-Jacques (Priest), Eulabelle Moore (Gramma Custis), Lynn Hamilton (Mrs. Custis), Alice Childress* (Mrs. Thurston), Clebert Ford (Foxy), Philip Hepburn (Mau Mau), George Gatlin (Cowboy), Martin Golar (Rod), Cheyenne Sorocki (Cherokee), Herb Coleman (Saint), Donald Blakely (Savage), Lamont Washington (Little Man), Calvin Lockhart (Blood), Alease Whittington (Lu Ann), Roscoe Lee Browne* (Royal Baron), Hilda Simms (Miss Dewpont), Wardell Saunders (Father Christmas), Melvin Stewart (Hermit), Cicely Tyson* (Girl), David Downing* (Boy), Maxwell Glanville* (Pusher), James Earl Jones* (Harrison Thurston), Harold Scott (Chester), Marvin Camillo (Bebop), Jim Oyster (Old Man), Art Aveilhe (Lucky), Ethel Ayler (Woman at the Beach).

*The New York Times* described *The Cool World* as "*West Side Story* without frosting." Unlike the recent musical, *The Cool World* had "no stylish dancing to take the sting out of its brutishness, no rhapsodic singing or rhythmic music to sugar-coat the ugliness of truth." This strong look at gang life in East Harlem both attracted and repelled the critics. The *Times* added: "It is exciting and shocking theatre once in a while, but it is more often recognizable as a piece of crusading journalism." Despite its brief run, *The Cool World* offered a showcase for the young Billy Dee Williams in the leading role of the gangleader Duke Custis.

**COP AND BLOW.** See BLACK VISIONS.

**THE CORNER** (Public, June 22, 1972, 46 p.). Producer: Joseph Papp and the New York Shakespeare Festival.

**Andrew.** Author: Clay Goss. Director: Rafic Bey.
Cast: Rafic Bey (Andrew), Frankie Russell Faison (Paul), Alfred Dean Irby (Billy).

**His First Step.** Author: Oyamo. Director: Kris Keiser.
Cast: Michael Coleman (Pritchard), Ilunga Adell (Country), Yoland Karr (Mary), Cornelius Suares (Sam).

**The Corner.** Author: Ed Bullins.* Director: Sonny Jim [J. E.] Gaines.*
Cast: Willard Reece, Jr. (Slick), Basil A. Wallace (Bummie), Petronia (Stella), Hampton Clanton (Blue), Michael Coleman (Silly Willy Clark), Bob Delegall (Cliff).

As the audience entered the Public Theatre for a performance of *The Corner*, a fight erupted when a man tried to enter without a ticket. Joseph Papp arrived to quell the disturbance and to discuss the nature of "theatre and reality." Most critics found this staged event the most exciting occurrence of the evening. *The Corner*, by Ed Bullins, sets the tone of the evening. Cliff (Bob Delegall), a character from *In the Wine Time** (1968), reappears and begins to question the meaning of a life spent on the street corner. *Andrew*, by Clay Goss, provides a symbolic view of ghetto life, as the deceased Andrew (Rafic Bey) confronts his murderers. *His First Step* offers a conversation between a college-educated young man (Ilunga Adell) and his street-wise companion (Michael Coleman). Most critics praised Bullins's work but, in general, dismissed the evening as "unsatisfying." Nevertheless, Mel Gussow commented in *The New York Times* that the "casts act with the conviction and forcefulness so frequently found in black theatre."

# D

**DADDY GOODNESS** (St. Marks, June 4, 1968, 64 p.). Producer: Negro Ensemble Company.* Author: Richard Wright.* Director: Douglas Turner Ward.*

Cast: Moses Gunn* (Daddy Goodness), Rosalind Cash* (Fanny), Bill Jay (Sam), Denise Nicholas (Lena), Douglas Turner [Ward]* (Thomas), Arthur French (Jeremiah), Allie Woods (A Preacher), Clarice Taylor* (Annie; Old Woman), Judyann Jonsson (Sarah), David Downing* (David), Richard Mason (Postman), Buddy Butler (Milkman), Norman Bush (Luke), Richard Mason (Chauffeur), Theodore Wilson (Young Man), Arthur French (The Mayor).

*Daddy Goodness*, Louis Sapin's adaptation of a work by Richard Wright, closed the first season of the Negro Ensemble Company. *The New Yorker* evaluated the first year's efforts (*Song of the Lusitanian Bogey*,* *Summer of the Seventeenth Doll*,* and *Kongi's Harvest**) and found it "an adventurous beginning that promises wonderful things to come. If ever a troupe was on the right track, it is this one." Nevertheless, critics had harsh words for this final play, with Edith Oliver noting that "as a whole it is a feeble affair, lacking satiric, comic, and dramatic force."

*Daddy Goodness*, based on the life of Father Divine, featured Moses Gunn as the newly resurrected Goodness. Actually, he is not revived from the dead, but merely from being dead drunk. His sudden return to life impresses his neighbors, and Goodness forms a religious cult to bilk these gullible souls out of their savings. A new musical version, starring Clifton James, Freda Payne, and Ted Ross, was aimed for Broadway in 1980, but it closed out of town.

**THE DARK TOWER.** See THE MOONLIGHT ARMS/THE DARK TOWER.

**THE DAUGHTERS OF THE MOCK** (St. Marks, December 20, 1978, 23 p.). Producer: Negro Ensemble Company.* Author: Judi Ann Mason. Director: Glenda Dickerson.

Cast: Frances Foster* (Maumau), Barbara Montgomery* (Oralia), Olivia Williams (Maneda), Michele Shay (Amanita), L. Scott Caldwell (Gail).

Judi Ann Mason's *Livin' Fat** had received dismal reviews in an earlier Negro Ensemble Company production, and *The Daughters of the Mock* followed suit. The mock is a vengeful voodoo power possessed by matriarch Maumau (Frances Foster) which she wishes to pass on to her daughter Amanita (Michele Shay), who would rather marry her college boyfriend. Despite the presence of five fine actresses, none was able to save *The Daughters of the Mock* from its disastrous reviews.

**DAY OF ABSENCE.** See HAPPY ENDING/DAY OF ABSENCE.

**DEEP ARE THE ROOTS** (Fulton, September 26, 1945, 477 p.). Producers: Kermit Bloomgarden and George Heller. Authors: Arnaud d'Usseau and James Gow. Director: Elia Kazan.

Cast: Gordon Heath (Brett Charles), Helen Martin (Honey Turner), Evelyn Ellis* (Bella Charles), Charles Waldron (Senator Langdon), Barbara Bel Geddes (Genevra Langdon), Carol Goodner (Alice Langdon), Harold Vermilyea (Roy Maxwell), Lloyd Gough (Howard Merrick), Andrew Leigh (Sheriff Serkin), George Dice (Chuck Warren), Douglas Rutherford (Bob Izay).

In the 1945-1946 Broadway season, three plays considered the problems of the black soldier returning home after World War II. Critics dismissed two (*Home Is the Hunter** and *On Whitman Avenue**), but praised *Deep Are the Roots* which ran for more than a year on Broadway.

Brett Charles (Gordon Heath), winner of a Distinguished Service Medal and an army lieutenant, returns home after being welcomed in the best homes in Europe and finds that race prejudice still exists. He visits his mother, who is in the employ of Senator Langdon (Charles Waldron), and gradually falls in love with his daughter Alice (Carol Goodner). When the senator learns of their relationship, he frames Charles in a crime and has him sent to jail. On his release, Alice suggests they go north and marry, but he refuses since they will always be subject to prejudice.

Lewis Nichols of *The New York Times* led the raves for the new play: "*Deep Are the Roots* is not only a plea for the understanding and final settlement through justice of one of America's problems, but it is . . . good theatre. It offers thought—and a show; it is well worth seeing."

**DEEP HARLEM** (Biltmore, January 7, 1929, 8 p.). Producer: Samuel Grisman. Book: Salem Whitney* and Homer Tutt.* Composer: Joe Jordan.* Lyrics: Homer Tutt and Henry Creamer.* Director: Henry Creamer.

Cast: Andrew Bishop (Author), Salem Whitney (King), Rosa White (Queen), Homer Tutt (Crown Prince), Juanita Stinette (Princess Lulu), Mabel Ridley (Princess Ola), Chappie Chapelle (Prince of Bataboula), Neeka Shaw (Temptress), Jimmy Baskette (Prophet), John Mason (Jethro), Columbus Jackson (Nebo), August Golden (African Native), Rookie Davis (Congo-Lulu), Harriet Williams (Crow Jane).

Songs: Deep Harlem; Mexican Blues; I Shall Love You; Deliver; Kentucky.

*Deep Harlem* preceded such 1960s musicals as *The Believers** which attempted to provide a musical history of black life. With music by Joe Jordan, Homer Tutt, and Henry Creamer, *Deep Harlem* traced black history from "the banquet halls of ancient Ethiopia to the jazz caverns of Harlem, with more than adequate stop-overs along the way in both the pre-war and post-war south." *Deep Harlem* strayed from the standard white conception of a black musical, and, as a result, critics dismissed it as "juvenile," "undisciplined," and "pretentious."

**DEEP RIVER** (Shubert, October 4, 1926, 32 p.). Producer and director: Arthur Hopkins. Author and lyricist: Laurence Stallings. Composer: Frank Harling.

Cast: Julius Bledsoe* (Tirzan), Rose McClendon* (Octavie), Bessie Allison (Sara), Gladys White (Julie), Rollo Dix (Henri), Andre Dumont (Paul), David Sager (Jules), Frederick McGuirk (Garcon), Luis Alberni (M. Brusard), Arthur Campbell (Hutchins), Lottice Howell (Mugette), Frederick Burton (Colonel Streatfield), Roberto Ardelli (Hazzard Streatfield), Antonio Salerno (Hercule), Frank Harrison (Announcer), Louisa Ronstadt (Mother of Mugette), Charlotte Murray (The Queen).

Songs: Ashes and Fire; Cherokee Rose; De Old Clay Road; Dis Is de Day; Love Lasts a Day; Po' Lil' Black Chile; Serenade Creole; Soft in de Moonlight; Two Little Stars.

*Deep River*, a "native opera" by Frank Harling and Laurence Stallings, explored life in New Orleans in 1835. Although primarily cast with white actors, *Deep River* offered three excellent performances by new black actors: Julius Bledsoe (Tirzan), Rose McClendon (Octavie), and Charlotte Murray (The Queen).

**DIXIE TO BROADWAY** (Broadhurst, October 29, 1924, 77 p.). Producer and director: Lew Leslie. Book: Walter De Leon, Tom Howard, Lew Leslie, and Sidney Lazarus. Composers: George W. Meyer and Arthur Johnston. Lyricists: Grant Clark and Roy Turk.

Cast: Florence Mills,* Hamtree Harrington, Cora Green, Maude Russell, Shelton Brooks,* Danny Small, Alma Smith, Juan Harrison, Billy Cain, Johnny Nit, U. S. Thompson, Byron Jones, Willie Covan, Lew Keene, Walter Crumbley, Winifred and Brown.

Songs: Put Your Old Bandanna On; Dixie Dreams; He Only Comes to See Me Once in a While; Jungle Nights in Dixieland; Prisoners Up to Date; Mandy, Make Up Your Mind; Hanging Around; Jazz Time Came from the South; If My Dream Came True; Darkest Russia; The Sailor and the Chink; Dixie Wildflowers; I'm a Little Blackbird Looking for a Bluebird; Trottin' to the Land of Cotton Melodies.

Florence Mills, now billed as the "Sensation of Two Continents," received top billing in *Dixie to Broadway*, and based on critics' reports she clearly deserved it. *Variety* commented: "Miss Mills received an ovation on her entrance which was cleverly designed. Just ahead, eight dancing boys . . . steamed up the house. The applause after an encore by the boys fused into that attending the appearance of Miss Mills, whose singing of 'Dixie Dreams' was charming. The colored song bird's fluty voice rose to high registers, a surprise to some who are not familiar with her varied talents." While all of Mills's songs were well received, "I'm a Little Blackbird Looking for a Bluebird" soon became her trademark.

*Dixie to Broadway* was soon able to command top prices ($3.30) for its seats on the basis of Mills's performance. Ticket brokers, who generally ignored black shows, began to demand seats for the new production.

*Variety* asked a black critic from Chicago to review *Dixie to Broadway*, and he praised it highly: ". . . the show is thoroughly well-done by a good company. It is a credit to the colored race rather than a ridicule."

**DON'T BOTHER ME, I CAN'T COPE** (Playhouse, April 19, 1972, 1,065 p.). Producers: Edward Padula, Arch Lustberg, and Vinnette Carroll's Urban Arts Corps. Author and composer: Micki Grant.* Director: Vinnette Carroll.*

Cast: Alex Bradford, Hope Clarke, Micki Grant, Bobby Hill, Arnold Wilkerson.

Songs: I Gotta Keep Movin'; Lookin' Over from Your Side; Don't Bother Me, I Can't Cope; When I Feel Like Moving; Help; Fighting for Pharaoh; Good Vibrations; Love Power; You Think I Got Rhythm; They Keep Coming; My Name Is Man; Questions; It Takes a Whole Lot of Human Feeling; Time Brings About a Change; So Little Time; Thank Heaven for You; So Long Sammy; All I Need.

*Don't Bother Me, I Can't Cope* emerged as the surprise hit of the 1971-1972 season, winning Drama Desk and Obie Awards for its author and composer Micki Grant. The show evolved in Vinnette Carroll's Urban Arts Theatre Workshop a year earlier, and later played Washington, D.C., Philadelphia, and Detroit before returning to New York City. Critics particularly praised Grant's vibrant music for the show. Clive Barnes of *The New York Times* commented: "Her music leans heavily on traditional black sources, such as the blues, calypsos, and spirituals, but from these sources she has written a charming and lovely score, and her lyrics, whether they be about love or the ghetto, have sweetness and wit." While Grant's performance in the second act of the show also received notice, Barnes added: "This show is full of talent working together with a cohesion rarely encountered outside the dance world."

**DON'T LET IT GO TO YOUR HEAD** (Henry Street, January 20, 1972, n.a.p.). Producers: Woodie King, Jr.,* Dick Williams,* and the New Federal Theatre.* Author: J. E. Gaines.* Director: Dick Williams.

Cast: J. Herbert Kerr, Jr. (Bubba), Peggy Kirkpatrick (Dorothy Lee), Lee Roy Giles (Dollar Bill), Bob Judd (Henry), Allegro Kane (Short Man), James Hainsworth (Rufus), Lellia Danette (Squatty Dotty), Barbara Montgomery* (Everlina), Mel Winkler (Herman), Hampton Clanton (Frank), Phylicia Ayers-Allen (Lena), Allia Schellander (Baby).

Sonny Jim had appeared in several plays by Ed Bullins.* As J. E. Gaines, he mastered new skills as a playwright, winning a Drama Desk Award for his first production at the Henry Street Playhouse. The theatre program revealed Gaines's debt to Bullins: "As a *writer*, I am a student of Ed Bullins; as an *actor*, I am a student of Robert Macbeth*; as a *man*, I am a student of black people."

*Don't Let It Go to Your Head* concerns the return of ex-con Bubba (J.

Herbert Kerr) to his wife (Peggy Kirkpatrick) after a lengthy absence. She is now living with her husband's best friend (Mel Winkler). Much of the play's action takes place in a bar where the audience witnesses Bubba's attempts to adjust to freedom. Mel Gussow, critic for *The New York Times*, praised the play, comparing it favorably to *No Place to Be Somebody*: "Like Charles Gordone,* Gaines has a sharp eye for atmospheric detail and a sharp ear for sardonic banter."

**DON'T PLAY US CHEAP!** (Barrymore, May 16, 1972, 164 p.). Producer, director, and author: Melvin Van Peebles.*

Cast: Avon Long* (David), Mabel King (Mrs. Bowser), Esther Rolle* (Miss Maybell), Rhetta Hughes (Earnestine), Thomas Anderson (Mr. Percy), Joshie Jo Armstead (Mrs. Washington), Nate Barnett (Harold Johnson; Rat), Frank Carey (Mr. Johnson; Cockroach), Robert Dunn (Mr. Bowser), Joe Keyes, Jr. (Trinity), Geo. "Ooppee" McCurn (Mr. Washington), Jay Vanleer (Mrs. Johnson).

Songs: Some Days It Seems That It Just Don't Even Pay to Get Out of Bed; Break That Party; 8 Day Week; Saturday Night; I'm a Bad Character; You Cut Up the Clothes in the Closet of My Dreams; It Makes No Difference; Quittin' Time; Ain't Love Grand; The Book of Life; Know Your Business; Big Future; Feast on Me; The Phoney Game; Smash Him.

*Don't Play Us Cheap!* was Melvin Van Peebles's second musical comedy of the 1971-1972 season. (Clive Barnes of *The New York Times* expressed mock surprise that Van Peebles did not design as well as write and direct his shows.) Unlike *Ain't Supposed to Die a Natural Death*,* *Don't Play Us Cheap!* provided a good-humored view of a Saturday night Harlem party. Inasmuch as this musical lacked the harshness of the earlier show for most critics, they embraced Van Peebles's new work much more readily. In the context of the party, Van Peebles provides a fantasy wherein two demons (a cockroach and a rat) assume human form and attempt to wreck the festivities. One demon repents and falls in love with the lady of the house.

Clive Barnes found the show had "fizz, guts, and honesty." Nikki Giovanni seconded Barnes's opinion in a *New York Times* column: "The ultimate genius of *Don't Play Us Cheap* is that it *is*. It *lives*. If you don't want to recognize the struggles of our people, you can wait to hear Rhetta Hughes, a meteorite on a star-studded stage, sing 'My Man.'" [May 28, 1972]

**THE DREAM ON MONKEY MOUNTAIN** (St. Marks, March 9, 1971, 48 p.). Producer: Negro Ensemble Company.* Author: Derek Walcott. Director: Michael A. Schultz.*

Cast: Ron O'Neal* (Cpl. Lestrade), Roscoe Lee Browne* (Makak), Afolabi Ajayi (Souris), Lawrence Cook (Tigre), Margaret Spear (The

Apparition), Antonio Fargas (Moustique), Robert Jackson (Basil), Esther Rolle* (Market Wife), David Downing* (Market Inspector).

*The Dream on Monkey Mountain*, by Trinidadian playwright Derek Walcott, climaxed the Negro Ensemble Company's 1970-1971 season of plays devoted to "Themes of Black Struggle." Walcott won an Obie Award for his mythical tale of an elderly black man, Makak (Roscoe Lee Browne), who searches for his identity at the behest of the white Moon Lady. Makak and his prison cohorts escape from jail as they begin this odyssey by climbing down Monkey Mountain. Makak eventually becomes an African chieftain, and slays the Moon Lady, and with it the colonial oppression of Western civilization. Critics praised the direction by Michael Schultz, as well as the performances of Makak's fellow prisoners, Ron O'Neal and Antonio Fargas.

**DREAMGIRLS** (Imperial, December 20, 1981, still running). Producers: Michael Bennett, Bob Avian, Geffen Records, and the Shubert Organization. Book and lyrics: Tom Eyen. Composer: Henry Krieger. Director: Michael Bennett.

Cast: Obba Babatunde (C. C. White), Cleavant Derricks (James Thunder Early), Loretta Devine (Lorrell Robinson), Ben Harney (Curtis Taylor, Jr.), Jennifer Holliday (Effie Melody White), Sheryl Lee Ralph (Deena Jones), Cheryl Alexander (Charlene), Linda Lloyd (Joanne), Vondie Curtis-Hall (Marty), Larry Stewart (M.C.), Joe Lynn (Tiny Joe Dixon), Sheila Ellis (Edna Burke), Tony Franklin (Wayne), David Thomé (Frank), Deborah Burrell (Michelle Morris), Joe Lynn (Jerry).

Songs: Move (You're Steppin' On My Heart); Fake Your Way to the Top; Cadillac Car; Steppin' to the Bad Side; Family; Dreamgirls; Press Conference; And I Am Telling You I'm Not Going; Ain't No Party; When I First Saw You; I Am Changing; I Meant You No Harm; The Rap; Firing of Jimmy; I Miss You Old Friend; One Night Only; Hard to Say Goodbye, My Love; I'm Looking for Something; Goin' Downtown; Takin' the Long Way Home; Party, Party; I Want You Baby; Only the Beginning; Heavy; It's All Over; Love Love You Baby; One More Picture Please; Got to Be Good Times; Quintette; I'm Somebody; Faith in Myself.

Michael Bennett's *Dreamgirls*, a pop history of black music of the 1960s with an emphasis on a Supremes-like singing group, received rave reviews from the critics. Jennifer Holliday won a Tony Award for her portrayal of Effie, who is left behind as "The Dreams" abandon rhythm and blues for a smoother and sleeker sound and look. Her performance of the Act I finale, "And I Am Telling You I'm Not Going," stopped the show nightly, and, as Frank Rich of *The New York Times* noted, made "Broadway history." While Holliday's performance dominated the evening, actors Ben Harney, as the manager, and Cleavant Derricks, as a James Brown figure, won Tony Awards as well.

**THE DUPLEX** (Forum, March 9, 1972, 28 p.). Producer: Repertory Theatre of Lincoln Center. Author: Ed Bullins.* Director: Gilbert Moses.*

Cast: Mary Alice* (Velma Best), Johnny Hartman (Montgomery Henderson), Albert Hall (Tootsie Franklin), Carl Mikal Franklin (Marco Polo Henderson), Les Roberts (Steve Benson), Clarice Taylor* (Mama), Phylicia Ayers-Allen (Sister Sukie), Joseph Attles (Pops), Frank Adu (O. D. Best), Kirk Kirksey* (Crook), Norma Donaldson (Marie Horton), Marie Thomas (Wanda).

Ed Bullins requested that the Repertory Theatre of Lincoln Center remove his name from the billing of *The Duplex*, or cancel the production. Bullins argued that the play had been altered in rehearsal by "hired artistic assassins" who had turned it into "just another darkie minstrel show." Nevertheless, the Public Theatre insisted on producing *The Duplex*, and it still received generally favorable reviews. Bullins revived Steve Benson from *In New England Winter** in this rendition of life in California in the early 1960s. Steve (Les Roberts) falls in love with his landlady Velma (Mary Alice), who returns his affections although she is married to the violent mobster O. D. (Frank Adu). John Lahr, in the *Village Voice*, praised Gilbert Moses for giving *The Duplex* "the most professional downtown production Bullins has yet received."

**DUTCHMAN** (Cherry Lane, March 23, 1964, 366 p.). Producers: Clinton Wilder, Richard Barr, and Edward Albee. Author: LeRoi Jones (Imamu Amiri Baraka).* Director: Edward Parone.

Cast: Robert Hooks* (Clay), Jennifer West (Lula).

LeRoi Jones's *Dutchman* moved from the Playwright's Unit Workshop to the Cherry Lane in March 1964. It appeared as a part of a triple bill which included Beckett's *Play* and Arrabal's *The Two Executioners*. New playwright Jones, however, grabbed the most attention. Critics' responses ranged from shock ("Dirt Hits Cherry Lane"—*Daily News*) to praise ("Mr. Jones is a writer of stunningly candid forcefulness"—*New York Post*).

Jones's reworking of the "Flying Dutchman" legend provided an encounter between Clay (Robert Hooks), a black intellectual, and Lula (Jennifer West), on a subway train. As she tries to interest him, a chain of events begins which will lead to his murder. Despite the critical furor, Jones won an Obie for his work. Critic Clayton Riley recalled the uproar five years later in *The New York Times*: "Jones' *Dutchman* is the best short play ever written in this country; black playwrighting began a new era with its production, an era that has not yet ended and has not yet seen the play's equal." [August 3, 1969]

# E

**EARTH** (Fifty-second Street, March 9, 1927, 24 p.). Producer: New Playwrights. Author: Em Jo Basshe. Directors: Russell Wright and Hemsley Winfield.

Cast: Inez Clough (Deborah), Daniel L. Haynes (Brother Elijah), Hayes Pryor (Abner), William Townsend (Senon), Marie Young (Mary), Ruth Carr (Sera), Dannie Morgan (Dinah), Elsie Winslow (Naomi), Geraldine Evans (Suzanna), Hemsley Winfield (Barnabas), H. Webster Elkins (Moses), Jerome N. Addison (Mathias), McKinley Reeves (Ebenezer), Harold Des Verney (Peter).

James Weldon Johnson described *Earth* as "a Negro play of considerable power, with religion and superstition as main themes." Inez Clough portrays Deborah, a mother who has lost her six children. She prays for the return of her favorite child, Walter, with the assistance of Brother Elijah (Daniel L. Haynes). At a religious shrine in the hills, her prayers are denied and she is killed by God's wrath. The play managed a three-week run, as most critics rejected the play but praised the performances.

Theophilus Lewis, black drama critic for *The Messenger*, called *Earth* "the best so-called Negro play since *The Emperor Jones*.*" He found "*Earth* the bunk when it is considered as a work bearing the slightest relation to Negro life or character; it is an intense and poignant piece of work when it is recognized as an oriental drama presented by colored actors." Lewis hoped that "white playwrights [would] ponder [his] words seriously, and that the next one who feels the urge to write a drama of Negro life will not rely solely on his own head for the concrete material he needs to work with."

**EDEN** (St. Marks, March 3, 1976, 181 p.). Producer: Negro Ensemble Company.* Author: Steve Carter.* Director: Edmund Cambridge.

Cast: Samm-Art Williams* (Eustace), Nate Ferrell (Nimrod), Laurence Fishburne III (Solomon), Barbara Montgomery* (Aunt Lizzie), Ramona King (Agnes), Shirley Brown (Annetta), Ethel Ayler (Florie), Graham Brown (Joseph Barton).

Clive Barnes of *The New York Times* called Steve Carter's *Eden* a "black *Hester Street*." Like the popular Joan Micklin Silver film, *Eden* explores the problems of immigrants in New York City. Here, however, the immigrants are well-educated and sophisticated West Indians who look down on the southern blacks living next door. Barriers seem to break down as Eustace Barton (Samm-Art Williams) begins to court Annetta (Shirley Brown), the youngest daughter of the West Indian family. They eventually marry, despite the senior Barton's unhappiness with the match, and the denouement reveals that the father may have been right in his initial assessment of Eustace.

Critics praised Carter's use of language, but *The New York Times* found several abrupt character changes somewhat disturbing. The acting, as in most Negro Ensemble Company (NEC) productions, was highly praised: ". . . we are watching a real family, not a company of actors. The cast plays with absolute conviction, even when credibility is being stretched." *Eden* moved from its NEC home to continue its run at the Theatre de Lys.

**EL HAJJ MALIK** (Martinique, November 29, 1971, 40 p.). Producer: Afro-American Studio. Author: N. R. Davidson, Jr. Director: Ernie McClintock.

Cast: Joan Bailey, Cindy Burroughs, Norman Butler, Woody Carter, Lee Cooper, James Harris, Deborah Howard, Augustus Keith, James Lee, Jim Mallette, Joan Seale.

N. R. Davidson's *El Hajj Malik* evoked the life of Malcolm X for New York theatre audiences. Davidson utilized Alex Haley's *Autobiogaphy of Malcolm X* and Malcolm's collected speeches to form the core of the play presented by the Afro-American Studio. Clayton Riley, who reviewed the original studio production for *The New York Times*, noted that "Davidson has woven these works into his own writing, which contains an extraordinarily rich and very Black lyricism. The combination is a fascinating piece of theatre-verité, an arresting work that is explosive in its examination of what America really stands for." Unlike other theatrical tributes to major black historical figures (see *Paul Robeson** or *I Have a Dream**), all the male performers in the ensemble assumed the role of Malcolm X for a portion of the evening. Although no individual dominated the character, Riley found that the actors brought "a special and personal quality to their versions of Malcolm." [October 4, 1970]

**THE ELECTRONIC NIGGER AND OTHERS** (American Place, March 6, 1968, 12 p.). Producer: American Place Theatre. Author: Ed Bullins.* Director: Robert Macbeth.*

**A Son, Come Home**

Cast: Estelle Evans (Mother), Wayne Grice (Son), Kelly-Marie Berry (Girl), Gary Bolling (Boy).

**The Electronic Nigger**

Cast: Wayne Grice (Mr. Jones), Warren Pincus (Lenard), Jeanne Kaplan (Miss Moskowitz), L. Errol Jaye (Mr. Carpenter), Roscoe Orman (Bill), Hedy Sontag (Sue), Helen Ellis (Martha), Roland Hirsch, Maie Mottus (Students).

**Clara's Ole Man**

Cast: Kelly-Marie Berry (Clara), Carolyn Y. Cardwell (Big Girl), Roscoe

Orman (Jack), Helen Ellis (Baby Girl), Estelle Evans (Miss Famie), Kris Keiser (Stoogie), George Miles (Bama), Gary Bolling (Hoss), L. Errol Jaye (C. C.).

After favorable reviews at the American Place Theatre, *The Electronic Nigger and Others* moved to the Martinique Theatre on March 28, 1968, under the title *Three Plays by Ed Bullins* (90 p.). Bullins won a Drama Desk Award for his three one-act plays and clearly identified himself as an up-and-coming playwright. The evening featured *A Son, Come Home*, a dramatic reunion between a mother and son after a nine-year separation, as well as two satiric comedies. *The Electronic Nigger* provides a classroom struggle between professor and student on the future of literature, while *Clara's Ole Man* turns out to be a woman, Big Girl (Carolyn Y. Cardwell). *The New Yorker* raved about Bullins's work, providing "three cheers" for his three new plays.

**THE EMPEROR JONES** (Neighborhood, November 1, 1920, 399 p.). Producer: Provincetown Players. Author: Eugene O'Neill. Director: George C. Cook.

Cast: Charles S. Gilpin* (Brutus Jones), Jasper Deeter (Harry Smithers), Christine Ell (An Old Native Woman), Charles Ellis (Lem).

Charles S. Gilpin's performance as Brutus Jones in *The Emperor Jones* was the surprise of the season. At first, white actors auditioned for the lead, but the Provincetown Players decided that they were unconvincing in the role. Gilpin, who had appeared previously in *Abraham Lincoln* (1919), won rave notices for his performance. The Drama League voted Gilpin one of the ten persons who had done the most for the American theatre in 1920. Nonetheless, when Gilpin was invited to the Drama League's dinner, public pressure called for the invitation to be withdrawn. The league refused to do so. Then people urged Gilpin not to attend. James Weldon Johnson recalled the furor in *Black Manhattan*: "The amount of noise and heat made, and of serious effort expended, was worthier of a weightier matter than the question of a dinner with a colored man present as guest." Gilpin attended the dinner without incident.

After the initial favorable reviews, *The Emperor Jones* moved uptown to the Princess Theatre to complete its run. It was revived three times in the 1920s on Broadway (February 11, 1925; February 16, 1926; and November 10, 1926). Paul Robeson* appeared in the 1925 revival as well as the 1933 film version.

**EUBIE!** (Ambassador, September 20, 1978, 439 p.). Producers: Ashton Springer, Frank C. Pierson, and Jay J. Cohen. Composer: Eubie Blake.* Director: Julianne Boyd.

Cast: Ethel Beatty, Terry Burrell, Leslie Dockery, Lynnie Godfrey, Gregory Hines,* Maurice Hines, Mel Johnson, Jr., Lonnie McNeil, Janet Powell, Marion Ramsey, Alaina Reed, Jeffrey V. Thompson.

Songs (all lyrics by Noble Sissle* unless otherwise noted): Good Night Angeline; Charleston Rag; Shuffle Along; In Honeysuckle Time; I'm Just Wild About Harry; Baltimore Buzz; Daddy; There's a Million Little Cupids in the Sky; I'm a Great Big Baby (Andy Razaf*); My Handyman Ain't Handy No More (Razaf); Low Down Blues; Gee, I Wish I Had Someone to Rock Me in the Cradle of Love; I'm Just Simply Full of Jazz; High Steppin' Days (Johnny Brandon); Dixie Moon; Weary (Razaf); Roll Jordan (Razaf); Memories of You (Razaf); If You've Never Been Vamped by a Brownskin, You've Never Been Vamped at All; You Got to Git the Gittin' While the Gittin's Good (F. E. Miller*); Oriental Blues; I'm Craving for That Kind of Love; Hot Feet.

*Eubie!*, a tribute to composer Eubie Blake, was 1978's second Broadway revue of the creative years of a noted black songwriter. *Eubie!*, unlike the earlier *Ain't Misbehavin'*,* opened in the midst of a newspaper strike and never managed to achieve the success of the former show. Nevertheless, critics found *Eubie!* a delight. The show chronicled Blake's career from 1919 ("Rock Me in the Cradle of Love") to 1978 ("High Steppin' Days"), with a tribute to *Shuffle Along** as well. The show reintroduced two dynamos, Gregory and Maurice Hines (the former child stars of Hines, Hines, and Dad), to Broadway audiences, and they stopped the show nightly with their elaborate revival of 1920s and 1930s tap-dancing routines. Despite its closing in 1979, *Eubie!* will be available to future generations as one of the first Broadway musicals on videotape and videodisc.

**AN EVENING OF ONE ACTS** (St. Marks, March 25, 1969, 32 p.). Producer: Negro Ensemble Company.*

**String.** Author: Alice Childress.* Director: Edmund Cambridge.
Cast: Esther Rolle* (Mrs. Beverly), Clarice Taylor* (Mrs. Rogers), Arthur French (Joe), Frances Foster* (Maydelle), Julius W. Harris (L. V. Craig), Stephanie Mills or Bambi Jones (Sadie).

**Contribution.** Author: Ted Shine. Director: Douglas Turner Ward.*
Cast: Esther Rolle (Katy Jones), Clarice Taylor (Mrs. Gracie Love), Allie Woods (Eugene Love).

**Malcochon.** Author: Derek Walcott. Director: Edmund Cambridge.
Cast: Rosalind Cash* (Conteur), Graham Brown (Charlemagne), Samual Blue, Jr. (Sonson), Norman Bush (Popo), Frances Foster (Madeleine), Arthur French (Chantal), Allie Woods (The Moumou), Sonny Morgan (Chorus Leader), Mari Toussaint, Theodore Wilson (Chorus).

Richard Watts, Jr., critic for *The New York Post*, judged *An Evening of One Acts* as "a fresh, striking, and richly varied assortment, all excellently done." Alice Childress presented *String*, based on the short story by Guy de Maupassant. Here the stingy Joe (Arthur French) interrupts a Block Association Picnic by picking up a piece of string. Soon everyone assumes that he is obviously a hobo and a thief as well. Derek Walcott provided *Malcochon*, a West Indian tale of six strangers who meet in a shed on a plantation during a rain storm. Ted Shine's *Contribution*, a tale of a grandmother's revenge, was compared to *Arsenic and Old Lace*. It later became the centerpiece of an evening of Shine plays at the Tambellini's Gate Theatre in 1970.

**EVERY NIGHT WHEN THE SUN GOES DOWN** (American Place, February 15, 1976, 46 p.). Producer: American Place Theatre. Author: Phillip Hayes Dean.* Director: Gilbert Moses.*

Cast: Frank Adu (Blood), Joe Senega (Sneaky Pete), Marge Eliot (Caledonia), Roscoe Orman (Pretty Eddie), Marki Bey (Ballerina), Les Roberts (Clean Sam), Norman Matlock (Jericho), Billie Allen (Cockeyed Rose).

Critics welcomed Phillip Hayes Dean's *Every Night When the Sun Goes Down*. Dean's play analyzes the lives of inhabitants of a rundown inner city Michigan hotel. Blood (Frank Adu), the former kingpin, returns from serving a three-year jail term for a crime he did not commit. He had accepted blame for his wife's murder of their retarded child. Everyone expects Blood to return to his former ways, but the prison experience has changed him. He now strongly objects to the exploitation of blacks by blacks. Clive Barnes of *The New York Times* led the favorable reviews for Dean's work: "The way Mr. Dean's political message falls into place is impressive. . . . The characterization of these flophouse denizens is very sharp; most of them are amusing, all of them well-observed."

# F

**THE FABULOUS MISS MARIE** (New Lafayette, March 9, 1971, 64 p.). Producer: New Lafayette Theatre.* Author: Ed Bullins.* Director: Robert Macbeth.*

Cast: Rosanna Carter (Marie Horton), Sonny Jim [Gaines]* (Bill Horton), Roscoe Orman (Art Garrison), Yvette Hawkins (Wanda), Bill Lathan (Marco Polo Henderson), Gary Bolling (Steve Benson), Vaughn Reddie (Ruth), Martha Charles (Toni), Whitman Mayo (Bud), George Miles (Gafney).

Ed Bullins won an Obie for his two 1970-1971 season plays, *In New England Winter** and *The Fabulous Miss Marie*. The latter play, Bullins's fourth in his projected twenty-play cycle, focused on Marie Horton (Rosanna Carter) and her three-day long Christmas party in the early 1960s. Marie's efforts to keep the party alive are often frustrated by news of riots and political activities that are continually emanating from the television in the background. Most of the party guests are oblivious to the news, but they are unhappy and express their feelings to the audience. Ironically, their problems might be resolved by joining the movements whose existence they ignore on the television. Critics found Bullins's play a "time capsule of the era," and Mel Gussow of *The New York Times* proclaimed it "the most composed play of the cycle."

**FAST AND FURIOUS** (New Yorker, September 15, 1931, 7 p.). Producer and director: Forbes Randolph.

Cast: Tim Moore,* Neeka Shaw, Clinton Fletcher, Melva Boden, Helmsley Winfield, Juano Hernandez,* Al Richards, Aurelia Wheeldin, Jackie Mabley, Baby Goins, Grace Smith, Lois Deppe, Emma Maitland, Edna Guy, Etta Moten, Midgie Lane, Forbes Randolph Choir.

Songs: Fast and Furious; Walking on Air; Rumbatism; Frowns; Doing the Dumbbell; Shadows on the Wall; Where's My Happy Ending?; Hot Feet (Mack Gordon-Harry Revel); So Lonesome; Boomerang (Joe Jordan*-J. Rosamond Johnson*); Dance of the Moods; Hot Hot Mama; Pansies on Parade; Let's Raise Hell (Porter Grainger); Modernistic (Grainger-John Dallavo); Ham What Am (Leighton Brill-Sigmund Herzig).

Producer and director Forbes Randolph assembled fifteen authors and composers to provide the material for *Fast and Furious*. Its thirty-seven scenes allowed Burns Mantle of the *Daily News* to praise it for "sheer bulk," if not necessarily high quality. Amidst the wide variety of musical numbers, J. Rosamond Johnson's "Jacob's Ladder" sequence was favorably reviewed, with the *Tribune* comparing him to Irving Berlin. Among the performers, Jackie "Moms" Mabley won honors for her rendition of "Rumbatism" and Neeka Shaw for "Walking On Air." Otherwise, *Fast and Furious* disappeared fast and furiously.

**LES FEMMES NOIRES** (Public, February 21, 1974, 57 p.). Producer: Joseph Papp and the New York Shakespeare Festival. Author: Edgar White. Director: Novella Nelson.*

Cast: Neil Harris (King Alfa), Gylan Kain (Hounsi), Norma Jean Darden (Miss Telephone Lady; Laverne), Rosemary Stewart (Carolyn), Laurie Carlos (High School Girl; Carla), Bob Diamond (Cop; Pee Wee), Rosanna Carter (Mrs. Carter), Ethel Ayler (Mrs. Thompson), Florene Wiley (Voice 1; Psychiatrist; Verna), Judyie Brandt (Voice 2; Didi), Juanita Clark (Mary Alice), Anna Horsford (Rita; Jackie), Barbara Montgomery* (Roberta), Trazana Beverley* (Erlene; Carolyn's Mother), Marshall Hutchinson (Cipo), Dewayne Oliver (Prophet), Willard Reece (Naphtali), Bill Cobbs (Hamm).

Critics tended to dismiss Edgar White's *Les Femmes Noires* ("The Black Women"), a series of vignettes concerning a cross-section of black women in America. *The New York Times* found it "small talk at its smallest," but the Associated Press's William Glover found some praise for the evening: "Director Novella Nelson deserves most of the praise for animating fragments of overheard talk among beggars, hookers, school girls, the lonely, lost, and frightened into an intriguing ritual of slow-motion choreographic movement and dark-lit sudden impressionistic halts."

**THE FIRST** (Martin Beck, November 17, 1981, 37 p.). Producers: Zev Bufman, Neil Bogart, Michael Harvey, and Peter A. Babley. Book: Joel Siegel and Martin Charnin. Composer: Bob Brush. Lyricist and director: Martin Charnin.

Cast: David Alan Grier (Jackie Robinson), Lonette McKee (Rachel Robinson), David Huddleston (Branch Rickey), Bill Buell (Patsy), Trey Wilson (Leo Durocher), Ray Gill (Clyde Sukeforth), Sam Stoneburner (Powers), Thomas Griffiths (Thurman), Jack Hallett (Cannon), Stephen Crain (Holmes), Paul Forrest (Sorrentino), Steven Bland (3rd Baseman), Michael Edward Steven (Junkyard Jones), Rodney Saulsberry (Jo-Jo), Clent Bowers (Cool Minnie), Paul Cook Tartt (Softball), Steven Boockvor (Swanee Rivers), Court Miller (Casey Higgins), D. Peter Samuel (Hatrack Harris), Bob Morrisey (Pee Wee Reese), Janet Hubert (Opal), Kim Criswell, Margaret Lamee (Dodger Wives).

Songs: Jack Roosevelt Robinson; Dancin' Off Third; The National Pastime; Will We Ever Know Each Other?; The First; Bloat; It Ain't Gonna Work; The Brooklyn Dodger Strike; You Do-Do-Do It Good; Is This Year Next Year?; There Are Days and There Are Days; It's A Beginning; The Opera Ain't Over.

*The First* presented Jackie Robinson's entry into major league baseball in musical comedy form. While critics praised the sincerity of the enterprise, most dismissed the book, music, lyrics, and direction as dull ("one long seventh inning stretch," according to *The New York Times*). Nevertheless, David Alan Grier won praise for his Broadway debut performance as Robinson, and Lonette McKee received kind words as his wife, Rachel.

**THE FIRST BREEZE OF SUMMER** (St. Marks, March 2, 1975, 70 p.). Producer: Negro Ensemble Company.* Author: Leslie Lee. Director: Douglas Turner Ward.*

Cast: Frances Foster* (Gremmar), Moses Gunn* (Milton Edwards), Douglas Turner Ward (Harper Edwards), Charles Brown (Nate Edwards), Reyno (Lou Edwards), Barbara Montgomery* (Aunt Edna), Ethel Ayler (Hattie), Janet League (Lucretia), Carl Crudup (Sam Greene), Anthony McKay (Briton Woodward), Lou Myers (Rev. Mosely), Petronia (Hope), Peter DeMaio (Joe Drake), Bebe Drake Hooks (Gloria Townes).

The critical and popular success of Leslie Lee's *The First Breeze of Summer* brought a swift move from the Negro Ensemble Company's St. Marks

Playhouse to Broadway's Palace Theatre (48 p.). Clive Barnes commented in *The New York Times* on its opening that "Mr. Lee is a new playwright of exceptional promise, and this first play is one of the most mature and rewarding works that the NEC has given us." Lee won an Obie for his efforts, as did lead performers Reyno and Moses Gunn.

*The First Breeze of Summer* exists in both present and past. The present scene involves Gremmar's (Frances Foster) visit to her grandchildren, and the past concerns flashbacks to Gremmar's memories of her three youthful loves. Reyno, as grandson Lou, won top acting honors for his portrayal of a sexually confused young man.

**FIVE ON THE BLACK HAND SIDE** (St. Clements Church, December 10, 1969, 62 p.). Producer: American Place Theatre. Author: Charlie L. Russell. Director: Barbara Ann Teer.*

Cast: L. Errol Jaye (Brooks), Clarice Taylor* (Mrs. Brooks), Jonelle Allen (Gail), Matthew Bernard Johnson, Jr. (Booker T.), William A. Stevenson III (Gideon), Patricia A. Edomy (Stephanie), Thabo Q. R. Gordon (Sampson), Nia Anderson (Nia), Theresa Merritt (Ruby), Judyann Elder (Stormy Monday), Gerry Black (Sweetmeat), Ed Bernard (Slim), Tchaka Almoravids (Fun Loving), Eugene Reynolds (Black Militant), Marilyn B. Coleman (Evangelist), Kirk Kirksey* (Rolls Royce), Demond Wilson (First Junkie), Lisle Wilson (Marvin).

Charlie Russell's *Five on the Black Hand Side*, directed by Barbara Ann Teer, received better reviews than its modest run would suggest. This domestic comedy features the conflict between the authoritarian Mr. Brooks (L. Errol Jaye) and his meek wife (Clarice Taylor), who suddenly begins to stand up for her rights. The *Village Voice* compared it to *Life with Father* written by a black Brendan Behan and staged by Joan Littlewood. Noting that this "beautifully orchestrated production celebrated the possibility of change and human renewal," critic Dick Brukenfeld urged his readers to see this play, but, apparently, few responded to his pleas.

**FLY BLACKBIRD** (Mayfair, February 5, 1962, 127 p.). Producer: Helen Jacobson. Composer, lyricist, and librettist: C. Jackson and James Hatch. Director: Jerome Eskow.

Cast: Avon Long* (William Piper), Robert Guillaume* (Carl), Mary Louise (Josie), Thelma Oliver (Susie), Chele Abel (Gladys), Micki Grant* (Camille), Elwood Smith (Police Officer Jonsen), William Sugihara (George), Paul Reid Roman (Paul), Jim Bailey (Lou), Gail Ziferstein (Gail), Jack Crowder (Palmer), Gilbert Price* (Roger), Glory Van Scott (Big Betty), Michael Kermoyan (Mr. Crocker), Helen Blount (Police Matron Jonsen).

Songs: Everything Comes to Those Who Wait; Now; Big Betty's Song; I'm Sick of the Whole Damned Problem; Who's the Fool?; Right Way;

Couldn't We; The Housing Cha-Cha; Natchitotches, Louisiana; Fly Blackbird; The Gong Song; Rivers to the South; Lilac Tree; Twilight Zone; The Love Elixir; Mister Boy; Old White Tom; Wake Up.

Authors C. Jackson and James Hatch claim to have been inspired to write this musical about integration after hearing a West Coast speech by Dr. Martin Luther King, Jr. This musical rendition of the struggle for civil rights in America faithfully echoed the climate of opinion of the age. On the one hand, William Piper (Avon Long) and his daughter, a Sarah Lawrence graduate, believe "Everything Comes to Those Who Wait." On the other hand, Carl (Robert Guillaume) sings that things have to be changed "Now." The events of *Fly Blackbird* cause Piper to change his mind when his daughter joins in the civil rights protests. In a poignant final scene, he sings "Who's the Fool?"

**FOR COLORED GIRLS WHO HAVE CONSIDERED SUICIDE/ WHEN THE RAINBOW IS ENUF** (Public, Anspacher, May 17, 1976, 120 p.). Producer: Joseph Papp and the New York Shakespeare Festival. Author: Ntozake Shange.* Director: Oz Scott.

Cast: Trazana Beverley* (Lady in Red), Paula Moss (Lady in Green), Janet League (Lady in Rose), Aku Kadago (Lady in Yellow), Risë Collins (Lady in Purple), Laurie Carlos (Lady in Blue), Ntozake Shange (Lady in Orange).

Ntozake Shange's *For Colored Girls Who Have Considered Suicide/ When the Rainbow Is Enuf* moved swiftly from West Coast workshop performances to Woodie King's* New Federal Theatre* and then uptown to the Public. A Broadway move to the Booth followed, with the show amassing a total run of 867 performances (747 at the Booth) in New York City.

Shange's "choreopoem" charmed the critics and won an Obie for the author and a Tony for Trazana Beverley. Critics praised the close collaboration of Shange, the performers, and director Oz Scott. Mel Gussow of *The New York Times* commented: "The words are Shange's, but each articulate actress invests her scenes with herself. It is her story she is confiding to us. It is the closeness, the intimacy, and the specificity of the revelations that make the play so tangible and so poignant." *For Colored Girls* finished its run in repertory with *Paul Robeson** and later was revised for Public Television's *American Playhouse* series.

**FOUR SAINTS IN THREE ACTS** (Forty-fourth Street, February 20, 1934, 48 p.). Producer: Harry Moses. Libretto: Gertrude Stein. Composer: Virgil Thomson. Director: John Houseman.

Cast: Altonell Hines (Commere), Abner Dorsey (Compere), Beatrice Robinson-Wayne (St. Teresa I), Bruce Howard (St. Teresa II), Edward Matthews (St. Ignatius), John Diggs (St. Chavez), Bertha Fitzhugh Baker

(St. Settlement), Leonard Franklin (St. Ferdinand), Randolph Robinson (St. Plan), David Bethe (St. Stephen), Kitty Mason (St. Cecilia), Thomas Anderson (St. Giuseppe), Charles Spinnard (St. Anselmo), Marguerite Perry (St. Sara), Flossie Roberts (St. Bernadine), Edward Batten (St. Absalon), Florence Hester (St. Answers), George Timber (St. Eustace).

After four weeks, *Four Saints in Three Acts* enjoyed the longest continuous run ever by an American opera. Virgil Thomson first had the idea for an opera based on the lives of Saint Ignatius and Saint Teresa in 1927, and he offered Gertrude Stein the opportunity to prepare the libretto. Thomson soon decided that the opera would be performed by blacks. Carl Van Vechten claimed that this decision was made during an intermission of Hall Johnson's* *Run Little Chillun!**: "Virgil turned and said to me, 'I am going to have *Four Saints* played by Negroes. They alone possess the dignity and poise, the lack of self-consciousness that proper interpretation of opera demands. And they are not ashamed of words.' " John Houseman acknowledges another version in his autobiography *Run-Through.* Here the same decision is reached in Jimmy Daniels's Harlem nightclub. Eva Jessye was then hired to recruit the choir for the show.

Critics were both dazzled and infuriated by the show, with Burns Mantle of the *Daily News* summing it up as: "Music—***; Libretto—0."

**FREDERICK DOUGLASS . . . THROUGH HIS OWN WORDS** (St. Marks, May 9, 1972, 32 p.). Producer: Negro Ensemble Company.* Program based on a play by Arthur Burghardt and Michael Egan, adapted from the works of Frederick Douglass. Director: Not credited.

Cast: Douglas Turner Ward,* Adolph Caesar,* Duane Jones (Frederick Douglass).

Three actors (Adolph Caesar, Duane Jones, and Douglas Turner Ward) portrayed Frederick Douglass in the final production of the 1971-1972 Negro Ensemble Company season. The evening comprises the history of ex-slave Douglass from his earliest memories (when his mother walks twelve miles to visit him on a neighboring plantation) to his later years when he becomes a foremost spokesman for the abolitionist cause. No director was credited for the evening, and, as a result, the actors tended to wander about the stage. Nevertheless, the power of Douglass's words carried the evening.

**FREEMAN** (American Place, February 5, 1973, 57 p.). Producer: American Place Theatre. Author: Phillip Hayes Dean.* Director: Lloyd Richards.*

Cast: Bill Cobbs (Freeman Aquila), J. A. Preston (Rex Coleman), Estelle Evans (Teresa Aquila), Dotts Johnson (Ned Aquila), Marjorie Barnes (Osa Lee Aquila).

Phillip Hayes Dean, author of the previous season's *The Sty of the Blind Pig,** turned to the American Place Theatre for his production of *Freeman. Freeman* looks at the contrasting lives of two young men in a smalltown

Michigan family. Freeman Aquila (Bill Cobbs) is apparently a loser. Unemployed and a high school dropout, he has returned home to live with his family. Rex (J. A. Preston), an orphan who has been raised by the Aquilas, has become a doctor and a pillar of the black professional community. Nevertheless, the audience comes to admire Freeman for his rebellious streak. Bill Cobbs won a Drama Desk Award for his performance of this difficult role.

**FUNNYHOUSE OF A NEGRO** (East End, January 14, 1964, 46 p.). Producers: Richard Barr, Clinton Wilder, and Edward Albee. Author: Adrienne Kennedy.* Director: Michael Kahn.

Cast: Ruth Volner (Funnyhouse Lady), Leonard Frey (Funnyhouse Man), Leslie Rivers (Mother), Billie Allen (Sarah), Cynthia Belgrave (Queen Victoria Regina), Ellen Holly (Duchess of Hapsburg), Gus Williams (Patrice Lumumba), Norman Bush (Jesus).

Despite a short run, *Funnyhouse of a Negro* brought author Adrienne Kennedy considerable attention. Richard Watts, Jr., of *The New York Post* commented: "It leaves no doubt that Edward Albee and his associates in Theatre 1964 have found in Miss Kennedy an original dramatist whose passionate voice demanded to be heard." The "funnyhouse" is the mind of a young black woman who is tormented by the desire to be white. Young Sarah's (Billie Allen) life wavers between reality and illusion throughout the play as she "meets" historical figures representing "blackness" and "whiteness." The tension becomes so strong that she is driven to madness and suicide. In an interview at the time, Kennedy confessed to a certain autobiographical element in the play. *Funnyhouse of a Negro* disappeared quickly, but Edith Oliver of *The New Yorker* found it a "strong and original" first play. Kennedy won an Obie for her premiere effort.

# G

**THE GENTLEMAN CALLER.** See A BLACK QUARTET.

**GETTIN' IT TOGETHER.** See BLACK VISIONS.

**GINGER SNAPS** (Belmont, December 31, 1929, n.a.p.). Book, lyrics, and direction: J. Homer Tutt,* Donald Heywood* and George Morris. Composer: Donald Heywood.

Cast: Vivian (Vivienne) Baber, Roscoe Simmons, J. Homer Tutt, Boots Swan, John Lee, Barrington Guy, Selma Smith, Bobby De Leon.

Critics found *Ginger Snaps* an "amateur night," with balky curtains and long stage waits slowing the action to a crawl. The audience dwindled as the show continued, and critics chided the producers for charging $3.50 for this claptrap. In the midst of the rubble, critics praised Barrington Guy's singing and the "Five Hot Shots'" dancing, but dismissed Swan and Lee as "two alleged comics." *Ginger Snaps* ended the decade on a sad note and signaled the continuing decline of the black musical revue.

**GOAT ALLEY** (Bijou, June 20, 1921, 5 p.). Producer: Alice Wade Mulhern. Author: Ernest Howard Culbertson. Director: Cecil Owen.

Cast: Lillian McKee (Lucy Belle Dorsey), Beulah Daniels (Aunt Rebecca), Louis Lang (Slim Dorsey), Daisey Garett (Lizzie Gibbs), Owen Lane (Chick Avery), Leonard Kennedy (Jeff Bisbee), Barrington Carter (Sam Reed), William H. Smith (Jeremiah Pocher), Plant Lang (Policeman), Gladys Munroe (Fanny Dorsey).

Most plays by white dramatists in the 1920s which concerned black life considered myths rather than reality. *Goat Alley*, however, attempted to be a realistic portrait of life in the ghettoes of Washington, D.C. The author, Ernest Howard Culbertson, explained in the program that his purpose was "primarily to present a view of primitive love and life in our very midst, which is totally unknown to the average intelligent New Yorker; and secondly, to enlist a helping hand to all the deserving human souls who are struggling to rise above Goat Alley."

Culbertson painted a tragic world in which a virtuous heroine Lucy Belle (Lillian McKee) is forced to compromise her morals due to the pressures of poverty. With her husband in jail and her job and money gone, she moves in with another man and bears his child. When her husband returns from jail, he discovers the illegitimate child and then kills his wife. *The New York Times* praised *Goat Alley*'s accuracy and "vivid dialogue." The show was revived on April 20, 1927, and, despite the fact that it was "greeted with applause," it lingered for only thirteen performances.

**GOD IS A (GUESS WHAT?)** (St. Marks, December 17, 1968, 32 p.). Producer: Negro Ensemble Company.* Author: Ray McIver. Composer: Coleridge-Taylor Perkinson. Director: Michael A. Schultz.*

Cast: Arthur French (First End Man), David Downing* (Second End Man), Julius W. Harris (Jim), Theodore Wilson (Officer), Clarice Taylor* (Reba), William Jay (Boy), Frances Foster* (Lady), Graham Brown (Voice), Allie Woods (A Man), Judyann Jonsson (First Spook), Hattie Winston* (Second Spook), Rosalind Cash* (Third Spook), Esther Rolle* (Cannibal), Norman Bush (Priest), Mari Toussaint (Acolyte).

Songs: A Mighty Fortress; The Lynch-Him Song; The Sonny-Boy Slave Song; The Black-Black Song; The Golden Rule Song; God Will Take Care; The Darkies' Song; The Sit Down Song; The Lynchers' Prayer.

*God Is a (Guess What?)* was billed as a "morality play," but to most critics it looked like a modernized minstrel show, or, as *The New York Times* claimed, "Son of Green Pastures." Ray McIver's second season opener for the Negro Ensemble Company actually stripped the hypocrisy from the surface of the minstrel show with such musical numbers as "The Lynch-Him Song," "The Sonny-Boy Slave Song," and "The Darkies' Song." Coleridge-Taylor Perkinson provided the music for McIver's "lively entertaiment."

**GOD'S TROMBONES.** See SHAKESPEARE IN HARLEM.

**GOLDEN BOY** (Majestic, October 20, 1964, 569 p.). Producer: Hillard Elkins. Book: Clifford Odets and William Gibson. Composer: Charles Strouse. Lyricist: Lee Adams. Director: Arthur Penn.

Cast: Sammy Davis* (Joe Wellington), Billy Daniels (Eddie Satin), Louis Gossett* (Frank), Johnny Brown (Ronny), Lola Falana (Lola), Paula Wayne (Lorna Moon), Kenneth Tobey (Tom Moody), Ted Beniades (Roxy Gottlieb), Charles Welch (Tokio), Roy Glenn (Mr. Wellington), Jeannette DuBois (Anna), Terrin Miles (Terry), Buck Heller (Hoodlum), Benny Payne (Benny), Albert Popwell (Al), Jaime Rogers (Lopez), Mabel Robinson (Mabel), Lester Wilson (Les), Don Crabtree (Drake), Maxwell Glanville* (Fight Announcer), Bob Daley (Reporter), Ralph Vucci (Driscoll).

Songs: Workout; Night Song; Everything's Great; Gimme Some; Stick Around; Don't Forget 127th Street; Lorna's Here; The Road Tour; This Is the Life; Golden Boy; While the City Sleeps; Colorful; I Want to Be with You; Can't You See It; No More; The Fight.

*Golden Boy* returned Sammy Davis to the Broadway stage where he had triumphed earlier in *Mr. Wonderful* (1956). Clifford Odets began the adaptation of his 1937 play, but William Gibson, author of *Two for the Seesaw* (1958), stepped in after Odets's death. Both reworked the play to fit Davis's talents and specifications, changing the milieu from Italian culture to black life in the modern fight game. Charles Strouse and Lee Adams, of *Bye Bye Birdie* (1960) fame, provided a serviceable score that showed Davis and co-star Billy Daniels to their best advantage. The hit songs included "While the City Sleeps," "No More," and a rousing ensemble number "Don't Forget 127th Street."

**GRANNY MAUMEE.** See THE RIDER OF DREAMS.

**GREAT GOODNESS OF LIFE.** See A BLACK QUARTET.

**THE GREAT MACDADDY** (St. Marks, February 12, 1974, 72 p.). Producer: Negro Ensemble Company.* Author: Paul Carter Harrison. Director: Douglas Turner Ward.*

Cast: David Downing* (MacDaddy), Al Freeman, Jr.* (Scag), Bebe Drake Hooks (Old Woman), Adolph Caesar* (Deacon Jones), Marjorie Barnes (Young Woman), Graham Brown (Wine), Martha Short-Goldsen (Momma), Sati Jamal (Shine), Hattie Winston* (Leionah), Charles Weldon (Skuleton), Victor Willis (Signifyin' Baby), Howard Porter (Cowboy), Alton Lathrop (Eagle), Freda T. Vanterpool (Red Woman), Alvin Ronn Pratt (Blood Son), Omar Clay (Drum), Phylicia Ayers-Allen, Dyane Harvey (Community Members).

Critics welcomed *The Great MacDaddy*, and Clive Barnes of *The New York Times* claimed that it represented "the birth of the black musical." Paul Carter Harrison's play is described as a "ritualized African-American event inspired by the African story-telling technique advanced by Amos Tutuola in his famous novel *The Palm Wine Drinkard.*" The musical follows the odyssey of MacDaddy (David Downing), who undertakes an eastward journey from Los Angeles to discover the formula for the palm wine that keeps his father's parishioners happy. MacDaddy has a rival, however, Scag (Al Freeman, Jr.), the villainous representative of heroine and white culture who wishes to thwart his quest. While critics praised Harrison's work (which won an Obie), differences surfaced on the direction. Clive Barnes found that Douglas Turner Ward did "a fine job," while Clayton Riley disagreed, calling it "flat, unfocused, undistinguished" in *The New York Times.* [March 3, 1974] The Negro Ensemble Company revived *The Great MacDaddy* on April 5, 1977.

**THE GREAT WHITE HOPE** (Alvin, October 3, 1968, 546 p.). Producer: Herman Levin. Author: Howard Sackler. Director: Edwin Sherin.

Cast: James Earl Jones* (Jack Jefferson), Jane Alexander (Eleanor Backman), Marlene Warfield (Clara), Lou Gilbert (Goldie), Peter Masterson (Smitty), Gil Rogers (Brady), Hector Elizondo (Blackface), George Ebeling (Fred), George Mathews (Cap'n Dan), Garwood Perkins (Deacon), Woodie King* (Young Negro), Antonio Fargas (Scipio), L. Errol Jaye (Pastor), Hilda Haynes (Mrs. Jefferson), Mel Winkler (Rudy), Eugene R. Wood (Pop Weaver), George Harris II (Waiter), Marshall Efron (Ragosy), Don Blakely (African Student), Jimmy Pelham (Tick), Yvonne Southerland (Signature Recorder).

*The Great White Hope* swept the best play honors for Howard Sackler; he won the Pulitzer Prize, a Tony Award, and a New York Drama Critics Circle Award. Some of the credit for the critical enthusiasm was no doubt due to the bravura performance of James Earl Jones in the role of champion boxer Jack Jefferson, closely modeled after Jack Johnson, the first black heavyweight champion of the world. Jones won a Drama Desk Award, a Tony Award, and a New York Drama Critics Circle Award for his portrayal. Clive Barnes declared Jones an "overnight star" in *The New*

*York Times*, although Jones had a lengthy and noteworthy theatrical career both on and Off-Broadway.

*The Great White Hope* exposed the racism that led to the champion's downfall in his 1915 bout with Jess Willard in Havana. The subplot featured Jefferson's affair with a white woman (Jane Alexander, another Tony winner), which led to his prosecution under the Mann Act. Both Jones and Alexander repeated their prize-winning roles in a 1970 film for Twentieth Century-Fox.

**THE GREEN PASTURES** (Mansfield, February 26, 1930, 557 p.). Producer: Laurence Rivers. Author and director: Marc Connelly.

Cast: Richard B. Harrison* (The Lord), McKinley Reeves (Choir Leader), Daniel L. Haynes (Adam), Inez Richardson Wilson (Eve), Lou Vernon (Cain), Charles H. Moore (Mr. Deshee; Isaac), Alicia Escamilla (Myrtle), Jazzlips Richardson, Jr., Howard Washington, Reginald Blythwood (The Boys), Joe Byrd (Randolph), Frances Smith (A Cook), Homer Tutt* (Custard Maker; Ham; High Priest), Anna Mae Fritz (Mammy Angel; Second Woman), Josephine Byrd (Stout Angel; Voice in Shanty; First Cleaner), Edna Thrower (Slender Angel), J. A. Shipp (Archangel; Abraham), Wesley Hill (Gabriel), Dorothy Randolph (Cain's Girl), Edna M. Harris (Zeba), James Fuller (Cain the Sixth), Louis Kelsey (Boy Gambler), Collington Hayes (First Gambler), Ivan Sharp (Second Gambler; First Scout), Susie Sutton (Noah's Wife), Milton Williams (Shem), Freddie Archibald (Flatfoot), Stanleigh Morrell (Japheth; Joshua), Florence Fields (Second Cleaner), Edgar Burks (Jacob), Alonzo Fenderson (Moses), Mercedes Gilbert (Zipporah), Reginald Fenderson (Magician), George Randol (Pharaoh), Walt McClane (General), Emory Richardson (First Magician), Arthur Porter (Head Magician), Ivan Sharp (First Scout), Billy Cumby (Master of Ceremonies), Jay Mondaaye (King of Babylon), Ivan Sharp (Prophet), Leona Winkler, Florence Lee, Constance Van Dyke, Mary Ella Hart, Inez Persand (The King's Favorites).

*The Green Pastures* has inspired mixed feelings in recent years. On one hand, Marc Connelly's play is censured for perpetuating black stereotypes inherited from the minstrel stage, and on the other, it has been praised for providing opportunities for black actors to display their talents. James Weldon Johnson noted in *Black Manhattan* that "the Negro established conclusively his capacity to get the utmost subtleties across the footlights, to convey the most delicate nuances of emotion, to create the atmosphere in which the seemingly unreal becomes for the audience the most real thing in life." The "unreal" notion was a black version of life in heaven based on the stories of Roark Bradford (*Ol' Man Adam and His Chillun*).

Brooks Atkinson declared the play a "masterpiece" in *The New York Times*, and *The World* noted: "It will move you to tears, and make you gasp with the simple beauty of Old Testament pageantry, and give you a sort of laughter that you never had before." Special praise went to Richard B. Harrison (The Lord) in a role that James Weldon Johnson found "perfectly played." *The Green Pastures* won the Pulitzer Prize. It continued its run until August 29, 1931, and toured the United States until 1935. Warner Brothers provided a film version of the play in 1936 with Rex Ingram* in the leading role.

**GUYS AND DOLLS** (Broadway, July 21, 1976, 239 p.). Producers: Moe Septee and Victor H. Potamkin. Book: Jo Swerling and Abe Burrows. Composer and lyricist: Frank Loesser. Director: Billy Wilson.

Cast: Robert Guillaume* (Nathan Detroit), Norma Donaldson (Miss Adelaide), Ken Page (Nicely-Nicely Johnson), Ernestine Jackson (Sister Sarah Brown), James Randolph (Sky Masterson), Christophe Pierre (Benny Southstreet), Sterling McQueen (Rusty Charlie), John Russell (Harry the Horse), Clark Morgan (Lt. Brannigan), Jymie Charles (Angie the Ox), Emett Wallace (Arvide Abernathy), Irene Datcher (Agatha), Alvin Davis (Calvin), Marion Moore (Martha), Derrick Bell (Joey Biltmore; Waiter), Andy Torres (M. C.; Drunk), Prudence Darby (Mimi), Edye Byrde (Gen. Cartwright), Walter White (Big Jule).

*Guys and Dolls* was one of several 1970s musicals which attempted to revive old chestnuts with black casts and modernized music. Since *Hello Dolly!* had attracted audiences earlier with Pearl Bailey* and Cab Calloway, other producers sought suitable vehicles for black performers. *Guys and Dolls*, a 1950 Frank Loesser and Abe Burrows smash, was reorchestrated and slightly rewritten for a black cast. The show displayed some of Broadways's top musical comedy performers—Robert Guillaume, Ernestine Jackson, and Ken Page—but it was to no avail. Even Billy Wilson, who shaped the previous season's *Bubbling Brown Sugar** into a hit, was unable to accomplish the same feat with *Guys and Dolls*.

# H

**HAITI** (Lafayette, March 2, 1938, 168 p.). Producer: James R. Ullman for the Federal Theatre Project* of the Works Progress Administration. Author: William Du Bois. Director: Maurice Clark.

Cast: Louis Sharp (Toussaint L'Ouverture), Rex Ingram* (Christophe), Alvin Childress (Jacques), Canada Lee* (Bertram), Louis Smith (Andre), Frederic Gibson (Guy), Zola King (Daughter), Mary Barnes (Mother),

Jacqueline Ghant Martin (First Woman), J. Louis Johnson (Old Man), Susie Sutton (Second Woman), Lulu King (Third Woman), Richard McCracken (Josef), Emile Hirsch (Boule), David Enton (Duval), Alfred Allegro (Phillipe), Lou Polan (Roche), William Sharon (Boucher), William Greene (Armand), Byron Lane (Jean), Bernard Paté (LeClerc), Elena Karam (Odette), Catherine Lawrence (Pauline), Lena Halsey (Aimee), Benny Tattnall, James Wright (Servants).

The Federal Theatre Project's production of William Du Bois's *Haiti* proved a "roaring melodrama" at the Lafayette Theatre. This evocation of the Haitian patriots Toussaint L'Ouverture and Christophe and their struggle against French colonialism in 1802 excited both critics and audiences. Critics gave special praise to Broadway veteran Rex Ingram. Brooks Atkinson noted in *The New York Times*: "Mr. Ingram has been a good actor for a long time. It is not very often, however, that he finds a heroic part like that of Christophe, the leader of a cause. Massive inside a gaudy uniform, active as a pole-vaulter, and gleaming with sincerity, Mr. Ingram gives a rattling good performance." His review concluded with specific subway directions to the Lafayette (131st Street and Seventh Avenue), so Broadway audiences would be sure to visit *Haiti*.

**HALLELUJAH, BABY!** (Martin Beck, April 26, 1967, 293 p.). Producers: Albert W. Selden, Hal James, Jane C. Nusbaum, and Harry Rigby. Book: Arthur Laurents. Composer: Jule Styne. Lyricists: Betty Comden and Adolph Green. Director: Burt Shevelove.

Cast: Leslie Uggams (Georgina), Lillian Hayman (Momma), Robert Hooks* (Clem), Allan Case (Harvey), Justin McDonough (Captain Yankee), Lou Angel (Calhoun), Barbara Sharma (Mary), Frank Hamilton (Mister Charles), Marilyn Cooper (Mrs. Charles), Winston DeWitt Hemsley, Alan Weeks (Tip and Tap), Bud Vest (Prince), Carol Flemming (Princess), Darrell Notara (Sugar Daddy), Chad Block (Official), Alan Peterson (Director), Ann Rachel (Brenda), Hope Clark (Maid), Clifford Allen, Garrett Morris, Kenneth Scott (Provers).

Songs: Back in the Kitchen; My Own Morning; The Slice; Farewell, Farewell; Feet Do Yo' Stuff; Watch My Dust; Smile, Smile; Witches Brew; Another Day; I Wanted to Change Him; Being Good Isn't Good Enough; Talking to Yourself; Hallelujah, Baby!; Not Mine; I Don't Know Where She Got It; Now's the Time.

Broadway's first musical look at black history was *Hallelujah, Baby!*, which followed stars Leslie Uggams and Robert Hooks through five decades of black life. While Walter Kerr noted in *The New York Times* that authors Arthur Laurents, Jule Styne, Betty Comden, and Adolph Green "put together [*Hallelujah, Baby!*] with the best intentions in the world, . . . [it] is a course in Civics One when everybody in the world has got to

Civics Six.'' Despite a weak and somewhat old-fashioned book, Leslie Uggams dazzled the critics in her Broadway debut. She won the Tony for the best performance by an actress in a musical in the 1967-1968 season.

**A HAND IS ON THE GATE** (Longacre, September 21, 1966, 21 p.). Producer: Ivor David Balding for the Establishment Theatre Company. Director: Roscoe Lee Browne.*

Cast: Leon Bibb, Roscoe Lee Browne, Gloria Foster,* Moses Gunn,* Ellen Holly, James Earl Jones,* Josephine Premice, Cicely Tyson.*

*A Hand Is on the Gate* almost folded after its second week. A ''Citizen's Committee to Open the Gate'' swiftly formed and managed to collect $7,000 in contributions (from Sidney Poitier,* Harry Belafonte, Alan Arkin, and others) to keep the play running. Despite the impressive talents involved, the show swiftly closed. Mixed reviews doomed the show, which was an ''evening of poetry and folk music.'' Richard Watts, Jr., of *The New York Post* found *A Hand Is on the Gate* an ''elegant affirmation of pride,'' while other critics found the evening spotty. *The Village Voice* compared it unfavorably to *In White America** ''which was straight documentation which didn't pull its punches.'' Nevertheless, *The New York Times* singled out several high points, such as Ellen Holly's reading of Gwendolyn Brooks's ''Meanwhile a Mississippi Mother Burns Bacon'' and Gloria Foster's rendition of Langston Hughes's* ''Bound No'th Blues.''

**HAPPY ENDING/DAY OF ABSENCE** (St. Marks, November 15, 1965, 504 p.). Producer: Robert Hooks Productions, Inc. Author: Douglas Turner Ward.* Director: Philip Meister.

**Happy Ending**

Cast: Esther Rolle* (Ellie), Frances Foster* (Vi), Robert Hooks* (Junie), Douglas Turner (Arthur).

**Day of Absence**

Cast: Lonne Elder* (Clem; Industrialist), Arthur French (Luke; Third Citizen; Mop Man), Robert Hooks (John; Brush Man), Barbara Ann Teer* (Mary), Hattie Winston* (First Operator), Maxine Griffith (Second Operator), Pamela Jones (Third Operator), Frances Foster (Supervisor; Aide), Adolph Caesar* (Jackson), Douglas Turner (Mayor; Clan), Moses Gunn* (First Citizen; Pious; Rastus), Esther Rolle (Club Woman), Bostic Van Felton (Courier), Mark Shapiro (Announcer).

Douglas Turner Ward's *Day of Absence* and *Happy Ending* won a Drama Desk Award for the author, and Ward (as Douglas Turner) also received an Obie for his performance in the show. These two one-act plays swiftly revealed the presence of ''a talented dramatist who deserves watching,'' said *The New York Times. Day of Absence*, played in white-face makeup by black actors, reveals the surprising events in a southern town when all the blacks strangely disappear. Ward's profile of the bewildered white citizens demonstrated "devastating comic inventiveness" to *The New York Post.*

*Happy Ending* presents a portrait of black maids bemoaning the marital breakup of their employers, the Harrisons. The Harrisons's nephew berates the maids for their servile attitude, but they soon reveal the real reasons for their sorrow: the loss of money, fine clothing, good food, and ample vacations. The *Happy Ending* is the reconciliation of the Harrisons. Edith Oliver of the *New Yorker* found Ward "equally adept at turning a telling phrase and inventing sly, satiric plots."

**THE HARANGUES** (St. Marks, December 30, 1969, 56 p.). Producer: Negro Ensemble Company.* Author: Joseph A. Walker.* Director: Israel Hicks.

**Tribal Harangue One/ Tribal Harangue Three**
Cast: Rosalind Cash* (Ayo), Damon W. Brazwell, Jr. (Obataiye).

**Tribal Harangue Two**
Cast: Robert Hooks* (Cal), David Downing* (Jake), Irene Bunde (Zoe Walton), Robert G. Murch (Walton), William Jay (Doctor), Julius W. Harris, Douglas Turner [Ward]* (Black Men).

**Harangue**
Cast: Julius W. Harris (Gorilla), William Jay (Lee), Elliot Cuker (Cooper), Linda Carlson (Billy Boy), Douglas Turner (Asura).

Joseph A. Walker's *The Harangues* opened the third season of the Negro Ensemble Company productions with mixed reviews. Clive Barnes commented in *The New York Times*: "Walker . . . has juxtaposed a remarkable series of white-black vignettes in an evening that makes a plea for . . . more racial understanding." Clayton Riley, critic for the *Manhattan Tribune*, lambasted the show: "There is virtually nothing about it one can honestly recommend. The writing fails for having no relevant information to impart." [*The New York Times*, January 25, 1970] This sharp division characterized the reviews, although all critics praised the performances of Robert Hooks and Douglas Turner.

*The Harangues* comprised two one-act plays and two "interludes." The interludes consider a mythical black past and a mythical future. "One" involves the decision of a fourteenth-century African couple to kill their son rather than let him become a slave. In "Three," the same couple decides to let the son live even though the father will soon be killed. The remaining Harangues return to the present. In "Two," Cal (Robert Hooks) gets his white girlfriend pregnant, and then decides to murder her rich stepfather and inherit his money. Finally, in "Harangue, " Asura (Douglas Turner), an elderly black man, becomes crazy after years of attempting to become a television director but being unable to get a job. He enters a bar and forces customers to prove their virtue or be killed. Asura thinks this is a television show and enjoys it enormously. His plans are frustrated as the virtuous die and the corrupt live.

**HARLEM** (Apollo, February 20, 1929, 93 p.). Producer: Edward A. Blatt. Authors: W. J. Rapp and Wallace Thurman.* Director: Chester Erskin.

Cast: Clarence Taylor (George Williams), Elise Thomas (Mazie Williams), Edna Wise Barr (Arabella Williams), Inez Clough (Ma Williams), Lew Payton (Pa Williams), Isabell Washington (Cordelia Williams), Richard Landers (Basil Venerable), Emory S. Richardson (Jasper Williams), Lillian Fairley (Effie), Hemsley Winfield (Jimmie), Collington Hayes (Thaddeus Jenkins), Hillis Walters (Ippy Jones), Carmen Marshall (Mary Lou), Billy Andrews (Roy Crowe), Frank Badham (Briggs), A. B. Walker (Will).

*Harlem* was Broadway's second visit to Harlem in 1929, as a musical entitled *Deep Harlem** had opened the previous month. Nevertheless, *Harlem* had been written first. It had floated from producer to producer, who wanted imitations of such hit plays as *Porgy** and *Lulu Belle*. Chester Erskin, a young actor and director, liked the play and interested Edward A. Blatt in producing it.

*Harlem* was a collaboration between a black author, Wallace Thurman, who provided the story and dialogue, and a white, William Jourdan Rapp, who shaped the play. Unlike earlier views of black life, *Harlem* attempted to provide a realistic portray of blacks in New York City. The theatre program even provided a "Glossary of Harlemisms" to guide white audiences to the patois of a nearby but, at the same time, alien culture.

*Harlem* presented the story of the Williams family, who had recently immigrated to New York City from South Carolina. Although the Williams clan is promised a new life, the family is slowly destroyed by economic hard times. The *Herald Tribune* praised all the performers: "Not a character is miscast or badly played, and the stage direction was uncommonly skillful. Isabell Washington stands out as the shameless Cordelia in whom the wayward blood coursed so fiercely. A splendid performance is the Kid Vamp of Ernest R. Whitman, an enormous black Negro who acts with an ease, subtlety, and restraint that many actors might envy. Inez Clough and Lew Payton, as Isabella's parents, also deserve mention." *Harlem* was revived on October 21, 1929, but it ran for only sixteen performances.

**HARLEM CAVALCADE** (Ritz, May 1, 1942, 49 p.). Producer: Ed Sullivan. Composer: Eubie Blake*; Lyricist: Noble Sissle. Directors: Ed Sullivan and Noble Sissle.*

Cast: Noble Sissle, Flournoy Miller,* Tim Moore,* Maude Russell, Johnny Lee, Moke and Poke, The Gingersnaps, Jesse Crior, Pops and Louie, Monte Hawley, Garland Wilson, Five Crackerjacks, Amanda Randolph, Una Mae Carlisle, The Peters Sisters, Jimmie Daniels, The Harlemaniacs, Tom Fletcher, Red and Curley, Edward Steele, Joe Byrd, Wini and Bob Johnson, Miller Brothers and Lois.

Songs: I'm Just Wild About Harry; Bandana Days.

In *Harlem Cavalcade* Ed Sullivan and Noble Sissle attempted to revive the popular black revues of the 1920s. Noble Sissle returned with "I'm Just Wild About Harry"; Flournoy Miller provided a skit about the draft; and Tim Moore and Joe Byrd, in black-face, enacted the obligatory graveyard sketch. Yet, many critics described the show as "monotonous," noting an unusually heavy emphasis on tap-dancing. *Harlem Cavalcade* expired with the traditional June exodus of Broadway shows.

**HEAVEN AND HELL'S AGREEMENT** (St. Marks, April 9, 1974, 8 p.). Producer: Negro Ensemble Company.* Author: J. E. Gaines.* Director: Anderson Johnson.

Cast: Nick Latour (Mr. Jackson), Lea Scott (Miss Vi), Michele Shay (Norma Jean), Leon Morenzie (Bert), Gary Bolling (Buddy), Roland Sanchez (Poor Boy), Mary Alice* (Mrs. Moore), Todd Davis (Western Union Boy).

*Heaven and Hell's Agreement*, J. E. (Sonny Jim) Gaines's "season-within-a-season" entry for the Negro Ensemble Company was billed as a "Myth." After seven years of hiding in Vietnam, a black soldier (Gary Bolling) returns home to find his wife of one month has a lover. The play considers the effect both on his parents, as well as the surprised lovers (Michele Shay and Leon Morenzie). Several critics praised Gaines's play, but found that the dialogue had a high proportion of speeches that rang untrue. *The New York Post* noted: "Mr. Gaines has marked talent; needs work."

**HIS FIRST STEP.** See THE CORNER.

**HIS HONOR THE BARBER** (Majestic, May 8, 1911, 8 p.). Producer: The Smart Set Company. Book: Edwin Hanaford. Composer: James Brymm. Director: S. H. Dudley.*

Cast: S. H. Dudley (Raspberry Snow), James Burris (Mose Lewis), Will Grundy (Captain Percival Dandelion), James Lightfoot (Wellington White), Elizabeth Hart (Lily White), Ella Anderson (Caroline Brown), Alberta Ormes (Ella Wheeler Wilson), Andrew Tribble (Babe Johnson), Will Everly (The Lion), George McClain (The Bear), John Warren (The Monkey), Aida Overton Walker* (In Her Specialties).

Songs: Leave 'Fore Supper Time; Corn Shucking Time; Merry Widow Brown; The Isles of Love; Rainbow Sue; Consolation Lane; Crybaby Moon.

The Smart Set Company was one of the few black acting companies to venture on Broadway between 1910 and 1920. *His Honor the Barber* features the dreams of a barber named Raspberry Snow. Snow wishes to shave the president of the United States and elope with the beautiful Lily White. His wishes come true in Act II, but it is only a dream sequence. Snow awakes to disappointment in Act III.

The highlights of the Smart Set shows were the performances of Dudley and Walker. The *New York Dramatic Mirror* commented: "S. H. Dudley and Aida Overton Walker lead the contingent with much assurance and allow no dull moments while they hold the stage. Dudley is a quiet comedian of much resourcefulness, while Miss Walker, as is well known, is the best Negro comedienne today. Her tomboy number, her Spanish song and dance, and her impersonation of a Negro 'chappie,' the last of which is the real hit of the play, are minutely favorable characterizations. With such material as Dudley and Miss Walker have, they do wonders."

**HOME** (St. Marks, December 14, 1979, 82 p.). Producer: Negro Ensemble Company.* Author: Samm-Art Williams.* Director: Dean Irby.

Cast: Charles Brown (Cephus Miles), L. Scott Caldwell (Woman One; Pattie Mae Wells), Michele Shay (Woman Two).

Samm-Art Williams's *Home* moved swiftly from the St. Marks Playhouse, home of the Negro Ensemble Company, to Broadway's Cort Theatre. The rhapsodic reviews encouraged the transfer. Mel Gussow noted in *The New York Times* that "in all respects—writing, direction, and performance—this is one of the happiest theatrical events of the season." Moving with the show was its cast—Charles Brown, L. Scott Caldwell, and Michele Shay—all relative newcomers to Broadway.

Williams claimed that he was trying to show a new side of black life in *Home*: "You know, all black characters don't have to be heroes. All black men do not have to be black macho strong leaders. . . . You can have very sensitive, very kind, and very gentle kinds of black men." [*The New York Times*, February 24, 1980] *Home*'s Cephus Miles fits this characterization. Cephus (Brown) leaves his North Carolina home after refusing to serve in the Vietnam War. After imprisonment, he drifts northward where he is both dazzled and disoriented by city life. Later, when he returns home, he finds that the South, too, has changed. Although only three people are onstage, Caldwell and Shay portray the various denizens of Cephus's world: a wino, a bus driver, a soldier, and the like.

**HOME IS THE HUNTER** (A.N.T. Playhouse, December 20, 1945, 18 p.). Producer: American Negro Theatre.* Author: Samuel M. Kootz. Director: Abram Hill.*

Cast: Evelio Grille (Dawson Drake, Sr.), Maxwell Glanville* (Rusty Saunders), Clarice Taylor* (Ann Drake), Elwood Smith (Dawson Drake, Jr.).

*Home Is the Hunter* opened the new home of the American Negro Theatre at 15 West 126th Street, a welcome change from the cramped basement theatre on West 135th Street. Elwood Smith, the lead actor, explained the goal of the new production: "Like *Anna Lucasta*,* it can be played by Negroes or whites. . . . [There are] no Negro twists . . . [It is] all in the good fight to prove that Negroes are like any other people—no better, no worse, and no different."

*Home Is the Hunter* concerns a soldier who goes to war to fight fascism, but on his return home, he embraces that ideology. Critics objected to the notion that American blacks might be attracted to fascism, and several newspapers, like the *New York World Telegram*, dismissed the play as "repugnant claptrap."

**HOT CHOCOLATES** (Hudson, June 20, 1929, 210 p.). Producer: Connie and George Immerman. Composers: Fats Waller* and Harry Brooks. Lyrics: Andy Razaf.* Comedy Sketches: Eddie Green.* Directors: George Immerman, Leonard Harper, and Danny Dare.

Cast: Baby Cox, Edith Wilson,* Jazzlips Richardson, Jimmie Baskette, Paul Bass, Paul Meers, Eddie Green, Billy Marey, Billy Higgins, Dick Campbell, Three Midnight Steppers, Thelma Meers, Margaret Simms, Louise Higgins, Madeline Belt, Dolly McCormick, and Russell Wooding's Jubilee Singers.

Songs: Pickaninny Land; Song of the Cotton Fields; Sweet Savannah Sue; Say It with Your Feet; Ain't Misbehavin'; Black and Blue; Redskinland; Can't We Get Together?; Snake Hips' Dance; Off-Time; That Rhythm Man; Dixie Cinderella; Goddess of Rain.

*Hot Chocolates* ("A New Tanskin Revel") arrived at the Hudson via the nightclub stage (Connie's Inn at 131st Street and Seventh Avenue) and the Bronx's Windsor Theatre. Featuring Baby Cox, Edith Wilson and Jazzlips Richardson, *Hot Chocolates* combined the music, dancing, and comedy that had made the black musical revue such a success in the 1920s.

The score by Thomas "Fats" Waller, Andy Razaf, and Harry Brooks received high praise, with "Black and Blue," "That Rhythm Man," and "Can't We Get Together?" mentioned most often. The best remembered song from *Hot Chocolates* is "Ain't Misbehavin'," but several critics were not wildly enthusiastic about it. The *New York World* commented: "There is a song called 'Ain't Misbehavin' ' on which much reliance is placed. Almost everybody in the show sings it at one time or another, and as there are a good many in the show, the song gets sung pretty often. It is tuneful and pleasant, and I should feel like giving everybody a great deal of credit for it were it not so strikingly reminiscent of something I seem to remember from a year or so ago." The Le Roy Smith Orchestra accompanied the cast, and an unbilled trumpeter by the name of Louis Armstrong attracted considerable attention.

**THE HOT MIKADO** (Broadhurst, March 23, 1939, 85 p.). Producer: Michael Todd. Based on the Gilbert and Sullivan operetta "The Mikado." Topical lyrics: Dave Greggory and William Tracy. Modern Orchestra Arrangements: Charles L. Cooke. Director: Hassard Short.

Cast: Bill Robinson* (The Mikado), Eddie Green* (Ko-Ko), Rosetta LeNoire (Peep-Bo), Bob Parrish (Nanki-Poo), James A. Lillard (Pish-Tush), Maurice Ellis (Pooh-Bah), Gwendolyn Reyde (Yum-Yum), Frances Brock (Pitti-Sing), Freddie Robinson (Messenger Boy), Rosa Brown (Katisha), Vincent Shields (Red Cap).

When Mike Todd failed to option the Federal Theatre Project's* *The Swing Mikado** for Broadway, he decided to bring his own black version of *The Mikado* to Broadway. Although *The Swing Mikado* opened a few weeks earlier, Todd proclaimed himself the victor with the casting coup of persuading Bill Robinson to appear in his show.

Although the critics liked *The Hot Mikado*, they missed the charm and subtlety of the earlier show. The Broadway showmanship of *The Hot Mikado* caused *Time*'s critic to explain: "It is less profitably compared with *The Swing Mikado* than with such spirited colored shows as *Blackbirds of 1928** and *Shuffle Along*.*"

The highlight of the new show was clearly the performance of sixty-one-year-old Bill Robinson as the Mikado. His reviews were almost love letters. Brooks Atkinson of *The New York Times* commented: "He has been a great man all these years in black dancing shoes and a black derby hanging on one ear. But Bojangles is a creature of wonderful effulgence when he is caparisoned in gold. Yes, that costume becomes him. He struts. He taps sharply and lightly according to the way he feels about a scene, and he gleams at the audience with the gusto that has crowded New York with his friends."

Although both Mike Todd and the Federal Theatre Project insisted on the novelty of their efforts, black versions of this Gilbert and Sullivan show appeared earlier. Thatcher, Primrose, and West's Minstrels did a black-face Mikado in 1886. The most recent version, *The Black Mikado*, opened in London in 1975.

**HOT RHYTHM** (Times Square, August 21, 1930, 73 p.). Producer: Max Rudnick. Sketches: Will Morrissey, Ballard Macdonald, and Edward Hurley. Composer: Porter Grainger. Lyricist: Donald Heywood.* Directors: Will Morrissey and Nat Cash.

Cast: Edith Wilson,* Ina Duncan, Revella Hughes, Mae Barnes, Eddie Rector, Johnny Lee Long, Dewey Markham, Sam Paige, Al Vigal, Mel Duncan, George Wiltshire, Arthur Bryson, Simms and Bowie, Nora Green, Hilda Perleno, Laura Duncan, Inez Seeley, Madeline Belt.

Songs: Mama's Gotta Get Her Rent; Say the Word That Will Make You Mine; Loving You the Way I Do (Eubie Blake*-Jack Scholl-Will

Morrissey); Since You Went Away; Jarahal; Alabamy; Up in the Sky, Tropical Moon; Hungry for Love; Hot Rhythm; The Penalty of Love; Steppin' on It.

Critics found that *Hot Rhythm* ("A Sepia-Tinted Little Show") attempted to copy "the elegance of contemporary Caucasian extravaganzas" much to its own detriment. At one point, during a tender love duet, director Will Morrissey walked on stage. "Look at them," he told the audience, "just like Jack Buchanan and Gertie Lawrence. Only a lot cheaper!" *Time* found the show "unfunny" but praised the song "Loving You the Way I Do," a Eubie Blake addition to the Grainger and Heywood score.

**HOUSE OF FLOWERS** (Alvin, December 30, 1954, 165 p.). Producer: Saint Subber. Book and lyrics: Truman Capote. Composer: Harold Arlen. Director: Peter Brook.

Cast: Pearl Bailey* (Madame Fleur), Diahann Carroll* (Ottilie alias Violet), Juanita Hall* (Madame Tango), Geoffrey Holder* (The Champion), Frederick O'Neal* (The Houngan), Alvin Ailey (Alvin), Dolores Harper (Tulip), Ada Moore (Gladiola), Enid Mosier (Pansy), Winston George Henriques (Do), Solomon Earl Green (Don't), Miriam Burton (Mother), Ray Walston (Captain Jonas), Leu Comacho, Margot Small (The Sisters Meringue), Mary Mon Toy (Mamselle Honolulu), Glory Van Scott (Mamselle Cigarette), Rawn Spearman (Royal), Don Redman (Chief of Police), Carmen de Lavallade (Carmen), Dino DiLuca (Monsieur Jameson).

Songs: Waitin'; One Man Ain't Quite Enough; Madame Tango's Tango; A Sleepin' Bee; Bamboo Cage; House of Flowers; Two Ladies in de Shade of de Banana Tree; What Is a Friend For?; Mardi Gras; I Never Has Seen Snow; Husband Cage; Has I Let You Down?; Voudou; Slide, Boy, Slide; Don't Like Goodbyes; Turtle Song; Bamboo Cage Finale.

Harold Arlen wrote two black musicals of Caribbean life in the 1950s. *Jamaica** (1957) provided a showcase for the talents of Lena Horne,* while *House of Flowers* gave strong roles to Pearl Bailey, Juanita Hall, Josephine Premice, and newcomer Diahann Carroll. The Truman Capote libretto provided a tale of two competing bordellos in the French West Indies. Bailey received ovations for her renditions of "One Man," "What Is a Friend For?," and "Has I Let You Down?" on opening night, while Diahann Carroll's "A Sleepin' Bee" also received raves. Critics dismissed the Capote book, however, and *House of Flowers* managed only a brief run.

**HOUSE PARTY** (American Place, October 16, 1973, 42 p.). Producer: American Place Theater. Author: Ed Bullins.* Director: Roscoe Orman.

Cast: Mary Alice* (Girl Friend; Woman; Poet; Loved One), Verona Barnes (Seduced and Abandoned; Fun Loving Wile Chile; Fried Brains),

Gary Bolling (Dopeseller; Working Man), Rosanna Carter (Soul Sister Rememberer; Confused and Lazy; Harlem Mother), Starletta De Paur (Virgin; Go-Go; Quitter), Earle Hyman* (Harlem Politician; Scrap Book Keeper; Black Critic; Reconciler), Andre Mtumi (Corner Brother; Explainer; Black Writer), Jimmy Pelham (M.C.; Groover; Rapper), Basil Wallace (Lover Man; West Indian Revolutionary).

Ed Bullins's *House Party*, "a soulful happening," resembled a musical revue. The scene is a nightclub in Harlem, where an M.C. (Jimmy Pelham) warms up the audience with the second-rate jokes and patter. Several skits (of varying quality) follow, with critics praising Rosanna Carter's portrayal of Josephine Baker's maid and Earl Hyman's impersonation of a smooth and corrupt politician. Despite several high points, most critics found it an evening of minor Bullins.

**HOW COME?** (Apollo, April 16, 1923, 32 p.). Producer: Criterion Productions. Book: Eddie Hunter.* Music and lyrics: Ben Harris and Eddie Hunter with additional songs by Henry Creamer* and Will Vodery. Director: Sam H. Grisman.

Cast: Eddie Hunter (Rastus Skunkton Lime), Andrew Fairchild (Deacon Long Tack), Alice Brown (Sarah Green), Leroy Broomfield (Brother Wire Nail), Nina Hunter (Dolores Love), Hilary Friend (Sister Doolittle), Amon Davis (Ebenezer Green), Alex Lovejoy (Brother Ham), Chappy Chapelle (Lawyer), Juanita Stinette (Malinda Joy), George W. Cooper (Rufus Wise), George C. Lane (Dandy Dan), Andrew Tribble (Ophelia Snow), James Dingbat (Brother Low Down), Betty Throck (Sister Whale), Sidney Bechet (Chief of Police), Harry Hunter, Adrian Joyce, Isaac Momen (Policemen), Helen Dunmore (Catherine Place), Vivian Harris (Laurette Wise), Mabel Kemp (Millie Johnson), Dorothy Lewis (Marie Fraine), Elvetta Davis (Ruth Johnson), Carrie Edwards (Hortense Carter).

Songs: Pretty Malindy; Certainly Is the Truth; Goodnight Brother Green; Syncopated Strain; Bandanna Anna; Pickaninny Vamp; Sweetheart Farewell; Dinah; Gingerena; Charleston Cut Out; In My Dixie Dreamland; When I'm Blue; Love Will Bring You Happiness; I Didn't Grieve Over Daniel; Keep the Man You've Got; Count Your Money: E-Gypsy-Ann; Some More Dancing; Charleston Finale.

*How Come?* was Broadway's fifth black musical of the season, and the *New York Mail* prophesied: "It promises to be even darker on old Broadway this summer." Eddie Hunter and the cast told the story of the Mobile Chicken Trust, whose members had been robbed of a great deal of money. In order to repay the group, the former treasurer sets up a bootleg liquor operation. Using a bootblack parlor as a front, customers would ask for white shoes if they wanted gin or tan shoes if they wanted whiskey.

*How Come?* was one of the few black musicals of the 1920s to allow blacks on the main floor of the theatre. The far right and far left of the orchestra were reserved for black patrons.

**HOW COME, LAWD?** (Forty-ninth Street, September 30, 1937, 2 p.). Producer: Negro Theatre Guild. Author: Donald Heywood.* Director: Charles J. Adler.

Cast: Rex Ingram* (Big Boy), Mercedes Gilbert (Mom), Homer Tutt* (Pa), Hilda Rogers (Clorinda), Alex Lovejoy (Slacks), Leigh Whipper* (Aloes), Harry D. Ingram (Sammy), Dan Michaels (Boots), Edgar Martin (Rasmus), George L. Ingram (Yamacraw), Dorothy Cadoza (Babes), Columbus Jackson (Wall Street), James Fuller (Jackknife).

Donald Heywood, author of *Black Rhythm*,* *Africana*,* and *Ol' Man Satan*,* displayed his diverse talents several times on Broadway during the 1930s. Unfortunately, he never enjoyed a successful show. *How Come, Lawd?*, billed as a "Negro folk-drama," followed in the footsteps of Heywood's previous works. This drama of black labor union recruitment managed only a two-performance run. Nevertheless, critics singled out Rex Ingram, once again, for dramatic honors, while Alex Lovejoy won praise for his comedic talents.

**HOW LONG TILL SUMMER** (Playhouse, December 27, 1949, 7 p.). Producers: Leon J. Bronsky and Edward M. Gilbert. Authors: Sarett and Herbert Rudley. Director: Herbert Rudley.

Cast: Josh White* (Mathew Jeffers), Ida James (Kate Jeffers), Frank Wilson* (Dr. Dan Benson), Leigh Whipper* (Al Gaige), Fredi Washington* (Mrs. Dexter), Josh White, Jr. (Josh Jeffers), Charles Taylor (Johnny Burns), Sam Gilman (Mr. Burns), Evelyn Davis (Mary), Milton Williams (Harold Carver), Arthur O'Connell (Fred Johnson), Maxwell Glanville* (Harlan), Peter Capell (A Man).

Herbert and Sarett Rudley's *How Long Till Summer* attempted to consider both racial intolerance and political corruption at the same time. An upwardly mobile black lawyer (Josh White) tries to shield his son from racial prejudice, but his efforts fail, and the son experiences a breakdown. Critics dismissed the play as "maudlin" and "inept," but praised black actors Josh White, Frank Wilson, Ida James, and long-time stage veteran Leigh Whipper.

**HUMMING SAM** (New Yorker, April 8, 1933, 1 p.). Producer: Allan K. Foster. Book: Eileen Nutter. Composer and lyricist: Alexander Hill. Directors: Carey and Davis.

Cast: Gertrude "Baby" Cox (Humming Sam), Madeline Belt (Madge Carter), Edith Wilson* (Nina May), Lionel Monagas* (Yellow George), Speedy Smith (Uncle Ned), Alonzo Bosan (Totem), Bunny Allen (Hot Cakes), Robert Underwood (Harlem Dan), Louise Lovelle (Louise), Dorothy Embry (Esmaraldae), Catherine Brooks (Emmaraldae), Mary Mason (Mamaraldae), Lorenzo Tucker (E. Bolton), John Lee (Mr. Connors), Sandy (Mike), Jones and Allen (Caesar and Cicero), Al Watts

(Mr. Carter), Flo Brown (Mae Carter), Cecil Rivers (Freddie Marlowe), Hannah Sylvester (Clara), J. Mardo Brown (Drum Major), Louise Cook (Miss Jitters).

Songs: Steppin' Along; Harlem Dan; How the First Song Was Born; They're Off; Pinching Yourself; Change Your Mind About Me; If I Didn't Have You; In the Stretch; Jubilee; A Little Bit of Quicksilver; Answer My Heart; Stompin' 'Em Down; I'll Be True, But I'll Be Blue; Jitters; Fifteen Minutes a Day; Ain'tcha Glad You Got Music?; Dancing, and I Mean Dancing.

Black musicals fared poorly in the 1930s, but *Humming Sam* would have flopped in any decade. Despite the presence of such veterans as Gertrude "Baby" Cox and Edith Wilson, *Humming Sam* folded after only one performance. *The New York Times* explained: "During their initial whispers, some of the performers looked a bit perplexed, and others appeared troubled. They had been in Negro musical comedies before. They knew."

# I

**I HAVE A DREAM** (Ambassador, September 20, 1976, 80 p.). Producers: Frank Von Zerneck, Mike Wise, Frankie Hewitt, and the Shubert Organization. Author: Josh Greenfield. Director: Robert Greenwald.

Cast: Billy Dee Williams* (Dr. Martin Luther King, Jr.), Judyann Elder (Woman), Sheila Ellis, Leata Galloway, Ramona Brooks, Millie Foster (Singer/Actress), Clinton Derricks-Carroll (Singer/Actor).

Coretta Scott King and the Reverend Martin Luther King, Sr., attended the opening night performance of *I Have a Dream* at the Ambassador Theatre. Billy Dee Williams impersonated King from the days in Alabama in 1955 to shortly before his assassination in 1968. *The New York Times* found Williams's performance a triumph: "He does a fascinating job, dominating, magnetic, even ebullient." Rather than a play, Clive Barnes of *The New York Times* found it a "theatrical tribute," based on King's speeches, letters, and conversations. Moses Gunn* replaced Williams late in the run.

**THE IMPRISONMENT OF OBATALA.** See PLAYS FROM AFRICA.

**IN ABRAHAM'S BOSOM** (Provincetown, December 30, 1926, 116 p.). Producer: Provincetown Players. Author: Paul Green. Director: Jasper Deeter.

Cast: Julius Bledsoe* (Abraham McCranie), Rose McClendon* (Goldie

McAllister), Frank Wilson* (Bud Gaskins), Thomas Moseley (Lije Hunneycutt), James Dunmore (Puny Avery), L. Rufus Hill (Colonel McCranie), H. Ben Smith (Lonnie McCranie), Abbie Mitchell* (Muh Mack), Richard Huey (Douglass McCranie), Melvin Greene (Eddie Williams), Armithine Lattimer (Lanie Horton), Stanley Greene (Neilly McNeill).

Although *In Abraham's Bosom* was written by Paul Green, a southern white dramatist, James Weldon Johnson in *Black Manhattan* found the play "closer and truer to actual Negro life . . . than any drama of the kind that had yet been produced." It opened to modest reviews at the Provincetown Playhouse, and later moved uptown to the Garrick, where it was reviewed favorably by the major critics. In May, it won the Pulitzer for the best play of the year. The play had closed by this time, so a revival was mounted, thus giving New Yorkers another chance to see the play in September 1927.

The Provincetown Players cast the top black dramatic actors of the day in *In Abraham's Bosom*. Julius Bledsoe (Abraham) moved swiftly from his acclaimed appearance in *Deep River** to the new play. When the show moved uptown, he was replaced by Frank Wilson. *The New York Times* noted: "Mr. Wilson suffused the drama with a passionate sincerity that pulled together the scattered scenes and gave a lucid meaning to the themes." Abbie Mitchell, Rose McClendon, and R. J. Huey also received words of praise.

Many black critics were less sympathetic to Green's play about a man who educates himself but is then driven to murder. Theophilus Lewis, critic for *The Messenger*, wrote: "the play is not only mechanically weak; it is constructed of rotten material. One of the implications . . . is that an erotic temperament and a lack of stamina go together. I suspect Massa Green attaches a racial significance to this, but since he doesn't say so, I won't charge him with it. The [play] is unsound on broader human grounds."

**IN AN UPSTATE MOTEL** (Theatre Four, May 8, 1981, 45 p.). Producer: Negro Ensemble Company.* Author: Larry Neal. Director: Paul Carter Harrison.

Cast: Phylicia Ayers-Allen (Female Shadow), Carl Gordon (Male Shadow), Donna Bailey (Queenie), Charles Henry Patterson (Duke).

Playwright Larry Neal died at age forty-three, before *In an Upstate Motel* could be fully revised for this Negro Ensemble Company production. As a result, critics noted several problems that might have been resolved with further work. Duke (Charles Henry Patterson) and Queenie (Donna Bailey) are on the lam from the mob and are stuck "in an upstate motel." Yet, critics asked whether this was an evocation of 1930s crime dramas or a dissertation on the meaning of life ("It's just a maze we can't get out of")? Despite this confusion, critics praised the strong direction of Paul Carter Harrison.

**IN DAHOMEY** (New York, February 18, 1903, 53 p.). Producers: Hurtig and Seamon. Book and direction: J. A. Shipp. Composer: Will Marion Cook.* Lyricist: Alex Rogers.*

Cast: Bert Williams* (Shylock Homestead), George W. Walker* (Rareback Pinkerton), Alex Rogers (George Reeder), J. A. Shipp (Hustling Charley), J. Leubrie Hill (Officer Still), Abbie Mitchell* (Pansy), Aida Overton Walker* (Rosetta Lightfoot), Chas. Moore (Je-Je), Wm. Elkins (Menuki), Wm. Barker (Mose Lightfoot), Pete Hampton (Hamilton Lightfoot), Fred Douglas (Dr. Straight), Walter Richardson (Henry Stampfield), George Catlin (Me Sing), Richard Conners (Leather), Green Tapley (White Wash Man), Theodore Pankey (Messenger Rush), Hattie McIntosh (Cecilia Lightfoot), Lottie Williams (Mrs. Stringer).

Songs: My Dahomian Queen (J. L. Hill-Frank Williams); Caboceers Chorale; Swing Along; When the Moon Shines; Me and De Minstrel Ban'; On Broadway in Dahomey (Al Johns-Alex Rogers); Why Adam Sinned; Society; I Want to Be an Actor Lady (Harry Von Tilzer-Vincent Bryan); I May Be Crazy, But I Am No Fool; A Rich Coon's Babe (Rogers); Dear Luzon (Tom Lemonier); The Czar; Emancipation Day; Jonah Man (B. Williams-Rogers); Evah Dahkey Is a King.

*In Dahomey* was a major success for the team of Bert Williams and George Walker. *Theatre Magazine* found it an "unquestionable success." Special praise was given to Bert Williams: "He is spontaneously and genuinely funny. Nature has endowed him with a comic mask, and he succeeds in obtaining with voice and gesture ludicrous effects that are irresistible." This show traveled to London, where Walker and Williams appeared before Edward VII, and later returned to America for a profitable tour in 1904 and 1905.

Despite the title, the new show spent little time in Africa. The first two acts concern Williams and Walker's efforts to find a missing silver box. In the third act, the comic team escapes to Africa a step ahead of the law. They enjoy their new life in Africa and decide to remain where "Evah Dahkey Is a King." Of course, a few changes will have to be made if they remain, as Williams and Walker explain in their hit song "On Broadway in Dahomey."

**IN NEW ENGLAND WINTER** (Henry Street, January 26, 1971, 8 p.). Producers: New Federal Theatre,* Woodie King, Jr.,* and Dick Williams.* Author: Ed Bullins.* Director: Dick Williams.

Cast: Mel Winkler (Cliff Dawson), Norman Bush (Steve Benson), Tony Major (Chuckie), J. Herbert Kerr, Jr. (Bummie), Gloria Edwards (Liz), Darryl W. Lee (Oscar), Donna O. Black (Carrie), Garrett Morris (Crook).

*In New England Winter*, the second play of Ed Bullins's "Twentieth Century Cycle," continues the saga of Cliff Dawson (Mel Winkler) and his half-brother Steve Benson (Norman Bush) from *In the Wine Time* (1968).*

The action takes place in two time periods. In 1960, the brothers plan a robbery that will enable Steve to return to Liz, the woman of his "New England winter" of 1955. Yet, the events of 1955 reveal that Steve has idealized his past. The rehearsal for the robbery is botched as Steve murders one of his cohorts. Nevertheless, the evening brings the brothers together as Steve and Cliff reveal secrets of the past to each other.

Bullins won an Obie for *In New England Winter* (and *The Fabulous Miss Marie**) as well as critical acclaim. Clive Barnes commented in *The New York Times*: "Bullins is one of the most interesting of American playwrights, and I think he may prove to be one of the most significant. . . . He copies no one. . . . The voice is entirely his own."

**IN SPLENDID ERROR** (Greenwich Mews, October 26, 1954, n.a.p.). Producers: Village Presbyterian Church and the Brotherhood Synagogue. Author: William Branch.* Director: Salem Ludwig.

Cast: William Marshall (Frederick Douglass), Alfred Sander (John Brown), Kenneth Manigault (Rev. Loguen), Lance Taylor (Joshua), Clarice Taylor* (Anna Douglass), Charles Harrigan (Lewis Douglass), Louis Guss (George Chatham), Howard Wierum (Theodore Tilton), Donna Liggins (Annie Douglass), Maxwell Glanville* (Shields Green), John Leighton (Col. Hugh Forbes), Albert M. Ottenheimer (Sanborn).

William Branch began his play on the confrontation between Frederick Douglass and John Brown while stationed in Germany with the U.S. Army. *The New York Times* found that Branch wrote with "eloquence and vigor," and the scenes between Douglass and Brown were "full of spirit and force." Yet, the reviewer lamented the fact that Douglass and Brown seemed to lose their humanity in the play and become historical symbols. Brown came to represent revolution and Douglass reform in the attempt to resolve the racial crisis in the era prior to the Civil War. Some have suggested that the play was also a historical metaphor for race relations in the 1950s.

William Marshall received considerable praise for his performance as Douglass. The *Times* noted: "It is difficult to imagine anyone who could have been more suited for the part. Mr. Marshall, a tall, powerful-looking man, plays with both regality and humility. Possessed of a deeply resonant voice that speaks in superb diction, he is able to bolster attention in a play that is given principally to long passages of dialogue and scanty action." A 1978 revival by the New Federal Theatre* featured Gilbert Lewis as Douglass.

**IN THE DEEPEST PART OF SLEEP** (St. Marks, June 4, 1974, 32 p.). Producer: Negro Ensemble Company.* Author: Charles Fuller.* Director: Israel Hicks.

Cast: Mary Alice* (Maybelle), Todd Davis (Reuben), Michele Shay (Lyla), Charles Weldon (Ashe).

Charles Fuller's *In the Deepest Part of Sleep* deals with the return of a mentally ill mother (Mary Alice) to her family after a nervous breakdown. As told by the son, Fuller's play recounts how the mother's excessive demands destroy the family. Mel Gussow, writing in *The New York Times*, argued that Fuller "is a playwright that should be heard from," but he lamented the fact that *In the Deepest Part of Sleep* "is stricken by bathos and never fully recovers."

**IN THE WINE TIME** (New Lafayette, December 10, 1968, n.a.p.). Producer: New Lafayette Theatre.* Author: Ed Bullins.* Director: Robert Macbeth.*

Cast: Sonny Jim [Gaines]* (Cliff Dawson), Bette Jean Howard (Lou Dawson), Gary Bolling (Ray), Rosanna Carter (Miss Minny Garrison), Helen Ellis (Bunny Gillette), Roberta Raysor (Beatrice), Yvette Hawkins (Tiny), Whitman Mayo (Silly Willy Clark), Kris Keiser (Red), George Miles (Bama), Peggy A. Kirkpatrick (Doris), Bill Lathan (Policeman).

Ed Bullins's *In the Wine Time* premiered at the New Lafayette Theatre, located in a converted movie house on Seventh Avenue near 138th Street after its previous site had been destroyed by fire. It was an auspicious debut for the new theatre. Lindsay Patterson, writing in *The New York Times*, heartily praised the playwright: "He has a deep sensitivity, love, and understanding for his characters that enable him to present a rare thing, a truthful presentation of ghetto dwellers." [December 22, 1968]

*In the Wine Time* takes place in a northern industrial city, where Cliff (Sonny Jim), his wife Lou (Bette Jean Howard), and sixteen-year-old nephew Ray (Gary Bolling) live together. Cliff and Lou spend most of their time drinking, and pin most of their hopes on young Ray, whom they feel will escape the family's pattern of failure. Ray accidentally becomes involved in a murder, and Cliff takes the blame. By this one noble act, he gives Ray the chance to succeed.

**IN WHITE AMERICA** (Sheridan Square, October 31, 1963, 499 p.). Producer: Judith Rutherford Marechal. Compiler: Martin Duberman. Director: Harold Stone.

Cast: Gloria Foster,* James Greene, Moses Gunn,* Claudette Nevins, Michael O'Sullivan, Fred Pinkard.

Historian Martin Duberman utilized the tools of his trade and provided an evening of dramatic readings of documents of black life in white America. From the beginnings of the slave trade to contemporary issues concerning civil rights, *In White America* presented a panoramic view of attitudes towards race in America. While the entire cast received praise, *The New York Times* singled out the readings of Gloria Foster. First, she is a slave who is forced to sell her thirteen children into bondage, then a woman whose husband is lynched by the Klan, and, finally, a young girl who is trying to integrate Central High School in Little Rock. Her scenes were clearly the most moving of the evening, and she won an Obie for her performance.

**INACENT BLACK** (Biltmore, May 6, 1981, 15 p.). Producers: Gloria Hope Sher, Marjorie Moon, Jay J. Cohen, Zaida Coles Edley, and Spirit Will Productions. Author: A. Marcus Hemphill. Director: Mikell Pinkney.

Cast: Melba Moore* (Inacent Black), Barbara Montgomery* (Mama Essie Rydell), Rosanna Carter (Waitress), Gregory Miller (Helwin), Reginald Vel Johnson (Marv Rydell), Count Stovall (Charles Rydell), Bruce Strickland (Percy), Ronald "Smokey" Stevens (Pretty Pete), Joyce Sylvester (Carmen Casteel), Lorey Hayes (Sally-Baby Washington), Ed Cambridge (Voice of Hamilton Rydell).

Melba Moore, of *Purlie** (1970) and *Timbuktu!** (1978) fame, returned to Broadway in *Inacent Black*, a comedy by A. Marcus Hemphill. Moore portrays Inacent Black, a domestic servant for the black upper-middle-class Rydell family. It is soon revealed that Inacent is not just a maid but, in reality, a servant of the Lord, who has been sent by God to help the Rydells change their greedy ways. Critics tended to dismiss the play, with Frank Rich of *The New York Times* declaring it an "anachronism" of "two generations ago."

**INNER CITY** (Barrymore, December 19, 1971, 97 p.). Producers: Joseph Kipness, Lawrence Kasha, and Tom O'Horgan. Book and lyrics: Eve Merriam. Composer: Helen Miller. Director: Tom O'Horgan.

Cast: Joy Garrett, Carl Hall, Delores Hall, Fluffer Hirsch, Linda Hopkins,* Paulette Ellen Jones, Larry Marshall, Allan Nichols, Florence Tarlow.

Songs: Fee Fi Fo Fum; Now I Lay Me; Locks; I Had a Little Teevee; Hushabye Baby; My Mother Said; Diddle Diddle Dumpling; Rub a Dub Dub; You'll Find Mice; Ding Dong Bell; The Brave Old City of New York; Urban Renewal; The Nub of the Nation; Mary, Mary; City Life; One Misty, Moisty Morning; Jack Be Nimble; If Wishes Were Horses; One Man; Simple Simon; Deep in the Night; Statistics; Twelve Rooftops, Leaping; Take a Tour, Congressman; Poverty Program; One, Two; Tom, Tom; Hickety, Pickety; Half Alive; This Is the Way We Go to School; The Spirit of Education; Little Jack Horner; Subway Dream; Christmas Is Coming; I'm Sorry Says the Machine; Jeremiah Obadiah; Riddle Song; Shadow of the Sun; Boys and Girls Come Out to Play; Summer Nights; Lucy Locket; Winter Nights; Wisdom; The Hooker; Wino Will; Man in the Doorway; Starlight, Starbright; The Cow Jumped Over the Moon; The Dealer; Taffy; Numbers; The Pickpocket; Law and Order; Kindness; As I

Went Over; There Was a Little Man; Who Killed Nobody; It's My Belief; Street Sermon; The Great If; On This Rock.

*Inner City* is best remembered for its talent rather than its libretto or music. Based on *The Inner City Mother Goose*, this collection of nursery rhymes for urban adults offered a showcase for such talents as Linda Hopkins, who won a Tony Award and a Drama Desk Award for her performance, Delores Hall, and Carl Hall. The songs by Helen Miller and Eve Merriam, however, failed to impress the critics, and *Inner City* managed only a brief run.

**IT'S SO NICE TO BE CIVILIZED** (Martin Beck, June 3, 1980, 8 p.). Producers: Jay Julien, Arnon Milchan, and Larry Kalish. Author: Micki Grant.* Director: Frank Corsaro.

Cast: Obba Babatunde (Sharky), Vivian Reed (Mollie), Mabel King (Grandma), Larry Stewart (Larry), Vickie D. Chappell (Sissy), Carol Lynn Maillard (LuAnne), Stephen Pender (Mr. Anderson), Dan Strayhorn (Blade), Eugene Edwards (Rev. Williams), Deborah Burrell (Mother), Juanita Grace Tyler (Dancing Bag Lady).

Songs: Step into My World; Keep Your Eye on the Red; Wake-up Sun; Subway Rider; God Help Us; Who's Going to Teach the Children?; Out on the Street; Welcome Mr. Anderson; Why Can't Me and You?; When I Rise; World Keeps Going Round; Antiquity; I've Still Got My Bite; Look at Us; The American Dream; Bright Lights; It's So Nice to Be Civilized; Like a Lady; Pass a Little Love Around.

*It's So Nice to Be Civilized* opened the same week that author Micki Grant's *Your Arms Too Short to Box with God** returned to the Ambassador Theatre for a 149-performance run. The new show suffered by comparison. Despite some excellent songs ("Look at Us" and "I've Still Got My Bite") and fine performances by Mabel King, Vivian Reed, and Obba Babatunde, critics lambasted the diffuse book and condemned *It's So Nice to Be Civilized* to a short run.

# J

**JAMAICA** (Imperial, October 31, 1957, 558 p.). Producer: David Merrick. Book: Fred Saidy and E. Y. Harburg. Composer: Harold Arlen. Lyricist: E. Y. Harburg. Director: Robert Lewis.

Cast: Lena Horne* (Savannah), Ricardo Montalban (Koli), Ossie Davis* (Cicero), Josephine Premice (Ginger), Adelaide Hall* (Grandma Obeah), Augustine Rios (Quico), Roy Thompson (Snodgrass), Hugh Dilworth

(Hucklebuck), Erik Rhodes (Governor), James E. Wall (Lancaster), Joe Adams (Nashua), Alvin Ailey and Christyne Lawson (Lead Dancers).

Songs: Savannah; Savannah's Wedding Day; Pretty to Walk With; Push De Button; Incompatibility; Little Biscuit; Cocoanut Sweet; Pity the Sunset; Yankee Dollar; What Good Does It Do?; Monkey in the Mango Tree; Take It Slow Joe; Ain't It the Truth; Leave the Atom Alone; For Every Fish; I Don't Think I'll End It All Today; Napoleon.

Although Lena Horne had featured billing in Lew Leslie's *Blackbirds of 1939,* Jamaica* was her first major musical on Broadway. Designed as a showcase for Horne's talents, *Jamaica* presented a weak tale of life on the Caribbean island. Nevertheless, no one noticed the plot as all attention was focused on Lena Horne. Walter Kerr praised her lavishly in the *Herald Tribune*: "Lena Horne is unconditionally dazzling. Everything about the lady has a downright phosphorescent radiance, a sheen and a shimmer that suggests she has been put together out of hummingbirds' wings."

Only *Variety* voiced some fears that the "racial aspects of the show" might keep theatregoers from *Jamaica*: "There may be raised eyebrows and perhaps increased blood pressure among Dixiecrats because of the love scenes between Miss Horne and Montalban, even though the latter appears to have been sun-lamped considerably." The critic noted that this "problem" could be corrected should there be a film version of the show.

**JAMIMMA** (New Federal, May 15, 1972, 48 p.). Producer: Woodie King, Jr.,* and Dick Williams.* Author: Martie Evans-Charles. Director: Shauneille Perry.*

Cast: Dick Williams (Omar Butler I), Marcella Lowery (Jameena Caine), Lucretia R. Collins (Vivian Williams), Roxie Roker (Viola Caine Robinson), Arnold Johnson (Crazy Man Johnson), Charles Weldon (Tyrone Jackson), Aston S. Young (Gil Washington), Lester Forte (Hussein), Vi Higgins (Radio Lady).

Jamimma is Jameena Caine's (Marcella Lowery) real name, which she changed to avoid ridicule. *Jamimma* focuses on Caine, her man Omar (Dick Williams), and neighbor Vivian (Roxie Roker) in a "toughly affectionate, wryly perceptive play about black people—that is genuinely engrossing," according to *The New York Times*. Critics praised playwright Martie Evans-Charles's "stage sense" and "perceptive ear," in this first produced play.

**JAZZBO BROWN** (City Lights, June 24, 1980, 44 p.). Producers: Barbara Gittler and Morris Jaffee. Author: Stephen H. Lemberg. Director and choreographer: Louis Johnson.

Cast: Andre DeShields (Billy "Jazzbo" Brown), Chris Calloway (Maxine McCall), Jerry Jarrett (D. D. Daniels), Zulema (Rachel Brown), Ned Wright (Rev. Brown), and Charles Bernard, Deborah Lynn Bridges, Rodney Green, Janice Nicki Harrison, Dennis A. Morgan, Gayle Samuels, Wyonna Smith, Allysia C. Sneed.

Songs: Jazzbo Brown; Broadway, I'm Bettin' on You; Million Songs; Born to Sing; He Had the Callin'; Bump, Bump, Bump; The Same Old Tune; When You've Loved Your Man; The Best Man; Give Me More; When I Die; Dancin' Shoes; Precious Patterns; Funky Bessie; Harlem Follies; First Time I Saw You; Pride and Freedom; Take a Bow.

*Jazzbo Brown* began as a workshop performance at the City Lights Theatre. Described as a black version of *The Jazz Singer*, it brought together Andre DeShields (of *The Wiz** and *Ain't Misbehavin'**) and Chris Calloway (Cab Calloway's daughter). The cantor of the Al Jolson film becomes a Harlem minister in conflict with his son who wants to perform on the Broadway stage. Despite praise for the music and performances, critics faulted the book, and *Jazzbo Brown* faded quickly in the hot New York summer.

**JAZZNITE.** See UNDERGROUND.

**JEB** (Martin Beck, February 21, 1946, 9 p.). Producer and director: Herman Shumlin. Author: Robert Ardrey.

Cast: Ossie Davis* (Jeb), Ruby Dee* (Libby George), Morris McKenney (Solly), Charles Holland (Don), Carolyn Hill Stewart (Cynthie), Wardell Saunders (Hazy Johnson), P. Jay Sidney (Bush), Percy Verwayne (Flabber), G. Harry Bolden (Simpson), W. J. Hackett (Mr. Touhy), Laura Bowman (Amanda Turner), Reri Grist (Rachel), Rudolph Whitaker (Libe), Christopher Bennett (Jefferson), Maurice Ellis (Julian), Santos Ortega (Paul Devoure), Grace McTarnahan (Mrs. Devoure), Frank M. Thomas (Charles Bard), Edwin Cushman (Dr. Hazelton), Grover Burgess (Mr. Gibney), Milton Shirah (Joseph), Edward Forbes (Mr. Dowd), Owen Hewitt (White Man).

*Jeb* and *Deep Are the Roots** (1945) considered the plight of black soldiers returning to American life after World War II. Jeb, played by Ossie Davis in his Broadway debut, learned accounting in the army and hoped to exercise his newfound skills on the adding machine in his small Louisiana hometown. Little has changed during the war years, and Jeb is denied a job. Although his family and girlfriend advise submission to the system, Jeb refuses and narrowly escapes lynching. He flees to New York for a dissolute life, but eventually decides to return home to fight racism in the South.

Miles Jefferson, writing in *Phylon*, proclaimed *Jeb* a success, at least during the first two-thirds of the play. After that point, "the engine of fury came to a sudden halt, and the blinding steam of monotonous repetition and sermonizing crept in. . . . Ardrey, the author, did not seem to know how to resolve the race dilemma he had built up—he did not know what to do with Jeb, his protagonist." Nevertheless, Jefferson found Ossie Davis's performance "moving," and the rest of the cast acted with "zest and skill."

**JERICO-JIM CROW** (Sanctuary, January 12, 1964, 31 p.). Producer: Greenwich Players, Inc. and Congress of Racial Equality, Student Nonviolent Coordinating Committee, and National Association for the Advancement of Colored People. Author: Langston Hughes.* Directors: Alvin Ailey and William Hairston.

Cast: Gilbert Price* (Young Man), Hilda Harris (Young Girl), Joseph Attles (Old Man), Rosalie King (Old Woman), William Cain (Jim Crow), Dorothy Drake (Woman).

Songs: A Meeting Here Tonight; I'm on My Way; I Been 'Buked and I Been Scorned; Such a Little King; Is Massa Gwine to Sell Us Tomorrow?; How Much Do You Want Me to Bear?; Where Will I Lie Down?; No More Auction Block for Me; John Brown's Body; Battle Hymn of the Republic; Slavery Chain Done Broke at Last; Oh, Freedom; Go Down, Moses; Ezekial Saw the Wheel; Stay in the Field; Freedom Land; God's Gonna Cut You Down; Don't You View That Ship?; Better Leave Segregation Alone; My Mind on Freedom; We Shall Overcome; The Battle of Old Jim Crow; Come and Go with Me.

*The New York Times* found Langston Hughes's *Jerico-Jim Crow* a musical counterpart to *In White America** which opened earlier the same season. *Jerico-Jim Crow* provided a musical history of segregation in American life from the time of slavery to the present. Hilda Harris and Gilbert Price represented the reaction of young blacks to segregation, while Joseph Attles and Rosalie King supplied the opinions of the older generation. William Cain, the only white in the cast, appeared alternately as a slave trader, a policeman, and a southern white singing "Better Leave Segregation Alone." Hughes supplied two new songs for *Jerico-Jim Crow* ("Freedom Land" and "Such a Little King") which complemented the traditional music utilized in the show.

**JOHN HENRY** (Forty-fourth Street, January 10, 1940, 7 p.). Producer: Sam Byrd. Author: Roark Bradford. Composer: Jacques Wolfe. Directors: Anthony Brown and Charles Friedman.

Cast: Paul Robeson* (John Henry), Ruby Elzy (Julie Anne), Joshua White* (Blind Lemon), Henrietta Lovelace (Julie Anne's Mamma), George Jones, Jr. (Julie Anne's Papa), Joe Attles (Sam), Robert Harvey (Hell Buster), Alexander Gray (Mate), Kenneth Spencer (Walking Boss), Minto Cato (Aunt Dinah), Musa Williams (Ruby), James Lightfoot (John Henry's Papa), Maude Simmons (John Henry's Mamma), George Dickson (Rucker), Sadie McGill (Rucker's Wife), Myra Johnson (Selma), Benveneta Washington (Carrie), Ray Yeates (Lead Heaver), Merritt Smith (Reader), Lou Gilbert, William Woolfolk (Callers), J. De Witt Spencer (Mink Eye), C. W. Scott (Roustabout).

Some critics debated whether *John Henry* was "a drama with music" or a "lyric drama," but there seemed to be no doubts concerning the talents of the show's star, Paul Robeson. Richard Lockridge of *The Sun* echoed the comments of the major critics: "Paul Robeson strides through the many scenes of *John Henry* . . . and his great voice rolls out in songs which have the authentic cadence of his race. Mr. Robeson is the positive virtue of *John Henry*. It is he, and not the fabulous hero of the title, who gives it such stature as it has. It is he, rather than Roark Bradford, the author, who is equal to the heroic legend."

Amidst the raves for Robeson, some critics managed to praise Ruby Elzy, as the woman who brings about John Henry's downfall, and Josh White. Despite the glowing notices for Robeson, the downbeat reviews for the play doomed *John Henry* to a brief run.

**JOLLY'S PROGRESS** (Longacre, December 5, 1959, 9 p.). Producers: Theatre Guild and Arthur Loew. Author: Lonnie Coleman. Director: Alex Segal.

Cast: Eartha Kitt* (Jolly Rivers), Vinnette Carroll* (Dora), Wendell Corey (David Adams), Charles McClelland (Robie Sellers), James Knight (Warren Holly), Peter Gumeny (Buford Williams), Joseph Boland (Charlie), Drummond Erskine (Lon Keller), Laurie Main (Mr. Scarborough), Nat Burns (Mr. Mendelsohn), Ellis Rabb (Reverend Furze), Anne Revere (Emma Ford), Joanne Barry (Portia Bates), Humphrey Davis (Thompson Bates), Eulabelle Moore (Thelma).

Lonnie Coleman adapted *Jolly's Progress* from his 1953 novel *Adams' Way*. However, to *The New York Times*, it seemed a combination of *Pygmalion* and *Pollyanna*. David Adams (Wendell Corey) discovers the poverty-stricken young Jolly Rivers (Eartha Kitt) in a small Alabama town. He begins to educate her and then realizes she is a genius. By the play's end, she is reciting Coleridge. After a confrontation with the Ku Klux Klan, Adams realizes that he has fallen in love with his student. He then sends her north to Philadelphia to continue her education.

Critics dismissed the play but managed to give Eartha Kitt a few kind words on her return to Broadway. Nevertheless, *Jolly's Progress* lasted only a week.

# K

**KEEP SHUFFLIN'** (Daly's, February 27, 1928, 104 p.). Producer: Con Conrad. Book: Flournoy Miller* and Aubrey Lyles.* Composers: J. C. ("Jimmy") Johnson,* Thomas "Fats" Waller,* and Clarence Todd. Lyrics: Henry Creamer* and Andy Razaf.* Director: Con Conrad.

Cast: Flournoy Miller (Steve Jenkins), Aubrey Lyles (Sam Peck), Jerry Mills (Boss), George Battles (Henry), John Gregg (Brother Jones), John

Vigal (Mose), Clarence Robinson (Walter), Byron Jones (Scrappy), Evelyn Keyes (Evelyn), Honey Brown (Honey), Jean Starr (Alice), Margaret Lee (Mrs. Jenkins), Josephine Hall (Ruth), Maude Russell (Maude), Billie Yarbough (Yarbo), Hazel Sheppard (Hazel), Gretta Anderson (Grit), Marie Dove (Marie), Gilbert Holland (Bill), Herman Listerino (Joseph). Orchestra includes: Fats Waller, Jimmy Johnson, and Jabbo Smith.

Songs: Teasin' Mama (Johnson-Creamer); Chocolate Bar (Waller-Razaf); Labor Day Parade (Todd-Razaf); Give Me the Sunshine (Johnson-Creamer-Conrad); Leg It (Todd-Creamer-Conrad); 'Sippi (Johnson-Creamer); How Jazz Was Born (Waller-Razaf); Keep Shufflin' (Waller-Razaf); Everybody's Happy in Jimtown (Waller-Razaf); Dusky Love (Will Vodery-Creamer); Charlie, My Back Door Man (Todd-Creamer-Conrad); On the Levee (Johnson-Creamer).

*Keep Shufflin'* returned Flournoy Miller and Aubrey Lyles to Daly's Sixty-third Street Theatre, the scene of their earlier triumph in *Shuffle Along*.* Although initial reviews were favorable, box office receipts diminished sharply after the opening of *Blackbirds of 1928*.* The competition among the new black musicals was clearly growing.

Miller and Lyles once again brought their classic vaudeville routines to *Keep Shufflin'*. This time they are the organizers of the utopian society, the Equal Got Club, which will entitle each of the members to an equal portion of the world's wealth. Needless to say, the pair's efforts to redistribute the wealth quickly bring the law in hot pursuit.

The orchestra also received high praise, and some critics even noticed the presence of "Fats" Waller at the piano.

**KONGI'S HARVEST** (St. Marks, April 14, 1968, 33 p.). Producer: Negro Ensemble Company.* Author: Wole Soyinka. Director: Michael A. Schultz.*

Cast: Moses Gunn* (Kongi), Frances Foster* (Ogbo Aweri or Segi), Rosalind Cash* (Ogbo Aweri or Segi), Douglas Turner [Ward]* (Oba Danlola), Clarice Taylor* (Sarumi), Roberta Raysor (Wuraola), Richard Mason (Dende), Judyann Jonsson (Superintendent), Denise Nicholas (Praise Singer), Hattie Winston* (Praise Singer), David Downing,* Norman Bush, Allie Woods, Carl Gordon, William Jay, Tom Brimm II (Aweris), Arthur French (Organizing Secretary), Robert Hooks* (Daoudu), Charles Greene, Jr. (Right Ear of State), Ozzie White (Left Ear of State), Bernard Marsh (Photographer), Afolabi Ajayi (Capt. of Carpenters).

The Negro Ensemble Company's third production of its first season featured the work of Nigerian playwright Wole Soyinka. *Kongi's Harvest* concerns the fictional African country of "Isma," where a maniacal dictator Kongi (Moses Gunn) has seized power from a traditional ruler (Douglas Turner). The deposed king is imprisoned, and he immediately plots a return to power. The king's assistant plans a scheme that eventually goes awry, but brings a pardon for the king and international recognition to

Kongi for his mercy. Critics found some weaknesses in the play, but, nevertheless, found the evening dazzling. Jack Kroll, *Newsweek*'s critic, spoke for the majority: "Under Michael A. Schultz, the large cast performs the juicy, chockablock, work with a splendid variety of drives, rhythms, styles, and savors. Douglas Turner Ward is superb as Danlola."

**KWAMINA** (Fifty-fourth Street, October 23, 1961, 32 p.). Producer: Alfred de Liagre, Jr. Composer and lyricist: Richard Adler. Book: Robert Alan Aurthur. Director: Robert Lewis.

Cast: Brock Peters* (Obitsebi), Robert Guillaume* (Ako), Sally Ann Howes (Eve), Norman Barrs (Blair), Ethel Ayler (Naii), Joseph Attles (Akufo), Terry Carter (Kwamina), Ainsley Sigmond (Kojo), Rex Ingram* (Nana Mwalla), Rosalie Maxwell (Alla), Lillian Hayman (Mammy Trader), Ronald Platts, Edward Thomas (Policemen).

Songs: The Cocoa Bean Song; Welcome Home; The Sun Is Beginning to Crow; Did You Hear That?; You're As English As; Seven Sheep, Four Red Shirts, and a Bottle of Gin; Nothing More to Look Forward To; What's Wrong with Me?; Something Big; Ordinary People; A Man Can Have No Choice; What Happened to Me Tonight?; One Wife; Another Time, Another Place.

Although *Kwamina* had only a brief run, it received plaudits for its portrayal of the conflict between old and new in a West African locale. One of the two musicals of the season to deal with an interracial love affair (*No Strings* was the other), *Kwamina* presented a talented black cast which, according to *The New York Times*, gave it a "mood of incantation and promise." Terry Carter, Brock Peters, Ethel Ayler, Robert Guillaume, and Broadway veteran Rex Ingram received raves for their performances.

# L

**LAGRIMA DEL DIABLO** (St. Marks, January 10, 1980, 30 p.). Producer: Negro Ensemble Company.* Author: Dan Owens. Director: Richard Gant.

Cast: Leon Morenzie (Dacius Soulimare), Graham Brown (Archbishop Stephen Emmanuel Pontiflax), Adolph Caesar* (Aquilo), Barbara Montgomery* (Belin), Chuck Patterson (Captain), Charles Brown (Soldier I), Zackie Taylor (Soldier II).

*Lagrima del Diablo* ("The Devil's Tear") presents a dialogue between a guerrilla leader (Leon Morenzie) and his captive, the archbishop (Graham Brown) of a mythical country. The guerrilla tries to convince the archbishop to support the revolution, but he refuses to cooperate. At first, each claims to represent the interests of morality, but later events reveal that each has a dark secret hidden in his past. The guerrilla has killed his best friend, and the archbishop has seduced and abandoned a virgin. Walter Kerr praised the performances of Brown and Morenzie in *The New York Times*, but found Dan Owens's play both static and cryptic.

**A LAND BEYOND THE RIVER** (Greenwich Mews, March 28, 1957, 99 p.). Producer: Greenwich Mews Theatre. Author: Loften Mitchell.* Director: Michael Howard.

Cast: Robert Graham Brown (Rev. Mr. Layne), Diana Sands* (Laura Turnham), Ted Butler (Philip Turnham), Eric Richmond (Willie Lee Waters), George Lucas (Glenn Raigen), Donald Julian (Ben Ellis), Howard Wierum (Dr. George Willis), Helen Martin (Martha Layne), Lionel Habas (Rev. Mr. Cloud), Richard Ward (Bill Raigen), Jacqueline Barnes (Mary Raigen), Clayton Corbin (Duff Waters), Charles Griffin (J. C. Langston), Albert Grant (Rev. Mr. Shell), Fran Bennett (Ruby Waters), Peggy Devello (Grandma).

*A Land Beyond the River* is Loften Mitchell's fictional version of the life of Reverend Joseph A. DeLaine and his fight for separate, but equal, schools in South Carolina in 1949. The Reverend DeLaine observed and approved of the opening night performance, but "felt a little unhappy about the 'damns' and 'hells' that popped up occasionally in the dialogue," according to *The New York Times*.

The characters in the play represent various viewpoints on the strategy for desegregation. Some proclaimed that the Reverend was moving too quickly, while others, such as Layne's wife, believed he was moving too slowly. The *Times* found the play somewhat "awkward in construction . . . but, thanks to the vigorous characterizations, it is human and likeable. Despite the seriousness of its theme, it flares into comedy repeatedly. Mr. Mitchell has not lost his sense of humor in the heat of a crusade."

**LIBERTY CALL** (St. Marks, April 29, 1975, 8 p.). Producer: Negro Ensemble Company.* Author: Buriel Clay II. Director: Douglas Turner Ward.*

Cast: Samm [Samm-Art] Williams* (John Wilheart), Michael Jameson (H.O.B. Rothschild II), Thelma Carter (Mama Sun), Ramon Rafiur (Lt. Priest), George Campbell (Opium Man; Bartender), Naola Adair (First Girl), Elaine Jackson (Second Girl), Sam Finch (First Marine), Suavae Mitchell (Second Marine).

*Liberty Call*, by Buriel Clay II, was a production of the Negro Ensemble Company's (NEC) "season-within-a-season," which featured works developed in their playwrights' workshop. Critics praised Clay's play concerning a friendship between a black boatswain (Samm Williams) and a white intellectual (Michael Jameson) in Southeast Asia, and they also took note of a remarkable performance by Samm Williams. While beginning his acting career with the NEC, Williams was also beginning his work as a dramatist, for his play *Welcome to Black River** would also appear in the series. Critics found the tale of friendship of interest, but thought a subsidiary plot (an investigation into the white sailor's suicide) somewhat tenuous.

**THE LIFE AND TIMES OF J. WALTER SMINTHEUS.** See UNDERGROUND.

**LIVIN' FAT** (St. Marks, June 1, 1976, 61 p.). Producer: Negro Ensemble Company.* Author: Judi Ann Mason. Director: Douglas Turner Ward.*

Cast: Minnie Gentry (Big Mama), Frances Foster* (Mama), Wayne Elbert (Daddy), Joyce Sylvester (Candy), Dean Irby (David Lee), Frankie Faison (Boo).

Judi Ann Mason's *Livin' Fat*, a Negro Ensemble Company production, was dismissed by the critics. This "soul farce" reveals a southern couple whose son "finds" two bags of money in a bank where he works as a janitor. After a few misgivings, the family decides to accept the money and "live fat." Despite excellent performances by Dean Irby and Frances Foster, *The New York Times* found the "jokes stale" and "the characters taken off a rack."

**LIZA** (Daly's, November 27, 1922, 169 p.). Producer: Al Davis. Book: Irvin C. Miller. Music and lyrics: Maceo Pinkard with additional lyrics by Nat Vincent. Director: Walter Brooks.

Cast: Irvin C. Miller (Ice Cream Charlie), Gertrude Saunders (Nora), Alonzo Fenderson (Squire Norris), Margaret Simms (Liza Norris), William Simms (Uncle Pete), Packer Ramsey (Parson Jordan), Quintard Miller (Judge Plummer), R. Eddie Greenlee (Ras Johnson), Thaddeus Drayton (Dandy), Will A. Cook (The Sheriff), Emmett Anthony (Bodiddily), Billy Mills (Tom Liggett), Doe Doe Green (John Jones), Elizabeth Terrill (Mammy), Maude Russell (Mandy), Snippy Mason (Harry Davis), Donald Fields (Bill Jones).

Songs: Tag Day; Pleasure; I'm the Sheriff; Liza; I'se Gwine to Talk; That Brownskin Flapper; Just a Barbershop Chord; Planning; On the Moonlit Swanee; Essence; Forget Your Troubles; My Old Man; Runnin' Wild Blues; The Charleston Dancy; Dandy; My Creole Girl; Love Me; Don't Be Blue.

After a tryout as *Bon Bon Buddy, Jr.* at the Lafayette Theatre in Harlem, *Liza* opened at the height of the season on Broadway. Its 169-performance run made it the most successful black musical of the 1922-1923 season. Part of the reason for its success may have been its willingness to copy the plot and format of *Shuffle Along*.*

The Irvin C. Miller book poses a political question for Jimtown, as Squire Norris (Alonzo Fenderson) attempts to have a monument built in honor of the late mayor. Young love complicates his plans as his daughter Liza (Margaret Simms) falls in love with the new school teacher, Dandy (Thaddeus Drayton). Soon the townspeople grow suspicious as they witness Dandy's new clothes and his hefty wad of money. Is he embezzling the money from the statue fund? His innocence is revealed in the last scene, as Norris announces the forthcoming marriage of Dandy and Liza.

While critics praised the specialty dance numbers of *Liza*, few took notice of "The Charleston Dancy" which was making its first formal appearance on the stage of Daly's Theatre.

**THE LONG DREAM** (Ambassador, February 17, 1960, 5 p.). Producers: Cheryl Crawford and Joel Schenker. Author: Ketti Frings. Director: Lloyd Richards.*

Cast: Al Freeman, Jr.* (Rex Tucker), Lawrence Winters (Tyree Tucker), Gertrude Jeannette (Emma Tucker), Josh White, Jr. (Tony), Clarence Williams III (Chris), Edward Phifer (Zeke), R. G. Armstrong (Chief of Police), Clifton James (Clem), Jim Jeter (Phil), Stanley Greene (Doc Bruce), Charles A. McDaniel (Lt. Harvey), Isabelle Cooley (Gladys), Helen Martin (Maude Carter), Joya Sherrill (Vera Mason), Walter Mason (Jim Bowers), Arthur Storch (Mr. McWilliams), John Garth III (Rev. Ragland), Barbara Loden (White Girl).

Ketti Frings adapted Richard Wright's* 1958 novel, *The Long Dream*, for Broadway audiences in 1960. Frings claimed that she became interested in the novel because "it clarified the enormous struggle for human dignity in this country." Nevertheless, Frings altered Wright's novel in a variety of ways that, according to most critics, weakened the stage version of the work. *The Long Dream* describes the plight of Tyree Tucker (Lawrence Winters), one of the richest black citizens in a southern town. Although an undertaker, Tucker also earns a living by supporting vice and corruption in the black sections of the town. Tucker has achieved his success by catering to the chief of police (R. G. Armstrong), but the friendship becomes unglued when Tucker's illegal dealings are revealed. Although critics praised the performances of Winters and Al Freeman, Jr., most found the drama weak. *The Long Dream* lingered only a short five performances.

**LOST IN THE STARS** (Music Box, October 30, 1949, 273 p.). Producer: Playwrights' Company. Composer: Kurt Weill. Librettist: Maxwell Anderson. Director: Rouben Mamoulian.

Cast: Todd Duncan* (Stephen Kumalo), Inez Matthews (Irina), Georgette Harvey* (Mrs. M'kise), Frank Roane (Leader), Joseph James (Answerer), Elayne Richards (Nita), Gertrude Jeannette (Grace Kumalo), Laverne French (The Young Man), Mabel Hart (The Young Woman), Leslie Banks (James Jarvis), Judson Rees (Edward Jarvis), John Morely (Arthur Jarvis), Warren Coleman (John Kumalo), Charles McRae (Paulus), Roy Allen (William), William C. Smith (Jared), Herbert Coleman (Alex), Jerome Shaw (Foreman), William Marshall (Hlabeni), Charles Grunwell (Eland), Sheila Guyse (Linda), Van Prince (Johannes Pafuri), William Greaves (Matthew Kumalo), Julian Mayfield (Absalom Kumalo), Gloria Smith (Rose), Robert Byrn (Policeman), Biruta Ramoska (White Woman), Mark Kramer (White Man), Jerome Shaw (The Guard), John W. Stanley (Burton), Guy Spaull (The Judge), Robert McFerrin (Villager).

Songs: The Hills of Ixopo; Thousands of Miles; Train to Johannesburg; The Search; The Little Gray House; Who'll Buy?; Trouble Man; Murder in Parkwold; Fear; Lost in the Stars; The Wild Justice; O Tixo, Tixo, Help Me; Stay Well; Cry, the Beloved Country; Big Mole; A Bird of Passage.

Although Kurt Weill and Maxwell Anderson originally wanted Paul Robeson* for the role of Stephen Kumalo in *Lost in the Stars*, they eventually chose Todd Duncan, of *Porgy and Bess** fame, for their lead. The authors felt that Duncan, like Robeson, could handle the arduous singing and dancing chores of the role. This musical adaptation of Alan Paton's *Cry, the Beloved Country* also borrowed the original Crown (Warren Coleman) from *Porgy and Bess*, as well as its director, Rouben Mamoulian.

Weill and Anderson conceived Paton's work as a "musical tragedy." Originally designed as a straight play with musical comment by a Greek chorus, song became a tool of musical expression as the show evolved. Brooks Atkinson of *The New York Times* stated that the music "carries through the theatre the fears and hatreds, the wildness, the anguish, and the heavy spiritual burdens of a big story."

The musical received mixed reviews. While *The New York Times* called it a "memorable musical drama," others found that librettist Anderson had great difficulty in adapting Paton's tale of racial hatred in South Africa to the stage. Nevertheless, both Duncan and Coleman received rave notices for their performances.

**LOUISIANA** (Forty-eighth Street, February 27, 1933, 8 p.). Producer: George L. Miller for the Negro Theatre Guild. Author: J. Augustus Smith.* Director: Samuel J. Park.

Cast: J. Augustus Smith (Amos Berry), Edna Barr (Myrtle Simpson), James Davis (Brother Zumee), Trixie Smith (Sister Marguerite), Morris McKenney (Thomas Catt), Alberta Perkins (Sister Knight), Fred Bonny (Brother Zero), Paul Johnson (Deacon August), Lionel Monagas* (Ebenezer), A. B. Comathiere* (Brother Dunson), Carrie Huff (Sister Zuzan), Ruth Morrison (Sister Gaghan), Harriet Daughtry (Sister Lauder), Bennie Small (Bou Bouce), Pedro Lopez (Marcon), Laura Bowman (Aunt Hagar).

The Negro Theatre Guild's production of *Louisiana* presented the struggle between Christianity and African religion, as did *Run, Little Chillun!** which opened only two days later. Author J. Augustus Smith portrayed the parson Amos Berry, while Aunt Hagar (Laura Bowman) represented the forces of voodoo. While critics praised Smith's "sincerity" in writing *Louisiana*, most dismissed it as amateurish. Nevertheless, the musical numbers, whether black spirituals or voodoo rhythms, won critical praise.

**LUCKY SAMBO** (Colonial, June 6, 1925, 9 p.). Producer: Harlem Productions, Inc. Book and songs: Porter Grainger and Freddie Johnson. Director: Leigh Whipper.*

Cast: Tim Moore* (Sambo Jenkins), Joe Byrd (Rufus Johnson), Wesley Hill (John Whitby), Gertie Moore (Mrs. Whitby), Monette Moore (June), Arthur Porter (Doc August), Freddie Johnson (Jack Stafford), Lena Wilson (Lena March), Happy Williams (Edith Simpson), Billy Ewing (John Law), Clarence Robinson (Jim Nightengale), Porter Grainger (Hitt Keys), Jean Starr (Vera Blues), Amelia Loomis (Nimble Foote), Mildred Brown (Minnie Tree), Anna White (Twilight Gadson), Johnny Hudgins (Shoo Nuff).

Songs: Happy; Stop; June; Don't Forget Bandana Days; Anybody's Man Will Be My Man; Aunt Jemima; Coal Oil; Charley from That Charleston Dancin' School; If You Can't Bring It, You've Got to Send It; Strolling; Dreary Dreary Rainy Days; Take Him to Jail; Legomania; Always on the Job; Singing Nurses; Dandy Dan; Porterology; Love Me While You're Gone; Keep A-Diggin'; Runnin'; Midnight Cabaret; Havin' a Wonderful Time; Not So Long Ago; Alexander's Ragtime Wedding Day.

*Lucky Sambo* toured as *Aces and Queens* on the Theatre Owners Bookings Association (TOBA) circuit before it arrived in New York City. Unfortunately, it opened in the midst of a heat wave. It was so hot at the Colonial Theatre that several men in the audience removed their shirts and collars. The house was half-filled on opening night, and attendance declined nightly. The show closed within a week as the orchestra refused to play without pay. As a result, few people saw Tim Moore's performance as "Lucky Sambo" in a plot concerning an oil-swindle scheme.

# M

**MAKE ME KNOW IT** (Wallack's, November 4, 1929, 4 p.). Producer: Wallace Davis. Author: D. Frank Marcus. Directors: D. Frank Marcus and Sam Rose.

Cast: Allen Gillard (Vendor), James Dunmore (Willie Weaver), Napoleon Whiting (Hop Abbott), Charles Hawkins (Joe Nippy), Philip

Martin (Policeman), Brevard Burnett (Eb Sneedy), Leo Bailey (Tagger Daly), Julia Moses (Georgia Peach), Edna Ellington (Sweet Mama), Ollie Burgoyne (Another Sweet Mama), Florence Lee (Jenny), George Howe (Noisey Knowles), Claude Hopkins (Jack Riggs), Enid Raphael (Mrs. Crouch), Paul C. Floyd (Ezra Gaines), Vivienne Baber (Mona Bannon), A. B. Comathiere* (Bulge Bannon), Barrington Guy (George Gaines), Louis Schooler (Reverend Stubbs), Lorenzo Tucker (Dr. Robbins).

*Make Me Know It* emerged as *Shuffle Along** without the music. This comedy of black political life revealed large-scale chicanery in "the Negro section of a large metropolis." Critics dismissed the play as humorless and welcomed the evening's one musical interlude, "Make Me Know It," sung by Vivienne Baber. As a result, *Make Me Know It* hardly lasted the week.

**MALCOCHON.** See AN EVENING OF ONE ACTS.

**MAMBA'S DAUGHTERS** (Empire, January 3, 1939, 162 p.). Producer and director: Guthrie McClintic. Authors: Dorothy and DuBose Heyward.

Cast: Georgette Harvey* (Mamba), Ethel Waters* (Hagar), Canada Lee* (Drayton), Anne Brown (Gardenia), Jimmy Wright (Tony), Maude Russell (Jane), Dorothy Paul (Tessie), Reginald Beane (Slim), Bob Coogan, John Rustad (Policemen), John Cornell (Clerk of the Court), Oliver Barbour (Prosecuting Attorney), Jose Ferrer (Saint), Harry Mestayer (Judge), Al Stokes (Davey), Hayes Pryor (Ned), Louis Sharp (Mingo), Ethel Purnello (Maum Vina), Georgia Burke (Eva), Helen Dowdy (Willie May), J. Rosamond Johnson* (Rev. Quintus Whaley), Willie Bryant (Gilly Bluton), Alberta Hunter (Dolly), Joyce Miller (Lissa—as a child), Rena Mitchell (Martha), Fredi Washington* (Lissa).

Although Dorothy and DuBose Heyward had several Broadway successes, they had trouble financing *Mamba's Daughters.* Several producers expressed doubts that Ethel Waters, "a singer," could portray the straight acting role of Hagar. The critical response proved the Heywards had made a correct choice. Richard Lockridge of *The Sun* wrote: "One of the imposing characters of fiction, and now of drama, is Hagar. . . . In the playing of Ethel Waters, Hagar becomes magnificently like a force of nature."

Although Mamba is the matriarch of the family, the play centers on the life of daughter Hagar. Hagar struggles to give her daughter Lissa (Fredi Washington) every opportunity that she never had. Lissa's success is threatened by the return of Gilly Bluton, who attempts to blackmail her. Hagar strangles Bluton, and, after hearing her daughter sing on the radio, she kills herself.

The only dissenter among the critics was Brooks Atkinson who liked neither the play nor Ethel Waters. Carl Van Vechten and several friends placed an ad in *The New York Times* to rebuke Atkinson: "We the undersigned feel that Ethel Waters' superb performance in *Mamba's*

*Daughters* . . . is a profound emotional experience which any playgoer would be the poorer for missing. It seems to be such a magnificent example of great acting, simple, deeply felt, moving on a plane of complete reality, that we are glad to pay for the privilege of saying so.'' Among the signers were Judith Anderson, Tallulah Bankhead, Dorothy Gish, and Oscar Hammerstein II. Atkinson then decided to revisit *Mamba's Daughters* and reversed his original opinion.

**MAN BETTER MAN** (St. Marks, July 2, 1969, 23 p.). Producer: Negro Ensemble Company.* Author: Errol Hill. Composer: Coleridge-Taylor Perkinson. Director: Douglas Turner Ward.*

Cast: Rosalind Cash* (Inez Briscoe), Esther Rolle* (Alice Sugar), David Downing* (Tim Briscoe), Graham Brown (Portagee Joe), Allie Woods (Swifty), Tony McKay (Hannibal), Samual Blue, Jr. (Tiny Satin), Arthur French (Crackerjack), Hattie Winston* (Petite Belle Lily), Julius W. Harris (Cutaway Rimbeau), Aston Young (Dagger Da Silva), Norman Bush (Coolie), Afolabi Ajayi (Peloo), William Jay (Pogo), Damon W. Brazwell (Diable Papa), Mari Toussaint (Minee Woopsa), Frances Foster* (First Village Woman), Clarice Taylor* (Second Village Woman).

Songs: Procession; Tiny, the Champion; I Love Petite Belle; One Day, One Day Congotay; One, Two, Three; Man Better Man; Petite Lily Belle; Thousand, Thousand; Me Alone; Girl in the Coffee; Coolie Gone; War and Rebellion; Beautiful Heaven; Briscoe, the Hero.

*Man Better Man* closed the second season of the Negro Ensemble Company (NEC) to mixed reviews. Richard F. Shepard, writing in *The New York Times*, welcomed Errol Hill and Coleridge-Taylor Perkinson's ''refreshing calypso tale,'' as ''a musical that shelves for the moment the brow-furrowing issues of the day.'' He compared this musical tale of life in Trinidad in 1900 to the colorful Brazilian novels of Jorge Amado, and he praised the cast headed by David Downing and Hattie Winston. Clayton Riley, drama critic of the *Manhattan Tribune*, strongly disagreed. He found the NEC's second-season plays assuming a ''safety-first, inoffensive stance.'' While the *Times* welcomed the light-hearted gaiety of the play, Riley was disturbed that the ''NEC found time and energy to spend on a piece of work that speaks to no significant issue of the day.'' [July 12, 1969]

**ME AND BESSIE** (Ambassador, October 22, 1975, 453 p.). Producer: Lee Apostoleris. ''Conceived and written by'': Linda Hopkins* and Will Holt. Director: Robert Greenwald.

Cast: Linda Hopkins (Bessie Smith), Lester Wilson, Gerri Dean.

Songs: I Feel Good; God Shall Wipe All Tears Away; Moan You Mourners; New Orleans Hop Scop Blues; Romance in the Dark; Preach Them Blues; A Good Man Is Hard to Find; 'Tain't Nobody's Biz-ness If I Do; Gimme a Pigfoot; Put It Right Here; You've Been a Good Ole Wagon;

Trombone Cholly; Jazzbo Brown; After You've Gone; There'll Be a Hot Time in the Old Town Tonight; Empty Bed Blues; Kitchen Man; Mama Don't 'Low; Do Your Duty; Fare Thee Well; Nobody Knows You When You're Down and Out; Trouble; The Man's All Right.

*Me and Bessie*, Linda Hopkins's and Will Holt's evocation of the life of Bessie Smith, was first produced at the Mark Taper Forum in Los Angeles. Hopkins admits as the show begins: "I ain't Bessie. But, you know there's a lot of Bessie in me." Then, via a combination of anecdotes, reminiscences, and songs, Hopkins brings the legend of Bessie Smith back to life. The show's hits included renditions of "Romance in the Dark," "There'll Be a Hot Time in the Old Town Tonight," and "Empty Bed Blues." The show eventually moved to the smaller Edison Theatre for the remainder of its lengthy run.

**THE ME NOBODY KNOWS** (Orpheum, May 18, 1970, 586 p.). Producer: Jeff Britton. Book: Stephen M. Joseph. Composer: Gary William Friedman. Lyricist: Will Holt. Director: Robert H. Livingston.

Cast: Melanie Henderson (Rhoda), Laura Michaels (Lillian), Jose Fernandez (Carlos), Irene Cara (Lillie Mae), Douglas Grant (Benjamin), Beverly Ann Bremers (Catherine), Gerri Dean (Melba), Paul Mace (Donald), Northern J. Calloway (Lloyd), Carl Thoma (Clorox), Kevin Lindsay (William), Hattie Winston* (Nell).

Songs: Dream Babies; Light Sings; This World; Numbers; What Happens to Life?; Take Hold the Crutch; Flying Milk and Runaway Plates; I Love What the Girls Have; How I Feel; If I Had a Million Dollars; Fugue for Four Girls; Rejoice; Sounds; The Tree; Robert, Alvin, Wendell and Jo Jo; Jail-Life Walk; Something Beautiful; Black; The Horse; Let Me Come In; War Babies.

After receiving an Obie Award for Best Musical in 1970, *The Me Nobody Knows* moved to Broadway to continue its triumphant run. The show originated in the mind of Stephen M. Joseph, a New York City schoolteacher. He asked his students to write their impressions of life in the ghetto, and the anthology was published to favorable reviews. Will Holt and Gary William Friedman added songs to the proceedings, and the show opened to warm reviews Off-Broadway, with Clive Barnes proclaiming, "I love it!" in *The New York Times*. Although descriptions of the show may have sounded "depressing," Barnes noted: "The sheer tenacity of the human spirit against oppression, against rats, against drugs, against the numbing, almost soothing grind of poverty, is glorious and triumphant."

**MEEK MOSE** (Princess, February 6, 1928, 24 p.). Producer: Lester A. Walton. Author: Frank Wilson.* Director: George MacEntee.

Cast: Charles H. Moore (Mose), Laura Bowman (Josephine), Arthur Ray (Ezra), J. Lawrence Criner (Nathan), Ruth Ellis (Penolia), Ruth Carl

(Claribel), Sidney Kirkpatrick (Enos Green), Olyve P. Hopkins (Madam Jones), Susie Sutton (Miss Minnie), Richard Gregg (Dave Roberts), Alston Burleigh (Cole Turner), Thomas Moseley (Dr. Slaughter), J. "Onion" Jeffry (Professor A. P.), Joe Chapman (Stanley Brown), William Edwards (Policeman), Oliver Sanderson (Dr. Strickland), George MacEntee (Mr. Harmon).

*Meek Mose* opened with considerable fanfare at the Princess Theatre in 1928. Mayor Jimmy Walker attended the premiere of what was announced as the beginning of a "Negro Repertory Theatre." Financed by banker Otto H. Kahn and black entrepreneur and newspaper editor Lester A. Walton, this enterprise chose as its first production *Meek Mose*, written by noted actor Frank Wilson. Wilson, who was currently performing in *Porgy*,* designed a "comedy drama of Negro life," which focused on Brother Mose (Charles H. Moore) and his flock. When the whites of the town urge the blacks to move to an undesirable part of the city, Mose encourages his followers to obey. Mose always turns the other cheek, no matter what happens, and is ultimately rewarded when oil is discovered on his land.

Unfortunately, the critics lambasted the play and derailed the plans for a repertory theatre. Brooks Atkinson of *The New York Times* commented: "With all the good-will in the world toward a Negro theatre as a necessity of drama and of contemporary American life, it is difficult to record *Meek Mose* as anything better than a childishly naive endeavor, full of sepia tint John Golden and depicting life only in the slightly shop-worn terms of the theatre." Despite the short run, *Meek Mose* was revived in 1934 as *Brother Mose*, which toured the theatres of the New York area during that year.

**MEMPHIS BOUND!** (Broadway, May 24, 1945, 36 p.). Producer: John Wildberg. Book: Albert Barker and Sally Benson. Composer: Don Walker. Lyricist: Clay Warnick. Directors: Vinton Freedly and Robert Ross with the assistance of Eva Jessye.

Cast: Bill Robinson* (Pilot Meriwether), Avon Long* (Winfield Carter), Edith Wilson* (Melissa Carter), Billy Daniels (Roy Baggott), William C. Smith (Hector), Ann Robinson (Chloe), Ada Brown (Mrs. Paradise), Sheila Guyse (Lily Valentine), Ida James (Penny), Thelma Carpenter (Henny), Frank Wilson* (Mr. Finch), Timothy Grace (Timmy), Oscar Plante (Sheriff McDaniels), Joy Merrimore (Eulalia), Harriet Jackson (Sarabelle), Charles Welch (Bill), William Dillard (Gabriel), the Delta Rhythm Boys.

Songs: Gilbert and Sullivan Blues; Big Old River; Stand Around the Band; Old Love and Brand New Love; Growing Pains. (The remainder of the score is adapted from Gilbert and Sullivan's *H. M. S. Pinafore*).

*Memphis Bound!* owed a major debt to *The Hot Mikado*.* If you can swing *The Mikado*, why not do the same for *H. M. S. Pinafore*? Bill Robinson returned to the stage as a jailbird who convinces a showboat owner to perform a jazz version of *Pinafore*.

Opening night was Robinson's sixty-seventh birthday, but his tap-dancing was that of a much younger man. John Chapman, critic for the *Daily News*, commented: "It's true all right, but I don't believe it anyhow. Nobody 67 years old could have such bounce, emanate such stage presence, and have such a happy time, and tap dance so wonderfully. Bill is famous for a stunt of running the 100 yard dash backward and beating opponents running forward, and this may be his secret. Maybe he is running backward inside, too, and is steadily becoming younger." Avon Long, Frank Wilson, Billy Daniels, Edith Wilson, and other veterans of earlier black musical shows gave Robinson able support.

**MESSIN' AROUND** (Hudson, April 22, 1929, 33 p.). Producer, director, and author: Louis Isquith. Composer: James P. Johnson.* Lyricist: Perry Bradford.

Cast: Sterling Grant, Paul Floyd, Billy McLaurin, James Thompson, Monette Moore, Cora La Redd, Audrey Thomas, Freda Jackson, Walter Brogsdale, Arthur Porter, James Dyer, Bamboo McCarver, Frank Lloyd, William McKelvey, Queenie Price, Hilda Perleno, Lena Shadney, Susie Wroten, Emma Maitland, Aurelia Wheeldin.

Songs: On to Harlem; Harlem Town; Your Love Is All I Crave; Get Away from My Window; Shout On; Skiddle-De-Scow; I Need You; I Don't Love Nobody; Roustabouts; Mississippi; Circus Time; Sorry; Put Your Mind Right on It; Yamekraw; Messin' Around.

*Messin' Around* played only briefly at the Hudson. Most critics admired parts of the show, but, in general, they found it "ordinary." Richard Watts, Jr., writing for the *Tribune*, lamented the lack of personalities, while the *Times* wished for the presence of a Bill Robinson* or Adelaide Hall* of *Blackbirds* fame. Nevertheless, both critics hailed lead Cora La Redd as a "rhythmic girl with a gift for getting gaiety into her dancing."

The score by James P. Johnson and Perry Bradford "saved the show" for the *Sun* critic. He noted that "Your Love Is All I Crave" sent the audience home "humming happily in a way which promised the song might be one of the season's hits." Others praised "Shout On," "Get Away from My Window," and "I Don't Love Nobody."

The most surprising scene of *Messin' Around* appeared in the second act. The curtains parted to reveal a regulation boxing ring with two female contenders, Aurelia Wheeldin, the "world's female bantamweight champion," and Emma Maitland, the "world's female junior lightweight champion." They shook hands and actually came out fighting. "It was a fight that had the audience on its toes," said one critic.

*Messin' Around* lasted only thirty-three performances, leaving the theatre vacant for *Hot Chocolates*.*

**THE MICHIGAN** (St. Marks, November 16, 1979, 22 p.). Producer: Negro Ensemble Company.* Author: Dan Owens. Director: Dean Irby.

Cast: Douglas Turner Ward* (Fletcher "Flick" Lacey), Hattie Winston* (Pilar Murray).

"The Michigan" is a gambling term that refers to a large bankroll with $50 and $100 bills on the outside, and blank paper on the inside. In a similar fashion, Dan Owens's *The Michigan* is about a series of scams. On one hand, Douglas Turner Ward is continually searching for the big con, while his girlfriend Hattie Winston is trying to con him into marrying her. Critics praised leads Ward and Winston, but *The New York Times* termed the play "a long and unprofitable evening." Michael Feingold disagreed in the *Village Voice*, finding several "virtues in the rough edges of this comedy."

**THE MIGHTY GENTS** (Ambassador, April 16, 1978, 9 p.). Producers: James Lipton Productions and Ron Dante and the Shubert Organization. Author: Richard Wesley.* Director: Harold Scott.

Cast: Morgan Freeman* (Zeke), Starletta DuPois (Rita), Dorian Harewood (Frankie), Brent Jennings (Tiny), Mansoor Najee-Ullah (Lucky), Richard Gant (Eldridge), Howard E. Rollins, Jr. (Braxton), Frank Adu (Father).

Richard Wesley's *The Mighty Gents* moved from the Manhattan Theatre Club, where it was called *The Last Street Play*, to Broadway's Ambassador Theatre. *The Mighty Gents* deals with the adult survivors of a Newark street gang ("the mighty gents"). The gang life was the high point of these characters' lives. Since then, all have become trapped in a life of poverty, crime, and despair. While the play focuses on the characters of Frankie, the gang leader (Dorian Harewood), and his wife Rita (Starletta DuPois), Morgan Freeman won acting honors and a Drama Desk Award for his portrayal of Zeke, an aging wino. Although *The New York Times* considered *The Mighty Gents* "moving and impressive," and several other critics agreed, Wesley's play managed only a week's run on Broadway.

**THE MINSTREL BOY.** See AMERICAN NIGHT CRY.

**MISTER JOHNSON** (Martin Beck, March 29, 1956, 44 p.). Producers: Cheryl Crawford and Robert Lewis. Author: Norman Rosten. Director: Robert Lewis.

Cast: Earle Hyman* (Mister Johnson), Josephine Premice (Bamu), James E. Wall (Aliu), Brock Peters* (Ajali), John Akar (Benjamin), Rosetta LeNoire (Matumbi), Thayer David (Gollup), Lawrence Fletcher (Bulteel), Charles McRae (Adamu), Rai Saunders (Audu), Earl Jones (Moma), William Sylvester (Rudbeck), Milton J. Williams (Brimah), Laverne French (Second Brother), David Berahzer (Uncle), Margie James (Girl), Ruth Attaway (Mother), Clayton Corbin (Policeman), Philip

Hepburn (Saleh), Jay Riley (Waziri), Harold Nurse (Isa), Gaby Rodgers (Celia), Percival Borde (Chief), Curtis James (Petitioner).

*Mister Johnson*, a 1956 adaptation of Joyce Cary's novel by Norman Rosten, received praise for its realistic portrayal of African life under the British colonial system. Mister Johnson, played by Earle Hyman, is caught between native and British culture. He helps his colonial masters complete a vital road link and is ironically fired for his efforts. He becomes a drunk and in a furor, kills a British storekeeper. As a result, Johnson is executed by his former cohorts.

The highlight of the show was clearly Hyman's performance. Miles Jefferson, critic for *Phylon*, wrote: "This young actor moves ahead with each performance to higher peaks, and promises even greater achievements. His mastery of the African dialect . . . was entirely admirable, and the pathos of his final tragic fate was overwhelmingly poignant. Hyman gave the best performance of the season by a Negro actor and was acclaimed for doing so. There were few performances, regardless of race, in a class with his compelling portrayal." Nevertheless, *Variety*'s critic offered a sobering note: "It's probably pertinent at this point, that having demonstrated unusual talent and versatility as an actor, Hyman will probably be limited to the typical small parts, such as servants, errand boys, and the like, that are habitually available for Negro actors. That's standard in the white man's theatre of Broadway, where a succession of fine Negro talents have been largely wasted for a lack of opportunity."

**MOON ON A RAINBOW SHAWL** (East Eleventh Street, January 15, 1962, 105 p.). Producers: Kermit Bloomgarden and Harry Joe Brown, Jr. Author: Errol John. Director: George Roy Hill.

Cast: James Earl Jones* (Ephraim), Cicely Tyson* (Mavis), Vinnette Carroll* (Sophia Adams), Robert Hill II (Ketch), Kelly-Marie Berry (Esther), Michael Barton (Sailor), Melvin Stewart (Old Mack), Ellen Holly (Rosa), Gertrude Jeannette (Fisherwoman), Ronald Mack (Policeman), Bill Gunn* (Prince), Robert Earl Jones (Charlie Adams), Peter Owens (Soldier), Carolyn Strictland (Janette), Wayne Grice (A Boy), Warren Berry (Taxi Driver).

Critics praised Trinidadian playwright Errol John's *Moon on a Rainbow Shawl* both for the interesting characters he created as well as the excellent performances by James Earl Jones, Vinnette Carroll, Cicely Tyson, and Bill Gunn. Both Jones and Carroll won Obie Awards for their performances. John's cross-section of Trinidadian life featured the problems of the Adams family, Sophia (Carroll), the rigid matriarch, Charlie (Robert Earl Jones), the ineffectual husband, and their daughter Esther (Kelly Marie Berry). As the play unfolds, these characters encounter a "Trinidadian gallery" of "brief lively portraits" of life in Port of Spain. James Earl Jones received great praise for his portrayal of Ephraim, a trolley bus conductor who wishes to escape to England rather than marry his pregnant mistress.

Vinnette Carroll, the original Sophia, directed a revival of *Moon on a Rainbow Shawl* at the Urban Arts Theatre in 1970. Maryce Carter portrayed Sophia, and James Hainesworth portrayed Ephraim. While Mel Gussow praised the play in *The New York Times*, he still fondly remembered the original performances of the 1962 production.

**THE MOONLIGHT ARMS/THE DARK TOWER** (St. Marks, May 13, 1975, 8 p.). Producer: Negro Ensemble Company.* Author: Rudy Wallace. Director: Osborne Scott.

**The Moonlight Arms**
Cast: Charliese Drakeford (Rena), Charles Brown (Roy).

**The Dark Tower**
Cast: Arthur French (Joe), Charles Brown (Philip).

During the 1974-1975 season, the Negro Ensemble Company presented two new one-act plays by Rudy Wallace in its "season-within-a-season." The curtain-raiser, *The Moonlight Arms*, featured a lengthy argument between Roy (Charles Brown), a scholar, and his low-brow wife (Charliese Drakeford) who refuses to sleep with him. *The Dark Tower* considered the confrontation between two artists, Philip (Charles Brown), a young poet, and Joe (Arthur French), a seedy old reprobate. While *The New York Times* considered Wallace "a playwright of promise," it criticized the dramatist's use of obvious stereotypes for his characters.

**MR. LODE OF KOAL** (Majestic, November 1, 1909, 40 p.). Producer: F. Ray Comstock. Composer: J. Rosamond Johnson.* Book and lyrics: Alex Rogers* and J. A. Shipp. Stage Manager: J. A. Shipp.

Cast: Bert Williams* (Chester A. Lode), Alex Rogers (Buggsy), Tom Brown (Gimlet), Siren Nevarro (Gluten), J. Leubrie Hill (Buttram), Charles H. Moore (Weedhead), Henry Troy ("Cap"), Chas. McKenzie (Singlink), J. E. Lightfoot (Sarg), Matt Housley (Blootch), Lottie Grady (Hysteria), Ada Banks (Saylor), Hattie Hopkins (Hoola), Georgia Gomez (Kinklets), Bessie Brady (What), Anita Bush (Ho), Lavinia Rogers (Rubeena), Maggie Davis (Diano), Jessie Ellis (Osee), Ida Day (Discretia), Katie Jones (Giddina).

Songs: The Start; The Can Song; My Old Man; The Harbor of Lost Dreams; Mum's the Word, Mister Moon (music: J. Leubrie Hill); In Far Off Mandelay (Al Johns); Hodge-Podge; By Gone Days in Dixie; Lament; Chink-Chink, Chink-Chink, Chinyman; The Fete of the Veiled Mugs; Believe Me.

Bert Williams appeared as a single for the first time in sixteen years in *Mr. Lode of Koal*. Despite the presence of veterans from the previous Williams and Walker* shows, Williams claimed that he felt apprehensive appearing without his partner. He found that his nerves calmed soon after he appeared on stage and heard the laughter of the audience. Nevertheless, it became apparent that critics and audiences missed the presence of George Walker, and, as a result, the show failed to duplicate the success of the team's earlier vehicles.

The *New York Dramatic Mirror* praised the show and explained the complicated plot: "Bert Williams is compelled to impersonate a king who has been kidnapped for political reasons. His reign is short, but eventful, and in the end, threatened with death as the real monarch returns, the imposter, looking for a means of escape, casts in his lot with the audience, and the last seen of him is a memory of coat tails as he disappears up the aisle of the theatre." After the brief run of *Mr. Lode of Koal*, Williams accepted an offer from Flo Ziegfeld, and left the world of the black musical theatre for the *Ziegfeld Follies*.

**MRS. PATTERSON** (National, December 1, 1954, 101 p.). Producer: Leonard Sillman. Authors: Charles Sebree and Greer Johnson. Composer: James Shelton. Director: Guthrie McClintic.

Cast: Eartha Kitt* (Teddy Hicks), Avon Long* (Mr. D.), Helen Dowdy (Bessie Bolt), Ruth Attaway (Anna Hicks), Vinie Burrows* (Selma Mae), Terry Carter (Willie B. Brayboy), Estelle Hemsley (Aunt Matt Crossy), Emory Richardson (Sylvanus), Enid Markey (Mrs. Patterson), Mary Ann Hoxworth (June Embree), Mary Harmon (Rose Embree), Joan Morgan (Fern Embree).

Songs: Mrs. Patterson; Tea in Chicago; If I Was a Boy; My Daddy Is a Dandy; Be Good, Be Good, Be Good; I Wish I Was a Bumble Bee.

*Mrs. Patterson* became Eartha Kitt's first starring vehicle since her triumph in *New Faces of 1952*. Black author Charles Sebree and Greer Johnson provided Kitt with a tale of a poverty-stricken young girl from Kentucky who yearns to be rich like her mother's employer, Mrs. Patterson. Teddy Hicks (Kitt) lives much of the play in a fantasy world, as she envisions what life would be like among the wealthy. She even encounters the devil (Avon Long) in her daydreams.

Miles Jefferson, writing in *Phylon*, dismissed *Mrs. Patterson* as "banal," while *The New York Times* considered it lacking in imagination. Nevertheless, Kitt received raves for her performance as Teddy. Brooks Atkinson wrote: "Miss Kitt deserves a career in the theatre. She is an incandescent young woman with lively intelligence, a darting style of movement, keen eyes, and an instinct for the stage."

**MULATTO** (Vanderbilt, October 24, 1935, 373 p.). Producer and director: Martin Jones. Author: Langston Hughes.*

Cast: Rose McClendon* (Cora Lewis), Morris McKenney (William Lewis), Stuart Beebe (Colonel Thomas Norwood), Jeanne Greene (Sally Lewis), John Boyd (Talbot), Frank Jaquet (Fred Higgins), Henry Forsberg (Henry Richards), Gertrude Bondhill (Grace Richards), Connie Gilchrist

(Mary Lowell), Hurst Amyx (Robert Lewis), Clark Poth (Storekeeper), Howard Negley (Undertaker).

The problem of race mixture had fascinated white dramatists in the 1920s in such plays as *All God's Chillun Got Wings** and *Roseanne.** Langston Hughes gave Broadway a black playwright's view of the phenomenon in *Mulatto*, a play that became the longest running play by a black dramatist until *A Raisin in the Sun** (1959).

*Mulatto* considers the plight of Robert Lewis (Hurst Amyx), the illegitimate son of Colonel Thomas Norwood (Stuart Beebe), a wealthy plantation owner, and Cora Lewis (Rose McClendon), the family servant. Norwood, who considers himself "kind to his darkies," sends Robert north for an education. When Robert returns, he demands full rights as a Norwood heir. The colonel objects to Robert's demands, explaining that he should "talk like a nigger should to a white man." The colonel attempts to shoot Robert, but Norwood is accidentally killed in the struggle. Robert, fearful of being lynched, flees from a mob. Robert then shoots himself before the mob arrives. As Talbot, the overseer, slaps Cora, who blocks the door to Robert's hiding place, she refuses to move in a final gesture of strength.

Critic Wilella Waldorf of *The New York Post* noted that "there was probably not a soul in the audience who did not feel indignation in his breast at the injustice displayed on the Vanderbilt stage." Yet, she reasoned, "the South should settle its own problems." Rose McClendon won raves for her performance as Cora, her last major role before her death the following year.

**MY MAGNOLIA** (Mansfield, July 8, 1926, 4 p.). Producer and director: Walter Campbell. Book: Alex Rogers* and Eddie Hunter.* Composer: C. "Luckey" Roberts.* Lyricist: Alex Rogers.

Cast: Eddie Hunter (Sherman), Adelaide Hall* (Jenny), Hilda Rogers (Peggy), Paul Bass (Harvey), Percy Colston (Jodey), Lionel Monagas* (Mr. Workem), Dink Stewart (Upson), Henry "Gang" Jines (Downson), Louis Sims (Johnny), Claude Lawson (Chef), Alberta Perkins (Dusty), Mabel Gant (Grenadine), Charles Davis (Lightfoot), George Randol (Detective), Paul Bass (Floor Manager), Estelle Floyd (Lulu Belle), George Nanton (A Member of Dominoes), Charles Davis and Clarence Peters (Two Winning Members), Catherine Parker (Magnolia), Lena Sanford Roberts (Widow Love), Barrington Carter (Constable Sapp), Charles Davis (Sherman's Brother), Snippy Mason (Snappy), Alex Rogers (Uncle Fi).

Songs: At Your Service; Baby Mine; Shake Your Duster; Pay Day; Magnolia; Hard Times; Spend It; Jazz Land Ball; Laugh Your Blues Away; Gallopin' Dominoes; Headin' South; Merry Christmas; Struttin' Time; Our Child; Gee Chee; Sundown Serenade; Parade of the Christmas Dinner; Baby Wants; The Oof Dah Man; Sweet Popopper.

*My Magnolia* was greeted warmly by opening night audiences and treated cooly by the critics. The "always present" applause continually stopped the show and encouraged numerous encores by Eddie Hunter, Adelaide Hall, and the rest of the cast. *Variety* found the "encore habit flagrant" and complained that it unduly lengthened the opening night performance. Despite the obvious audience pleasure, noted by several reviewers, the critics killed *My Magnolia*, dooming it to a four-performance run.

**MY SISTER, MY SISTER** (Little, April 30, 1974, 119 p.). Producers: Jay J. Cohen, Myra L. Burns, and Chesmark Productions. Author: Ray Aranha.* Director: Paul Weidner.

Cast: Barbara Montgomery* (Mama), Seret Scott (Sue Belle), Jessie Saunders (Evalina), Lowell Copeland (Jesus), David Downing* (Eddie).

Although *My Sister, My Sister* had only a modest run, its author and cast received several awards. Ray Aranha and Seret Scott won Drama Desk Awards and Barbara Montgomery received an Obie. *My Sister, My Sister* received raves at its Hartford Stage Company premiere, and it was soon optioned for a Broadway production. It was lodged at the new Little Theatre, formerly a television production studio.

*My Sister, My Sister* moves backward and forward through the life of Sue Belle (Seret Scott) at ages six, twelve, and sixteen. As Sue Belle waits for her lover Eddie (David Downing), she recalls her drunken father, her pious mother, and her prostitute sister. While Clive Barnes of *The New York Times* found the time jumps "disconcerting," he claimed *My Sister, My Sister* was "strong and demanding theatre."

# N

**NATIVE SON** (St. James, March 24, 1941, 114 p.). Producers: Orson Welles, John Houseman, and Bern Bernard. Authors: Richard Wright* and Paul Green. Director: Orson Welles.

Cast: Canada Lee* (Bigger Thomas), Evelyn Ellis* (Hannah Thomas), Helen Martin (Vera), Lloyd Warren (Buddy), Jacqueline Ghant Andre (A Neighbor), Eileen Burns (Miss Emmett), J. Flashe Riley (Jack), Rodester Timmons (G. H. Rankin), Rena Mitchell (Clara), Wardell Saunders (Gus Mitchell), C. M. Bootsie Davis (Ernie Jones), Erskine Sanford (Mr. Dalton), Nell Harrison (Mrs. Dalton), Everett Sloane (Britten), Frances Bavier (Peggy), Anne Burr (Mary Dalton), Joseph Pevney (Jan Erlone), Philip Bourneuf (Buckley), Ray Collins (Paul Max), Paul Stewart (A Newspaper Man), William Malone (Judge), John Berry (Reporter).

Paul Green, author of the Pulitzer Prize play *In Abraham's Bosom**

(1926), collaborated with Richard Wright in the stage adaptation of Wright's 1940 novel. Green wrote most of the dialogue for the play, while Wright aided in the revisions. The show received rave reviews when it opened on Broadway. Brooks Atkinson wrote in *The New York Times*: "Mr. Wright and Paul Green have written a powerful drama. Orson Welles has staged it with imagination and force. Those are the first things to be said about the overwhelming play that opened at the St. James last evening. But they hardly convey the excitement of the first performance of a play that represents experience of life and conviction in thought and a production that represents a dynamic use of the stage."

Canada Lee portrayed the difficult leading role of Bigger Thomas, a man who accidentally kills the daughter of his white employer. The *Times* praised his "clean, honest, driving performance of remarkable versatility."

The 114-performance run underestimates *Native Son*'s appeal. The show returned to Broadway in October 1942 for an 84-performance revival. During this run, the Catholic Theatre Movement declared *Native Son* "objectionable," for its "glorification of licentiousness and crime" and urged Lee Shubert to close the play. Shubert agreed, and Broadway's leading lights protested. Actors Equity, the Theatre Guild, and Mayor La Guardia joined with the National Association for the Advancement of Colored People in challenging Shubert's decision. Shubert reversed himself, and *Native Son* continued its run.

**NATURAL MAN** (Library, May 7, 1941, n.a.p.). Producer: American Negro Theatre.* Author: Theodore Browne. Director: Benjamin Zemach.

Cast: Stanley Greene (John Henry), James Jackson (Charley Boy), Maxwell Glanville* (Bign' Me), William Lopez Daniels (Hard Tack), Howard Augusta (Jim), George Lewis (Britt), Ruby Wallace (Polly Ann), Alvin Childress (Capt. Tommy), Kenneth Manigault (The Creeper), Claude Sloan (The Salesman), Letitia Toole (The Singer), Claire Leyba (Cleo), Mildred Meekins (Susie), Frederick O'Neal* (The Preacher), Alice Childress* (Sistuh Bessie).

During the 1939-1940 season, Broadway saw a musical version of the life of "John Henry,* the steel-driving man," starring Paul Robeson.* Despite raves for Robeson, the Roark Bradford drama lasted barely a week. *Natural Man*, originally produced by the Federal Theatre Project in Seattle, opened in New York in 1941, and critics compared it favorably to the Broadway version. George Freedly of the *Morning-Telegram* even found Stanley Greene's performance a rival to Robeson's: "As John Henry, Greene contributed a highly physical and often vocal performance which was interesting to behold." Theodore Browne's play, "a Negro folk opera," was the second major production of the new American Negro Theatre, and it won the author a 1941 Rockefeller Playwrighting Fellowship.

**NEVER NO MORE** (Hudson, January 7, 1932, 12 p.). Producer: Robert Sparks. Author: James Knox Millen. Director: Chester Erskin.

Cast: Rose McClendon* (Mammy), Lew Payton (Deacon), Leigh Whipper* (Neighbor), Morris McKenny (Tom), William L. Andrews (Joe), Enid Raphael (Milly), James Dunmore (Ike), Viola Dean (Laura), Rudolph Toombs (Solomon), Dorothy Paul (Susie).

A twelve-performance run usually connotes a second-rate play that has been drubbed by the critics. Yet, *Never No More* received some of the best reviews of the 1931-1932 season. Robert Garland of the *World-Telegram* concluded his review as follows: "Mr. Millen has written a play in which are bravery and bitterness and a rather splendid courage. . . . *Never No More* is for the proud and none-too-profitable playgoer who takes his drama straight and tragic."

*Never No More* avoided the colorful myths of the black dramas of the era and concentrated on the lynching problem. A lynching is staged in the second act, and in *The New York Times* Brooks Atkinson declared it "one of the most harrowing scenes ever put on stage." This was strong medicine for the depression years, and audiences avoided *Never No More* despite favorable reviews.

Rose McClendon again attracted notice for her portrayal of the mother of the man who is to be lynched. Again Garland commented: "There were those in last night's audience who felt that Miss Rose McClendon is guilty of underacting as the mammy. . . . With this I cannot agree. To my way of thinking it is the sheer simplicity of her portrayal which makes *Never No More* so difficult to bear. As in *In Abraham's Bosom*,* *Deep River*,* *Porgy*,* and *The House of Connelly*, Miss McClendon's art has breadth and height and human understanding. I would not have her Mammy otherwise."

*Never No More* was the first of a series of dramas concerning the lynching problem. Both John Wexley's *They Shall Not Die* and Dennis Donoghue's *Legal Murder* considered the Scottsboro Case in 1934, and both experienced the briefest of runs.

**NEVIS MOUNTAIN DEW** (St. Marks, December 7, 1978, 61 p.). Producer: Negro Ensemble Company.* Author: Steve Carter.* Director: Horacena J. Taylor.

Cast: Frances Foster* (Everalda Griffin), Ethel Ayler (Zepora Philibert), Arthur French (Ayton Morris), Graham Brown (Jared Philibert), Barbara Montgomery* (Billie Philibert), Charles Brown (Lud Gaithers), Samm-Art Williams* (Boise McCanles).

*Nevis Mountain Dew*, Steve Carter's successor to *Eden** (1976), also considers the transplantation of a West Indian family to New York City, but there the resemblance ends. Jared Philibert (Graham Brown), an adult victim of polio, is encased in an iron lung. As the play opens, his loyal wife (Barbara Montgomery) and two sisters (Frances Foster and Ethel Ayler) celebrate his fiftieth birthday. As everyone drinks the "Nevis Mountain

Dew," the family's underlying unhappiness is revealed. *The New York Times* hoped that *Nevis Mountain Dew* had a "long life and a wide public." Critic Mel Gussow added: "[Mr. Carter] has a natural gift for the theatre, writing dialogue that is hearty, flavorful, and lightened with West Indian rhythms and humor. This is a serious play with moments that make us laugh out loud, and, it must be emphasized, this is laughter that rises directly from character."

**NO PLACE TO BE SOMEBODY** (Public, May 4, 1969, 312 p.). Producer: Joseph Papp and the New York Shakespeare Festival. Author: Charles Gordone.* Director: Ted Cornell.

Cast: Ron O'Neal* (Gabe Gabriel), Ronnie Thompson (Shanty Mulligan), Nathan George (Johnny Williams), Susan Pearson (Dee Jacobson), Lynda Wescott (Evie Ames), Marge Eliot (Cora Beasely), Henry Baker (Melvin Smelts), Paul Benjamin (Machine Dog), Laurie Crews (Mary Lou Bolton), Iris Gemma (Ellen), Walter Jones (Sweets Crane), Nick Lewis (Mike Maffucci), Ed VanNuys (Judge Bolton), Charles Seals (Sergeant), Malcolm Hurd (Harry), Martin Shakar (Louie).

Charles Gordone's *No Place to Be Somebody* won a Pulitzer Prize before it opened on Broadway for a regular run in September 1971. It began as a workshop production at The Other Stage in 1969 and then moved to the New York Shakespeare Festival's Public Theatre. In 1970 it appeared at the American National Theatre and Academy (ANTA) Festival of non-Broadway theatre and then moved Off-Broadway to the Promenade Theatre. Before opening at the Morosco in 1971, *No Place to Be Somebody* had already played 572 performances in the New York area. Gordone continued to revise the play during its travels, and by the time it reached the ANTA, Clive Barnes of *The New York Times* began comparing the play to *The Iceman Cometh.*

Like the O'Neill play, *No Place to Be Somebody* takes place in a bar, where the customers are waiting and talking of their dreams. Johnny Williams (Nathan George), a small-time crook, dreams of the day when his idol, gangster Sweets Crane (Walter Jones), will return from prison. Sweets returns, but as a two-bit pickpocket. Johnny attempts to become a rival of a local Mafia chieftain but is killed by his friend Gabe (Ron O'Neal) as a result of his efforts.

The performances received raves, especially those of O'Neal and George. Clive Barnes noted that "there are few better casts than this on or off-Broadway."

**NOWHERE TO RUN, NOWHERE TO HIDE** (St. Marks, March 26, 1974, 8 p.). Producer: Negro Ensemble Company.* Author: Herman Johnson. Director: Dean Irby.

Cast: Frankie Faison (Sam Wilde), Leon Morenzie (Frank Wilson), Roland Sanchez (Jesse Graves), Todd Davis (Willie Stewart), Joyce Hanley

(Lucia Ferguson), Lea Scott (Ida Mae Stewart), Samm [Samm-Art] Williams* (Chester Pearce), Michele Shay (Clarissa Ferguson), Robert Stocking (Paul Ferguson), Adolph Caesar* (Newscaster's Voice).

Critics welcomed *Nowhere to Run, Nowhere to Hide*, a 1973-1974 "season-within-a-season" workshop production of the Negro Ensemble Company. Herman Johnson's drama depicts the difficult life of a Harlem youth (Todd Davis) who is framed in a murder by two dope-dealing policemen (Leon Morenzie and Frankie Faison). *The New York Times* praised Johnson's ability to allow the audience to know the characters in a short period of time. Calling Johnson "a born playwright," Howard Thompson added that "he simply must be heard from again."

# O

**ODODO** (St. Marks, November 17, 1970, 48 p.). Producer: Negro Ensemble Company.* Book, lyrics, and direction: Joseph A. Walker.* Composer: Dorothy A. Dinroe.

Cast: Ethel Ayler, Garrett Morris, Marilyn B. Coleman, Ray Aranha,* Deloris Gaskins, Tonice Gwathney, Robert Jackson, Jack Landron, Roxie Roker, Garrett Saunders, Charles Weldon, Anita Wilson.

Critics for the major newspapers greeted *Ododo* (Yoruba for "truth") with a mixture of admiration and hatred. On one hand, reviewers praised the libretto of this "militant musical," but rejected its message of black nationalism. *Ododo* celebrates the history of black life from Africa to Harlem. Although the play resembles Walker's earlier musical, *The Believers** (1968), it is less hopeful in outlook. Clive Barnes's praise of Walker in *The New York Times* revealed the critics' ambivalence about the show: "Walker . . . is a real talent. For a lot of time here he is content to write propaganda, but even then it is beautifully written propaganda. And when he writes from the heart rather than the mind, he conveys emotions that strike deeper than rhetoric."

**THE OFFERING** (St. Marks, November 26, 1977, 59 p.). Producer: Negro Ensemble Company.* Author: Gus Edwards.* Director: Douglas Turner Ward.*

Cast: Douglas Turner Ward (Bob Tyrone), Olivia Williams (Princess), Charles Weldon (Martin), Katherine Knowles (Ginny).

*The New York Times* found Gus Edwards's *The Offering* a "remarkable first play," which was "dramatically literate, observant, and most worthwhile." This Negro Ensemble Company production concerns the visit of a young hired killer, Martin (Charles Weldon), and his white mistress (Katherine Knowles) to his aging mentor Bob Tyrone (Douglas Turner

Ward). Tyrone seems somewhat listless as he sits in front of the television set, but he soon manages to turn the tables on Martin and, for a short time, win his mistress. Ward received praise for both his performance and his directon of *The Offering*, with Olivia Williams, as Tyrone's long-suffering wife, stealing the acting honors.

**OH JOY!** (Bamboo Isle, August 3, 1922, n.a.p.). Producer: Lewis Rogers. Book and lyrics: J. Homer Tutt* and S. T. Whitney.* Composers: James J. Vaughn and Edgar Dowell.

Cast: S. T. Whitney, J. Homer Tutt, Amon Davis, Margaret Simms, Leroy Broomfield, Julia Moody, Julian Costello, Andrew Tribble, Emmett Anthony, J. Anthony Mores, Johnnie Nit.

Songs: Smile on Sue; Sally Sue; Da Da Strain; Valley of the Nile; My Dog; What's the Use?; At the Old Stage Door; Brown Boys Go Marching By.

When *Oh Joy!* opened in New York City, its producers hoped to capitalize on the new interest in black musical comedies. Unfortunately, no theatre was available, so the producers converted a tennis stadium at Fifty-seventh Street and Eighth Avenue into a tent-covered theatre dubbed the "Bamboo Isle." The seats were benches with individual cushions. The conversion cost a mere $3,000.

Ethel Waters* first appeared as a name performer in *Oh Joy!* in Boston. She was initially excited that the show would open in New York. But when Whitney and Tutt explained that it would be opening in a tent, Waters replied, "The days when I worked in a tent are over forever. I have slept with horses for the last time, I trust." Waters refused to appear in the show, and it managed only a short run.

**OL' MAN SATAN** (Forrest, October 3, 1932, 24 p.). Producer: Shillwood Productions. Author: Donald Heywood.* Director: William A. Shilling.

Cast: A. B. Comathiere* (Satan), Dan Michaels (Saul), Lionel Monagas* (Peter), Georgette Harvey* (Ma Jackson), Phyllis Hunt (Josh), Edna Thomas (Maggie), Mike Jackson (Gabriel), Laurence Chenault (Moses), Hayes L. Pryor (Noah), Walter Richardson (David), Alice Ramsey (Sister Bright), Tressie Legge (Sister Crabtree), Lorenzo Tucker (Teacher), Freeman Fairley (Number Three Imp), Mary Jane Watkins (Becky), Kolly Mitchell (Soldier), Hilda Offley, Bee Freeman (David's Temptresses), Herbert Ellis (Keeper of the Souls), Fred Miller (Farmer), Walter Robinson (Paul), DeKoven Thompson (James), James McPheeters (John), Taylor Gordon, Luther Henderson, David Bethe (Disciples), Clyde Faison (Noah's Temptress), Florence Lee (Jezebel), Arthur McLean (Maggie's Protector), Ismay Andrews (Sister Johnson), James Cook (Hunchback), Ralph Ramson (Blind Man), Helen Nelson (Mother), Wandolf Saunders (Racketeer), Ellen Baylor (Primrose), Cleo Harris (Merrie).

Spirituals: Watermelon Time; Trouble Don't Last Always; Time Ain't Long; I Know the Lord; I Know the Word; Hol' On; Go Down, Moses;

Ain't It a Shame; Home Beyond the River; Te Deum Laude Amus; Blind Man; Smiles; Angel Song.

Most critics found *Ol' Man Satan* an attempt to copy the success of *The Green Pastures*.* Here the central figure is Satan (A. B. Comathiere) rather than the Lord. Although Comathiere won praise for his performance, most found this Donald Heywood production an inferior effort.

**OLD PHANTOMS** (St. Marks, February 7, 1979, 15 p.). Producer: Negro Ensemble Company.* Author: Gus Edwards.* Director: Horacena J. Taylor.

Cast: Samm-Art Williams* (James), L. Scott Caldwell (Ruth), Chuck Patterson (Nick), Douglas Turner Ward* (Jack Hamilton), Olivia Williams (Grace Hamilton), Barbara Montgomery* (Mavis), Charles Brown (Blake Walters), Leon Morenzie (Sgt. Russell).

Gus Edwards's first two plays for the Negro Ensemble Company (*The Offering** and *Black Body Blues**) brought comparisons to Harold Pinter. *Old Phantoms* had critics evoking Ibsen and O'Neill in praise of "the richness of Mr. Edwards' dramatic talent." This family study begins after the death of father Jack Hamilton (Douglas Turner Ward), as two brothers (Samm-Art Williams and Chuck Patterson) discuss their feelings with sister Ruth (L. Scott Caldwell). The play then moves between past and present as Jack is revealed as a tyrant, whose children are unable to live up to his high standards. While Douglas Turner Ward received praise for his "restrained and forceful performance," critic Mel Gussow of *The New York Times* admired the difficult roles of the children, who had to change from adult to child and back again without the use of makeup or costume changes. Their acting skills alone made the transition believable.

**ON STRIVER'S ROW** (ANT, February 28, 1946, 27 p.). Producer: American Negro Theatre.* Author and director: Abram Hill.*

Cast: Stanley Greene (Oscar Van Striven), Dorothy Carter (Dolly Van Striven), Isabell Sanford (Sophie), Draynard Clinton (Prof. Hennypest), Letitia Toole (Tillie Petunia), Oliver Pitcher (Chuck), Javotte Sutton (Cobina Van Striven), Hattie King-Reavis (Mrs. Pace), Verneda La Selle (Lily Livingston), Hilda Haynes (Louise Davis), Charles Henderson (Dr. Leon Davis), Courtenaye Olden (Rowena).

Abram Hill's *On Striver's Row* had a lengthy history before its 1946 production at the American Negro Theatre (ANT) in Harlem. It was first presented by the Rose McClendon Players in Harlem in 1939, and the ANT gave it a brief run in 1940. The Apollo saw a musical version in 1941, but the revised play dropped its songs in 1946. Some critics faulted Hill for reviving a play that had continually received mixed reviews, but he responded that Harlem's audiences "demanded" it.

Hill's satire of a social-climbing family on Harlem's fashionable Striver's Row examines a crisis that takes place on the day of the Radcliffe-educated daughter's coming-out party. The daughter refuses to marry the "aristocratic" young man her mother has selected for her. Most critics dismissed the play as weak, but *PM*'s Louis Kronenberger praised its "mixture of a good-hearted spoof and the sobriety of real social criticism."

**ON WHITMAN AVENUE** (Cort, May 8, 1946, 150 p.). Producers: Canada Lee,* Mark Marvin, and George McLain. Author: Maxine Wood. Director: Margo Jones.

Cast: Canada Lee (David Bennett), Abbie Mitchell* (Cora Bennett), Richard Williams (Owen Bennett), Augustus Smith (Gramp Bennett), Martin Miller (Johnnie Tilden), Ernestine Barrier (Kate Tilden), Will Geer (Ed Tilden), Vivienne Baber (Wini Bennett), Kenneth Terry (Bernie Lund), Hilda Vaughn (Aurie Anderson), Perry Wilson (Toni Tilden), Philip Clarke (Jeff Hall), Betty Greene Little (Belle Hall), Robert Simon (Walter Lund), Jean Cleveland (Ellen Lund), Stephen Roberts (Wilbur Reed), Joanna Albus (Edna Reed).

*On Whitman Avenue* foreshadowed *A Raisin in the Sun** by thirteen years. White playwright Maxine Wood focuses on the effect of the arrival of a black family into a hitherto white area of town. Toni Tilden (Perry Wilson), a liberal young girl, rents an apartment to a returning black war hero and his family while her parents are out of town. The town slowly mobilizes to oust the "intruders." Canada Lee co-produced and starred in *On Whitman Avenue* because it explored a vital social issue, but white critics found the play "flattish propaganda." Nevertheless, Wood's play managed a modest run.

**ONE MO' TIME** (Village Gate, October 22, 1979, still running). Producers: Art D'Lugoff, Burt D'Lugoff, Jerry Wexler, and Shari Upbin. Author and director: Vernel Bagneris.

Cast: Vernel Bagneris (Papa Du), Sylvia "Kuumba" Williams (Bertha), Thais Clark (Ma Reed), Topsy Chapman (Thelma), John Stell (Theatre Owner).

Songs: Down in Honky Tonk Town (Charles McCarron-Chris Smith); Kiss Me Sweet (A. J. Piron-Steve Lewis); Miss Jenny's Ball (Reed); Cake Walkin' Babies from Home (Smith-Henry Troy-Clarence Williams); I've Got What It Takes (C. Williams-Hezekiah Jenkins); C. C. Rider; The Graveyard (Clifford Hayes); He's Funny That Way (Richard Whiting-Neil Moret); Kitchen Man (Alex Belledna-Andy Razaf*); Wait Till You See My Baby Do the Charleston (C. Williams-Clarence Todd-Rousseau Simmons); Love (Jabbo Smith); Louise; New Orleans Hop Scop Blues (George W. Thomas); Everybody Loves My Baby (Jack Palmer-Spencer Williams); You've Got the Right Key, But the Wrong Keyhole (C. Williams-Lil Green); After You've Gone (Henry Creamer*-Turner Layton); My Man Blues (Bessie Smith); Papa De Da Da (S. Williams-C. Williams-C. Todd); Muddy

Water (Peter De Rose-Harry Richman-Jo Trent); There'll Be a Hot Time in the Old Town Tonight (Theodore A. Metz).

Vernel Bagneris (Papa Du) has recreated a 1927 New Orleans black vaudeville show in *One Mo' Time.* Recalling such talents as Bessie Smith, Ethel Waters,* and Ma Rainey, Bagneris successfully reconstructs life on the TOBA (Theatre Owners Booking Agency, or "Tough on Black Actors") circuit. The evening at first was primarily musical, featuring such hits as "C. C. Rider," "Papa De Da Da," and "Cake Walkin' Babies from Home." As *One Mo' Time* spun off both a touring version and a London edition, it was lengthened somewhat to explore the relationships of the black vaudeville troupers and the white theatre manager. Most critics praised the evening, with *Time* noting that "from one minute to the next, *One Mo' Time* is a hot, wild, ribald and rousing delight."

**ORRIN/SUGAR-MOUTH SAM DON'T DANCE NO MORE** (St. Marks, May 6, 1975, 8 p.). Producer: Negro Ensemble Company.* Author: Don Evans. Director: Helaine Head.

**Orrin**

Cast: Taurean Blacque (Orrin), Lea Scott (Wilma), Eric Coleman (Kenny), Carl Gordon (Alex).

**Sugar-Mouth Sam Don't Dance No More**

Cast: Lea Scott (Verda Mae Hollis), Carl Gordon (Sammy).

Don Evans's "season-within-a-season" entry for the Negro Ensemble Company presented the effects of two unexpected reunions on family life. In *Orrin*, an elder son (Taurean Blacque), now a drug dealer, returns home to his middle-class Philadelphia family, much to the displeasure of his moralistic father. *Sugar-Mouth Sam Don't Dance No More* concerns the return of a former lover (Carl Gordon) who now claims that he will at last be faithful. In both one-act plays, the surprise guest retreats, leaving others in confusion. *Orrin* received the better reviews, with the critics praising Blacque's performance in the title role.

**OUR LAN'** (Royale, September 27, 1947, 41 p.). Producers: Eddie Dowling and Louis J. Singer. Author: Theodore Ward.* Directors: Eddie Dowling and Edward R. Mitchell.

Cast: Muriel Smith (Delphine), Louis Peterson (Emanuel Price), Theresa Merritt (Patsy Ross), Irving Barnes (Edgar Price), Ferman Phillips (Gabe Peltier), Augustus Smith, Sr.* (Joe Ross), Emory Richardson (Charlie Setlow), Valerie Black (Ellen), Harold Conklin (James), Service Bell (Daddy Sykes), Margo Washington (Roxanna), Dolores Woodward (Beaulah), Martha Evans (Ruth), Paula Oliver (Martha), Mary Lucille McBride (Alice), Augustus Smith, Jr. (Fred Douglas), Jay Brooks (Tom Taggart), Blanche Christopher (Minnie), Estelle Rolle Evans (Sarah),

William Veasey (Joshua Tain), Virginia Chapman (Georgana), Edith Atuka Reid (Dosia), Richard Angarola (Ollie Webster), Chauncey Reynolds (Lem), Edmund Cambridge (Chester), Charles Lillienthal (Hank Saunders), Jack Becker (Captain Bryant), Julie Haydon (Libeth), James Harwood (Oliver Webster), Stuart Hoover (Yank Sergeant), Gene O'Donnell (Capt. Stewart), Frank Tweddell (John Burkhardt), Graham Velsey (Cotton Broker), Nathan Adler, Michael Higgins (Rebel Soldiers).

*Our Lan'*, by black playwright Theodore Ward, originated at the Henry Street Settlement as an experimental work. Eddie Dowling and Louis Singer joined with the Associated Playwrights to give the work a Broadway showcase. Ward's play presented a Reconstruction drama with contemporary overtones. A group of freed slaves are given a former plantation after the Civil War. Through political chicanery on the part of northern and southern whites, the land is returned to the original owners. The lead character, Joshua (William Veasey), hopes that "someday the land will belong to those who till it," but he is killed by a soldier as the curtain falls.

The reviews of *Our Lan'* were generally favorable, although several critics complained that the play was not yet ready for commercial production. *Variety* led the raves: "*Our Lan'* . . . is a powerful piece of stagecraft, powerful enough to merit being lifted out of obscurity . . . to a Broadway showcase. . . . As enacted by the predominately Negro cast, the play becomes brilliantly alive with the pride, the suffering, and courage of a submerged people fighting for dignity." Muriel Smith, fresh from her triumph in *Carmen Jones*,* won praise for her "exceptional dramatic and singing talent," as did William Veasey for his "inspired performance" as Joshua.

**THE OWL ANSWERS.** See CITIES IN BEZIQUE.

**THE OYSTER MAN** (Yorkville, November 23, 1907, 8 p.). Producer and director: Ernest Hogan.* Composers: Ernest Hogan and Will Vodery. Lyricist: Henry Creamer.* Book: Flournoy Miller and Aubrey Lyles.*

Cast: Ernest Hogan (Rufus; Baltimore Oyster Vendor), Muriel Ringgold (Matilda), John Rucker (Sunny Sam), Harry Reed (Useless), Robert R. Kelley (Brother Peter Smith), Al F. Watts (Aunt Jemima), Lawrence Deas (Samuel Austin), Creg Williams (George Oramos), George Lynnier (Policeman), Charles Foster (Panama Jack), Carita Day (Angelea Gailiard), Ella Deas (Belle Cown), Billie Moore (Gazook Seventh Eleventh), George Lynnier (Ho Bo), Gus Hall (Gazabo), Newell Morse (Keno), J. H. Bolden (Bazo), James Worles (Debility), J. L. Grant (Delivery), Ella Anderson (Princess Itto), Blanche Arlington (Ba La), Louise Salisbury (La La), Ora Henry (Zamazi).

Songs: Meet Me at the Barber Shop; A Yankee Doodle Coon; Mina; Tomorrow; The White-Wash Brigade; I Just Can't Keep My Eyes Off You;

Contribution Box; Blazasus Chorus; Mermaid's Chorus; Swanee River; Hail to the King; No, You Didn't, Yes I Did; When Buffalo Bill and His Wild West Show Came to Baltimore.

Ernest Hogan ("The Unbleached American") turned from minstrelsy to the musical comedy stage shortly after the turn of the century. With a talented ensemble, which included Carita Day and John Rucker, Hogan toured the United States with shows he produced and directed. *The Oyster Man* was a fanciful affair according to the *Toledo Blade*: "The first act shows scenes on the Atlantic Coast at Baltimore. Later the whole company is transferred to the mystic and marvelous island of Blazasus, where chickens grow on trees, and gin rickeys sprout from the rocks. Scenes of barbaric splendor, painful escapes in which Sunny Sam and the Oyster Man fall into the clutches of bloodthirsty savages, and other developments are sufficient for the company to exhibit their talents to the best advantage."

# P

**PANSY** (Belmont, May 14, 1929, 3 p.). Producer, composer, and lyricist: Maceo Pinkard. Book: Alex Belledna. Director: Frank Rye.

Cast: Ralph Harris (Dean Liggett), Al Frisco (James), Tom and Austin Cole (Campus "Cut Ups"), Ida Anderson (Miss Wright), Alfred Chester (Bill), Elizabeth Taylor (Miss Merritt), Pearl McCormack (Pansy), Speedy Wilson (Ulysses Grant Green), Amon Davis (Mrs. Green), Billy Andrews (Bob), Jackie Young (Sadie), W. Crumbley, L. Randall, H. Mattingly, and D. Davis (Penn Comedy Four), and Bessie Smith as herself.

Songs: It's Commencement Day; Break'n the Rhythm; Pansy; Campus Walk; I'd Be Happy; Gettin' Together; Shake a Leg; If the Blues Don't Get You; A Stranger Interlude; A Bouquet of Fond Memories.

The major highlight of *Pansy* was the appearance of Bessie Smith, who, unfortunately, did not perform until the middle of the second act. At that point, *Pansy*, a college musical modeled after *Good News*, virtually disappeared. The restless audience gave Smith a standing ovation and greeted "If the Blues Don't Get You" to "wild applause." After several encores, she retired and returned only briefly in "A Stranger Interlude," a parody of the Eugene O'Neill play. Otherwise, *Pansy* was quite forgettable.

**PAUL ROBESON** (Lunt-Fontanne, January 19, 1978, 77 p.). Producer: Don Gregory. Author: Phillip Hayes Dean.* Director: Lloyd Richards.*

Cast: James Earl Jones* (Paul Robeson*), Burt Wallace (Lawrence Brown).

Prominent black personalities denounced *Paul Robeson* in a two-page ad in *Variety* before this Broadway opening. Signed by James Baldwin,* Julian Bond, Nikki Giovanni, Alvin Ailey, Coretta Scott King, and others, the ad claimed that the "revolutionary" Robeson was "sentimentalized" in the new Phillip Hayes Dean play. Baldwin later claimed that the play turned Robeson into a "chocolate John Wayne." Carl Stokes, of National Broadcasting Company news, opposed this viewpoint: "This is a play Americans need to see, not because an actor rises to superlative heights in his portrayal of a character, which James Earl Jones does, but because this play reintroduces Paul Robeson to the American public and causes white and black Americans to confront the atrocious treatment they accorded this remarkable man." [*The New York Times*]

Critics tended to ignore the debate and assessed the play on its own merits. Despite a brilliant performance by James Earl Jones, the play emerged more as a dramatic reading than as an attempt to probe Robeson's personality. After foundering at the box office, Joseph Papp moved *Paul Robeson* into repertory with *For Colored Girls** on March 9, 1978.

**THE PERFECT PARTY** (Tambellini's Gate, March 20, 1969, 21 p.). Producer: Jeff G. Britton. Author: Charles Fuller.* Director: Perry Brushkin.

Cast: Woodie King* (Ed), Moses Gunn* (Nick), Susan Willerman (Laura), Art Wallace (Cornish), Ceci Perrin (Kate), Virginia Kiser (Helen), Tracee Lyles (Bella), Victor Eschbach (Mark), Beverly Hayes (Jill), Harold Miller (Leon).

Despite respectable reviews, *The Perfect Party* managed only a brief run at the Tambellini's Gate Theatre. Charles Fuller designed a far from perfect party, where five integrated married couples meet to discuss the success of their marriages. Nick, the host, played by Moses Gunn, interrupts the surface tranquillity of the evening by announcing that he is leaving his wife to live with a black woman. *The New York Times* noted: "There is no one in the cast undeserving of praise. Mr. Fuller has served them well with his many gifts, which augur well for the future."

**PERRY'S MISSION/ROSALEE PRITCHETT** (St. Marks, January 12, 1971, 44 p.). Producer: Negro Ensemble Company.*

**Perry's Mission.** Author: Clarence Young III. Director: Douglas Turner Ward.*

Cast: William Jay (Charles Stripling), Adolph Caesar* (Lester Johnson), Katherine McGrath (Susie Collett), Charles Weldon (Henry Jorden), Jeff David (Bob Hinton), Win Wilford (Boosie Taylor), Charles Grant (Pookie Fields), David Downing* (A Black Man), Arthur French (Jouba Spinter), Harold Triggs (Bus Driver).

**Rosalee Pritchett.** Authors: Carlton and Barbara Molette. Director: Shauneille Perry.*

Cast: Frances Foster* (Rosalee Pritchett), Roxie Roker (Doretha Ellen), Esther Rolle* (Maybelle Johnson), Clarice Taylor* (Dolly Mae Anderson), Adolph Caesar (Robert Barron), Arthur French (Augustin Lowe), William Jay (Donald King), David Downing (Wilbur Wittner), Anita Wilson (Thelma Franklin).

*Perry's Mission* joined *Rosalee Pritchett* as a double bill in the Negro Ensemble Company's fourth season of "themes of black struggle." In *Perry's Mission*, a group of diverse characters find shelter in a bar during a storm. While *The New York Times* initially found the black businessman, the militant, and the wino to be "stereotypes," critic Mel Gussow was surprised at how quickly they grew into characters. He praised Young's dialogue for this transformation, as well as the performances by Charles Grant, Win Wilford, and David Downing.

While Atlanta burns in the middle of a race riot, Carlton and Barbara Molette's *Rosalee Pritchett* presents a bridge party attended by upper class blacks who are totally unaware of the chaos around them. One of the card party members, Rosalee Pritchett, is raped by a member of the National Guard, but the game continues. Gussow also found this play "provocative" and the playwrights "promising."

**A PHOTOGRAPH** (Public, December 1, 1977, 62 p.). Producer: New York Shakespeare Festival. Author: Ntozake Shange.* Director: Oz Scott.

Cast: Michele Shay (Michael), Avery Brooks (Sean David), Petronia Paley (Nevada), Count Stovall (Earl), Hattie Winston* (Claire).

*A Photograph: A Study of Cruelty* was Ntozake Shange's followup to her smash *For Colored Girls** (1976). Reviewers were somewhat more reserved in their assessment of *A Photograph*. One argued that the play was caught in a "theatrical purgatory" between drama and poetry, while Edith Oliver of the *New Yorker* argued that "Shange's poetic talent and passion carry the show, and her characters are given flesh and blood by the actors."

*A Photograph* concerns the relationship between Sean (Avery Brooks) and his three women: Michael (Michele Shay), who loves him the most, the wealthy Nevada (Petronia Paley), and the poor, but witty, Claire (Hattie Winston). The relationship becomes a "study of cruelty" when Sean loses his self-esteem because he is rejected for a fellowship.

**THE PIG PEN** (St. Clements Church, April 29, 1970, 46 p.). Producer: American Place Theatre. Author: Ed Bullins.* Director: Dick Williams.*

Cast: Basil A. Wallace (Ray Crawford), Tony Thomas (Len Stover), Laura Esterman (Sharon Stover), Avis McCarther (Margie), Lou Courtney (Bobo Carroll), Milton Earl Forrest (John Carroll), Elbert Bernard Pair (Henry Carroll), Edward Clinton (Mackman), Michael Coleman (Ernie Butler), J. Herbert Kerr, Jr. (Carlos), Robert Patterson (Pig Pen).

Ed Bullins's *The Pig Pen* takes place on the day of the assassination of Malcolm X in 1965. The characters in the play are unaware of this fact until the final moments of the drama. Thus, this day is much like any other for Len (Tony Thomas), his white wife Sharon (Laura Esterman), and itinerant poet Ray (Basil A. Wallace). As a day-long party develops, Len, Ray, and several neighbors begin to discuss black nationalism, but the talk is halted by the radio bulletin. Therefore, little happens at this party, but several critics enjoyed the experience. Clive Barnes of *The New York Times* led the praise of Bullins: ". . . in this strangely unstructured play . . . there is a real feeling for time and a place. . . . Mr. Bullins' play is the most meaningful nothing experience—and I intend this as a compliment—of the season."

**PLANTATION.** See CONTRIBUTIONS.

**PLANTATION REVUE** (Forty-eighth Street, July 17, 1922, 40 p.). Producer: Lew Leslie. Music and lyrics: Roy Turk and Russell J. Robinson. Director: Lew Leslie.

Cast: Shelton Brooks,* Edith Wilson,* Will Vodery, Chappy Chapelle, Florence Mills,* Juanita Stinette, Will Vodery's Plantation Orchestra.

Songs: Bugle Call Blues; Old Black Joe; A Southern Hobby; Robert E. Lee; Swanee River; Southland; Mandy; Hawaiian Night in Dixie Land; I Want to be Vamped in Georgia; Minstrels on Parade.

Lew Leslie, known in the late 1920s for his *Blackbirds* revues, began his producing career with *Plantation Revue*. Following the pattern of the minstrel show, this new revue featured Shelton Brooks as the master of ceremonies who introduced a variety of acts. Dominating the stage was "a large imitation half of watermelon," which *The Globe* claimed added "conviviality to the atmosphere."

The true casting coup of *Plantation Revue* was the presentation of Florence Mills, who would soon be hailed as "the world's greatest colored entertainer." She had appeared in a replacement role in *Shuffle Along*,* but her sensual rendition of "I'm Craving for That Kind of Love" quickly attracted notice. Her performance in *Plantation Revue*, claimed one critic, became the must-see performance of the year.

**PLAYERS INN.** See BLACK VISIONS.

**PLAYS FROM AFRICA (EVERYMAN and THE IMPRISONMENT OF OBATALA)** (St. Marks, January 10, 1979, 15 p.). Producer: Negro Ensemble Company.* Author: Obotunde Ijimere. Director: Dean Irby.

Cast: Samm-Art Williams,* Graham Brown, Charles Brown, Leon Morenzie, Adolph Caesar,* Frances Foster,* Chuck Patterson, Olivia Williams, Ethel Ayler, Barbara Montgomery,* L. Scott Caldwell.

Critics were impressed by the wide variety of Negro Ensemble Company productions in the 1978-1979 season. *Plays from Africa*, a Nigerian import by Obotunde Ijimere, presented a dramatization of two African folk tales. *Everyman* features the dilemma of a wealthy man (Leon Morenzie) who begins to travel the road to death and finds that his fair-weather friends have disappeared. *The Imprisonment of Obatala* offers a king's (Graham Brown) journey in search of truth. Critics praised the play, but especially enjoyed the lavish masks and costumes designed by Alvin Perry and the versatile sets by Wynn Thomas.

**THE POLICY PLAYERS** (Koster and Bial's, April 3, 1900, 8 p.). Producers, authors, and composers: Bert Williams* and George Walker.*

Cast: George Walker, Bert Williams, Mattie Wilkes, Ada Overton [Walker],* Reese Bros., Fred Douglas, George Catlin, Mallory Bros., Mazie Brooks, Lottie Thompson, Edward Harris.

Songs: Whose Gwine to Get the Money?; Dream Interpreter; I Cert'nly Was a Very Busy Man (Bennett and Northrup); Gwine to Catch a Gig Today; Ghost of a Coon; The Colored Band; The Broadway Coon; Honolulu Belles; The Man in the Moon Might Tell (Jessie Shipp); The Medicine Man; Gladys (Theo. Northrup); Take Me As I Am (Joe Hurtig-Andy Lewis); The Policy Players.

*The Policy Players*, Bert Williams and George Walker's first major show, toured from Lawrence, Kansas, to Brooklyn before opening at Koster and Bial's to a favorable reception. *The New York Times* found the plot, which deals with Williams's attempts to become a social success, merely an excuse for an enjoyable variety show: "The musical farce-comedy has little or nothing to do with policy-playing, but serves an excellent means to present Williams and Walker, about whom are surrounded a large company who indulge in solos, duets, acrobatic feats, yarn-spinning, and negro eccentricities." The critic also singled out Ada Overton, who had become Mrs. George Walker the previous year, for her excellent performance in the second act.

**PORGY** (Guild, October 10, 1927, 367 p.). Producer: Theatre Guild. Authors: Dorothy and DuBose Heyward. Director: Rouben Mamoulian.

Cast: Frank Wilson* (Porgy), Evelyn Ellis* (Crown's Bess), Percy Verwayne (Sporting Life), Jack Carter (Crown), Georgette Harvey* (Maria), Wesley Hill (Jake), Dorothy Paul (Lily), Richard Huey (Mingo), Ella Madison (Annie), Rose McClendon* (Serena), Lloyd Gray (Robbins), Peter Clark (Jim), Marie Young (Clara), Hayes Pryor (Peter), Stanley de Wolfe (Detective), Hugh Rennie and Maurice McRae (Policemen), Leigh Whipper* (Undertaker), Melville Greene (Scipio), A. B. Comathiere* (Simon Frazier), G. Edward Brown (Nelson), Edward Fielding (Alan Archdale), Leigh Whipper (Undertaker; Crab Man), Garret Minturn (Coroner).

DuBose and Dorothy Heyward's *Porgy* was transformed from a novel to a play within two years' time. This work, and *Porgy and Bess** as well, have now attained classic stature, but in 1927 *Time* had to explain to its readers that *Porgy* is pronounced "with the sharp, hard 'g' of porgy, the fish."

In order to cast *Porgy*, the Theatre Guild, the Heywards, and director Rouben Mamoulian observed the recent plays of the 1920s performed by blacks. Frank Wilson (whose work filled Heyward with "emotional power") came from *In Abraham's Bosom*,* as did Richard Huey. Rose McClendon was remembered for her "distinguished stairway descent" in *Deep River* (1926) before she joined the cast of *Porgy* as Serena.

This story of a legless cripple, Porgy (Frank Wilson), his love for Bess (Evelyn Ellis) on Catfish Row in Charleston, South Carolina, won favorable reviews from the critics. James Weldon Johnson, author of *Black Manhattan* (1930), claimed "*Porgy* loomed high above every Negro drama that had ever been produced." He also believed that this production was of major historical importance: "In *Porgy* the Negro performer removed all doubts as to his ability to do acting that requires thoughtful interpretation and intelligent skill. Here was more than the achievement of one or two individuals who might be set down as exceptions. Here was a large company giving a first-rate, even performance, with eight or ten reaching a high mark. The evidence was massive and indisputable."

**PORGY AND BESS** (Alvin, October 10, 1935, 124 p.). Producer: Theatre Guild. Composer: George Gershwin. Libretto: Ira Gershwin and DuBose Heyward. Director: Rouben Mamoulian.

Cast: Todd Duncan* (Porgy), Anne Wiggins Brown (Bess), John W. Bubbles* (Sportin' Life), Georgette Harvey* (Maria), J. Rosamond Johnson* (Frazier), Ford L. Buck (Mingo), Abbie Mitchell* (Clara), Edward Matthews (Jake), Olive Ball (Annie), Helen Dowdy (Lily; Strawberry Woman), Ruby Elzy (Serena), Henry Davis (Robbins), Jack Carr (Jim), Gus Simons (Peter), Warren Coleman (Crown), Alexander Campbell (Detective), Harold Woolf, Burton McEvilly (Policemen), John Garth (Undertaker), George Lessey (Mr. Archdale), Ray Yeates (Nelson; Crab Man), George Carleton (Coroner).

Songs: Summertime; A Woman Is a Sometime Thing; They Pass By Singing; Crap Game Fugue; Gone, Gone, Gone!; Overflow; My Man's Gone Now; Leavin' fo' de Promis' Lan'; It Take a Long Pull to Get There; I Got Plenty o' Nuttin'; Woman to Lady; Bess, You is My Woman Now; Oh, I Can't Sit Down; It Ain't Necessarily So; What You Want with Bess?; Time and Time Again; Street Cries; I Loves You, Porgy; Oh, de Lawd Shake de Heaven; A Red Headed Woman; Oh, Doctor Jesus; Clara, Don't You Be Downhearted; There's a Boat Dat's Leavin' Soon for New York; Oh, Bess, Where's My Bess?; I'm on My Way.

DuBose and Dorothy Heyward's tale of "Porgy" first appeared as a novel and was later presented by the Theatre Guild in 1927. George Gershwin expressed interest in preparing an operatic version as early as 1926, but his plans would not come to fruition until 1935. In the meantime, Jerome Kern and Oscar Hammerstein II dropped a plan to produce a musical comedy of the work with Al Jolson!

Gershwin's version of the Porgy story cunningly used a remarkable mixture of talented newcomers to Broadway as well as seasoned veterans. Todd Duncan (Porgy) made his Broadway debut in the show. He had formerly been a Washington, D.C., music teacher. On the other hand, *Porgy and Bess* utilized some of the top stars of the early days of the black musical, such as Abbie Mitchell and J. Rosamond Johnson, who appeared in *Red Moon** in 1909.

Reviews for Gershwin's show were mixed, and *Porgy and Bess* managed only a 124-performance run. Despite its initial failure, *Porgy and Bess* slowly became a classic. Revived periodically on Broadway, the show has continually risen in critical esteem. A 1952 revival, which featured Leontyne Price, toured the world until 1958. By 1975, the Metropolitan Opera was planning a production of the show. When these plans fizzled, the Houston Grand Opera revived the show and brought its production to the Uris Theatre in 1976. Despite the presence of a 1959 film version with Dorothy Dandridge and Sidney Poitier,* stage performances of *Porgy and Bess* continue to attract audiences. Its music, particularly "Summertime," has become an enduring part of the American cultural heritage.

**PRAYER MEETING OR THE FIRST MILITANT MINISTER.** See A BLACK QUARTET.

**THE PRODIGAL SISTER** (De Lys, November 25, 1974, 40 p.). Producer: Woodie King, Jr.* Book: J. E. Franklin.* Composer: Micki Grant.* Lyricists: J. E. Franklin and Micki Grant. Director: Shauneille Perry.*

Cast: Paula Desmond (Jackie), Frances Salisbury (Mother), Esther Brown (Mrs. Johnson), Ethel Beatty (Sissie), Leonard Jackson (Jack), Louise Stubbs (Essie; Baltimore Bessie), Saundra McClain (Lucille), Kirk Kirksey* (Slick; Pallbearer), Frank Carey (Rev. Wynn; Employment Man), Joyce Griffen (Hot Pants Harriet), Victor Willis (Dr. Patten; Caesar; Jackie's Boyfriend).

Songs: Slip Away; Talk, Talk, Talk; Ain't Marryin' Nobody; If You Know What's Good for You; First Born; Woman Child; Big City Dance; Sister Love; Remember Caesar; Superwoman; Look at Me; I Been Up in Hell; Thank You Lord; Remember; Celebration; The Prodigal Has Returned.

Micki Grant, author of *Don't Bother Me, I Can't Cope,** returned to the world of musical comedy with *The Prodigal Sister*, written with J. E. Franklin. First produced by the New Federal Theatre,* *The Prodigal Sister* soon moved to the Theatre de Lys. Grant and Franklin modernized the biblical tale of the prodigal son and changed the sex. Here, Jackie (Paula Desmond), a high school girl, becomes pregnant and leaves for the city. She encounters disaster, but she eventually returns home to her family's love and forgiveness. The reviews praised the "talented and charming cast," the authors, and the director, Shauneille Perry, but *The Prodigal Sister* had only a brief run.

**THE PRODIGAL SON** (Greenwich Mews, May 20, 1965, 141 p.). Producers: Beverly Landau, Stella Holt, Henrietta Stein, and the Greenwich Players, Inc. Author: Langston Hughes.* Director: Vinnette Carroll.*

Cast: Philip A. Stamps (The Prodigal Son), Dorothy Drake (Sister Lord), Robert Pinkston (Brother Callius), Joseph Attles (Exhorter), Ronald Platts (Father), Clayton Corbin (Minister), Jeannette Hodge (Mother), Glory Van Scott (Jezebel), Marion Franklin (Brother John), Johnny Harris (Brother Alex), Jean Perry (Sister Anna), Sylvia Terry (Sister Waddy), Teddy Williams (Brother Jacob), Jeffrey Wilson (Brother Joseph), Hattie Winston* (Sister Fatima).

Songs: How Am I Gonna Make It?; You Better Take Time to Pray (Langston Hughes); Rock with Jezebel (Billy Eaton-Hughes); Devil, Take Yourself Away (Jobe Huntley-Hughes); and the following traditional songs: Wade in the Water; Take the Lord God; I Look Down the Road; Feast at the Welcome Table; When I Touch His Garment; Fly Away (Wings); I'm Waiting for the Child; Done Found My Lost Sheep; Come on in the House.

Langston Hughes's *The Prodigal Son* opened on a double bill with Brecht's *The Exception and the Rule.* This "gospel song-play" of the biblical story received rhapsodic reviews from the critics. Edith Oliver of the *New Yorker* proclaimed it an "exciting and stirring production" and hoped it would "run forever." *The Prodigal Son* combined new songs by Hughes with traditional gospel music which flooded the theatre with "elation," according to *The New York Times.* Special notice went to Dorothy Drake, Glory Van Scott, and Philip A. Stamps as the Prodigal Son.

**PURLIE** (Broadway, March 15, 1970, 688 p.). Producer and director: Philip Rose. Book: Ossie Davis,* Philip Rose, and Peter Udell. Composer: Gary Geld. Lyricist: Peter Udell.

Cast: Cleavon Little* (Purlie), Melba Moore* (Lutiebelle), Linda Hopkins* (Church Soloist), Novella Nelson* (Missy), Sherman Hemsley (Gitlow), C. David Colson (Charlie), Helen Martin (Idella), John Heffernan (Ol' Cap'n).

Songs: Walk Him Up the Stairs; New Fangled Preacher Man; Skinnin' a Cat; Purlie; The Harder They Fall; Charlie's Songs; Big Fish, Little Fish; I Got Love; Great White Father; Down Home; First Thing Monday Mornin'; He Can Do It; The World Is Comin' to a Start.

This musical version of Ossie Davis's 1961 play, *Purlie Victorious,** brought several awards to its leads Cleavon Little and Melba Moore. Both won Tony and Drama Desk Awards for their performances, and both topped *Variety*'s Drama Critics Poll. Moore also won a Theatre World Award, and Little a New York Drama Critics Circle Award. Clive Barnes of *The New York Times* also praised the stars: "She is a delight. Miss Moore has an irresistibly knowing innocence, the timing of a superb comedian, and the God-given ability to walk straight into an audience's heart and hang around there. Cleavon Little's Purlie is a strutting, gutsy, guy. . . . His voice was pleasant, his acting and presence both splendid, and he handled the gospel-speaking with a virtuoso verve." The strength of *Purlie* was based on the retention of most of Davis's earlier version, the new music and excellent choreography of Louis Johnson, as well as the performances of the leads plus Sherman Hemsley, Linda Hopkins, and Novella Nelson.

**PURLIE VICTORIOUS** (Cort, September 28, 1961, 261 p.). Producer: Philip Rose. Author: Ossie Davis.* Director: Howard Da Silva.

Cast: Ossie Davis (Purlie Victorious Judson), Ruby Dee* (Lutiebelle), Helen Martin (Missy Judson), Godfrey Cambridge (Gitlow Judson), Alan Alda (Charley Cotchipee), Beah Richards* (Idella Landy), Sorrell Booke (Ol' Cap'n Cotchipee), Ci Herzog (The Sheriff), Roger C. Carmel (Deputy).

Ossie Davis claimed that the inspiration for *Purlie Victorious* was, strange as it may seem, *The World of Sholom Aleichem* (1953), directed by Howard Da Silva. Davis, then a fledgling stage manager, admired the vivid characters with "their gaiety, their fecklessness, the unembarrassed exhibition of their frailties, and their unity under terrible, sometimes terrifying, conditions." *Purlie Victorious* provided similar portrayals in a satire of race relations in modern America. [*The New York Times*, September 24, 1961]

Purlie (Davis) returns home to the plantation with the hope of buying an old house for conversion to a church. He had hoped to receive $500 from his cousin's inheritance, but she unfortunately died before receiving the money. Purlie finds a look-alike, Lutiebelle Gussie Mae Jenkins (Ruby Dee), whose name is "an insult to the Negro people," in order to pry the money from staunch segregationist Ol' Cap'n Cotchipee (Sorrell Booke). With the help of the Cap'n's son (Alan Alda), Purlie obtains the money for the church. Critics enjoyed Davis's playful treatment of stereotypes of both blacks and whites. Howard Taubman, writing in *The New York Times*, admired Davis's humor as well as his message: "While *Purlie Victorious* keeps you laughing, chuckling, and guffawing, it unrelentingly forces you to feel how it is to inhabit a dark skin in a hostile, or at best, grudgingly benevolent world."

*Purlie Victorious* was later filmed as *Gone Are the Days!* (1963) with limited success, but Davis's play found a new life in a musical version, *Purlie,** in 1970.

**PUT AND TAKE** (Town Hall, August 23, 1921, 34 p.). Producer: McCormick Amusement Company. Author and director: Irvin C. Miller. Songs: Spencer Williams, Tim Brymm, and Perry Bradford.

Cast: Irvin C. Miller, Hamtree Harrington, Earl Dancer, Bernie Barber, Andrew Tribble, Cora Green, Mildred Smallwood, Emmett Anthony, Fred La Joy, Florence Parham, Hobart Shand, Lillian Goodner, Mae Crowder, Violet Branch, Virgie Cousins, Essie Worth, Joe Peterson, George Braxton, Al Pizarro, John Roecoe, Julius Foxworth, Roscoe Wickham, Chappell and Stinette, Percy William, Walter Richardson, Claude Lawson, Arthur Ford, Maxie.

Songs: Wedding Day in Georgia; Broadway Down in Dixieland (Bernie Barber); Stop and Rest Awhile; Georgia Rose; Dog; Wedding Bells; June Love; Snagem Blues; Beedle 'Em Boo; Put and Take; Creole Gal; Chocolate Brown; Yodle; Old Time Blues.

Although *Put and Take* opened three months after *Shuffle Along*,* it had actually been on tour for almost a year. Known initially as *Broadway Rastus*, it had appeared in over forty-five cities, from New Orleans to Chicago.

*Put and Take* avoided the stereotypes of the minstrel stage and, as a result, received hostile comments from the critics. *Variety* explained it bluntly: "There is too much effort to be dressed up and dignified. . . . Colored performers cannot vie with white ones, and colored producers cannot play within an apple's throw of Ziegfeld and try to compete with him. . . . Here the colored folks seem to have set out to show the whites that they're just as white as anybody. They may be as good, but they're different, and, in their entertainment they should remain different, distinct, and indigenous."

Despite a profitable first two weeks, objections were made to the presence of a "colored company" at Town Hall. The show closed on September 23 and did not move to another Broadway house.

# R

**RAISIN** (Forty-sixth Street, October 18, 1973, 847 p.). Producer: Robert Nemiroff. Book: Robert Nemiroff and Charlotte Zaltzberg. Composer: Judd Woldin. Lyricist: Robert Brittan. Director: Donald McKayle.*

Cast: Virginia Capers (Lena Younger), Joe Morton (Walter Lee Younger), Ernestine Jackson (Ruth Younger), Robert Jackson (Joseph Asagai), Deborah Allen (Beneatha Younger), Helen Martin (Mrs. Johnson), Al Perryman (Pusher), Loretta Abbott (Victim), Ralph Carter (Travis Younger),

Elaine Beener (Bar Girl), Ted Ross (Bobo Jones), Walter P. Brown (Willie Harris), Chief Bey (Drummer), Herb Downer (Pastor), Marenda Perry (Pastor's Wife), Richard Sanders (Karl Lindner).

Songs: Man Say; Whose Little Angry Man; Runnin' to Meet the Man; A Whole Lotta Sunlight; Booze; Alaiyo; African Dance; Sweet Time; You Done Right; Same Old Color Scheme; He Came Down This Morning; It's a Deal; Sidewalk Tree; Not Anymore; Measure the Valleys.

*Raisin*, a musical based on Lorraine Hansberry's* *A Raisin in the Sun** (1959), swept the awards for the 1973-1974 season. It won a Tony for the best musical of the year, and Virginia Capers received a similar honor for her performance as Lena Younger. The Theatre World Awards picked up the slack, providing honors for Joe Morton, Ralph Carter, and Ernestine Jackson.

Clive Barnes of *The New York Times* found *Raisin* "one of those unusual musicals that should not only delight people who love musicals, but might well also delight people who don't." One of the strengths of *Raisin*, according to Barnes, was that it retained the best of Hansberry's earlier play as well as adding excellent staging and performances. As a result, it became "a show with a heartbeat very much of its own."

**A RAISIN IN THE SUN** (Ethel Barrymore, March 11, 1959, 530 p.). Producers: Philip Rose and David J. Cogan. Author: Lorraine Hansberry.* Director: Lloyd Richards.*

Cast: Ruby Dee* (Ruth Younger), Glynn Turman (Travis Younger), Sidney Poitier* (Walter Lee Younger), Diana Sands* (Beneatha Younger), Claudia McNeil* (Lena Younger), Ivan Dixon (Joseph Asagai), Louis Gossett* (George Murchison), Lonne Elder III* (Bobo), John Fiedler (Karl Lindner), and Douglas Turner,* Ed Hall (Moving Men).

Lorraine Hansberry won the Drama Critics Circle Award for the best play of the season against such formidable competition as Tennessee Williams's *Sweet Bird of Youth*, Archibald Macleish's *J.B.*, and Eugene O'Neill's *A Touch of the Poet*. The twenty-eight-year-old playwright was the first black to win this honor.

The title of Hansberry's play is derived from a Langston Hughes* poem ("What happens to a dream deferred/Does it dry up/Like a raisin in the sun?"). The deferred dream is Lena Younger's (Claudia McNeil) desire to move her family out of Chicago's slums to a small house in the suburbs. A $10,000 life insurance policy gives Lena the opportunity, despite the objections of son Walter (Sidney Poitier) who wishes to open his own business. A representative of the new neighborhood visits the Youngers and tries to bribe them not to move into the all-white neighborhood. Walter orders him out of the apartment. Soon afterwards, the doorbell rings, and Walter discovers that his partner has absconded with the $10,000 he was supposed to put into the bank. In Act III Walter toys with the idea of accepting the bribe from the neighborhood association, but Lena forbids it.

("Ain't nobody in my family never let nobody pay 'em no money that was a way of telling us we wasn't fit to walk the earth. We ain't never been that poor.") Walter finally agrees with his mother, and once again he tells his suburban friend to leave.

Claudia McNeil and Sidney Poitier received raves for their leading roles, while cast members Diana Sands, Ivan Dixon, Ruby Dee, and Louis Gossett provided able support. *A Raisin in the Sun* returned to Broadway in 1973 as the musical comedy *Raisin.**

**RANG TANG** (Royale, July 12, 1927, 119 p.). Producers: Walker and Kavanaugh. Book: Kaj Gynt. Composer: Ford Dabney. Lyricist: Jo Trent. Directors: Charles Davis, Flournoy Miller,* and Aubrey Lyles.*

Cast: Miller & Lyles, Daniel Haynes, Zaidee Jackson, James Strange, Josephine Hall, Marie Mahood, Inez Draw, Le'etta Revells, George Battles, Evelyn Preer,* Josephine Jackson, Lillian Westmoreland, Mae Barnes, Lavinia Mack, Crawford Jackson, Edward Thompson, Jo Willis, Byron Jones, Gilbert Holland.

Songs: Everybody Shout; Sammy and Topsy; Brown; Pay Me; Sambo's Banjo; Some Day; Come to Africa; Zulu Fifth Avenue; Jungle Rose; Monkey Land; Sweet Evening Breeze; Summer Nights; Tramps of the Desert; Voo Doo; Harlem; Rang Tang.

*Rang Tang* was the third black musical comedy to open in the summer of 1927. *The Evening World* noted this trend and commented, "One or two more Negro revues and we'll rename Broadway 'The Great Black Way.' " The critics welcomed Miller and Lyles's new show, although one critic feared that the cast might "all die of the heat as a result of its superhuman efforts to amuse."

Miller and Lyles utilized old vaudeville routines (as they did in *Shuffle Along**) to construct the plot of *Rang Tang*. Steve and Sam, once again escaping their creditors, flee to Africa in search of treasure. Although their airplane falls into the Atlantic, they manage to reach Africa where they "make love to the Queen of Sheba; meet a savage Zulu tribe; and experience strange interludes in a marriage market." They find a treasure and return to Harlem "in regal fashion."

In addition to Miller and Lyles's comic routines, the *Evening World* praised *Rang Tang*'s melodious score: "Ford Dabney wrote some music which makes the feet crazy to dance. The lyrics by Jo Trent are bright and rhythmical. . . . Among the numbers which go over the strongest are 'Sambo's Banjo,' 'Jungle Rose,' 'Sweet Evening Breeze,' 'Summer Nights,' 'Zulu Fifth Avenue,' and 'Rang Tang,' the latter a new dance number that is certain to be popular in the restaurants and nightclubs."

**A RECENT KILLING** (New Federal, January 26, 1973, 10 p.). Producers: Woodie King* and Dick Williams.* Author: LeRoi Jones* (Imamu Amiri Baraka). Director: Irving Vincent.

Cast: Gary Bolling (Lennie Pearson), Gil Rogers (General Comb), Sharon Devonish (Cynthia), Carl Willis Crudup (T. T. Jackson), Mba Acaz (Sgt. Milton Butler), Robert McLane (Nijinski), John Blanda (Sgt. Clay), Keith Perry (Lt. Pyle), Elisha Ignatoff (Leopold Bloom), Stephen Alan Itkin (Stanley Laffkowitz), Rick Livert (Corporal), Marcella Lowery (Barbara Butler), E. Jaye Tracey, Millie Rudin (Whores), Bruce Thomson (Sebastian Flyte), Obako Adedunyo (Busted Sgt.), A. B. Grant (Black Faggot), Del Willard (Sgt. in Latrine), Ed Wheeler (Prisoner), Alexander Paul (Stockade Lt.), Joseph A. Bosco (Stockade Sgt.).

*A Recent Killing* had been making the rounds since 1964. LeRoi Jones claimed that producers rejected it because of his strong views on black nationalism. A 1968 option by Ray Stark came to naught, and the first production finally appeared in 1973. Jones confessed to having doubts about the play on its premiere, since it was a play about the 1950s written in the 1960s, and, as a result, somewhat dated. Jones compared himself to the lead character Lennie Pearson (Gary Bolling), "a young black airman who wants to be a poet; trying to learn about himself through a totally alien set of references—Joyce, Eliot, Bartok, Wittgenstein, Beethoven." Lennie, a soldier of the Strategic Air Command stationed on a Caribbean island slowly turns from a poet to a fighter as he realizes the true meaning of American life. Harold Clurman, critic for *The Nation*, found *A Recent Killing* "a play of considerable scope, power, and, despite its harshness, sensibility."

**THE RECKONING** (St. Marks, September 4, 1969, 94 p.). Producer: Hooks Productions Inc. Author: Douglas Turner Ward.* Director: Michael A. Schultz.*

Cast: Douglas Turner (Scar), Jeannette DuBois (Baby), Richard Pyatt (News Announcer), Lester Rawlins (Governor), Conrad Fowkes (Son), Louise Stubbs (Missy), Joseph Attles (Josh).

*The Reckoning*, billed as a "Surreal Southern Fable," presents a confrontation between a pimp and a white southern governor on the eve of a black march on the state capital. Douglas Turner Ward both wrote and starred in this drama, and won praise for his performance as Scar, the pimp. Lester Rawlins, as the George Wallace-like governor, proved an able foil as the all-white (from shoes to hair) representative of southern bigotry.

While Walter Kerr dismissed *The Reckoning* as a "tired play," Larry Neal responded in *The New York Times* that it "is a magical, poetic one." He argued, "The play . . . is absolutely fantastic. And mean, too. This work not only establishes Ward as an excellent playwright, but as an exciting poet as well." [September 14, 1969]

**THE RED MOON** (Majestic, May 3, 1909, 32 p.). Producer: A. J. Wilbur. Composer: J. Rosamond Johnson.* Book, lyrics, and direction: Bob Cole.*

Cast: Bob Cole (Slim Brown), J. Rosamond Johnson (Plunk Green), Ada Overton Walker* (Phoebe Brown), Abbie Mitchell* (Minnehaha), Henry Gant (Bill Gibson), Wesley Jenkins (Bill Armour), Sam Lucas (Bill Webster), Benny Jones (Bill Simmons), Arthur Talbot (John Lowdog), Frank Brown (Red Feather), Harry Watson (Eagle Eye), Sam Lucas (Spread Eagle), Elizabeth Williams (Lucretia Martin), Mollie Dill (Amanda Gibson), Rebecca Delk (Lilly White), Fanny Wise (Truscalina White), Marie Young (Waneta).

Songs: Checkers; Keep on Smilin'; Don't Tell Tales Out of School; Pickinniny Days; Ada; Bleeding Moon; Big Red Shawl; As Long as the World Rolls on; On the Road to Monterey; Wildfire Dance; Red Moon; To-da-lo Two Step; Sambo; Pianologue "Coola-Woo-La"; Run, Billy Possum, Run; Phoebe Brown.

Bob Cole and J. Rosamond Johnson began to write *The Red Moon* while performing in *The Shoo-Fly Regiment.** Billed as a "sensation in red and black," *The Red Moon* combined the folklore of two of America's minorities—blacks and Indians—in a new musical comedy.

The red moon of the title was an omen of bad luck to the blacks in the cast and a call to war for the Indians. Needless to say, this dual meaning led to several plot complications. Minnehaha, half-Indian and half-black, lives with her mother on a Virginia farm. Her delinquent father, Chief Lowdog, decides that he misses his long-lost daughter, so he kidnaps her to his reservation. Slim Brown (Cole) and Plunk Green (Johnson) try to rescue the chief's daughter from her father's clutches. Brown and Green disguise themselves as Indians and depart for the West. After several Indian war dances in the second act, Plunk rescues Minnehaha, and the chief and his wife are reconciled.

The *New York Dramatic Mirror* called *The Red Moon* "brilliant," and the *Mirror* found it "well worth seeing." Johnson's score was consistently praised as "ambitious," with special attention called to the Indian songs "Land of the Setting Sun," "Big Red Shawl," and "I Want to Be an Indian."

**REGGAE** (Biltmore, March 27, 1980, 21 p.). Producers: Michael Butler, Eric Nezhad, and David Cogan. Book: Melvin Van Peebles,* Kendrew Lascelles, and Stafford Harrison. Composers and lyricists: Ras Karbi, Michael Kamen, Kendrew Lascelles, Max Romeo, Randy Bishop, Jackie Mittoo, and Stafford Harrison. Director: Glenda Dickerson.

Cast: Calvin Lockhart (Ras Joseph), Alvin McDuffie (Anancy), Sheryl Lee Ralph (Faith), Philip Michael Thomas (Esau), Obba Babatunde (Rockets), Fran Salisbury (Mrs. Brown), Louise Robinson (Louise), Ras Karbi (Natty), Charles Wisnet (Gorson), Sam Harkness (Binghi Maytal).

Songs: Jamaica Is Waiting (Karbi-Romeo-Kamen); Rise Tafari (Karbi); Farmer (Romeo); Hey Man (Karbi-Kamen); Mash Em Up (Lascelles-Karbi-Mittoo-Kamen); Mrs. Brown (Harrison-Kamen); Everything That Touches

You (Kamen); Mash Ethiopia (Lascelles-Harrison-Karbi-Mittoo-Kamen); Star of Zion (Kamen); Reggae Music Got Soul (Mittoo); Talkin' 'Bout Reggae (Lascelles-Harrison-Kamen-Mittoo); Rise Up Jah-Jah Children (Karbi); No Sinners in Jah Yard (Romeo-Karbi); Banana, Banana, Banana (Karbi-Kamen); Promised Land (Karbi); Rasta Roll Call (Karbi); Ethiopian Pageant (Kamen); Rastafari (Kamen); Roots of the Tree (Lascelles-Karbi); I and I (Lascelles-Romeo); Gotta Take a Chance (Romeo-Kamen); Chase the Devil (Romeo); Now I See It (Lascelles-Bishop).

Michael Butler, producer of the hit rock musical *Hair*, hoped that the popular music of Jamaica would also win over Broadway. While many critics did praise the score, others, including *Variety*, suggested that the producer "throw away the book" and provide a concert. The libretto involved the return of a Jamaican singer to her home after her career begins to soar in the United States. She meets her ex-lover who is now a marijuana farmer, and they get in trouble with local mobsters. They are saved by local Rastafarians who also bring them spiritual enlightenment. Although Calvin Lockhart received praise for his performance as the Rastafarian leader, most other actors were dismissed by the critics. After dismal reviews, *Reggae* swiftly faded from the scene.

**RHAPSODY IN BLACK** (Harris, May 4, 1931, 40 p.). Producer, author, and director: Lew Leslie.

Cast: Ethel Waters,* Valaida, Cecil Mack's Choir, The Berry Bros., Eddie Rector, Blue McAllister, Al Moore.

Songs: Wash Tub Rub-sidy; Till the Real Thing Comes Along; Dance Hall Hostess; Where's My Prince Charming?; Pullman Porter's Lament; You Can't Stop Me from Loving You (Mann Holiner-Alberta Nichols); Harlem Rhumbola; I'm Feeling Blue (Jimmy McHugh-Dorothy Fields); Harlem Interlude (Nat Dorfman); Rhapsody in Blue (George Gershwin); St. Louis Blues (W. C. Handy); Dream of the Chocolate Soldier (Victor Herbert); Rhapsody in Black (Ken Macomber-Pat Carroll); Soul of a Trumpet (Demus Dean); Eli, Eli (Traditional).

After *Blackbirds of 1930** closed abruptly, Lew Leslie lured Ethel Waters to his latest show, *Rhapsody in Black*. When Waters arrived for rehearsals, she discovered that the show had been built around Valaida [Snow], and no new material had been prepared for her. Waters's lawyer suggested a husband-and-wife songwriting team, Mann Holiner and Alberta Nichols, to provide new songs. The composers worked day and night, and even wrote songs as the train headed to the Washington opening. The four songs they prepared for Waters became the hits of the show: "Wash Tub Rub-sidy," "Dance Hall Hostess," "Where's My Prince Charming?" and "You Can't Stop Me from Loving You." For the first time Ethel Waters received a percentage of the gross receipts, which brought her her highest salary ever.

One of the highlights of opening night occurred when Avis Andrews, Eloise Uggams, and Cecil Mack's Choir sang the Yiddish tune "Eli, Eli" to cries of "sacrilege" from the audience. Robert Garland of the *World-Telegram*, after seeing the show a second time, noted that audiences were now taking it "very calmly."

The wide variety of songs impressed the critics. *The New York Times* noted: "What Mr. Leslie has evidently attempted to do is escape the usual clichés of the Negro revue by producing a simple unpretentious show whose entertainment value depends on the persons and material contributing to it. . . . There were no sketches in which a big Negro draws a formidable razor from his pocket and starts after his smaller companion. There was likewise no chorus of tawny Harlem belles specializing in stomping and other abandoned exercises calling for a display of hot feet, and there were no elaborate production effects." The results were electric. As the *Washington Post* commented: "*Rhapsody in Black* blew the theatre roof off with applause."

**RIDE A BLACK HORSE** (St. Marks, May 25, 1971, 32 p.). Producer: Negro Ensemble Company.* Author: John Scott. Director: Douglas Turner Ward.*

Cast: Graham Brown (Carl Blanks), Madison Arnold (Bob), Marilyn Chris (Edie), Adolph Caesar* (Harold), William Countryman (Max), Bill Cobbs (Lloyd), Esther Rolle* (Faye), David Downing* (Junior Bonner), Charles Grant (Alfred), Charles Weldon (Rudy), Deloris Gaskins (Sharon), Barbara Clarke (Sandy), Jay Montgomery (Harley).

John Scott's *Ride a Black Horse* is a symbolic look at a black professor of sociology caught between black and white culture. When Junior Bonner (David Downing), a radical ghetto leader, convinces the sociologist that he has a plan for improving race relations in America, Carl (Graham Brown) agrees to convince his colleagues of its worth. The plan, a one-month takeover of the city by blacks, falls on deaf ears and Carl loses his university post. When Carl announces his failure to his ghetto friends, they strip him and humiliate him. While critics praised the performances and Scott's dialogue, they found the basic premise of the play absurd. As Clive Barnes noted in *The New York Times:* "You can't hear the play for the clash of symbols."

**THE RIDER OF DREAMS** (Garden, April 5, 1917, 18 p.). Producer: Emily Hapgood. Author: Ridgely Torrence. Director: Robert Edmond Jones.

**The Rider of Dreams**

Cast: Blanche Deas (Lucy Sparrow), Joseph Burt (Booker Sparrow), Opal Cooper (Madison Sparrow), Alexander Rogers* (Dr. Williams).

**Granny Maumee**

Cast: Marie Jackson Stuart (Granny Maumee), Fannie Tarkington (Pearl), Blanche Deas (Sapphie).

**Simon the Cyrenian**

Cast: Inez Clough (Procula), Andrew Bishop (Drusus), Lottie Grady (Acté), Theodore Roosevelt Bolin (Battus), John T. Butler (Simon), Alexander Rogers (Pilate), Jesse Shipp (Barabbas), Robert Atkin, Thomas William (Mockers), Frederick Slade (Herald), Jerome Osborne, Jr. (Centurion), Ralph Hernandez (Longius).

James Weldon Johnson, writing in *Black Manhattan* (1930), proclaimed April 5, 1917, to be "the date of the most important single event in the entire history of the Negro in the American theatre. . . . On that date a performance of three dramatic plays was given by the Coloured Players at the Garden Theatre in Madison Square Garden, New York, and the stereotyped traditions regarding the Negro's histrionic limitations were smashed."

These three one-act plays by Ridgely Torrence provided a wide variety of roles for several prominent black actors and actresses: *The Rider of Dreams* presented a comic vision of a get-rich-quick scheme; *Granny Maumee* featured a tale of voodoo and vengeance; and *Simon the Cyrenian* displayed a biblical account of the man who bore Christ's cross. George Jean Nathan singled out Opal Cooper and Inez Clough in his yearly compilation of best performances. Also receiving great praise was J. Rosamond Johnson,* the musical director, who provided orchestral settings of black folk songs for the show.

**THE RIVER NIGER** (Brooks Atkinson, March 27, 1973, 400 p.). Producer: Negro Ensemble Company.* Author: Joseph A. Walker.* Director: Douglas Turner Ward.*

Cast: Douglas Turner Ward (Johnny Williams), Frances Foster* (Grandma Wilhelmina Brown), Graham Brown (Dr. Dudley Stanton), Grenna Whitaker (Ann Vanderguild), Roxie Roker (Mattie Williams), Lennal Wainwright (Chips), Neville Richen (Mo), Saundra McClain (Gail), Charles Weldon (Skeeter), Dean Irby (Al), Les Roberts (Jeff Williams).

*The River Niger*, by Joseph A. Walker, was one of the most important productions of the Negro Ensemble Company. After a regular season run at the St. Marks, the play moved to Broadway's Brooks Atkinson Theatre, where it received accolades from the critics. It also won the Tony Award for best play, and playwright Walker won an Obie, a Dramatists Guild Award, and a Guggenheim Fellowship. The cast remained the same as the original production, with Douglas Turner Ward repeating his directorial duties.

*The New York Times* praised all the actors in the production. Clive Barnes was forced to single out Ward for special praise, proclaiming him "craggy, vulnerable, human, and magnificent." Ward, as Johnny Williams, portrays a Harlem housepainter and poet who is waiting for his son to return from air force duty. Ward received an Obie Award for his depiction of the disillusioned yet optimistic father.

**ROLL, SWEET CHARIOT** (Cort, October 2, 1934, 7 p.). Producer: Margaret Hewes. Author: Paul Green. Incidental Music: Dolphe Martin. Directors: Margaret Hewes, Emjo Basshe, and Stanley Pratt.

Cast: Lionel Monagas* (Ed Uzzell), Rose McClendon* (Sudie Wilson), Frank Wilson* (Levin Farrow), Eleanor Wallace (Quiviene Lockley), Lucius Carter, Jr. (Willie Lockley), Billy Andrews (Zeb Lockley), Dorothea Archie (Milly Wilson), Luoneal Mason (Bantam Wilson), Ralf Coleman (Tom Sterling), Pearl Gaines (Seeny Gray), Philip Carter (Bad Eye Smith), Warren Coleman (John Henry), Fred Miller (Jim Parr), Lillian Norris (Belle Utley), Willard DeCosta (Sport Womack), Lucian Ayers (Dode Wilson), Marguerite Cartwright (Flossie Tucker), John Morrissey (First Guard), Bigelow Sayre (Second Guard).

Paul Green, author of the Pulitzer Prize play *In Abraham's Bosom*,* designed *Roll, Sweet Chariot* as a "symphonic play of the Negro people." Although a study of the disintegration of a black shantytown, *Roll, Sweet Chariot* utilized the town as a metaphor for the modernizing South. While critics found *Roll, Sweet Chariot* of interest, they found Green's ambitious structure of the play confusing. Once again, the cast was praised at the expense of the play. Frank Wilson and Rose McClendon, veterans of *In Abraham's Bosom*, were singled out by most reviewers, but Green's play lasted only a week.

**ROSALEE PRITCHETT.** See PERRY'S MISSION/ROSALEE PRITCHETT.

**ROSEANNE** (Greenwich Village, December 29, 1923, 41 p.). Producer: Mary H. Kirkpatrick. Author: Nan Bagby Stephens. Director: John A. Kirkpatrick.

Cast: Chrystal Herne (Roseanne), Blaine Cordner (Son), Kathleen Comegya (Leola), Murray Bennett (Rodney), John Harrington (Cicero Brown), Marie Taylor (Sis Tempy Snow), Terry L'Engle (Sis Lindy Gray), Irma Caldwell (Winnie Caldwell), Robert Strauss (Alec Gray), Leslie M. Hunt (Dacas Snow), Conway Sawyer (Morninglory Trimble).

Although *Roseanne* was billed as "a drama about colored people by Nan Bagby Stephens," it was actually performed by a cast of white actors in burnt-cork makeup. After tepid reviews, the show was given an all-black cast with Charles Gilpin* (Rev. Cicero Brown) and Rose McClendon* (Roseanne) in the leading roles. Paul Robeson* replaced Gilpin before *Roseanne* ended its brief run.

**RUFUS RASTUS** (American, January 29, 1906, n.a.p.). Producers: Hurtig and Seamon. Book: W. D. Hall. Composers: Ernest Hogan* and Tom Lemonier. Lyricist: Frank Williams. Director: J. Ed Green.

Cast: Ernest Hogan (Rufus Rastus), Carita Day (Selina Giltedge), J. Leubrie Hill (Dr. Fo-Fo), J. F. Morres (John Drake), Anna Cooke Pankey (Sophronia), Harry Fiddler (Hugo), J. Ed Green (Noah Beasley), A. D.

Byrd (Angelica Newcomb), Will Wilkins (Billy B. Dam), Robt. A. Kelley (Rev. Nightline), Alice Mackey (Frederica), Muriel Ringgold (Snowflake), Theo. Pankey (Enoch), Henry Troy (Lazarus Tuttle), Mamie Emerson (Mandy Jones), Harry Gilliam (Samson Strong), Wm. Spicer (Officer), Pauline Hackney (Balmoral), Bill Moore (Floor Manager).

Songs: What We're Supposed to Do; Mammy; My Mobile Mandy; Oh! Wouldn't It Be a Dream; Cockadoodle Doo; Watermelon; Consolation; Is Everybody Happy?; The Isle of Repose; If Peter Was a Colored Man; Good-bye Old Dixie Land; Newsboys' Life; The Hornet and the Bee; Lilly's Wedding Day.

Ernest Hogan ("The Unbleached American") began his career on the minstrel stage and shortly after the turn of the century moved into musical comedy. *Rufus Rastus* was his first Broadway hit, and critics singled out "Oh! Wouldn't It Be a Dream" as the show's best song.

*Rufus Rastus* featured Hogan as an out-of-work actor with a debt of $22 which he must work off at the rate of $2 per week in a second-rate Florida hotel. As the play continues, the debt increases instead of decreases. As Rufus is about to be imprisoned for non-payment of his debt, he inherits $50,000 and is able to marry the girl of his dreams (Carita Day). The *New York Dramatic Mirror* noted that Hogan asked "Is everybody happy?" at the end of the show, and the audience answered him with "hearty applause."

**RUN, LITTLE CHILLUN!** (Lyric, March 1, 1933, 126 p.). Producer: Robert Rockmore. Author: Hall Johnson.* Director: Frank Merlin.

Cast: Edna Thomas (Ella), Olive Ball (Luella Strong), Mattie Shaw (Sister Mattie Fullilove), Bertha Powell (Sister Flossie Lou Little), Ray Yeates (Bartholomew Little), Walter Price (Esau Redd), Rosalie King (Mahalie Ockletree), Pauline Rivers (Judy Ann Hicks), Lulu Hunt (Lulu Jane Hunt), Carolyn Hughes (Susie May Hunt), Esther Hall, Marietta Canty, Jimmie Waters, Henri Wood, Bennie Tattnall, Nell Taylor, Edna Commodore (Children), Edward Broadnax (George W. Jenkins), Milton Lacey (Jeremiah Johnson), Service Bell (Goliath Simpson), Harry Bolden (Rev. Jones), Alston Burleigh (Jim), Fredi Washington* (Sulamai), Harold Sneed (Elder Tongala), Jack Carr (Brother Moses), Olga Burgoyne (Mother Kanda), Waldine Williams (Reba), Ethel Purnello (Sister Mata), James Boxwill (Brother-Lu-Te), Gus Simons (Brother Jo-Ba).

*Run, Little Chillun!*, Hall Johnson's drama of the conflict between the Christian and African religious heritage, managed a healthy run during the worst days of the Depression. Sulamai (Fredi Washington) tempts the Pastor Jones's son Jim (Alston Burleigh) to leave his wife and religion. She introduces Jim to the rituals of the New Day Pilgrims, but he eventually returns to the fold. In the climactic scene, the pregnant Sulamai confronts Jim in the Baptist Church and is struck by lightning as her lover rejects her.

Critics tended to ignore the plot, for the true genius of the evening was the marvelous choral music. Both *Variety* and *Time* suggested that Johnson had written an opera. *Variety* noted: "But when Mr. Johnson . . . reaches the spirituals, he is on familiar ground. Some of them deserve—without the usual equivocation—the adjective superb, and all of them are more than good. Partly they are haunting and wistful, and partly ringing; partly they take their tempo from the old church litanies. And in their singing the voices of men, women, and children are blended perfectly."

**RUNNIN' WILD** (Colonial, October 29, 1923, 213 p.). Producer: George White. Book: Flournoy E. Miller* and Aubrey Lyles.* Composer: James P. Johnson.* Lyricist: Cecil Mack.* Choreography: Lyda Webb.

Cast: Flournoy Miller (Steve Jenkins), Aubrey Lyles (Sam Peck), Ina Duncan (Mandy Little), Revella Hughes (Ethel Hill), Adalade [Adelaide] Hall* (Adalade), C. Wesley Hill (Uncle Mose), Arthur D. Porter (Uncle Amos), Lionel Monagas* (Tom Sharper), George Stephens (Jack Penn), Paul C. Floyd (Detective Wise), Mattie Wilkes (Mrs. Silas Green), Eddie Gray (Willie Live), Tommy Woods (Chief Red Cap), Charles Olden (Head Waiter), Elizabeth Welsh* [Welch] (Ruth Little), J. Wesley Jeffrey (Silas Green), James H.Woodson (Boat Captain), George Stamper (Sam Slocum), Katherine Yarborough (Lucy Lanky), Georgette Harvey* (Angelina Brown).

Songs: Set 'Em Sadie; Open Your Heart; Gingerbrown; Red Caps Cappers; Old Fashion(ed) Love; Snowtime; Charston (Charleston); Roustabouts; Log Cabin Days; Ghost Recitative; Lazy Dance; Pay Day on Levee; Swanee River; Song Birds Quartette; Ghost Ensemble; Juba Dance; Jazz Your Troubles Away.

George White, the young producer of the *Scandals* revues, noted the success of *Shuffle Along** (1921) and decided to capitalize on the new interest in black musical comedies. He lured comedians Flournoy Miller and Aubrey Lyles from the former show with hefty salary hikes and a promise of total control of a new revue, *Shuffle Along of 1923*. Noble Sissle* and Eubie Blake,* composers of the original *Shuffle Along*, claimed title infringement, and the courts agreed. After dismissing the title *George White's Black Scandals*, Miller and Lyles selected *Runnin' Wild* as the title of their new show. Much to Sissle and Blake's dismay, Miller and Lyles lured the most talented members from the *Shuffle Along* company. Paul Floyd, Arthur Porter, C. Wesley Hill, Ina Duncan, Tommy Woods, and Adelaide Hall led the parade of *Shuffle Along* alumni to the new show.

White hired James P. Johnson and Cecil Mack to provide the score for *Runnin' Wild*. It was a first collaboration, although each had contributed songs to earlier Broadway shows. Critics relished the score, and praised "Old Fashion(ed) Love," "Gingerbrown," and "Open Your Heart" as the show's hits. Interestingly, critics initially ignored the classic "Charston," which came to symbolize the mood of the Roaring Twenties as "The Charleston."

Miller and Lyles crafted a loosely structured libretto which allowed them to display their favorite vaudeville routines, such as "Fisticuffs," without the restrictions of a rigid plot. Their comedy skits combined verbal humor, based on extensive use of malapropisms, with physical humor which delighted their audiences. In *Runnin' Wild* Miller and Lyles portray Steve Jenkins and Sam Peck, two petty swindlers who are forced to flee their Jimtown home before the law arrives.

Several critics proclaimed *Runnin' Wild* equal in quality to *Shuffle Along*, while one suggested it was better because of its "faster pace and lavish scenery." After a profitable twenty-seven-week run on Broadway, *Runnin' Wild* continued its success on the road.

# S

**SAFARI 300** (Mayfair, July 12, 1972, 17 p.). Producer: Richie Havens. Book: Tad Truesdale. Director: Hugh Gittens.

Cast: Tad Truesdale, Lari Becham, Ernest Andrews, Joyce Griffin, Holly Hamilton, Onike Lee, Fredi Orange, Andre Robinson, Grenna Whitaker, Dorian Williams.

*Safari 300* may have been a few years ahead of its time. While Broadway welcomed such "cavalcade" shows as *Bubbling Brown Sugar** by 1976, this "300 year musical experience of black culture, song, and dance" was dismissed by both critics and audiences. Act I featured songs of the slavery era, while Act II presented a potpourri of items from minstrel shows, Cotton Club Revues, and even rock music of the 1970s. *Safari 300* disappeared swiftly in the summer of 1972.

**ST. LOUIS WOMAN** (Martin Beck, March 30, 1946, 113 p.). Producer: Edward Gross. Book: Arna Bontemps and Countee Cullen. Composer: Harold Arlen. Lyricist: Johnny Mercer. Director: Rouben Mamoulian.

Cast: Ruby Hill (Della Green), Harold Nicholas (Little Augie), Rex Ingram* (Bigelow Brown), Pearl Bailey* (Butterfly), Juanita Hall* (Leah), Robert Pope (Barfoot), Fayard Nicholas (Barney), June Hawkins (Lila), Louis Sharp (Slim), Elwood Smith (Ragsdale), Merritt Smith (Pembroke), Charles Welch (Jasper), Maude Russell (The Hostess), J. Mardo Brown (Drum Major), Milton J. Williams (Mississippi), Frank Green (Dandy Dave), Joseph Eady (Jackie), Yvonne Coleman (Celestine), Herbert Coleman (Piggie), Lorenzo Fuller (Joshua), Milton Wood (Mr. Hopkins), Creighton Thompson (Preacher), Carrington Lewis (Waiter).

Songs: L'il Augie Is a Natural Man; Any Place I Hang My Hat Is Home; I Feel My Luck Comin' Down; True Love; Legalize My Name; Cake Walk Your Lady; Come Rain or Come Shine; Chinquapin Bush; We Shall Meet to Part, No Never; Lullaby; Sleep Peaceful; Leavin' Time; A Woman's Prerogative; Ridin' on the Moon; Least That's My Opinion; Racin' Form; Come on, L'il Augie.

*St. Louis Woman*, based on the novel *God Sends Sunday* by Arna Bontemps, experienced trouble in its out-of-town tryout. The cast complained to director Rouben Mamoulian about the stereotypes utilized in *St. Louis Woman*. In particular, the cast objected to the bawdiness of the lead character, Della Green, who owns a St. Louis saloon. The character was modified as a result of the complaints, and rehearsals resumed.

*St. Louis Woman* concerns the ill-fated love affair between L'il Augie (Harold Nicholas), a jockey, and Della Green (Ruby Hill). Della shoots her current boyfriend, Bigelow Brown (Rex Ingram), after he beats her. Brown, thinking that Augie has shot him, curses him before he dies. The jinxed Augie now finds his horses losing, and Della fears remaining with him. Augie eventually returns to his winning ways, and after a climactic horse racing scene, he and Della are reunited.

Although Ruby Hill and Harold Nicholas received praise in the leading roles, a secondary performer, Pearl Bailey, won raves for her rendition of the two show-stoppers, "Legalize My Name" and "A Woman's Prerogative."

**SAMBO** (Public, December 12, 1969, 37 p.). Producer: Joseph Papp and the New York Shakespeare Festival. Book and lyrics: Ron Steward. Composers: Ron Steward and Neal Tate. Director: Gerald Freeman.

Cast: Ron Steward (Sambo), Gerri Dean (Untogether Cinderella), Janice Lynne Montgomery (Miss Sally Muffat), Kenneth Carr (Little Boy Blue), George Turner (Jack Horney), Hattie Winston* (Bo Peep), Camille Yarborough, Rob Barnes, Jenny O'Hara, Robert La Tourneaux, Sid Marshall, Henry Baker (Tigers).

Songs: Sing a Song of Sambo; Hey Boy; I Am Child; Young Enough to Dream; Mama Always Said; Baddest Mammyjammy; Sambo Was a Bad Boy; Pretty Flower; I Could Dig You; Do You Care Too Much?; Be Black; Let's Go Down; Astrology; The Eternal Virgin; Boy Blue; The Piscean; Aries; Untogether Cinderella; Peace Love and Good Damn; Come on Home; Black Man; Get an Education; Ask and You Shall Receive; Son of Africa.

*Sambo*, billed as a "black opera with white spots," received mixed reviews. Howard Thompson, critic for *The New York Times*, praised Ron Steward's "marvelous" score: "Vibrant, pulsating, and real, with inventive melodies intricately developed—but never lost—and founded on sound musical knowledge." Larry Neal, however, found this show "stale Papp, with diluted black sound and frail choreography." [*The New York Times*, January 11, 1970] The New York Shakespeare Festival production moved from Lincoln Center to a successful tour of the city's parks and neighborhoods at the end of its run.

**SAVAGE RHYTHM** (John Golden, December 31, 1931, 12 p.). Producer: John Golden. Authors: Harry Hamilton and Norman Foster. Director: Robert Burton.

Cast: Georgette Harvey* and Mamie Cartier (Conjur-Women), Vivian [Vivienne] Baber (Star), Juano Hernandez* (Roustabout), Ernest R. Whitman (Sweetback), Inez Clough (Sweetback's Wife), Venezuela Jones (Waitress), Joe Sobers, Raymond Bishop (Grandchildren), Olive Wanamaker (Flirt), John Robinson (Boy Neighbor), J. W. Mobley (Parson), Al F. Watts (Barbecue Man), James Daniels (Fighting Boy), Alvin Childress (Another), Fred Miller (Old Church Man).

After the success of *The Green Pastures*,* white authors continued to copy the earlier hit with its emphasis on black myth and religion. The authors explained in the program: "Here certain magic rites, which are not considered voodooistic, persist and are believed to be a part of the Christian religion. Superstitions are accepted as dogma and self-hypnosis is believed to be a manifestation of God's grace."

*Savage Rhythm* is a tale of murder and vengeance. When a local woman is killed, a conjur-woman is called to find the murderer. She decides that the "shiftless, drunken Sweetback" (Ernest R. Whitman) is the cause of the crime, even though he did not wield the knife. He tries to resist his fate, but the townspeople chase him into the poisonous swamp.

While *The New York Times* dismissed the play as "virtually themeless," critic Brooks Atkinson praised the cast: "Among the dark-skinned players, there are several interesting performers. Georgette Harvey has a sort of resigned good-humored patience as the mother of a scrambled family. Venezuela Jones is as picturesque as her name . . . and Vivian (Vivienne) Baber makes the Harlem singer becomingly torrid. As a village swain, Juano Hernandez has an engaging frankness and Ernest R. Whitman is flaring and swagger as the village swell."

**A SEASON TO UNRAVEL** (St. Marks, January 24, 1979, 15 p.). Producer: Negro Ensemble Company.* Author: Alexis De Veaux. Director: Glenda Dickerson.

Cast: Olivia Williams (Erzula), Barbara Montgomery* (Bandit), Michele Shay (Cortez), L. Scott Caldwell (Aphrodite), Graham Brown (Her Father), Adolph Caesar* (Garrison).

*A Season to Unravel* must have been a difficult play for Glenda Dickerson to direct since the entire play takes place in the mind of the heroine Erzula (Olivia Williams), a psychologist. Critics dismissed the play as "tiresome" and "pretentious," but *The New York Times* had praise for Barbara Montgomery's performance as "Bandit," one of Erzula's alter egos.

**THE SECOND COMIN'** (Provincetown, December 8, 1931, 8 p.). Producer: Jerome H. Wallace. Author: George Bryant. Director: William Sunderman.

Cast: Irving Hopkins (Wilbur), A. B. Comathiere* (Nicodemus), Enid Raphael (Glory), Lillian Butler (Helen), Ruth Peterson (Elaine), Gordon Fallows (Dr. Evans), Alice Ramsey (Manny), Hayes Pryor (Sam), Lloyd Russell (Old Joe), Maggie Elliott (Fanny), Anis Davis (Susie).

White dramatist George Bryant described his play, *The Second Comin'*, as an attempt to "present an authentic study of the emotional stages of the Negro as they are expressed in their search for religion." It involves Reverend Wilbur, a white preacher, who attempts to bring religion to the Deep South. He endeavors to convince a doubter, Nicodemus (A. B. Comathiere), of his sincerity, but he fails. Wilbur then hypnotizes and rapes Nicodemus's girlfriend, and convinces her that she will give birth to a black Jesus. The baby is white, and Nicodemus discovers the ruse. Before the climactic fight begins, Wilbur dies of a heart attack as the curtain falls. Brooks Atkinson of *The New York Times* found this "a weird brew," but praised A. B. Comathiere for giving every scene in which he appeared "a solid structure."

**SET MY PEOPLE FREE** (Hudson, November 3, 1948, 36 p.). Producer: Theatre Guild. Author: Dorothy Heyward. Director: Martin Ritt.

Cast: Canada Lee* (George, Head Slave), Juano Hernandez* (Denmark), Mildred Joanne Smith (Rose), Blaine Cordner (Captain Wilson), Marion Scanlon (Phyllis), Gail Gladstone (Eliza), Leigh Whipper* (Gullah Jack), Somer Alberg (Trader Henri), Frank Wilson* (Morris Brown), Tyler Carpenter (Patrolman), Bertha T. Powell (Mauma), Alonzo Bosan (Pompey), Edith Atuka-Reid (Tina), William Warfield (Aneas), William McDaniel (Pharaoh), Wanza L. King (Benbow), Fredye Marshall (Rachel), Merritt Smith (Adam), Theodore Hines (Cuppy), Harry Bolden (Belleisle), Louis Sharp (Lot), George Dosher (Jemmy), Musa Williams (Sinah), Urylee Leonardos (Blanche), Earl Sydnor (Peter Piyas), Thomas Anderson (Jesse Blackwood), Earl Jones (Ned Bennett), William Marshall (Rolla Bennett), Charles McRae (Monday Gell), John Bouie (Perault Prioleau), Eric Burroughs (Mingo Harth), Harold Des Verney (Blind Philip), Richard Silver (Frank Ferguson), Samuel Brown, Moses Mianns (Drummers).

Dorothy Heyward and the Theatre Guild returned to the successful terrain of *Porgy and Bess** with *Set My People Free* and received mixed results. This sprawling historical drama revived the Denmark Vesey slave revolt in Charleston, South Carolina. The play came alive in the scenes in which Denmark (Juano Hernandez) and George (Canada Lee), a house slave, debate the merits of freedom, but Heyward's attempt to display the entire historical event onstage often slowed the proceedings. *Billboard* compared the play to a "pageant."

Nevertheless, *Billboard* praised the entire cast for their performances.

Juano Hernandez, who had triumphed recently in *Strange Fruit* (1945), played the role of Vesey in a "remarkable" fashion, and Canada Lee, who portrayed the slave who betrayed the rebellion, was alternately praised as "masterly" and "brilliant." The minor roles were also "beautifully cast," featuring such veterans as Frank Wilson of *Porgy** fame and Leigh Whipper.

**SHAKESPEARE IN HARLEM** (Forty-first Street, February 9, 1960, 32 p.). Producers: Robert Glenn and Howard Gottfried. Director: Robert Glenn.

**Shakespeare in Harlem.** Author: Langston Hughes.*

Cast: Jay Riley (Narrator), John McCurry (Blues Man; Preacher), Alma Hubbard (Alberta K. Johnson), Ted Butler (Old Man), Calden Marsh (Young Man), Frank Glass (Cat; Killer Boy), Richard Ward (Sick Man; Bartender), Isabell Sanford (Girl in Bar), Royce Wallace (Chippie).

**God's Trombones.** Authors: Adapted from James Weldon Johnson's *God's Trombones* by Robert Glenn.

Cast: Frederick O'Neal* (The Preacher), Ted Butler (The Creation), Richard Ward (Noah and the Ark), Jay Riley, Frank Glass, Royce Wallace (The Prodigal Son), Ted Butler, John McCurry, Isabell Sanford (Let My People Go), Ted Butler (The Judgment).

*Shakespeare in Harlem*, originally presented in an ANTA matinee series, moved to the Forty-first Street Theatre for a brief run. Robert Glenn's adaptation of Langston Hughes's poems provided a glimpse of life in Harlem. These vignettes included an older man pondering the problems of migrating to Harlem from the South; a college student wondering how to convey his ideas to his white instructor; and a madam explaining how she started her illegal business. Brooks Atkinson heartily praised this endeavor in *The New York Times*: ". . . the delicacy of feeling it discloses, the idiomatic music of the times, and the immaculate taste of the performance endow it with thoughtful beauty."

*God's Trombones*, a musical version of James Weldon Johnson's book, concluded the evening, garnering raves for Frederick O'Neal as "The Preacher." This was the less successful half of the show, but Vinnette Carroll* brought Johnson's book to life once again in 1963 as *Trumpets of the Lord.**

**SHOES.** See CONTRIBUTIONS.

**THE SHOO-FLY REGIMENT** (Bijou, August 6, 1907, 15 p.). Book: Bob Cole.* Composers: Bob Cole, J. Rosamond Johnson,* and James Weldon Johnson.*

Cast: Bob Cole (Hunter Wilson), J. Rosamond Johnson (Edward Jackson), Arthur Talbot (Professor Maxwell), Frank De Lyons (Williamson), Nettie Glenn (Virginia), Henry Gant (Uncle July Jackson), Elizabeth

Williams (Aunt Phebe Jackson), Fannie Wise (Rose Maxwell), Andrew Tribble (Ophelia), J. T. Porter (Mailman), Sam Lucas (Bro. Doolittle), Wesley Jenkins (Bro. Doless), Mollie Dill (Dilsey Lumpkins), Arthur Ray (Napoleon Bonaparte Lumpkins; Filipino Spy), Anna Cook (Martha Jones), Mamie Butler (Truscolina), Theo. Pankey (Lieutenant Dixon), Wm. Phelps (Orderly).

Songs: I Think an Awful Lot of You; Won't You Be My Little Brown Bear?; On the Gay Luneta; De Bo'rd of Education; Floating Down the Nile; The Ghost of Deacon Brown; If Adam Hadn't Seen the Apple Tree; I'll Always Love Old Dixie; Who Do You Love?; Run, Brudder Rabbit, Run; There's Always Something Wrong.

The songwriting team of Bob Cole, James Weldon Johnson, and J. Rosamond Johnson initially gained fame by supplying songs for others' Broadway shows, such as *Sally in Our Alley* (1902) and *Humpty Dumpty* (1904). In 1907, the three writers began work on an all-black musical comedy, *The Shoo-Fly Regiment.* James joined the consular service before the show's premiere, and Cole and J. Rosamond Johnson starred in their latest effort.

*The Shoo-Fly Regiment* concerned Hunter Wilson, a young graduate of Tuskegee Institute, who was about to become a teacher. The Spanish-American War erupts, and Hunter goes to war before he can begin his professorial duties. While his friends and neighbors are pleased by his patriotic zeal, his sweetheart feels he should remain at home. Nevertheless, Hunter enlists and becomes a hero in the Philippine campaign. He returns home and marries his girlfriend as the curtain falls.

Cole and Johnson won praise for their performances as well as for their "jingling catchy songs." The *New York Dramatic Mirror* singled out "There's Always Something Wrong," "If Adam Hadn't Seen the Apple Tree," and "Won't You Be My Little Brown Bear?" as probable hits.

**SHUFFLE ALONG** (Sixty-third Street Music Hall, May 23, 1921, 504 p.). Producer: Shuffle Along Company. Book: Flournoy Miller* and Aubrey Lyles.* Composer: Eubie Blake.* Lyricist: Noble Sissle.* Director: Walter Brooks.

Cast: Eubie Blake (At the Piano), Flournoy Miller (Steve Jenkins), Aubrey Lyles (Sam Peck), Noble Sissle (Tom Sharper), Paul Floyd (Jim Williams), Lottie Gee (Jessie Williams), Gertrude Saunders (Ruth Little), Roger Matthews (Harry Walton), Richard Cooper, Arthur Porter, Arthur Woodson, Snippy Mason (Board of Aldermen), "Onion" Jeffrey (Grocery Clerk), Mattie Wilkes (Mrs. Sam Peck), Lawrence Deas (Jack Penrose), C. Wesley Hill (Rufus Loose), A. E. Baldwin (Soakum Flat), Billy Williams (Strutt), Charles Davis (Uncle Tom), Bob Williams (Old Black Joe), Ina Duncan (Secretary to the Mayor), Adelaide Hall* (Jazz Jasmine).

Songs: I'm Just Simply Full of Jazz; Love Will Find a Way; Bandana Days; Uncle Tom and Old Black Joe; Honeysuckle Time; Gypsy Blues;

Shuffle Along; I'm Just Wild About Harry; Sing Me to Sleep, Dear Mammy; Everything Reminds Me of You; Syncopation Stenos; If You've Never Been Vamped by a Brownskin, You Haven't Been Vamped at All; Oriental Blues; I'm Craving for That Kind of Love; Baltimore Buzz; African Dip.

When *Shuffle Along* opened in the spring of 1921, Broadway had not seen a successful all-black show for almost twelve years. *Shuffle Along* seemed an unlikely candidate for a run. The composer and cast were virtually unknown in New York, and the dilapidated Sixty-Third Street Theatre was unprepared to handle a major musical. After a brief out-of-town try-out, the show arrived in New York $18,000 in debt.

Despite these difficulties, *Shuffle Along* became the surprise hit of the season. Composer Eubie Blake and lyricist Noble Sissle produced an outstanding score that delighted critics and audiences with its modern tempos. The cast of unknowns was quicky catapulted to stardom. Leads Flournoy Miller and Aubrey Lyles, who also wrote the libretto, appeared on Broadway almost every season throughout the 1920s. Even members of the replacement cast (Florence Mills*) and the chorus (Josephine Baker, Paul Robeson,* and Adelaide Hall) found *Shuffle Along* the first step to international stardom.

Critics responded warmly to the libretto of *Shuffle Along*. Writers Miller and Lyles revived their stock characters Steve Jenkins and Sam Peck from their vaudeville act and placed them at the center of the new show. In Act I, Sam and Steve decide to enter Jimtown's mayoralty race with the winner promising to name the other the chief of police. Sam wins with the help of a crooked campaign manager (played by Sissle), and appoints Steve his chief of police. The former allies begin to bicker over the division of the spoils in Jimtown, and a rip-snorting twenty-minute fight sequence erupts in Act II. Meanwhile, a reform candidate, Harry Walton (Roger Matthews), promises to end the corrupt regime of Sam and Steve as the townspeople sing the classic "I'm Just Wild About Harry." Harry wins the next election and the ingenue (Lottie Gee) as well, while Sam and Steve are run out of town.

*Shuffle Along* legitimized the black musical on Broadway. It proved to producers and theatre managers that audiences would pay to see black talent on the Great White Way. As a result of the success of *Shuffle Along*, black musicals swiftly became a Broadway staple.

**SHUFFLE ALONG OF 1933** (Mansfield, December 26, 1932, 17 p.). Producer: Mawin Productions. Book: Flournoy Miller.* Composer: Eubie Blake.* Lyricist: Noble Sissle.* Director: Walter Brooks.

Cast: Noble Sissle (Tom Sharp), Flournoy Miller (Steve Jenkins), Mantan Moreland* (Caesar Jones), Edith Wilson* (Mrs. Jones), Lavada Carter (Edith Wilkes), Marshall Rodgers (Taxi Ben), Louise Williams (A Customer), George McClennon (Dave Coffey), Clarence Robinson (Harry

Walton), Vivienne Baber (Alice Walker), Howard Hill (Sam), Taps Miller (Farmer Taps), Joe Willis (Sheriff), James Arnold (Summons Server), Catherine Brooks (Stenographer), Herman Reed (Office Boy), Ida Brown (Telephone Girl), Romaine Johns (Shipping Clerk), Adolph Henderson (Waiter), and Eubie Blake (At the Piano).

Songs: Labor Day Parade; Sing and Dance Your Troubles Away; You Don't Look for Love; Bandanna Ways; Keep Your Chin Up; Breakin' 'Em In; In the Land of Sunny Sunflowers; Sugar Babe; Chickens Come Home to Roost; Waiting for the Whistle to Blow; Saturday Afternoon; Here 'Tis; Lonesome Man; Falling in Love; We're a Couple of Salesmen; Dusting Around; Arabian Moon; If It's Any News to You; You've Got to Have Koo Wah; "Reminiscing" (medley by Sissle and Blake).

Noble Sissle, Eubie Blake, and Flournoy Miller attempted to regain their former triumphs with a new version of *Shuffle Along*.* Absent from the pantheon was the name of Aubrey Lyles, who died of tuberculosis in 1932. Although *Shuffle Along of 1933* received mixed to favorable notices, it had the misfortune to open during the darkest days of the depression. It expired quickly, as did all the new musicals of that season.

Flournoy Miller, teamed with his new partner Mantan Moreland, returned the *Shuffle Along* troupe to Jimtown, where he owned a molasses factory. The high spots of the show, however, tended to ignore the libretto. Robert Garland of the *World-Telegram* praised Noble Sissle for leaving his role of Tom Sharp in order to conduct the orchestra through the "twists and turns" of the "St. Louis Blues." Blake's music presented no new standards, but critics praised "Sing and Dance Your Troubles Away," "Breakin' 'Em In," "Saturday Afternoon" "Here 'Tis," and "Bandanna Ways," with the last-named sung by Edith Wilson.

**SHUFFLE ALONG OF 1952** (Broadway, May 8, 1952, 4 p.). Producers: Irving Gaumont and Grace Rosenfeld. Book: Flournoy Miller* and Paul Gerard Smith. Composer: Eubie Blake.* Lyricist: Noble Sissle.* Directors: George Hale and Paul Gerard Smith.

Cast: Avon Long* (Lt. Jim Crocker), Thelma Carpenter (Cpl. Betty Lee), Flournoy Miller (Cyphus Brown), Hamtree Harrington (Longitude Lane), William Dillard (Bugler), James E. Wall (M/Sgt.), Earl Sydnor (Alexander Popham), William McDaniel (Joseph Gantt), T. S. Krigarin (Frederick Graham), Delores Martin (Lucy Duke), Leslie Scott (Louie Bauche), Napoleon Reed (Harry Gaillard), Laurence Watson (Chaplain), Mabel Lee (Mabel), Henry Sherwood (Fifeto), Louise Woods (Rosa Pasini), Harro Meller (SS Trooper), Urylee Leonardos (Laura Popham), Marie Young (Sgt. Mabel Powers), Noble Sissle, Eubie Blake.

Songs: Falling; City Called Heaven; Bongo-Boola; Swanee Moon; Rhythm of America; Farewell with Love; I'm Just Wild About Harry; Love Will Find a Way; It's the Gown That Makes the Gal That Makes the Guy (lyricist: Joan Javits); Bitten by Love; You Can't Overdo a Good Thing; My Day; Give It Love (Joseph Meyer-Floyd Huddleston).

Noble Sissle and Eubie Blake never managed to duplicate the success of their original *Shuffle Along*.* Most critics dismissed their 1952 effort to update the show. A hasty revision of the script changed the setting from Jimtown to Italy during World War II. Original star Pearl Bailey* left when she saw the new script, and Noble Sissle was injured during rehearsals. The chaos evident on opening night doomed the show, although many critics relished such song-and-dance numbers as "I'm Just Wild About Harry" and "Love Will Find a Way."

Black critic Miles Jefferson of *Phylon* also found the comedy of *Shuffle Along of 1952* in poor taste: "The *Shuffle Along* brand of humor has long since been happily buried—the humor of two shambling comedians murdering the English language and indulging in 'Negroisms' is painfully embarrassing in a much more enlightened 1952." He agreed with Richard Watts, Jr., of the *Post* who argued that "it would have been wiser to let the sleeping dog lie unmolested in the happy dream of its original success."

**THE SIGN IN SIDNEY BRUSTEIN'S WINDOW** (Longacre, October 15, 1964, 101 p.). Producers: Burt C. D'Lugoff, Robert Nemiroff, and J. I. Jahre. Author: Lorraine Hansberry.* Director: Peter Kass.

Cast: Gabriel Dell (Sidney Brustein), Rita Moreno (Iris Brustein), Ben Aliza (Alton Scales), Frank Schofield (Wally O'Hara), John Alderman (David Ragin), Dolph Sweet (Max), Alice Ghostley (Mavis Parodus Bryson), Cynthia O'Neal (Gloria Parodus), Josip Elic (Policeman).

*The Sign in Sidney Brustein's Window* was playwright Lorraine Hansberry's last drama. She died of cancer at age thirty-four shortly after the play opened. The play moved from the black world of the Chicago ghetto of *A Raisin in the Sun** to the interracial world of Greenwich Village in the 1950s and early 1960s. Although the play received some favorable reviews, it faded from the Broadway scene fairly quickly. A 1972 revival with Hal Linden and Zohra Lampert reinforced original opinions of the play. Clive Barnes commented in *The New York Times*: "This is not a particularly profound play, and it is certainly a far from perfect play, but I think a lot of people will find it an entertaining play that is at times even provocative."

**SIMON THE CYRENIAN.** See THE RIDER OF DREAMS.

**SIMPLY HEAVENLY** (Playhouse, August 20, 1957, 62 p.). Producer: Playhouse Heavenly Company. Book and lyrics: Langston Hughes.* Composer: Dave Martin. Director: Joshua Shelley.

Cast: Melvin Stewart (Simple), Claudia McNeil* (Mamie), Wilhelmina Gray (Madam Butler), Stanley Greene (Boyd), Dagmar Craig (Mrs. Caddy;

Nurse), Marilyn Berry (Joyce Lane), Duke Williams (Hopkins), Willie Pritchett (Bar Pianist), Charles A. McRae (Bodiddly), Allegro Kane (Character), John Bouie (Melon), Brownie McGhee (Gitfiddle), Anna English (Zarita), Josephine Woods (Arcie), Charles Harrigan (John Jasper), Maxwell Glanville* (Big Boy; Cop).

Songs: Love Is Simply Heavenly; Let Me Take You for a Ride; Broken String Blues; Did You Ever Hear the Blues?; I'm Gonna Be John Henry; When I'm in a Quiet Mood; Look for the Morning Star; Let's Ball Awhile; The Men in My Life; I'm a Good Old Girl.

*Simply Heavenly* was based on "Simple Takes a Wife" and other "Simple" stories by Langston Hughes. Claudia McNeil, who had just received raves for her performance in *The Crucible*, joined with Melvin Stewart in this musical version of Hughes's stories. Here Simple attempts to raise enough money to obtain a divorce and marry his new love Joyce (Marilyn Berry). The plot line fails to describe the experience of *Simply Heavenly*, as much of the action takes place in Paddy's Bar, where the customers spend considerable time discussing the state of the world. Brooks Atkinson of *The New York Times* led the praise for the show: "Mr. Hughes loves Harlem. He loves the humor, the quarrels, the intrigues, the crises and the native shrewdness that makes life possible from day to day. He has written *Simply Heavenly* like a Harlem man. If it were a tidier show, it would probably be a good deal less enjoyable. It would seem like something that has been improvised out of high spirits for the sake of a good time."

**SINGIN' THE BLUES** (Liberty, September 16, 1931, 45 p.). Producers: Alex Aarons and Vinton Freedley. Author: John McGowan. Director: Bertram Harrison.

Cast: Mantan Moreland* (Knuckles Lincoln), Isabell Washington (Susan Blake), Fredi Washington* (Elise Joyce), Ashley Cooper (Potato-Eyes Johnson), Frank Wilson* (Jim Williams), John Sims (Bad Alley Joe), James Young (Dooley), Joe Byrd (Colored Policeman), Johnny Reid (Rocky), Shirley Jordan (Eddie), Jennie Sammons (Mazie), S. W. Warren (Jay), Jack Carter (Dave Crocker), Estelle Bernier (Edith), Ralph Theodore (Sam Mason), Millard Mitchell (Whitey Henderson), C. C. Gill (Tod), Percy Wade (Sid), Percy Verwayne (Jack Wilson), Maude Russell (Sizzles Brown), James Stark (Officer Frank), Susaye Brown (A Singer), and the Eubie Blake* Orchestra.

Songs: Singin' the Blues; It's the Darndest Thing (Jimmy McHugh-Dorothy Fields).

*Singin' the Blues* combined black melodrama and black musical, and received praise for its treatment of each genre. Yet, when both parts were combined, critics claimed the seams were showing. Jim Williams (Frank Wilson) kills a Chicago policeman and then flees to Harlem. As detectives begin to ask questions in New York City, Jim delays his flight because he has fallen in love. As Williams evades the police, he travels through Harlem's top nightclubs, thus providing the musical background for *Singin' the Blues*. Eubie Blake's Orchestra provided the music for the new Jimmy McHugh and Dorothy Fields songs performed by Isabell Washington, Maude Russell, and Fredi Washington. *The New York Times* found *Singin' the Blues* "picturesque and pungent in the best style of theatrical shows," but the show nevertheless failed to find an audience for a long run.

**SISTER SON/JI.** See BLACK VISIONS.

**THE SIXTEENTH ROUND** (Theatre Four, September 30, 1980, 48 p.). Producer: Negro Ensemble Company.* Author: Samm-Art Williams.* Director: Horacena J. Taylor.

Cast: Paul Benjamin (Jesse), Rosalind Cash* (Marsha), Roscoe Orman (Lemar).

After receiving raves for *Home** (1979), Samm-Art Williams turned to a portrait of a down-and-out fighter in *The Sixteenth Round*. This study of a failed boxer (Paul Benjamin) and his girlfriend (Rosalind Cash), who always wanted to be a ballet dancer, was dismissed by the critics. Despite some moments of interest, Mel Gussow of *The New York Times* found it "an inert play about an inarticulate man."

**THE SLAVE.** See THE TOILET/THE SLAVE.

**SLAVE SHIP** (Theater-in-the-Church, January 13, 1970, 4 p.). Producer: Oliver Rea and the Chelsea Theatre Center. Author: LeRoi Jones (Imamu Amiri Baraka).* Director: Gilbert Moses.*

Cast: Frank Adu (Atowoda; Auctioneer), Gwen D. Anderson (Tawa), Preston Bradley (Akoowa; Preacher), Lee Chamberlin (Iyalosa), Bill Duke (Akano), Jackie Earley (Segilola), Phyllis Espinosa (Adufe), Ralph Espinosa (Olala), Maxine Griffith (Dademi), Garrett Morris (Lalu), Tim Pelt (Salako; Rev. Turner), C. Robert Scott (Sailor), Seret Scott (Noliwe), Marilyn Thomas (Imani), Reeta White (Oyo).

LeRoi Jones's play, *Slave Ship*, divided the critics when it moved from the Brooklyn Academy of Music to Off-Broadway. Clive Barnes in *The New York Times* found it "ugly, militant, and racist," [November 22, 1969] while John Lahr declared it "thrilling" in *The Village Voice*. Clayton Riley, of the *Manhattan Tribune*, responded to Barnes in the *Times* and declared *Slave Ship* a "masterpiece." [November 23, 1969]

The first act of *Slave Ship* presents the voyage of slaves to America. There is little dialogue except shouts and screams in the Yoruban dialect. The second act provides vignettes of slavery in America, with one of the most moving scenes being the slave auction. *Slave Ship* concludes with the beginnings of slave rebellions. Gilbert Moses's direction earned favorable reviews (and an Obie), as did his score (which he composed with Archie Shepp).

**SO NICE, THEY NAMED IT TWICE** (Public, December 26, 1975, 8 p.). Producer: New York Shakespeare Festival. Author: Neil Harris. Director: Bill Lathan.

Cast: Bill Jay (Abe), Veronica Redd (Betty), Dianne Kirksey (Doris), Nick Smith (Dr. Harris), Joanna Featherstone (Mrs. Jones), Nadyne Spratt (Go Go Dancer), Neil Harris (Reggie), J. W. Smith (Gunn), Starletta DuPois (Henrietta), Robbie McCauley (Kitty), Brent Jennings (Larry), Taurean Blacque (Lee), Alfre Woodard (Terry), Allen Ayers (Miji), Hank Ross (Country Bill).

*So Nice, They Named It Twice* refers to the Big Apple, New York, New York, with more than a touch of irony. Neil Harris's play considers the life of a middle-class black family, and the problems of upward social mobility. As Harris compares the family members to junkies and pushers, the social distance between classes begins to fade. Critics praised the performances of Bill Jay as the husband, Veronica Redd as the wife, Dianne Kirksey as the daughter, and especially Alfre Woodard as the mistress. Critics tended to admire the play, but several felt it needed additional work.

**A SOLDIER'S PLAY** (Theatre Four, November 28, 1981, 481 p.). Producer Negro Ensemble Company.* Author: Charles Fuller.* Director: Douglas Turner Ward.*

Cast: Adolph Caesar* (Tech. Sgt. Vernon C. Waters), Peter Friedman (Capt. Charles Taylor), Eugene Lee (Col. Bernard Cobb), Denzel Washington (Pfc. Melvin Peterson), James Pickens, Jr. (Corp. Ellis), Samuel L. Jackson (Pvt. Louis Henson), Steven Jones (Pvt. James Wilkie), Brent Jennings (Pvt. Tony Smalls), Charles Brown (Capt. Richard Davenport), Larry Riley (Pvt. C. J. Memphis), Cotter Smith (Lt. Byrd), Stephen Zettler (Capt. Wilcox).

Charles Fuller's *A Soldier's Play* won the 1981 Pulitzer Prize for Drama and embarked on a lengthy run in the Negro Ensemble Company's new home at Theatre Four. Fuller's play is a courtroom drama which involves the search for the murderer of Tech. Sgt. Vernon Waters (Adolph Caesar), and, indirectly, the search for the meaning of his last words, "They still hate you!" An inquiry at Fort Neal, Louisiana, reveals a multitude of suspects from the rednecks in the nearby town to Waters's own soldiers. The search for the culprit soon becomes secondary to the analysis of black roles in white society.

Frank Rich of *The New York Times* acclaimed the play and its lead actor: "Mr. Caesar is able to make Waters a hateful Queeg one moment and a sympathetic, pitiful wreck the next. It's a fascinating performance, full of contradictions that always leave the audience on edge. As such, it emblemizes Mr. Fuller's play, which tirelessly insists on embracing volatile contradictions because that is the way to arrive at the shattering truth."

**SOMEONE'S COMIN' HUNGRY** (Pocket, March 31, 1969, 16 p.). Producers: Preston Fischer and Bruce W. Paltrow. Authors: McCrea Imbrie and Neil Selden. Director: Burt Brinckerhoff.

Cast: Cleavon Little* (Paul Odum), Jonelle Allen (Tamara Bissy), W. Bendon Terry (James C. Odum), Blythe Danner (Connie Odum), Jane Hoffman (Mrs. Gershon).

*Someone's Comin' Hungry*, by McCrea Imbrie and Neil Selden, was Off-Broadway's second miscegenation drama within the month, and it disappeared as quickly as its predecessor (*The Perfect Party**). While critics praised the authors' sincerity, some found them dealing in stereotypes. While Paul Odum (Cleavon Little) is waiting for his wife (Blythe Danner) to give birth, he has an affair with Tamara (Jonelle Allen), the black woman upstairs. *The New York Times* dismissed the play as "superficial," but credited Cleavon Little for "kicking his stereotyped role into a human being."

**A SON COME HOME.** See THE ELECTRONIC NIGGER AND OTHERS.

**SONG OF THE LUSITANIAN BOGEY** (St. Marks, January 2, 1968, 40 p.). Producer: Negro Ensemble Company.* Author: Peter Weiss. Director: Michael A. Schultz.*

Cast: Rosalind Cash,* Moses Gunn,* David Downing,* Arthur French, William Jay, Judyann Jonsson, Denise Nicholas, Hattie Winston,* Allie Woods.

The Negro Ensemble Company opened its first season with the American premiere of German playwright Peter Weiss's *Song of the Lusitanian Bogey*. Weiss, author of *Marat/Sade* and *The Investigation*, presented a harsh indictment of Portuguese colonial policy in Angola. While some critics found Weiss's play "tedious" and "old-fashioned," several had kind words for the new repertory group. Jack Kroll noted in *Newsweek*: "This first production should be taken as a proclamation, a manifesto of a gallant, sensitive, and open militancy that will seek dramatic form. As such the seeds of something important have been planted."

**SONS OF HAM** (Grand Opera House, March 3, 1902, 8 p.). Producers: Bert Williams* and George Walker.* Book: Jesse Shipp, Bert Williams, and George Walker. Composer: Will Marion Cook.* Lyricist: Alex Rogers.*

Cast: Bert Williams, George Walker, Ada Overton Walker,* Lottie Thompson, Hattie McIntosh, Jesse Shipp.

Songs: My Castle on the Nile; The Phrenologist Coon; Zulu Babe; The Leader of the Ball; Beyond the Gates of Paradise.

Bert Williams and George Walker toured in *Sons of Ham* for two seasons, beginning in September 1900. During this period, the show evolved through improvisation as writer Jesse Shipp remained on hand to copy down the funniest ad-libs. *Sons of Ham* concerned the efforts of Williams and Walker to masquerade as twins in a Colorado mining town in order to inherit a fortune. The masquerade proceeds well until it is learned that the real twins had mastered "acrobatics and gun-juggling" while at school. The fake twins spend much of their time trying to avoid a display of these talents. The real twins arrive in the final act, and Williams and Walker are forced to flee.

**SOPHISTICATED LADIES** (Lunt-Fontanne, March 1, 1981, 767 p.). Producers: Robert S. Berlind, Manheim Fox, Sondra Gilman, Burton Litwin, and Louise Westergaard. Concept: Donald McKayle.* Composer: Duke Ellington.* Director: Michael Smuin.

Cast: Gregory Hines,* Judith Jameson, Hinton Battle, Terri Klausner, P. J. Benjamin, Gregg Burge, Mercedes Ellington, Phyllis Hyman, Priscilla Baskerville.

Songs: I've Got to Be a Rug Cutter (Duke Ellington); Music Is a Woman (Ellington-John Guare); The Mooche (Ellington-Irving Mills); Hit Me with a Hot Note and Watch Me Bounce (Ellington-Don George); Love You Madly (Ellington); It Don't Mean a Thing (Ellington-Mills); Bli-Blip (Ellington-Sid Kuller); Solitude (Ellington-Eddie De Lange-Mills); Don't Get Around Much Anymore (Ellington-Bob Russell); I Let a Song Go Out of My Heart (Ellington-Henry Nemo-Mills-John Redmond); Caravan (Ellington-Juan Tizol-Mills); Something to Live For (Ellington-Billy Strayhorn); Rockin' in Rhythm (Ellington-Mills-Harry Carney); In a Sentimental Mood (Ellington-Manny Kurtz-Mills); I'm Beginning to See the Light (Ellington-George-Johnnie Hodges-Harry James); Satin Doll (Ellington-Strayhorn-Johnny Mercer); Just Squeeze Me (Ellington-Lee Gaines); Dancers in Love; Cotton Tail; Drop Me Off in Harlem (Ellington-Nick Kenny); Echoes of Harlem; I'm a Lucky So-and-So (Ellington-Mack David); Hey Baby (Ellington); Imagine My Frustration (Ellington-Strayhorn-Gerald Wilson); Kinda Dukish; I'm Checking Out Goombye (Ellington-Strayhorn); Do Nothing 'Til You Hear from Me (Ellington-Russell); I Got It Bad and That Ain't Good (Ellington-Paul Francis Webster); Mood Indigo (Ellington-Mills-Albany "Barney" Bigard); Sophisticated Lady (Ellington-Mitchell Parish-Mills); Perdido (Juan Tizol-Ervin Drake-Hans Lengfelder); Fat and Forty (Skeets Tolbert); Take the 'A' Train (Strayhorn).

Duke Ellington never had a hit show on Broadway, and, for a while, it seemed that *Sophisticated Ladies* might continue the trend. After a catastrophic Washington, D.C., tryout, Michael Smuin, co-director of the San Francisco Ballet, was called in to rescue the faltering production. Smuin accomplished the virtually impossible, by turning a potential flop into a smash hit. *Sophisticated Ladies* received rave reviews and began a lengthy run to full houses.

*Sophisticated Ladies* combined the skills of talented dancers (Gregory Hines and Judith Jameson) with the Ellington music. The sumptuous sets and gorgeous costumes provided an elegant setting for the evening's musical cavalcade of Ellington tunes. While the leading cast members received raves, featured actor Hinton Battle won a Tony Award for his distinguished dancing, and Phyllis Hyman received a Theatre World Award.

**THE SOUTHERNERS** (New York, May 23, 1904, 36 p.). Producer and director: George W. Lederer. Composer: Will Marion Cook.* Book and lyrics: Will Mercer and Richard Grant.

Cast: Junie McCree (Brannigan Bey), Albert Hart (Bob Rutledge), William Gould (Le Roy Preston), Eddie Leonard (Dandy Dan), W. Wallace Black (Col. Maximillian Easy), Jos. W. Standish (Judge Budge), Wilmer Bentley (Cyril Osborn), Paul Decker (Phil Fuller), Charles Wentz (Cecil Brown), Theodore Peters (Lewis Middleton), Cecil Somers (Harry Stetson), Wheeler Earl (Sam Blossom), Theodore Peters (Sing Hi), Charles H. Moore (Uncle Mose), Walter Dixon (Aunt Matilda), Elfie Fay (Polly Drayton), Vinie Daly (Parthenia), Reine Davies (Japonica Preston), Louisa Lathrop (Olivia Pemberton), Bertyne Mortimer (Magnolia Preston), Abbie Mitchell* (Mandy Lou), Mildred De Vere (Violet), Mabel Verne (Rose), Irene Cameron (Pansy), Florence Arkell (Lily), Belva Don Kersley (Daisy), Lorayne Osborne (Marguerite), Sallie Loomis (Virginia), Ethel Davies (Florida), Hattie Burde (Louisiana), Edith Girvin (Alabama), Ella Ray (Carolina), Lillian Rice (Orleana), Averta Sanchez (Maryland), Bessie Moulton (Georgia), Violette Pearl (Atlanta).

Songs: As the Sunflower Turns to the Sun; Mandy Lou; Where the Lotus Blossoms Grow; Darktown Barbecue; Allus De Same in Dixie; Daisy Deane; Dandy Dan; Sweet Dreams, Dear One of Thee; Good Evenin'; Julep Song; The Amorous Star (Marie Sutherland).

Will Marion Cook, fresh from his triumph with *Clorindy*, returned to Broadway with *The Southerners*, "a musical study in black and white." An integrated show on Broadway was not unique in 1904, but it often brought fears of trouble. During the previous year, one Broadway management attempted to hire an actual black man to portray a porter, and the entire cast walked out in protest. *The New York Times* critic described the tension on opening night: "When the chorus of real live coons walked in for the cake (walk) last night at the New York Theatre, mingling with the white members of the cast, there were those in the audience who trembled in their seats, as if expecting an . . . explosion. . . . But it presently became evident that the spirit of harmony reigned. The magician was discovered on inquiry to be the Negro composer Will Marion Cook, who all alone had succeeded in harmonizing the racial broth as skillfully as he had harmonized the accompanying score."

Also deserving praise was Abbie Mitchell. While the *New York Dramatic Mirror* despised this musical of life on the old plantation, it raved about Mitchell: "Miss Mitchell won her laurels by singing a quaint, wistful Negro song called 'Mandy Lou' in so sincere a fashion that for the moment the artificiality of the rest of the performance was forgotten and the audience was surprised into genuine feeling. The song was demanded again and again. The singer had actually touched the hearts of Broadway playgoers." This performance propelled Miss Mitchell to a successful acting career that lasted almost fifty years.

**SPELL #7** (Public, July 15, 1979, 175 p.). Producer: Joseph Papp and the New York Shakespeare Festival. Author: Ntozake Shange.* Composers: Butch Morris and David Murray. Director: Oz Scott.

Cast: Larry Marshall (Player #1), Avery Brooks (Player #2), Ellis Williams (Player #3), Dyane Harvey (Player #4), Laurie Carlos (Player #5), Beth Shorter (Player #6), La Tanya Richardson (Player #7), Reyno (Player #8), Mary Alice* (Player #9).

*Spell #7* revived the form of the successful *For Colored Girls Who Have Considered Suicide/When the Rainbow Is Enuf** (1976) in a new setting. Here actors and actresses gather after hours in a show business bar and recite the dramatic poetry that reveals the difficulties of their profession. Later, the themes pass from show business to the problems of the individuals themselves. Although Richard Eder, writing in *The New York Times*, claimed that *Spell #7* was "an uneven work," he added that "it is a talented and often beautiful work, excitingly performed; and there is reason to hope that if it continues to evolve, it will become a remarkable one."

**THE SQUARE ROOT OF SOUL** (De Lys, June 14, 1977, 28 p.). Producer: Negro Ensemble Company.* Conceived by: Adolph Caesar.* Director: Perry Schwartz.

Cast: Adolph Caesar.

*The Square Root of Soul* presented Adolph Caesar's dramatic reading of "forty poems on the black experience in America." These included the works of Langston Hughes,* Gwendolyn Brooks, Joseph A. Walker,* Richard Wright,* and James Weldon Johnson.* Caesar won praise for his efforts, as Richard Eder noted in *The New York Times*: "He can be a good performer, sometimes wry, sometimes harsh, often moving; and he is best when he is not simply reciting the poems, but acting out some character or attitude in them." Nevertheless, most critics found *The Square Root of Soul* lacking as an evening of theatre.

**STEVEDORE** (Civic Repertory, April 18, 1934, 111 p.). Producer: Theatre Union, Inc. Authors: Paul Peters and George Sklar. Directors: Michael Blankfort and Irving Gordon.

Cast: Millicent Green (Florrie), Jack Hartley (Bill Larkin; Mitch), Jack

Daley (Sergeant), Carrington Lewis (Bobo Valentine), Alonzo Fenderson (Rag Williams), Ray Yeates (Angrum), Jack Carter (Lonnie Thompson), (G.] Harry Bolden (Joe Crump), Frank Gabrielson (Steve), Georgette Harvey* (Binnie), Edna Thomas (Ruby Oxley), Al Watts (Sam Oxley), William C. Elkins (Uncle Cato; Mose Venable), Leigh Whipper* (Jim Veal), Rex Ingram* (Blacksnake), Dodson Mitchell (Walcott), Robert Caille (Mike; Pons), Jack Williams (Detective; Marty Fox; Cop), Neill O'Malley (Lem Morris), Frank Gabrielson (Al Regan), Irving Gordon (Charley Freedman), Susie Sutton (Bertha Williams), Gena Brown (Nanny), Arthur Bruce (Sherman).

*Stevedore*, by Paul Peters and George Sklar, is a drama of racial conflict on the docks in a southern port city. Lonnie Thompson (Jack Carter), a black union organizer, is framed in an assault on a white woman because of his attempts to form a longshoreman's union. Peters and Sklar gave their drama realism by basing it on a variety of actual historical episodes concerning black union organization.

The authors received praise for their writing, and the predominantly black cast received rave reviews. Brooks Atkinson of *The New York Times* noted: "The white actors are good . . . but the Negroes give their scenes a robustiousness and an earthiness that are wholly exhilarating. Whether it is the manliness of Jack Carter . . . , or the black brawniness of Rex Ingram as Blacksnake, or the broad-beamed callousness of Georgette Harvey—it is acting with tang and bite and raciness."

**STRING.** See AN EVENING OF ONE ACTS.

**THE STRONG BREED/THE TRIALS OF BROTHER JERO** (Greenwich Mews, November 9, 1967, 115 p.). Producers: Farris-Belgrave Productions and Afolabi Ajayi. Author: Wole Soyinka. Director: Cynthia Belgrave.

**The Strong Breed**

Cast: Harold Scott (Eman), Mary Alice* (Sunma), Edward Luis Espinosa (Ifada), Yvette Hawkins (Sick Girl), James Spruill (Jaguna), Dennis Tate (Orage), Robert Earl Jones (Eman's Father), Willie Woods (Attendant), Lauren Jones (Omae), G. Tito Shaw (Young Eman), Vernon Washington (Tutor), Roger Robinson (Priest).

**The Trials of Brother Jero**

Cast: Harold Scott (Brother Jero), Dennis Tate (Old Prophet), Afolabi Ajayi (Chume), Cynthia Belgrave (Amope), Peggy Kirkpatrick (A Trader Woman), Lauren Jones (Girl Who Passes By), Edward Luis Espinosa (Drummer Boy), Yvonne Warden (Penitent), Roger Robinson (Member of Parliament).

This double bill by Nigerian playwright Wole Soyinka was presented at the Greenwich Mews Theatre with an American cast. Dan Sullivan, of *The*

*New York Times*, praised the evening and proclaimed the author "one of the continent's leading artistic natural resources."

The curtain-raiser, *The Trials of Brother Jero*, provides a comic look at a phony cleric and his gullible flock. The evening's main entry, *The Strong Breed*, offers a parable concerning a young educated Nigerian who is forced to become the "carrier" (ritual scapegoat) for the town where he is serving as a teacher. As he flees from his executioners, visions from his past continue to haunt him. The play achieved an added poignance as author Soyinka had just been arrested by Nigerian authorities. Harold Scott received raves for his performances in both plays, but critics had harsh words for director Belgrave's staging of these works.

**STRUT MISS LIZZIE** (Times Square Theatre, June 19, 1922, 32 p.). Producer: Minsky Brothers. Music and lyrics: Henry Creamer* and Turner Layton.* Director: Henry Creamer.

Cast: Henry Creamer, Turner Layton, Hamtree Harrington, Brevard Burnett, George Harve, James Barrett, James Moore, Alice Brown, Cora Green, Grace Rector, Jean Rountree, Charles Frederick, Henderson and Halliday, Williams and Taylor.

Songs: Dear Old Southland; Buzz Mirandy (Dave Franklin); Darktown Poker Club; Nobody's Gal; My Hometown; Creole Blues; Dixie; Lovesick Blues; In Yama; Crooning; Wyoming Lullaby; 'Way Down Yonder (in New Orleans); Breakin' a Leg; Brother-in-Law Dan; Lonesome Longing Blues; New Orleans; Hoola from Coney Isle; Mandy; I Wana Dance; Fan Tan Fannie; When You Look in the Eyes of a Mule; Four Fo' Me; Jazz Blues; Sweet Angeline.

Following the success of *Shuffle Along*,* several black musical shows opened in the early 1920s. In the first act of *Strut Miss Lizzie*, the hero returns to his southern home. "Have you come home to stay?," asks his mother. "No," says the lad, "I have come to take you back up North with me. . . . This is a colored year on Broadway." *Strut Miss Lizzie*, like the other black musicals of the period, premiered during the dog days of summer, which was the only time theatre managers would take a chance on a black show.

Billed as "Glorifying the Creole Beauty," the show parodied Ziegfeld's slogan "Glorifying the American Girl." Songwriters Henry Creamer and Turner Layton provided the high point of the show by performing a medley of their hits, including "Dear Old Southland," "Lizzie," and "'Way Down Yonder (in New Orleans)."

Despite some favorable reviews, the show immediately encountered financial difficulties. The cast went unpaid, and the court seized the props for nonpayment of debts.

**THE STY OF THE BLIND PIG** (St. Marks, November 16, 1971, 64 p.). Producer: Negro Ensemble Company.* Author: Phillip Hayes Dean.* Director: Shauneille Perry.*

Cast: Clarice Taylor* (Weedy), Moses Gunn* (Blind Jordan), Frances Foster* (Alberta Warren), Adolph Caesar* (Doe).

Playwright Philip Hayes Dean won a Drama Desk Award for the Negro Ensemble Company production of *The Sty of the Blind Pig.* Set in Chicago in the late 1950s, this play examined the life of Alberta Warren (Frances Foster), a thirty-year-old spinster, who lives with her possessive mother. Alberta falls in love with Blind Jordan (Moses Gunn), who was born of a blind father who lived in a house of ill-repute ("a blind pig"). Alberta's mother, however, resents this intruder and forces him to leave her daughter alone. *The Nation* praised the debut of playwright Dean, noting that *The Sty of the Blind Pig* "is honest realism with the kind of clearsighted, compassionate observation that is one of the chief contributions the black theatre has to offer our stage."

**SUGAR HILL** (Forrest, December 25, 1931, 11 p.). Producer: Moveing (sic) Day Company. Book: Charles Tazewell. Composer: James P. Johnson.* Lyricist: Jo Trent. Director: Not designated.

Cast: Flournoy Miller* (Steve Jenkins), Aubrey Lyles* (Sam Peck), Juanita Stinette (Loucinda), Chappy Chapelle (Jasper), Broadway Jones (Gyp Penrose), Carrie Huff (Sister Huff), Margaret Lee (Matilda Small), Albert Chester (Joe), Kay Mason (Mitzie), Edna Moten (Cleo), Tressa Mitchell (Tress), Harrison Blackburn (Uncle Henry), Andrew Copeland (Officer Brown), Ina Duncan (Cleo's Mother), J. Louis Johnson (Parson Johnson).

Songs: Noisy Neighbors; I Love You Honey; Hanging Around Yo' Door; Hot Harlem; Boston; What Have I Done?; Hot Rhythm; Fooling Around with Love; Rumbola; Something's Going to Happen to You; Moving Day.

*Sugar Hill*, "an Epoch of Negro Life in Harlem," received mixed reviews from the critics because it strayed from the standard formula of black musicals of the 1920s. It veered between comedy and drama in what one critic called a combination of *Street Scene*, *Grand Hotel*, and *The Bandwagon.* Miller and Lyles reappeared as Steve Jenkins and Sam Peck, their stock vaudeville characters, in the guise of janitors. Miller drops Lyles down a dumbwaiter shaft, which *The New York Times* found "a lusty piece of horseplay the first two times you see it." Yet, after the typical Miller and Lyles horseplay, the story moves to the tale of a gangster who tries to shoot a rival, but accidentally kills a little girl instead. Thus, song and comedy become interspersed with the attempt to bring the murderer to justice.

**SUGAR-MOUTH SAM DON'T DANCE NO MORE.** See ORRIN/SUGAR-MOUTH SAM DON'T DANCE NO MORE.

**SUMMER OF THE SEVENTEENTH DOLL** (St. Marks, February 20, 1968, 40 p.). Producer: Negro Ensemble Company.* Author: Ray Lawler. Director: Edmund Cambridge.

Cast: Esther Rolle* (Pearl Cunningham), Hattie Winston* (Bubba Ryan), Frances Foster* (Olive Leech), Norman Bush (Barney Ibbot), Moses Gunn* (Roo Webber), Clarice Taylor* (Emma Leech), William Jay (Johnnie Dowd).

Broadway had already seen Australian playwright Ray Lawler's *Summer of the Seventeenth Doll* in 1958. Therefore, it seemed somewhat surprising for the Negro Ensemble Company (NEC) to choose the play for its second production. The NEC moved the play from its Melbourne locale and placed it in the sugar cane fields outside New Orleans with appropriate changes in dialogue. Clive Barnes wrote in *The New York Times* that he enjoyed the NEC version better than the original production. Even at this early date, individual performers began to shine at the NEC, as Moses Gunn and Frances Foster received praise for their leading performances as Roo Webber and Olive Leech.

**SWEET CHARIOT** (Ambassador, October 23, 1930, 3 p.). Producer: Michael Mindlin. Author: Robert Wilder. Director: Jose Ruben.

Cast: Frank Wilson* (Marius Harvey), Fredi Washington* (Lola), Vivian [Vivienne] Baber (Delia), Alex Lovejoy (King), Harrison Blackburn (Futch), Percy Verwayne (Troll), Martin Mallory (Ship's Captain), Clay Cody (Port Officer), Dixie Reid (First Negro), Hubert Browne (Second Negro), Clara Smith (A Worker), Billy Andrews (Peter), Victor Esker (First White Man), George Dryden (Second White Man).

Frank Wilson, star of *In Abraham's Bosom** and *Porgy*,* won praise once again in *Sweet Chariot*. As Marius Harvey (read Marcus Garvey), Wilson portrays an unscrupulous real estate speculator who sells shares in a back-to-Africa scheme for a quick profit. Harvey comes to believe the tales he is spinning for his investors, and he envisions himself as the emperor of an African kingdom. Once everyone arrives in Africa, disillusionment sets in, and all return to America except Harvey and Lola (Fredi Washington), the woman who loves him. While Wilson received the lion's share of the critical praise, Alex Lovejoy and Harrison Blackburn also won acclaim.

**SWING IT** (Adelphi, July 22, 1937, 60 p.). Producer: Variety Theatre Unit of the Federal Theatre Project* of the Works Progress Administration. Composer: Eubie Blake.* Librettists and lyricists: J. Milton Reddie and Cecil Mack.* Directors: Cecil Mack and Jack Mason.

Cast: Edward Frye (Jake Frye), George Booker (Gabby), Genora English

(Mame), Frances Everett (Sadie), James Mordecai (Ginger), Olena Williams (Gladys), Marion Brantley (Ethel), James Boxwill (Jasper), Ernest Mickens (Skadmoose), Blanche Young (Miranda), Walter Crumbley (Nate Smith), Joe Loomis (Bud), Sonny Thompson (Steve), Sherman Dirkson (Bob), Henry Jines (Rusty), James Green (Dusty), Al Young (Chin Chin; Sheriff), Dorothy Turner (Su San), John Fortune (Jamaica Joe), Cora Parks (Mom Brown), Richard Webb (Smoky), Leo Bailey (Sonny), Norman Barksdale (Bill), Lawrence Lomax (Swipes), Frank Jackson (Flatfut), Anita Bush (Amy).

Songs: The Susan Belle; What Do I Want with Love?; It's the Youth in Me; Ain't We Got Love; Old Time Swing; Sons and Daughters of the Sea; Green and Blue; By the Sweat of Your Brow; Captain, Mate, and Crew; Huggin' and Muggin'; Rhythm Is a Racket; Shine (Ford Dabney-Lew Brown-Cecil Mack).

The Federal Theatre Project brought Eubie Blake (*Shuffle Along**) and Cecil Mack (*Runnin' Wild**) back to Broadway for *Swing It*, an evocation of the popular black musicals of the early 1920s. *The New York Times* strongly recommended Blake's latest show: "*Swing It* is a pot-pourri of minstrelsy, singing, dancing, mugging, clowning, spirituals, jazz, swing, tapping, and the carrying of Harlem's throaty torch." *Swing It* marked the Broadway debut of Blake's newest lyricist, Milton Reddie, whom the Broadway veteran later claimed was his most talented partner. "Ain't We Got Love" seemed the critics' choice for the most popular of the new team's efforts.

**THE SWING MIKADO** (Forty-fourth Street, May 1, 1939, 24 p.). Producer: The Marolin Corporation. Based on the Gilbert and Sullivan operetta "The Mikado." Swing arrangements by Charles Levy and Gentry Warden. Director: Harry Minturn.

Cast: Edward Fraction (The Mikado), Maurice Cooper (Nanki-Poo), Lewis White (Pish-Tush), Herman Greene (Ko-Ko), William Franklin (Poo-Bah), Gladys Boucree (Yum-Yum), Frankie Fambro (Pitti-Sing), Mabel Carter (Peep-Bo), Mabel Walker (Katisha).

The Federal Theatre Project* (FTP) staged a black version of *The Mikado* in Chicago and suddenly had a smash hit on its hands. In five months, the show played to 250,000 people at $1.10 top price. The success lured Broadway producers, and Mike Todd decided to stage his own black version of *The Mikado* on Broadway starring Bill Robinson.* In response, the FTP moved its *Swing Mikado* to Broadway three weeks before Todd's *Hot Mikado** opened. Thus, Broadway was treated to two black versions of *The Mikado* in one season. Eleanor Roosevelt attended on opening night, in an action designed to lend continued attention to her protest of the D.A.R. ban on Marian Anderson's appearance in Washington, D.C.

Although *The Swing Mikado* was a success, several critics carped that the show did not "swing" enough. In fact, with few exceptions, the show was played as the D'Oyly Carte troupe might have done it. *The New York Times* felt the show came alive as the Mikado (Edward Fraction) "burst out into a cakewalk" and the Three Little Maids from school "strutted what they had learned there."

**SWINGIN' THE DREAM** (Center, November 29, 1939, 13 p.). Producer and director: Erik Charell. Book: Gilbert Seldes and Erik Charell (based on Shakespeare's "A Midsummer Night's Dream"). Composer: Jimmy Van Heusen. Lyricist: Eddie De Lange.

Cast: Benny Goodman, Louis Armstrong (Bottom, Pyramus), Maxine Sullivan (Titania), Jackie Mabley (Quince), Oscar Polk (Flute), Troy Brown (Snout), Nicodemus (Starveling), Gerald de la Fontaine (Snug), Bill Bailey (Cupid), Juan Hernandez* (Oberon), Herman Green (Majordomo), Joseph Holland (Theodore, Governor of Louisiana), Ruth Ford (Polly), Catheryn Laughlin (Crimson), George LeSoir (Egbert), Eleanor Lynn (Gloria), Thomas Coley (Cornelius), Boyd Crawford (Alexander), Dorothy McGuire (Helena), Alberta Perkins (Peaceful Pearl), Butterfly McQueen (Puck), Vivian, Dorothy, and Etta Dandridge (Pixies), Sunny Payne (Drummer Boy).

Songs: Peace, Brother; There's Gotta Be a Wedding; Swingin' a Dream; Moonland; Love's a Riddle; Darn That Dream; Doing the Saboo; Jumpin' at the Woodside; Pick-a-Rib.

During the previous season, New Yorkers viewed *The Swing Mikado**; now Shakespeare would join the swing parade with a musical version of *A Midsummer Night's Dream*. The play was moved to New Orleans in 1890, with Billy Bottom (Louis Armstrong) and his cast of "simple artisans" leading the revelry.

Despite the presence of an excellent cast, most critics dismissed the new *Dream*. John Chapman of *The News* objected strongly to the show: "For foolish casting, take Louis Armstrong, dressed as a fireman and always carrying his trumpet, as Bottom. Or Maxine Sullivan, with a World's Fair Guide chair as her throne, as Titania. Butterfly McQueen as Puck—carrying a flit gun with which to charm her sleeping victims. . . . Juan Hernandez as Oberon, who slides down a hollow tree on a fireman's pole . . ." *Swingin' the Dream* closed swiftly and helped to cure the swing fever that was sweeping Broadway.

# T

**TABOO** (Sam H. Harris, April 4, 1922, 3 p.). Producer and director: Augustin Duncan. Author: Mary Hoyt Wiborg.

Cast: Marie Stuart (Aunt Angy), Fannie Belle de Knight (Mammy

Dorcas), Master Junior Tiernan (The Child), Margaret Wycherly (Mrs. Gaylord), Henry O'Neill (Charles), Ruth Taylor (Sadie), Alex Rogers* (Tom), Paul L. Robeson* (Jim), Harold Simmelkjaer (Steve), Milton Dees (Lemuel Johnson), F. H. Wilson (Joseph), Harold McGee (Cartwright), Walter Downing (Wheeler), David A. Leonard (Dr. Elder), C. Kamba Simango (The Beze).

While *Goat Alley** (1921) considered life in the Washington ghetto, *Taboo* examined the world of black myth and superstition, a favorite theme of 1920s dramas about blacks. Mary Hoyt Wiborg, the white dramatist, structured her first play to "examine the effect of superstition on colored people." Most of *Taboo* is an extended dream sequence, as Jim, a plantation worker, falls asleep and pictures himself a king in Africa, where "all superstitions began." *Taboo* disappeared in three days, but critics began to take notice of the actor who played Jim, Paul Robeson, who was appearing on Broadway in his first major role.

**TAKE A GIANT STEP** (Lyceum, September 24, 1953, 76 p.). Producers: Lyn Austin and Thomas Noyes. Author: Louis Peterson.* Director: John Stix.

Cast: Louis Gossett* (Spencer Scott), Estelle Hemsley (Grandmother), Fred Vogel (Tony), Bernard Rich (Iggie), Frank Wilson* (Frank), Maxwell Glanville* (Man), Pauline Myers (Violet), Helen Martin (Poppy), Margaret Williams (Rose), Jane White (Carol), Frederick O'Neal* (Lem Scott), Estelle Evans (May Scott), Dorothy Carter (Christine), Robert Brivic (Gussie), Warren Berlinger (Johnny Reynolds), Tarry Green (Bobby Reynolds).

Louis Peterson's autobiographical first play, *Take a Giant Step*, concerns Spencer Scott's (Louis Gossett) growth from adolescence to adulthood in white middle-class America. Spencer's awakening begins when his history teacher explains that all "Negro slaves were stupid" which was the reason they waited for the Northerners to free them during the Civil War. When Spencer objects to this curious brand of history, he is expelled from school. During this "vacation," Spencer is forced to reevaluate his relations with his father (Frederick O'Neal), his grandmother (Estelle Hemsley), his girlfriend (Dorothy Carter) and his white friends.

Critics praised this "original and poignant drama," and honored virtually the entire cast. Brooks Atkinson of *The New York Times* found that Louis Gossett conveyed "the whole range of Spencer's turbulence—manly and boyish at the same time, wild and disciplined, cruel and pitying. It is a composite of opposite impulses."

Despite several glowing reviews, *Take a Giant Step* faded quickly from the Broadway scene. A 1956 Off-Broadway revival, with Bill Gunn* in the leading role, brought a "robust and knowing second hearing" to theatre audiences.

**THE TAKING OF MISS JANIE** (Mitzi E. Newhouse, May 4, 1975, 42 p.). Producers: New York Shakespeare Festival and the Henry Street Settlement's New Federal Theatre.* Author: Ed Bullins.* Director: Gilbert Moses.*

Cast: Kirk Kirksey* (Rick), Hilary Jean Beane (Janie), Adeyemi Lythcott (Monty), Darryl Croxton (Len), Robbie McCauley (Peggy), Lin Shaye (Sharon), Sam McMurray (Lonnie), Dianne Oyama Dixon (Flossy), Robert B. Silver (Mort Silberstein).

*The Taking of Miss Janie* moved from the Henry Street Settlement to Lincoln Center, marking the first collaboration between Joseph Papp's New York Shakespeare Festival and Woodie King, Jr.'s* New Federal Theatre. Ed Bullins had troubles with Lincoln Center with *The Duplex*, but all problems seemed to be forgotten with *Miss Janie*. Clive Barnes of *The New York Times* claimed Bullins wrote "like an angel," and the playwright garnered a New York Drama Critics Circle Award and an Obie for his latest effort. Gilbert Moses, who also directed *The Duplex*, received an Obie as well.

*The Taking of Miss Janie*, a sequel to *The Pig Pen** (1970), continues the adventures of a white California coed (Hilary Jean Beane) and her relationship with a black militant (Kirk Kirksey) during the 1960s. The relationship is finally consummated several years later by rape, with Janie symbolizing "Miss White America."

**TAMBOURINES TO GLORY** (Little, November 23, 1963, 24 p.). Producers: S. & H. Venture and Sydney S. Baron. Composer: Jobe Huntley. Librettist and lyricist: Langston Hughes.* Director: Nikos Psacharopoulos.

Cast: Robert Guillaume* (C. J. Moore), Rosetta LeNoire (Essie Belle Johnson), Louis Gossett* (Buddy Lomax), Micki Grant* (Marietta Johnson), Joseph Attles (Chicken-Crow-for Day), Clara Ward (Birdie Lee), Anna English (Gloria Dawn), Clyde Williams (Youth), Rosalie King (Mattie Morningside), Hilda Simms (Laura Wright Reed), Garwood Perkins (Bartender), Helen Ferguson, Tina Sattin (The Glorietas), Brother John Sellers (Brother Bud), Lynn Hamilton (Deaconess Lucy Mae Hobbs), Rudy Challenger (Windus).

Songs: Nobody Knows the Trouble I Seen; O, What Blessings to Receive; Travelling Slow; The New York Blues; Scat with Me; Moon Outside My Window; As I Go; Just to Be a Flower in the Garden of the Lord; I've Come Back to the Fold; I'm Goin' to Testify; Away from Temptation; Devil, Devil, Take Yourself Away; Yes, Ma'am; Fix Me; Just Trust in Him; God's Got a Way; Let the Church Say 'Amen'; God's Love Can Save; If You've Got a Tambourine; Shake It for the Glory of God.

*Tambourines to Glory* had an extremely long trip to Broadway. When Langston Hughes first became interested in gospel music, he decided to utilize it in a forthcoming play, but no producer would touch it. Hughes rewrote the play as a novel in 1958, and then several producers called and asked Hughes to dramatize it. The Theatre Guild optioned the play, but dropped it when producer Lawrence Langner died. By 1963, Joel Schenker decided to produce it.

*Tambourines* was an oddity in 1963 as one of the few nonintegrated shows in town, and, as a result, several potential backers refused to participate. In addition, Hughes mentioned the fear that white actors might picket the show because there were none in the company. Hughes slyly suggested that there might be a role for a white actor as a chauffeur.

Critics praised the musical elements of *Tambourines to Glory*, but had reservations about the book. The plot concerned the efforts of Essie Belle Johnson (Rosetta LeNoire) and Laura Wright Reed (Hilda Simms) to establish a gospel church in Harlem. The hypocritical Reed is involved in a murder, and, as a result, she changes her ways. *The New York Times* praised Lou Gossett, Rosetta LeNoire, Robert Guillaume, Clara Ward, and Micki Grant, but "wished they had more songs to sing, and less story to tell."

**TERRACES** (St. Marks, April 2, 1974, 8 p.). Producer: Negro Ensemble Company.* Author: Steve Carter.* Director: Frances Foster.*

Cast: First: Leon Morenzie (Manager), Joyce Hanley (Wife-to-Be), Roland Sanchez (Husband-to-Be); Second: Michele Shay (Wife), Robert Christian (Husband); Third: Mary Alice* (Older Wife), Leon Morenzie (Older Husband); Fourth: Joyce Hanley (Fleur), Roland Sanchez (Zan), Mary Alice (Octavia), Michele Shay (Marigold), Robert Christian (Nicky), Leon Morenzie (Man).

Steve Carter's *Terraces* appeared for a week's run upstairs at the St. Marks Playhouse during its "season-within-a-season" of experimental plays. The novelty of *Terraces* was its subject of wealthy blacks living in a "pseudo-posh multi-terraced housing complex, smack in the middle of Harlem, U. S. of A." Carter's harsh disapproval of Harlem's wealthy denizens is revealed in four sketches of varying moods. The tone remains critical, however, as demonstrated by the wealthy couple who celebrate their birthdays by killing a wino, since he brings scandal on the name of blacks everywhere. Clive Barnes of *The New York Times* assessed the evening in a favorable fashion: "[These sketches] reveal a playwright of some originality and style. Mr. Carter writes with a sharp pen, and these dramatic episodes maintain the interest."

**THIS BIRD OF DAWNING SINGETH ALL NIGHT LONG.** See AMERICAN NIGHT CRY.

**THOUGHTS** (De Lys, March 19, 1973, 24 p.). Producers: Arthur Whitelaw, Seth Harrison, and Dallas Alinder. Author and composer: Lamar Alford. Lyricists: Lamar Alford, Megan Terry, and José Tapla. Director: Michael Schultz.*

Cast: Mary Alice,* Barbara Montgomery,* Jean Andalman, Jeffrey Mylett, Howard Porter, Sarallen, E. H. Wright, Martha Flowers, Robin Lamont, Baruk Levi, Bob Molock.

Songs: Opening; Blues Was a Pastime; At the Bottom of Your Heart; Ain't That Something; Accepting the Tolls; One of the Boys; Trying Hard; Separate But Equal; Gone; Jesus Is My Main Man; Bad Whitey; Thoughts; Strange Fruit; I Can Do It to Myself; Walking in Strange and New Places; Music in the Air; Sunshine; Many Men Like You; Roofs; Day Oh Day.

Lamar Alford's *Thoughts* received rave reviews at the Cafe La Mama and moved to Off-Broadway's Theatre De Lys for a short run. This musical features a successful black musician's reminiscences of his childhood in Alabama. Critics praised Alford's clever and original songs, especially "Sunshine," "Accepting the Tolls," and "Blues Was a Pastime." Mary Alice and Barbara Montgomery provided most of the evening's musical high spots.

**THREE PLAYS BY ED BULLINS.** See THE ELECTRONIC NIGGER AND OTHERS.

**THUNDER IN THE INDEX.** See AMERICAN NIGHT CRY.

**TIGER, TIGER BURNING BRIGHT** (Booth, December 22, 1962, 33 p.). Producers: Oliver Smith, Roger L. Stevens, Lyn Austin, and Victor Samrock. Author: Peter S. Feibleman. Director: Joshua Logan.

Cast: Claudia McNeil* (Mama), Diana Sands* (Adelaide Smith), Alvin Ailey (Clarence Morris), Al Freeman, Jr.* (Dan Morris), Ellen Holly (Cille Morris), Cicely Tyson* (Celeste Chipley), Roscoe Lee Browne* (Deacon Morris), Bobby Dean [Robert] Hooks* (Dewey Chipley), Paul Barry (Mr. Keres), Robert Macbeth* (Sergeant Jameson), Janet MacLachlan, Rudy Challenger (Neighbors).

*Tiger, Tiger Burning Bright*, by white dramatist Peter S. Feibleman, managed a brief run at the Booth during the 1962-1963 Broadway season. *Theatre Arts* complained that the play "conventionalizes the Southern colored community once again." Nevertheless, *Tiger, Tiger Burning Bright* won praise for its performers. *The New York Herald Tribune* said that Claudia McNeil was as "fine an actress as a playwright ever had to read his lines," and *Theatre Arts* found Diana Sands's performance one of the main reasons to see the play.

**TIMBUKTU!** (Mark Hellinger, March 1, 1978, 221 p.). Producer and librettist: Luther Davis. Composer and lyricist: Robert Wright and George Forrest (based on the themes of Alexander Borodin). Director and choreographer: Geoffrey Holder.*

Cast: Eartha Kitt* (Sahleem-La-Lume), Ira Hawkins (Hadji), Melba Moore* (Marsinah), Gilbert Price* (Mansa of Mali), Obba Babatunde

(Chakaba; Orange Merchant; Antelope), Harold Pierson (Beggar; Witch-doctor), Shezawae Powell (Beggar; Woman in Garden), Louis Tucker (Beggar), Deborah Waller (Child), Daniel Barton (M'Ballah), Eleanor McCoy (Najua; Bird in Paradise), George Bell (Wazir), Bruce A. Hubbard (Chief Policeman), Miguel Godreau (Munshi; Bird in Paradise), Luther Fontaine (Antelope), Vanessa Shaw (Zubbediya).

Songs: Rhymes Have I; Fate; In the Beginning, Woman; Baubles, Bangles, and Beads; Stranger in Paradise; Gesticulate; Night of My Nights; My Magic Lamp; Rahadlakum; And This Is My Beloved; Golden Land, Golden Life; Zubbediya; Sands of Time.

Geoffrey Holder, who directed and designed the new version of *The Wizard of Oz, The Wiz,** in 1975, attempted to breathe new life into a 1953 Broadway musical, *Kismet*. A white show became black by moving the locale from Baghdad to Timbuktu and rewriting the original play. Some new songs by Robert Wright and George Forrest (the original composers) were added, and others received an African beat, but the weaknesses of the original show remained. The show was notable for Eartha Kitt's return to Broadway after a lengthy absence. Her performance of "In the Beginning, Woman" and "Rahadlakum" stopped the show nightly. Gilbert Price and Melba Moore also brought distinction to the roles of the young lovers.

**TO BE YOUNG, GIFTED, AND BLACK** (Cherry Lane, January 2, 1969, 380 p.). Producers: Harry Belafonte, Chiz Schultz, Edgar Lansbury, and Robert Nemiroff. Author: Lorraine Hansberry.* Adapted: Robert Nemiroff. Director: Gene Frankel.

Cast: Cicely Tyson,* Barbara Baxley, John Beal, Rita Gardner, Gertrude Jeannette, Janet League, Stephen Strimpell, Andre Womble.

At twenty-eight Lorraine Hansberry was the youngest American playwright and the first black to win the New York Drama Critics Circle Award for Best Play, *A Raisin in the Sun*.* She died at age thirty-four while her second play, *The Sign in Sidney Brustein's Window*,* was running on Broadway. *To Be Young, Gifted, and Black* is a tribute to Hansberry's work, featuring excerpts from her plays, journals, letters, and a novel. Robert Nemiroff, Miss Hansberry's husband, selected the readings for the show, and a talented cast gave new meaning to her writings. Cicely Tyson, Barbara Baxley, Gertrude Jeannette, and others recalled Hansberry's works on a bare stage with photographic backdrops.

**TOBACCO ROAD** (Forty-eighth Street, March 6, 1950, 7 p.). Producer: Negro Drama Group. Author: Jack Kirkland. Director: Evelyn Ellis.*

Cast: Powell Lindsay (Jeeter Lester), Jimmy Wright (Dude Lester), Evelyn Ellis (Ada Lester), Baby Joyce (Ellie May), Estelle Hemsley (Grandma Lester), John Tate (Lov Bensey), Cherokee Thornton (Henry Peabody),

Mercedes Gilbert (Sister Bessie Rice), Delores Mack (Pearl), John Mark (Captain Tim), John Bouie (George Payne).

Critics generally dismissed this all-black version of Jack Kirkland's *Tobacco Road* presented by the Negro Drama Group. Nevertheless, Brooks Atkinson of *The New York Times* found praise for the lead actors Evelyn Ellis (who also directed) and John Tate: ". . . there is a certain pathetic beauty in the part of the mother as Miss Ellis acts her. Under the grime and the tatters there is a perceptible pride and a rebellious strength of character. . . . And Mr. Tate is a forceful and honest actor who respects the part of the rejected husband, describes his dilemma seriously, and speaks his lines with some feeling." Despite the admiration for some of the performances, *Tobacco Road* failed to match the long-run success of the original 1933 production.

**THE TOILET/THE SLAVE** (St. Marks, December 16, 1964, 151 p.). Producers: Leo Garen, Stan Swerdlow, Gene Persson, and Rita Fredricks. Author: LeRoi Jones (Imamu Amiri Baraka).* Director: Leo Garen.

**The Toilet**

Cast: James Spruill (Ora), Gary Bolling (Willie Love), D'Urville Martin (Hines), Bostic Van Felton (Johnny Holmes), Norman Bush (Perry), Antonio Fargas (George Davis), Gary Haynes (Donald Farrell), Walter Jones (Knowles), Tony Hudson (Skippy), Jaime Sanchez (Karolis), Hampton Clanton (Foots).

**The Slave**

Cast: Al Freeman, Jr.* (Walker Vessels), Nan Martin (Grace Easely), Jerome Raphel (Bradford Easely).

LeRoi Jones's *Dutchman** both shocked and impressed the major critics, and the double bill of *The Toilet* and *The Slave* followed suit. Once critics vented their wrath at the torrent of four-letter words, they could not help but admit, as Howard Taubman did in *The New York Times*, that "Jones is a writer who cannot be ignored."

*The Toilet* provides a view of life in a high school men's room. As students assault each other, it is revealed that Karolis (Jaime Sanchez) has sent a love letter to Foots (Hampton Clanton), the brightest student in the class. In the final scene, Karolis and Foots do battle. Karolis is left alone and bloodied, but Foots later returns and comforts his admirer. *The Slave* shifts the focus to a college campus in the midst of revolution, as a liberal white professor and his wife are confronted with difficult questions by the wife's black ex-husband Walker Vessels (Al Freeman, Jr.). The acting received high marks, with Taubman called Freeman "brilliant."

**TOUCHSTONE** (Music Box, February 3, 1953, 7 p.). Producer: Elaine Perry. Author: William Stucky. Director: Hale McKeen.

Cast: Ossie Davis* (Dr. Joseph Clay), Josh White, Jr. (Jimmy Clay), Evelyn Ellis* (Aunt Emma), Patty McCormick (Cathy Roberts), Ian Keith (Major Robert Spaulding), Ann Dere (Dr. Gwendolyn Taliafero), Guy Arbury (Rev. Ronald Thompson), Paul McGrath (Langdon Spaulding), Carl Low (Charles Tutwell).

William Stucky, a Kentucky newspaperman, wrote *Touchstone*, a play Walter Kerr termed "intelligent" but not "moving." As a young black boy (Josh White, Jr.) begins to see visions, his father, a successful Los Angeles doctor (Ossie Davis), is forced to search for their cause. While the plot was generally dismissed by the critics, the "honest acting" of White, Davis, and Evelyn Ellis was praised. Nevertheless, *Touchstone* managed only a one-week run.

**TREEMONISHA.** See JOPLIN, SCOTT.

**THE TRIAL OF DR. BECK** (Maxine Elliot, August 10, 1937, n.a.p.). Producer: New Jersey Federal Theatre Project.* Author: Hughes Allison. Director: Louis M. Simon.

Cast: Kenneth Renwick (Dr. John Beck), Earl Sydnor (Collings), Clifford Dempsey (Judge Archer), Frank Harrington (District Attorney), George C. Williams (Dr. Hicks), Kenneth Woodruff (Ass't D.A.), Jethro Webb (James James), Thomas McKenna (O'Malley), Jane Ferrell (Ella Gordon), Slim Mason (George Doolittle), Carrie Adams (Lulu Doolittle), Lulu King (Hilda Redd), Kermit Augustine (Oscar Brooks), Stewart Ward (Dr. Simms), Tessie Green (Carrie Jones), Dorothy Washington (Elenore Hopkins), H. Blanche Harris (Ruth Ellen), Howard Arthur (Ralph Judd), Norman Lewis (Herman Philips), Claire Vernon (Mary Hudson), William Bendix (George B. Shaw).

Black author Hughes Allison presented *The Trial of Dr. Beck* to New York audiences under the auspices of the New Jersey Federal Theatre Project. This courtroom drama concerns the murder of the wife of Dr. Beck (Kenneth Renwick), a Harlem physician. Investigators first suspect the doctor, since he had often expressed the view that blacks should marry women with light complexions. Mrs. Beck, as witnesses reveal, was extremely dark-skinned. Beck is freed at the last moment, as another admits to murdering Mrs. Beck after she spurned his advances. While most critics rejected the courtroom drama as inferior to recent entries such as *Libel* (1935) and *The Trial of Mary Dugan* (1927), several noted another aspect of the play. At many points in the drama, particularly in a speech by the trial judge, Allison injected the notion that "race prejudice may sway a judge" or a jury. In this regard, several critics found that *The Trial of Dr. Beck* featured interesting social commentary.

**THE TRIALS OF BROTHER JERO.** See THE STRONG BREED.

**TRIBAL HARANGUE ONE/TWO/THREE.** See THE HARANGUES.

**A TRIP TO COONTOWN** (Third Avenue, April 4, 1898, 8 p.). Producers and authors: Bob Cole* and Billy Johnson.

Cast: Bob Cole (Willie Wayside), Billy Johnson (Jim Flimflammer), Tom Brown (Rube), Bob A. Kelley (Silas Green), J. A. Shipp (Silas Green, Jr.), Lloyd G. Gibbs (Opera Singer), Geo. Brown (Sam), Walter Dixon (Captain Fleetfoot), Jim Wilson (Boarder), Sam King (Boarder), Molly Dill (Mrs. Fannie Brown), Pauline Freeman (Fannie Brown), Clara Freeman (Flotinda), Marguerite Rhodes (Marinda), Jennie Sheper (Clotinda), Maggie Davis (Florinda), Estella Ware (Aminda), Jennie Hillman (Dudinda), Juvia Roan (Opera Singer).

Songs: The Coontown Regiment; Miss Arabella Jones; I Hope These Few Lines Will Find You Well; Old Kentucky Home; A Jolly Old Rube; Two Bold Bad Men; A Trip to Coontown; The Italian Man; Meet Me at the Gin Spring; 4-11-44; When the Chickens Go to Sleep; The Wedding of the Chinee and the Coon; Coontown Frolique; There's a Warm Spot in My Heart for You Babe; I Wonder What Is Dat Coon's Game; For All Eternity; Sweet Savannah; In Dahomey; Ma Chickens; Ika Hula; Trio from Attila; Stars and Stripes Forever.

*A Trip to Coontown* was the first full-length musical comedy written, directed, performed, and produced by black artists. The show's title bore a striking resemblance to an earlier musical hit, *A Trip to Chinatown* (1891), which remained Broadway's long-run champion for almost twenty-five years. Like the earlier show, *A Trip to Coontown* offered a visit to one of New York City's regional enclaves, but there the similarity ended.

Bob Cole's script provided a loosely structured plot concerning Jim Flimflammer, a con artist, who tries to bilk old Silas Green out of a $5,000 pension. At the last moment, Willie Wayside saves Green from Flimflammer's schemes. The plot was ignored throughout most of the evening, since the visit to Coontown allowed the appearance of several specialty acts, such as contortionists, jugglers, and opera singers. Although *A Trip to Coontown* had a brief run, Cole and Johnson toured with the show for several weeks. The show returned to Broadway in 1899, with Cole and Johnson now billed as "The Kings of Koon-dom."

**TROUBLE IN MIND** (Greenwich Mews, November 4, 1955, 91 p.). Producer: Greenwich Mews Theatre. Author: Alice Childress.* Directors: Clarice Taylor* and Alice Childress.

Cast: Clarice Taylor (Wiletta Mayor), Louise Kemp (Singer), Liam Lenihan (Pop), Charles Bettis (John Neville), Hilda Haynes (Millie Davis),

Howard Augusta (Sheldon Forrester), Stephanie Elliot (Judith Sears), James McMahon (Al Manners), Hal England (Eddie Fenton).

*Trouble in Mind* drew on Alice Childress's experience as an actress in such plays as *On Striver's Row** (1940), *Natural Man** (1941), and *Anna Lucasta** (1944). Childress's play presents the tensions that occur among black and white cast members during a rehearsal of a fictitious Broadway show, *Chaos in Belleville.* As rehearsals continue, the black actors become increasingly uncomfortable with the standard stage stereotypes the white author and director continue to utilize in *Chaos.* A walkout is narrowly averted in the third act as the cast and director agree to talk to the author about the problems with the play.

*The New York Times* found *Trouble in Mind* an "original play, full of vitality," which "is well worth the trip downtown." Clarice Taylor also received praise for her "beautiful performance" as a "resigned veteran of numerous maid's roles . . . who finds that she must speak her mind at last."

**TRUMPETS OF THE LORD** (Astor Place, December 21, 1963, 160 p.). Producers: Theodore Mann and Will B. Sandler. Author: Vinnette Carroll.* Director: Donald McKayle.*

Cast: Al Freeman, Jr.* (Rev. Ridgley Washington), Theresa Merritt (Henrietta Pinkston), Lex Monson (Rev. Bradford Parham), Cicely Tyson* (Rev. Marion Alexander).

Songs: So Glad I'm Here; Call to Prayer; Listen Lord—A Prayer; Amen Response; In His Care; The Creation; God Lead Us Along; Noah Built the Ark; Run Sinner Run; Didn't It Rain; The Judgment Day; In That Great Gettin' Up Morning; God Almighty Is Gonna Cut You Down; Soon One Morning; There's a Man; Go Down Death; He'll Understand; Were You There?; Calvary; Crucifixion; Reap What You Sow; We Shall Not Be Moved; We Are Soldiers; Woke Up This Morning; Let My People Go; We Shall Overcome; Jacob's Ladder; God Be with You.

*Trumpets of the Lord*, like *Tambourines to Glory** (1963), utilized gospel music and spirituals in its exploration of black life. Based on James Weldon Johnson's *God's Trombones—Seven Negro Sermons in Verse* (1927), *Trumpets of the Lord* attempted to recapture "the dignity and fervor" of black evangelist preachers during the 1920s. Vinnette Carroll adapted the work for the theatre and used an earlier title of the Johnson book. *The New York Times* praised the show: "It has a built-in impact that is stimulating, inspiring, and contagiously exciting." Lewis Funke also singled out Al Freeman, Jr., Theresa Merritt, and Cicely Tyson for special praise. Merritt and Tyson returned for a Broadway revival in April 1969 at the Brooks Atkinson Theatre.

**TURPENTINE** (Lafayette, June 27, 1936, n.a.p.). Producer: Negro Theatre Division of Works Progress Administration. Authors: J. A. Smith* and Peter Morell. Directors: J. A. Smith and Emjo Basshe.

Cast: Gus [J. Augustus] Smith (Forty-four), Estelle Hemsley (Granny), Charles Wayne (Mr. Safford), Alonzo Bosan (Burrhead), Louis Sharp (Shine Sommers), Viola Dean (Sally May), Charles Taylor (Turtle Eyes), Edward H. Loeffler (Mr. Chase), Charles Leack (Mr. Forsythe), Muriel McCrory (Sissie Jones), Bertram Miller (Bill Austin), Herbert Jelley (Crawford), William Melville (Mr. Jenkins), Thomas Moseley (Col. Dutton).

Triple threat J. Augustus (Gus) Smith co-authored, co-directed, and starred in *Turpentine*, presented on the stage of the Lafayette Theatre under the auspices of the Federal Theatre Project.* Smith, a native of Gainesville, Florida, wrote of the workers in a turpentine camp in his home state. The workers are starving and underpaid, so "Forty-four" (Smith) begins to unionize the laborers. His efforts are brutally repressed by the owners of the camp and the local police. Both Robert Garland of the *World-Telegram* and Lewis Nichols of *The New York Times* praised *Turpentine* in virtually identical words. Nichols said: "As played at the Lafayette, *Turpentine* is exciting as melodrama and just as much as a social document." The *Times* added that Harlem's audiences evidently enjoyed the play as well, as theatregoers supplied "cheers, hisses, and applause" at appropriate intervals.

**THE TWILIGHT DINNER** (St. Marks, April 14, 1978. 27 p.). Producer: Negro Ensemble Company.* Author: Lennox Brown. Director: Douglas Turner Ward.*

Cast: Leon Morenzie (Jimmy), Karen Bernhard (Elissa), Reuben Green (Ray).

The *New Yorker* called Lennox Brown's *The Twilight Dinner* "an elegy for the sixties." This play examines a reunion between Jimmy (Leon Morenzie) and Ray (Reuben Green), two idealistic college students of the 1960s, who meet again in a posh restaurant that has passed its prime. The optimism of the early years has faded, as Jimmy has become a successful businessman and Ray a cynical politician. Douglas Watt of the *Daily News* said that the writing was "witty, sophisticated, and delicately probing," and that "the acting couldn't be better."

# U

**UNDERGROUND** (Public, April 18, 1971, 38 p.). Producer: Joseph Papp and the New York Shakespeare Festival. Director: Walter Jones.

**The Life and Times of J. Walter Smintheus**. Author: Edgar White.

Cast: Dennis Tate (J. Walter Smintheus), Edward Seamon (Edward), Walter Jones (Robert), Norma Darden (Joyce), John McCants Trotter

(Dr. Comma), Robin Braxton (Margie), MacArthur Flack (Walter), John Gallagher (Bob).

**Jazznite.** Author: Walter Jones.

Cast: Robin Braxton (Leola), Demond Wilson (Dudder), Lennal Wainwright (Slick), Sam Singleton (Eligah), Walter Cotton (Baylock), MacArthur Flack (Heavy), Norma Darden (Barbara).

*Underground* featured two one-act plays which considered the plight of the black intellectual in modern America. Edgar White's *The Life and Times of J. Walter Smintheus* concerns a Cornell-educated sociologist who is writing a six-volume history of black intellectuals in America. Engulfed in white culture (even the furniture is white), the sociologist (Dennis Tate) begins to write a prisoner convicted of a drug charge (Walter Jones). As the correspondence continues, the intellectual begins to question his values.

Walter Jones, the prisoner of the first play, provided *Jazznite*, the story of the return of a Yale-educated man to his ghetto family. He hopes to teach his relatives what he has learned of the "white man's games," but they studiously ignore him. He, too, is forced to reconsider his ideas. The evening received generally favorable reviews, with the nod going to *Jazznite*. Clive Barnes of *The New York Times* noted: "*Jazznite* is a fascinating vignette of black ghetto life, with a beautiful feel for reality and a heightened sense of the world around us."

**WAITING FOR MONGO** (St. Marks, May 18, 1975, 33 p.). Producer: Negro Ensemble Company.* Author: Silas Jones. Director: Douglas Turner Ward.*

Cast: Bill Cobbs (Preach; Mongo), Reyno (Virgil), Bebe Drake Hooks (Viana), Barbara Montgomery* (Sadie Mae), Roland Sanchez (Bill), Ethel Ayler (Teach), Adolph Caesar* (Doodybug), Graham Brown (Doc), Samm Williams* (Argus).

Silas Jones's *Waiting for Mongo*, a Negro Ensemble Company "season-within-a-season" production, is a "nightmare comedy" that deals with the confusion of fantasy and reality. Mel Gussow, writing in *The New York Times*, called Jones's play a black version of *Billy Liar*. Virgil (Reyno), who has raped a white woman, hides in a church and slowly loses all contact with reality. He calls for Mongo (Bill Cobbs) to help him out, using his boot as a telephone, and the black freedom fighter finally arrives. While the two leads received favorable notices, most critics found Jones's play "an unfunny comedy."

**WALK HARD** (Chanin Auditorium, March 27, 1946, 17 p.). Producer: Gustav Blum. Author: Abram Hill.* Directors: Gustav Blum and Gilbert Weiss.

Cast: Maxwell Glanville* (Andy Whitman), Jacqueline Andre (Becky), Richard Kraft (Bobby), Leonard Yorr (Mack Jeffris), Fred C. Carter (Mr. Berry), Joseph Kamm (Lou Foster), Howard Augusta (Happy), Stephen Elliott (Mickey), Mickey Walker (Larry Batcheller), Maurice Lisby (Charlie), Lulu Mae Ward (Susie), Dorothy Carter (Ruth Lawson), John O. Hewitt (Bartender), Jean Normandy (Sadie), Miriam Pullen (Dorothy), Leslie Jones (George, the Bellhop), Richard Kraft (Hotel Clerk), Fiona O'Shiel (Lady Friend), Edward Kreisler (Reporter).

Abram Hill based *Walk Hard* on the novel of the boxing world, *Walk Hard—Talk Loud* by Len Zinberg. *Walk Hard* features the plight of Andy Whitman (Maxwell Glanville), a former Harlem shoeshine boy, who eventually becomes a great fighter. En route to success, Whitman is continually plagued by prejudice, as he is denied lodging in hotels and is given bad calls in the ring. Yet, as some critics complained, the dramatics of the fight game overshadowed the social commentary "which is implicit in the situation." As a result of the focus on the boxing milieu, critics emphasized the debut of ex-fighter Mickey Walker as Whitman's coach, friend, and confidant. Nevertheless, George Freedly of the *Morning-Telegram* found *Walk Hard* "an honest and sincere effort."

**WALK TOGETHER CHILDREN** (Greenwich Mews, November 11, 1968, 24 p.). Producer: Ananse Productions. Author and director: Vinie Burrows.*

Cast: Vinie Burrows.

Vinie Burrows described *Walk Together Children* as "the black scene in prose, poetry, and song." This one-woman show featured dramatic readings from the works of such black writers as Paul Laurence Dunbar, Richard Wright,* Langston Hughes,* LeRoi Jones,* Nikki Giovanni, and Angela Davis. Clive Barnes, writing in *The New York Times*, found Burrows a "magnificent performer," and commented: "Miss Burrows has a strange, fine face. Expressive, mobile, and yet also beautiful, it is ideal for interpreting the whole range of emotions . . . involved in the black scene." A 1972 revival played eighty-nine performances.

**WALK TOGETHER CHILLUN** (Lafayette, February 2, 1936, 29 p.). Producer: Negro Theatre Unit of the Federal Theatre Project* of the Works Progress Administration. Author: Frank Wilson.* Directors: Frank Wilson, J. De Witt Spencer, and John Houseman.

Cast: Lionel Monagas* (Willy James), Gus Smith* (Eli Jackson), Percy Verwayne (Mr. Primero), Alonzo Bosan (Blibbie Jones), J. Francis O'Reilly (Judge Walters), Cornelius Donnelly (Dr. Stratton), Bertram Miller (K. C. Hawkes), John Hayden (Jim Manderville), Bebe Townsend

(Bessie Holden), Oliver Foster (Reverend Smiley), Hilda Offley (Martha Ray Browne), Charles Taylor (Alexander), Julian Costello (Aubrey Gladman), Abner Dorsey (Hot Rock), Al Watts (Old Face), Alberta Perkins (Tiny), Hudson Prince (Henry), Christola H. Williams (Hermantine), Wilhelmina Williams (Blibbie's Wife), Frances Smith (Mrs. Stallings).

The veteran Broadway actor Frank Wilson had received raves for his performances in *In Abraham's Bosom*,* *Porgy*,* *Sweet Chariot*,* *Singin' the Blues*,* and several others. His new play, *Walk Together Chillun*, became the first production of the Negro Theatre Unit of the Federal Theatre Project. The controversial play noted the divisions between northern and southern blacks in a northern city. Wilson urged the blacks to forget their sectional differences in the face of white hostility. Wilson's play was directed to black audiences, and *The New York Times* noted that they particularly enjoyed "the attacks upon the duplicity of the whites, the complacence of the colored clergy, and the cultivated manners of the Negro leaders in the North." Brooks Atkinson added that *Walk Together Chillun* was "simple, direct, and sincere."

**THE WARNING—A THEME FOR LINDA.** See A BLACK QUARTET.

**WEDDING BAND** (Public, September 26, 1972, 175 p.). Producer: Joseph Papp and the New York Shakespeare Festival. Author: Alice Childress.* Directors: Joseph Papp and Alice Childress.

Cast: Ruby Dee* (Julia Augustine), James Broderick (Herman), Calisse Dinwiddie (Teeta), Juanita Clark (Mattie), Hilda Haynes (Lula Green), Clarice Taylor* (Fanny Johnson), Albert Hall (Nelson Green), Brandon Maggart (The Bell Man), Vicky Geyer (Princess), Polly Holliday (Annabelle), Jean David (Herman's Mother).

Joseph Papp and Alice Childress co-directed *Wedding Band*, which was first produced at the University of Michigan in 1966. Childress's play is set in a coastal South Carolina town during the influenza epidemic of 1918. Two star-crossed lovers, one black (Ruby Dee) and one white (James Broderick), have been seeing each other for years but are unable to marry because of the state's anti-miscegenation laws. They attempt to flee north, but poverty prevents their escape. Critics approved this treatment of miscegenation in the South, with Harold Clurman leading the raves in *The Nation*: "There is an honest pathos in the telling of this simple story, and some humorous and touching thumbnail sketches, [which] reveal knowledge and understanding of the people dealt with." A television version starring Ruby Dee and J. D. Cannon received similar acclaim in 1974.

**WEEP NOT FOR ME** (Theatre Four, January 27, 1981, 48 p.). Producer: Negro Ensemble Company.* Author: Gus Edwards.* Director: Douglas Turner Ward.*

Cast: Ethel Ayler (Lillian), Bill Cobbs (Jake), Seret Scott (Crissie), Elaine Graham (Deanie), Chuck Patterson (Willy), Phylicia Ayers-Allen (Janet), Robert Gossett (Mel), Brian Evaret Chandler (Henry), Sarallen (Sylvie).

Gus Edwards, author of *Old Phantoms** (1979), turned to a family portrait of life in the South Bronx in *Weep Not for Me*, his latest Negro Ensemble Company production. The play analyzes the life of the Hendricks family, headed by matriarch Lillian (Ethel Ayler), who is unfaithful to her husband, and Jake (Bill Cobbs), the loving but deceived father. Critics praised the character study in Act I, but found that the play lapsed into melodrama in Act II. Both Ayler and Cobbs received praise in *The New York Times* for their "fine" performances.

**WELCOME TO BLACK RIVER** (St. Marks, May 20, 1975, 8 p.). Producer: Negro Ensemble Company.* Author: Samm-Art Williams.* Director: Dean Irby.

Cast: Juanita Bethea (Mama Liza), Marcella Lowery (Lou Mae), Lea Scott (Anna Lee), Taurean Blacque (D. J.), Clayton Corbin (David Jack), Peter DeMaio (Mordicah), Carl Gordon (Amos).

Samm Williams appeared first as an actor with the Negro Ensemble Company, but soon revealed himself to be a playwright of promise. In the 1974-1975 "season-within-a-season," Williams received praise for his performance as a seaman in *Liberty Call,** and his name reappeared later in the season as the author of *Welcome to Black River*. Mel Gussow, writing in *The New York Times*, identified Williams as a playwright of promise, despite the fact that this portrait of North Carolina sharecroppers in 1958 was "deeply flawed." Gussow added: "The play needs work, but its rawness is one of its assets. It is packed with honest emotion and moral fervor."

**WHAT IF IT HAD TURNED UP HEADS?** (New Lafayette, October 13, 1972, 8 p.). Producer: New Federal Theatre.* Author: J. E. Gaines.* Director: William E. Lathan.

Cast: Whitman Mayo (Jacob Jones), Carol Cole (Jennie Louise Harris), Sonny Jim (Mose), Gary Bolling (Bimbo), George Miles (Dizzy).

J. E. Gaines's second production of 1972 brought considerable attention to the actor (Sonny Jim) turned playwright. *What If It Had Turned Up Heads?* earned an Obie for both playwright Gaines and director William E. Lathan. This character study provides a portrait of an old man (Whitman Mayo) who lives in a cheap basement apartment. His home is invaded by a vagrant (Carol Cole), as well as other disreputable folk (including the playwright in a cameo role). Critics praised both Gaines and the cast for the ability to create characters that come alive for the audience.

**WHAT THE WINE-SELLERS BUY** (Vivian Beaumont, February 14, 1974, 37 p.). Producer: Joseph Papp and the New York Shakespeare Festival. Author: Ron Milner.* Director: Michael Schultz.*

Cast: Dick A. Williams* (Rico), Glynn Turman (Steve Carlton), Loretta Greene (Mae Harris), Marilyn B. Coleman (Mrs. Laura Carlton), Gloria Edwards (Candy; Mrs. Copeland), Frank Adu (Hustler; Old Bob), Steve Laws (Slim; Cab Driver), Ron Rayford (Tate; Pete), Ray Vitte (Joe), Jean DuShon (Voice; Mrs. Harris), Sonny Jim Gaines* (Jim Aaron), Lonny Stevens (Melvin), Berlinda Tolbert (Francis), Debbie Morgan (Helen), Sheila Goldsmith (Marilyn), Starletta De Paur (Phyllis), Kyle Duncan (Red), Harris David (Hunt), Kirk Kirksey* (George), Bill Wintersole (White Cop; Coach), Garrett Morris (Black Cop).

After productions at the Henry Street Playhouse and in Los Angeles, Ron Milner's *What the Wine-Sellers Buy* moved to the Vivian Beaumont at Lincoln Center. Milner's portrait of ghetto life in Detroit involves young Steve Carlton (Glynn Turman) who has a sick mother. A pimp, Rico (Dick A. Williams), fascinates the boy and suggests that he make his girlfriend into a prostitute in order to obtain money for his mother. Steve struggles with his conscience and decides that the cost would be too great for him and his girlfriend Mae (Loretta Greene). After all, he notes, "What do the wine-sellers buy, one-half as precious as they sell?"

Critics found the plot lodged in the movie melodramas of the 1930s, but they praised Milner's way with language and his observation of character. The acting also received praise, with Dick A. Williams earning a Drama Desk Award for his portrayal of Rico.

**WHO'S GOT HIS OWN?** (St. Clement's Church, October 12, 1966, 19 p.). Producer: American Place Theater. Author: Ronald Milner.* Director: Lloyd Richards.*

Cast: Glynn Turman (Tim, Jr.), Barbara Ann Teer* (Clara), Estelle Evans (Mother), L. Errol Jaye (Rev. Calver), Sam Laws (First Deacon), Roger Robinson (Second Deacon).

Critics found much to admire in *Who's Got His Own?* Ron Milner's play concerns a family's recollections of Tim, Sr., on the day of his funeral. Tim, Jr. (Glynn Turman) remembers the day he discovered his father was a janitor; Clara (Barbara Ann Teer) ponders her father's reactions to her relationship with a white man in college; and Mother (Estelle Evans) recalls how her husband beat her, but failed to stand up to the Ku Klux Klan. The monologues and performances were praised, but most critics found the evening somewhat lacking. *The Newark Evening News* summarized these sentiments: "Milner's play is of high literary quality and his rich and pungent use of a lean hard language mark him as a talented and promising young writer capable of bringing great beauty to the stage and to the use of words. But words are not enough. . . . While *Who's Got His Own?* is often moving and always intense, it is not always sustained."

**THE WIZ** (Majestic, January 5, 1975, 556 p.). Producer: Ken Harper. Book: William F. Brown. Score: Charlie Smalls. Director: Geoffrey Holder.*

Cast: Stephanie Mills (Dorothy), Hinton Battle (Scarecrow), Tiger Haynes (Tinman), Ted Ross (Lion), Andre De Shields (The Wiz), Mabel King (Evillene), Dee Dee Bridgewater (Glinda), Tasha Thomas (Aunt Em), Ralph Wilcox (Uncle Henry), Evelyn Thomas (Tornado), Clarice Taylor* (Addaperle), Danny Beard (Gatekeeper), Carl Weaver (Soldier Messenger), Andy Torres (Winged Monkey).

Songs: The Feeling We Once Had; He's the Wizard; Soon as I Get Home; I Was Born on the Day Before Yesterday; Ease on Down the Road; Slide Some Oil to Me; Mean Ole Lion; Be a Lion; So You Wanted to Meet the Wizard; To Be Able to Feel; No Bad News; Everybody Rejoice (Luther Vandros); Who Do You Think You Are?; Believe in Yourself; Y'all Got It!; A Rested Body Is a Rested Mind; Home.

*The Wiz*, a black version of *The Wizard of Oz*, swept the Tony Awards in 1975. As Best Musical, *The Wiz* also enjoyed awards for its music (Charlie Smalls), its direction (Geoffrey Holder), its choreography (George Faison), and two of its stars (Dee Dee Bridgewater and Ted Ross). Although the story is familiar to all via the 1939 Metro-Goldwyn-Mayer film, librettist Brown and composer Smalls modernized it and provided Broadway magic to replace the memories of cinematic wizardry.

Despite the success of *The Wiz*, initial reviews were poor, with a thumbs down from *The New York Times*. Fortunately, the major backer, Twentieth Century-Fox, gave the show a reprieve as aggressive selling techniques, especially television ads, attempted to win audiences. Word of mouth also contributed to the success of *The Wiz*, which soon moved into the sellout column. In addition to the several Tony Awards, *The Wiz* also boosted the careers of stars Stephanie Mills and Andre De Shields, and spawned a popular standard "Ease on Down the Road." Sidney Lumet directed a 1978 film version with Diana Ross, Richard Pryor, and Lena Horne* in a sparkling cameo as Glinda the Good Witch.

**YEAH MAN** (Park Lane, May 26, 1932, 4 p.). Producers: Walter Campbell and Jesse Wank. Book: Leigh Whipper* and Billy Mills. Composers and lyricists: Al Wilson, Charles Weinberg, and Ken Macomber. Director: Walter Campbell.

Cast: Mantan Moreland,* Eddie Rector, Billy Mills, Leigh Whipper, Rose Henderson, Lily Yuen, Hilda Perleno, Peggy Phillips, Marcus Slayter,

Adele Hargraves, "Jarahal," Walter Brogsdale, Russell Graves, Harry Fiddler and the Melodee Four.

Songs: Mississippi Joys; Gotta Get de Boat Loaded; Dancing Fool; At the Barbecue; I'm Always Happy When I'm in Your Arms; I've Got What It Takes; Crazy Idea of Love; Come to Harlem; The Spell of Those Harlem Nights; Baby, I Could Do It for You; Shady Dan; Give Me Your Love; Shake Your Music; That's Religion; Qualifications (Porter Grainger).

*Yeah Man* opened at the Park Lane Theatre, formerly Daly's Sixty-third Street, the home of *Shuffle Along*.* The critics fondly remembered the earlier show and found *Yeah Man* an unworthy successor. After four postponements, *Yeah Man* still appeared somewhat ragged on opening night. Amidst the ruins, *The New York Times* found some saving grace in the appearance of Mantan Moreland: "The head man is Mantan Moreland, without whom none of these blackamoor capers is quite official. Mr. Moreland is still tireless. His smile is one of the friendliest omens the theatre has to offer, and he can smoke a cigar, take the falls, or feign wide-eyed terror with stout results."

**YOUR ARMS TOO SHORT TO BOX WITH GOD** (Lyceum, December 22, 1976, 429 p.). Producer: Frankie Hewitt and the Shubert Organization. Author and director: Vinnette Carroll.* Composer and lyricist: Alex Bradford with additional songs by Micki Grant.*

Cast: Adrian Bailey, Salome Bey, Deborah Lynn Bridges, Sharon Brooks, Clinton Derricks-Carroll, Sheila Ellis, Thomas Jefferson Fouse, Jr., Michael Gray, Delores Hall, Cardell Hall, William Hardy, Jr., Bobby Hill, Edna M. Krider, Hector Jaime Mercado, Mabel Robinson, William Thomas, Jr., Leone Washington, Derek Williams, Marilyn Winbush.

Songs: Beatitudes; We're Gonna Have a Good Time; There's a Stranger in Town; Do You Know Jesus?/He's a Wonder; Just a Little Bit of Jesus Goes a Long Way; We Are the Priests and Elders; Something Is Wrong in Jerusalem; It Was Alone; I Know I Have to Leave Here; Be Careful Whom You Kiss; It's Too Late; Judas Dance; Your Arms Too Short to Box with God; Give Us Barabbas; See How They Done My Lord; Come On Down; Can't No Grave Hold My Body Down; Didn't I Tell You; When the Power Comes; Everybody Has His Own Way; I Love You So Much Jesus; The Band.

Vinnette Carroll, Alex Bradford, and Micki Grant, veterans of *Don't Bother Me, I Can't Cope** (1972), returned to Broadway shortly before Christmas with a new surprise package. Ms. Carroll developed the show, a gospel version of the Book of Matthew, for the Festival of Two Worlds in Spoleto in 1975, and had it ready for Broadway in 1977. From the opening number, "We're Gonna Have a Good Time," which set the tone for the evening, critics and audiences welcomed the show. Critics were dazzled by the voices of William Hardy, Jr., and Delores Hall, who won a Tony Award for her performance. After a lengthy Broadway run, *Your Arms Too Short* visited sixty-six American cities, and then returned to Broadway in June 1980 at the Ambassador Theatre.

# Z

**ZOOMAN AND THE SIGN** (Theatre Four, November 25, 1980, 48 p.). Producer: Negro Ensemble Company.* Author: Charles Fuller.* Director: Douglas Turner Ward.*

Cast: Alvin Alexis (Victor Tate), Mary Alice* (Rachel Tate), Ray Aranha* (Reuben Tate), Terrance Terry Ellis (Russell), Giancarlo Esposito (Zooman), Frances Foster* (Ash), Carl Gordon (Emmett Tate), Steven A. Jones (Donald Jackson), Carol Lynn Maillard (Grace).

Philadelphia playwright Charles Fuller presented an important dilemma of urban life in the Negro Ensemble Company's production of *Zooman and the Sign.* Zooman (Giancarlo Esposito), a psychotic teenager, reveals that he has killed a little girl, but none of the neighbors will identify the murderer to Reuben (Ray Aranha), the girl's father. Reuben then places a large sign on his front porch which harshly criticizes the neighbors for their cowardice. The neighbors, however, still refuse to testify and fear that the sign will give their neighborhood a bad name. Critics gave the actors in this drama high marks. Ray Aranha (author of *My Sister, My Sister** [1974]) gave the evening "its conscience and its heart" according to *The New York Times*, while Giancarlo Esposito won a Theatre World Award for his portrayal of the violent teenager.

# Part II:

# PERSONALITIES AND ORGANIZATIONS

**ALICE, MARY** (1941-    ). Mary Alice (Smith) was born in Indianola, Mississippi, but was raised in Chicago. She arrived in New York City in 1967 and made her debut in *The Strong Breed** by Athol Fugard. She was accepted into the Negro Ensemble Company's* training program, and soon made her Broadway debut in *No Place to Be Somebody** in 1971. She won an Obie in 1979 for her work in Fugard's *Nongogo* at the Manhattan Theatre Club and a Joseph Papp production of *Julius Caesar*.

Credits: *The Strong Breed* (1967); *A Rat's Mass* (1969); *Street Sounds* (1970); *No Place to Be Somebody* (1971); *The Duplex** (1972); *Thoughts**; *House Party**; *Miss Julie* (1973); *Black Sunlight**; *Terraces**; *Heaven and Hell's Agreement**; *In the Deepest Part of Sleep** (1974); *Cockfight** (1977); *Nongogo* (1978); *Second Thoughts*; *Julius Caesar*; *Spell #7** (1979); *Zooman and the Sign** (1980); *Glasshouse* (1981).

Reference: *Encore* 5 (March 8, 1976).

**AMERICAN NEGRO THEATRE (ANT).** Abram Hill* and Frederick O'Neal* founded the American Negro Theatre in Harlem as the Federal Theatre Project* was ending. The ANT provided training for blacks interested in acting, playwrighting, directing, and the technical aspects of production. After the premiere of *Hits, Bits, and Skits* on July 17, 1940, the company produced eighteen plays of varying merit during the decade. These included Abram Hill's *Walk Hard** and *On Striver's Row*,* Philip Yordan's *Anna Lucasta*,* Curtis Cooksey's *Starlight*, Owen Dodson's *Garden of Time*, Dan Hammerman's *Henri Christophe*, Samuel Kootz's *Home Is the Hunter*,* Katherine Garrison's *Sojourner Truth*, Walter Carroll's *Tin Top Valley*, Nat Sherman's *The Washington Years*, Jonathan Tree's *The Fisherman*, Kurt Unkelbach's *The Peacemakers*, Kenneth White's *Freight*, Theodore Browne's *Natural Man*,* and Phoebe and Henry Ephron's *Three's a Family*. The Ephrons's play, a Broadway import, had the distinction of having two simultaneous New York City productions, one with a white cast and one with a black cast.

Four of the ANT's productions (*On Striver's Row*, *Anna Lucasta*, *Walk Hard*, and *Freight*) transferred theatres for commercial runs. The major black playwrights who had shows presented by the ANT were Abram Hill, Theodore Browne, and Owen Dodson. The ANT ran into difficulties in the late 1940s as a Rockefeller Foundation Grant ended and as many of its participants moved on to Broadway work.

Reference: Walker, Ethel Pitts, "The American Negro Theatre: 1940-1949," Ph.D. diss., University of Missouri, Columbia, 1975.

**ANDERSON, GARLAND** (1887–1939). Anderson wrote the first full-length drama produced on Broadway by a black author. While working as a bellhop in a San Francisco hotel, Anderson wrote a courtroom drama concerning a black man falsely accused of a crime by a white woman. Through his public relations skills he interested Al Jolson in the project, and a reading by Richard Harrison (later of *The Green Pastures** fame) was held in New York. Lester W. Sagar produced *Appearances** in 1925, and a London version (starring Doe Doe Green) opened in 1930.

Reference: Anderson, Garland, *From Newsboy and Bellhop to Playwright*, San Francisco: Author, 1926.

**ARANHA, RAY** (1939– ). An actor as well as a playwright, Aranha gained fame with his Broadway production of *My Sister, My Sister** (1974), originally produced by the Hartford Theatre Company. He received a Rockefeller Foundation Grant in 1974 and was named Playwright in Residence for the Hartford Company. During this period, he completed *The Estate*, a play about Thomas Jefferson's attitudes concerning slavery. It was produced in 1976. He recently appeared with the Negro Ensemble Company* in *Zooman and the Sign** (1980).

Reference: "Ray Aranha" File, NYPL/TC.

# B

**BAILEY, PEARL** (1918– ). Virginia-born Pearl Bailey first attracted notice at the Village Vanguard in New York City. Her first Broadway appearance was in *St. Louis Woman** (1946) which won her a Donaldson Award. She was featured in *Arms and the Girl* and *Bless You All* in 1950, and received top billing in *House of Flowers** in 1954. She returned to Broadway as Dolly Levi in 1967 in an all-black version of *Hello Dolly!*, which featured Cab Calloway.

Reference: Bailey, Pearl, *The Raw Pearl*, New York: Harcourt, Brace, and World, 1968.

**BALDWIN, JAMES ARTHUR** (1924– ). Black American novelist, essayist, and dramatist, Baldwin was born and reared in New York City. Baldwin attended Frederick Douglass Junior High School and De Witt Clinton High School where he published several stories and editorials and shared the job of newspaper editor-in-chief with classmate Richard Avedon. Baldwin's religious family background led him to serve briefly in the ministry, but he soon renounced this vocation to pursue a career in writing.

Over the past thirty years, Baldwin has published nineteen books, including six novels, six essay collections, one volume of short stories, two plays, and numerous uncollected essays and book reviews. His writings have outsold those of every black writer in the last three decades. In 1961, *Nobody Knows My Name* sold over 2 million copies, while *Another Country* (1962) soared to 4 million. Following these successes, *The Fire Next Time* (1963) reached the 1 million mark.

Although Baldwin dramatized *Giovanni's Room* for the Actors Studio Workshop in 1958, his reputation as a playwright rests on *Blues for Mister Charlie** (1964) and *The Amen Corner** (1965). Viewed in Aristotelian terms, Baldwin's artistic philosophy considers the audience as an active observer whose behavior must be changed by the action of the play: "I want to shock the people; I want to wake them up. . . . I want the people to think and feel, to feel and think. . . . I want the people to get upset. I want to send them home annoyed" (*New York Times*, April 19, 1964). The drama, then, becomes a vehicle that leads us into a heightened state of awareness while the playwright wages perennial warfare against our complacency and indifference.

Although Baldwin set a record among black playwrights by having two plays produced on Broadway in as many years, the critical reception of his dramas has been reserved. The gamut of criticism extends from Fred Lumley's observation that Baldwin's "cardboard characters in the end offend our sensitivities" to Carlton W. Molette's praise of those characters for their "depth and complexity." But perhaps it is Kay Boyle who captures the impact and special significance of Baldwin's accomplishments: "He is the eloquence of the silent throughout our land. For the man of genius in all ages is he who, like an Aeolian harp, catches the sound of the longing and hopes of men who cannot give them shape or sound."

References: Boyle, Kay, "Introducing James Baldwin," in *Contemporary American Novelists*, Harry T. Moore, ed., Carbondale: Southern Illinois University Press, 1964; Gansberg, Martin, "James Baldwin Turns to Broadway with a Play About Our Times," *The New York Times*, April 19, 1964; Lumley, Fred, *New Trends in Twentieth Century Drama*, New York: Oxford University Press, 1972; Molette, Carlton W., "James Baldwin as Playwright," in *James Baldwin: A Critical Evaluation*, Therman B. O'Daniel, ed., Washington, D.C.: Howard University Press, 1977.

LOUIS H. PRATT

**BARAKA, IMAMU AMIRI.** See JONES, LEROI.

**BEVERLEY, TRAZANA** (1945- ). Beverley, a New York University graduate from Baltimore, Maryland, recently attracted attention for her performance in *For Colored Girls Who Have Considered Suicide/When the Rainbow Is Enuf** (1976), which won her a Theatre World Award. She made her Off-Broadway debut in *Rules for Running Trains* (1969) and then appeared in *Les Femmes Noires** and *Geronimo* (1974). She also won rave notices for her Broadway performance in *My Sister, My Sister** in 1974.

Reference: "Trazana Beverley" File, NYPL/TC.

**BLACK PATTI.** See JONES, SISSIERETTA.

**BLAKE, EUBIE** (1883-1983) **and NOBLE SISSLE** (1889-1975). Songwriters James Herbert (Eubie) Blake and Noble Sissle revived the black musical in the 1920s with their long-running hit *Shuffle Along** (1921).

Sissle and Blake met at a Baltimore party in 1915. Blake needed a lyricist, and Sissle, a composer. They shook hands and immediately joined forces. Both had considerable musical experience at this time. Sissle, born in Indianapolis in 1889, first exercised his singing talents in his high school glee club. After graduation, he toured with the Thomas Jubilee Singers in order to earn money for college. Sissle's college career was brief, as the lure of singing jobs with dance bands proved too great. In 1916, Sissle joined James Reese Europe's Society Orchestra.

Blake was born in Baltimore, Maryland, in 1883. He claims that he was reading music and playing piano at age six. By 1899, he had already written the "Charleston Rag" and other ragtime melodies, much to the distress of his mother who refused to have the "devil's music" in the house. Blake polished his performing style in Atlantic City, New Jersey, where he met such ragtime greats as Willie "the Lion" Smith and James P. Johnson.*

Sissle and Blake's initial partnership was brief but successful. Sophie Tucker sang the team's first song, "It's All Your Fault." World War I interrupted the collaboration, as Sissle joined James Europe overseas. After the war, Sissle and Blake renewed their partnership and performed their latest compositions in a promising vaudeville act, "The Dixie Duo." It was during this period that Flournoy Miller* and Aubrey Lyles* approached them with a unique proposition—the creation of a musical comedy for Broadway audiences.

Despite many obstacles, *Shuffle Along* had 504 performances and returned a healthy profit to the creators, performers, and financial backers. The surprise success of the show legitimized the black musical on Broadway and spawned a host of imitators.

Sissle and Blake continued their collaboration with *Elsie* (1923), performed by a white cast, before returning to the terrain of *Shuffle Along* with *The Chocolate Dandies** in 1924. Attempts to revive *Shuffle Along* in 1932* and 1952* were unsuccessful. Blake also collaborated with Andy Razaf* (*Blackbirds of 1930**) and Cecil Mack* and Milton Reddie (*Swing It** [1937]). Sissle and Blake were recently honored in the 1979 Broadway musical *Eubie!**

Reference: Kimball, Robert, and William Bolcom, *Reminiscing with Sissle and Blake*, New York: Viking Press, 1973.

**BLEDSOE, JULIUS (JULES)** (1898-1943). Bledsoe was born in Waco, Texas, and came north to study medicine at Columbia University. Sol Hurok heard him at a glee club performance and suggested that he change careers. Bledsoe made his singing debut in 1924 and soon turned to acting as well.

Bledsoe replaced Charles Gilpin* in Eugene O'Neill's *The Emperor Jones** and won praise for his performances in *Deep River* and *In Abraham's Bosom** in 1926. As the original "Jim" in *Show Boat* (1927), Bledsoe estimated that he sang "Ol' Man River" more than 3,600 times.

After his Broadway success, Bledsoe moved to the world of opera, appearing at the Metropolitan Opera as well as with several major European companies. His promising career on the concert stage was cut short by a cerebral hemorrhage in 1943.

Reference: *The New York Times*, July 16, 1943.

**BRANCH, WILLIAM BLACKWELL** (1927- ). Branch was born in New Haven, Connecticut, the sixth of seven sons of A.M.E. Zion minister James Matthew and Iola Douglas Branch. The family moved from parish to parish in New York State and settled in Charlotte, North Carolina. Young Branch went to high school in Washington, D.C., received a B.S. in Speech from Northwestern University in 1949, and went to New York intending to be an actor. Parts for black actors were scarce, and he soon became convinced that he should write plays about the black experience.

William Branch's first play, *A Medal for Willie*, opened in October 1951 at Harlem's Club Baron, produced by the Committee for the Negro in the Arts. It is a play that dramatically underscores the ironies of a black American soldier fighting abroad for freedoms he is not allowed to enjoy at home. An additional irony was that Branch was inducted into the U.S. Army the day after *A Medal for Willie* opened. It was on a troopship that Branch wrote the first few pages of what was to become a historical drama about John Brown and Frederick Douglass. Originally copyrighted as *Frederick Douglass* in 1953, the play opened as *In Splendid Error** at the Greenwich Mews on October 26, 1954, and ran through January 1955.

For the stage in 1960 he wrote *A Wreath for Udomo*, based on Peter Abraham's prophetic novel about the rise and fall of an African prime minister. Its world premiere at Cleveland's Karamu Theatre in the spring of

1960 led to a Broadway option and a London production at the Lyric Hammersmith Theatre in November 1961. His most recent play, *Baccalaureate*, a chilling family drama, had its premiere in Bermuda in 1975 and then dropped out of sight.

Currently as founder and president of his own consulting and production firm, William Branch Associates, Branch is working on new projects for theatre, films, and television from his home and office in New Rochelle, New York. Since September 1979, he has also been visiting professor of Afro-American Studies at the University of Maryland, Baltimore County.

Reference: Abramson, Doris E., *Negro Playwrights in the American Theatre*, New York: Columbia University Press, 1969.

DORIS E. ABRAMSON

**BROOKS, SHELTON** (1886–1975). Brooks was born in Cleveland, Ohio, of theatrical parents. He toured the South with his family in musical companies that performed for black audiences.

Brooks met Al Jolson in Chicago and wrote a song for him ("You Ain't Talking to Me") which started a new career for Brooks. Brooks's hits include two classic songs, "Some of These Days" (1910) and "Darktown Strutters' Ball" (1917). He later appeared on the Broadway stage in the classic black revues of the 1920s and other musical comedies.

Credits: *Plantation Revue** (1922); *Dixie To Broadway** (1924); *Brown Buddies** (1930); and *Ken Murray's Blackouts of 1949.*

Reference: *The New York Herald*, July 25, 1922.

**BROWNE, ROSCOE LEE** (1925– ). Browne was born in New Jersey. He was successful at a variety of occupations (college professor, track star, and businessman) before turning to acting in a 1956 production of *Julius Caesar* at the New York Shakespeare Festival. Browne's career has also embraced television (*All in the Family*) as well as motion pictures (*The Connection* [1962], *Black Like Me* [1964], and *The Comedians* [1967]). He first achieved notice in Off-Broadway's long-running production of *The Blacks** in 1961.

Credits: *Julius Caesar*; *Titus Andronicus* (1956); *Romeo and Juliet* (1957); *Aria Da Capo* (1958); *Antigone* (1959); *The Cool World**; *The Pretender* (1960); *The Blacks* (1961); *General Seeger*; *King Lear*; *Tiger, Tiger Burning Bright** (1962); *The Winter's Tale*; *Ballad of the Sad Cafe* (1963); *Benito Cereno* (1964); *Troilus and Cressida*; *Danton's Death*; *A Hand Is on the Gate** (1965); *Volpone*; *Tartuffe* (1967); *Remembrance* (1979).

Reference: *The Philadelphia Inquirer*, February 27, 1972.

**BUBBLES, JOHN W.** (1902– ). Bubbles of Louisville, Kentucky, achieved fame as a tap-dancer on the vaudeville stage with Ford Lee "Buck" Washington ("Buck and Bubbles"), and later as the original

"Sportin' Life" in *Porgy and Bess** (1935). He brought his talents to other Broadway musicals, television, and films (such as *Cabin in the Sky* [1943]). He recently performed "I Got Plenty O' Nuttin' " from *Porgy and Bess* in *Black Broadway** (1980), a tribute to the black musicals of the first half of this century.

Credits: *Weather Clear, Track Fast* (1927); *Blackbirds of 1930**; *The Dance of Death* (1932); *Porgy and Bess* (1935); *Virginia* (1937); *Laugh Time* (1943); *Carmen Jones** (1945); *Judy Garland* (1959); *At Home at the Palace* (1967); *Black Broadway* (1980).

Reference: Stearns, Marshall and Jean, *Jazz Dance*, New York: Schirmer, 1979.

**BULLINS, ED** (1935- ). Playwright, novelist, fiction writer, and poet, Ed Bullins grew up in a rough neighborhood in north Philadelphia. In 1952, after dropping out of Franklin High School, he joined the U.S. Navy. The young Bullins left Philadelphia in 1958 and moved to Los Angeles where he enrolled in Los Angeles City College. In 1961, while attending classes part-time, he started writing seriously. At this time, he wrote mainly fiction, essays, and poetry. In 1964, after visiting several cities, he moved to the San Francisco Bay area. While registered in a college writing program in San Francisco, he began writing plays. He thought writing plays was the best way to communicate with black people.

After some discouraging experiences, he saw a production of *Dutchman** and *The Slave** by Imamu Amiri Baraka* in the Bay area. He cites this experience as the greatest inspiration in his career. Baraka was dealing with the same qualities and conditions of black life that influenced Bullins. Shortly afterwards, Bullins joined with others inspired by Baraka to organize a militant cultural-political group called Black House. Active in this group were Huey Newton, Bobby Seale, and Eldridge Cleaver, all of whom later became nationally known as Black Panther leaders. Bullins served for a brief time as the minister of culture for the Panthers. A conflict in ideology between the artists and the revolutionaries led to a split with this group. Bullins says that the artists were interested in cultural awakening, while the revolutionaries thought that poems and plays should inspire people to pick up guns.

In 1967, the thirty-two-year-old Bullins was making plans to leave the country when he heard of the New Lafayette Theatre in Harlem, New York. This was the turning point in his career. Although he started writing in 1961 on the coast, it was not until he was embraced by New York producers, artists, publishers, and audiences that his plays placed him in the national and international theatre arena.

In March 1968, the New Lafayette Theatre produced three one-act plays by Bullins. In December 1968, it produced the premiere production of *In the Wine Time.** For approximately six years following these events, audiences were treated to a steady diet of his plays at the New Lafayette. In addition, from 1969 to 1972, the New Lafayette published a biannual periodical entitled *Black Theatre*, edited by Ed Bullins.

Bullins has now written more than fifty plays which have been produced throughout the United States, in London, Paris, Kingston, and Prague. He is currently developing a "Twentieth-Century Cycle"—twenty full-length plays about a group of blacks and their friends and relatives. Among those completed are *In the Wine Time*, *In New England Winter*,* *The Duplex*,* *The Fabulous Miss Marie*,* *Homeboy*, and *Daddy*. Other celebrated plays by Bullins are *The Taking of Miss Janie*,* *The Electronic Nigger*,* and *A Son, Come Home*,* all award winners.

Bullins, a playwright of the black experience, a people's playwright, is at his best in his full-length "theatre of reality" plays. He is a pioneer developing new forms for the black theatre, that is, the black ritual and street theatre. However, Bullins's rituals, street theatre plays, and agitation-propaganda plays remain in the shadows of the "theatre of reality" plays. Although influenced by Baraka, Bullins developed his own style, his own distinct voice. While Baraka is concerned with "teaching the white eyes their deaths," Bullins is concerned with revealing the black man to himself. He is the poet/playwright of the black masses. Many of his characters are those struggling to survive "by any means necessary." He takes these characters and develops their song and their story; he reveals their hopes, fears, and dreams.

Credits: *Dialectic Determinism or The Rally*; *How Do You Do*; *It Has No Choice* (1965); *Goin' a Buffalo*; *A Minor Scene*; *The Theme Is Blackness* (1966); *The Man Who Dug Fish* (1967); *Clara's Ole Man**; *The Electronic Nigger*; *A Son, Come Home*; *In the Wine Time*; *The Helper* (1968); *The Gentleman Caller** (1969); *The Pig Pen**; *Deathlist*; *It Bees Dat Way*; *Street Sounds* (1970); *In New England Winter*; *The Fabulous Miss Marie* (1971); *The Corner**; *The Duplex*; *Homeboy* (1972); *House Party** (1973); *The Mystery of Phyllis Wheatley*; *The Taking of Miss Janie* (1975); *I Am Lucy Terry*; *JoAnne!* (1976); *Daddy*; *Sepia Star* (songs: Mildred Kayden); *Storyville* (songs: Mildred Kayden) (1977); *Michael* (1978); *Leavings* (1980).

Reference: Hay, Samuel A., "Structural Elements in Ed Bullins' Plays," *Black World* 6 (April 1974), 20-26.

SANDRA MAYO

**BURROWS, VINIE** (1928- ). New York-born Vinie Burrows made her acting debut with Helen Hayes in *The Wisteria Trees* in 1950, while she was still a student at New York University. After a lengthy acting career, Burrows assembled a one-woman show, *Walk Together Children** (1968), which chronicled the black experience in America. The show received wide acclaim in its initial showing, and it was revived in 1972.

Credits: *The Wisteria Trees* (1950); *The Green Pastures** (1951); *Mrs. Patterson** (1954); *The Skin of Our Teeth* (1955); *The Ponder Heart* (1956); *Come Share My House*; *Nat Turner* (1960); *Mandingo* (1961); *Walk Together Children*; *The Worlds of Shakespeare* (1968/1972).

Reference: *Essence*, May 1972.

# C

**CAESAR ADOLPH** (1934- ). Although an acting veteran for many years, Caesar finally became a star with his performance as Technical Sergeant Vernon Waters in Charles Fuller's* Pulitzer Prize winning *A Soldier's Play** (1981). He began his Broadway career with Shakespearean roles in 1966, and by 1971 he initiated his lengthy relationship with the Negro Ensemble Company.* He also wrote and starred in a one-man show, *The Square Root of Soul** (1977), a dramatic reading of the works of black poets and novelists.

Credits: *Day of Absence** (1965); *Falstaff*; *Murder in the Cathedral*; *Twelfth Night*; *Julius Caesar* (1966); *Harper's Ferry*; *The Visit* (1967); *Perry's Mission/Rosalee Pritchett**; *Ride a Black Horse**; *The Sty of the Blind Pig** (1971); *A Ballet Behind the Bridge**; *Frederick Douglass . . . Through His Own Words** (1972); *The Great MacDaddy**; *Nowhere to Run, Nowhere to Hide** (1974); *Waiting for Mongo** (1975); *The Brownsville Raid** (1976); *The Square Root of Soul* (1977); *Plays From Africa**; *A Season to Unravel** (1979); *Lagrima del Diablo** (1980); *A Soldier's Play* (1981).

Reference: "Adolph Caesar" File, NYPL/TC.

**CALDWELL, BEN** (?- ). Caldwell has been active in Harlem theatre since the beginning of the Black Arts Movement in the 1960s. He first gained attention as a playwright when four of his plays (*The Job*, *Riot Sale or Dollar Psyche Fake Out*, *Top Secret or a Few Million Years after B.C.*, and *Mission Accomplished*) were included in the Black Theatre issue of *The Drama Review*. He served as a contributing editor to the short-lived *Black Theatre* periodical, and his plays have been presented by various Harlem groups, Spirit House in Newark, New Jersey, and the Black Arts Alliance in San Francisco. His best known play, *Prayer Meeting or The First Militant Minister*,* was produced in 1969 as part of *A Black Quartet** by the Chelsea Theatre Center.

Among the playwrights of the Black Arts Movement, Caldwell stands out as a satirist whose ridicule of white society and unliberated blacks aims at raising the consciousness of his audience and moving them toward a revolutionary attitude. As a satirist, however, he ranges from incisive to heavy-handed, and most of his short dramas take the form of agit-prop cartoons that drive his message home through broad comedy and biting social comment.

One of Caldwell's best plays is *Prayer Meeting or The First Militant Minister*, a relatively restrained comedy based upon the classical device of mistaken identity. It offers the incongruous situation of an Uncle Tom preacher having his consciousness raised by a hidden burglar who pretends to be God answering the prayers of the unsuspecting preacher. The burglar is a wrathful voice of black vengeance that orders the minister to stop preaching nonviolence and to start caring for his people rather than feathering his own nest. The comedy is broad but the revolutionary point is clear, as Caldwell calls for black solidarity.

Throughout the 1960s, Caldwell was a prolific playwright and provided a number of short plays for local black groups. In later plays such as *The King of Soul or the Devil and Otis Redding* and *All White Caste*, he moved beyond the simplistic exhortations of the agit-prop form to explore a more ambiguous and complex world. As a playwright, Caldwell brings to his dramas a broad sense of humor and an often bitter satirical thrust.

References: Caldwell, Ben, *Four Plays* in *The Drama Review* 12 (Summer 1968), 40-51; Ladwig, Ronald V., "The Black Comedy of Ben Caldwell," *Players* 51 (February-March 1976), 89-91; Neal, Larry, "The Black Arts Movement," *The Drama Review* 12 (Summer 1968), 29-39.

GERALD T. GOODMAN

**CARROLL, DIAHANN** (1935- ). Diahann Carroll, a native of New York, stopped the show in *House of Flowers** (1954) with her rendition of "A Sleepin' Bee." She returned to Broadway in Richard Rodgers's musical *No Strings* (1962), which concerned an interracial love affair (although the topic was hardly mentioned in the show). Carroll shared a Tony with Anna Maria Alberghetti (*Carnival*) for the best performance by a female in a musical comedy. In 1962 Carroll appeared in NBC Television's *Julia*, a series that attempted to present a nonstereotypical view of the life of a single middle-class black woman and her family. Carroll also appeared in such films as *Carmen Jones** (1954), *Porgy and Bess** (1969), and *Claudine* (1974).

Reference: "Diahann Carroll" File, PFL/TC.

**CARROLL, VINNETTE** (1922- ). Harlem-born Vinnette Carroll first became a psychologist before turning to acting. She began studying drama at the New School at the same time as Marlon Brando and Rod Steiger.

In the 1950s she taught acting at the High School of Performing Arts, where she became interested in directing. She currently teaches theatre at her Urban Arts Corps, a training center for minority youths. Many of Carroll's shows were presented in workshop format at this center.

Although Carroll is best known for *Don't Bother Me, I Can't Cope** (1972) and *Your Arms Too Short to Box with God** (1976) on Broadway, she has also appeared on television (as "Sojourner Truth" on CBS) and in films.

Credits (Acting): *Outside the Door* (1949); *A Streetcar Named Desire* (1956); *Small War on Murray Hill* (1957); *The Crucible* (1958); *Jolly's Progress** (1959); *The Octoroon* (1961); *Moon on a Rainbow Shawl** (1962).

(Directing): *Black Nativity** (1961); *The Prodigal Son** (1965); *But Never Jam Today**; *Old Judge Mose Is Dead*; *Moon on a Rainbow Shawl* (1969); *Don't Bother*

*Me, I Can't Cope* (1972); *All the King's Men* (1974); *Your Arms Too Short to Box with God* (1976).

(Playwright): *Trumpets of the Lord** (1963); *But Never Jam Today* (1969/1979); *Don't Bother Me, I Can't Cope* (1972); *Your Arms Too Short to Box with God* (1976).

Reference: *Philadelphia Bulletin*, January 13, 1974.

**CARTER, NELL** (?- ). Carter was born in Birmingham, Alabama. She achieved star status in *Ain't Misbehavin'** (1978), for which she won a Theatre World and Tony Award. She made her debut in 1971 in *Soon*, and her most recent Broadway appearance was *Black Broadway** (1980). She is currently appearing on the National Broadcasting company television series *Gimme a Break*.

Credits: *Soon*; *The Wedding of Iphigenia* (1971); *Dude* (1972); *Be Kind to People Week* (1975); *Ain't Misbehavin'* (1978); *Black Broadway* (1980).

Reference: "Nell Carter" File, NYPL/TC.

**CARTER, STEVE** (1930- ). Carter was born in New York City's San Juan Hill and later moved to Harlem. He joined the Negro Ensemble Company* in the late 1960s as Lonne Elder III's* assistant in the playwright's workshop. When Elder left for California to write the screenplay for *Sounder*, Carter filled his position. Carter's most acclaimed play was *Eden** (1976), and his most recent work, *Dame Lorraine* (1981), was produced in Chicago with Esther Rolle* in the leading role.

Credits: *Terraces** (1974); *Eden* (1976); *Nevis Mountain Dew** (1978).

Reference: "Steve Carter" File, NYPL/TC.

**CASH, ROSALIND** (1938- ). Cash hails from Atlantic City, New Jersey, and has acted in both theatre and films. She made her debut in Langston Hughes's* *Soul Gone Home* at the Harlem YMCA in 1958. She studied drama with Vinnette Carroll* and Edmund Cambridge before joining the Negro Ensemble Company* (NEC). After a lengthy hiatus in Hollywood (*Melinda* [1972], *Uptown Saturday Night* [1974], and *Cornbread, Earl, and Me* [1975]), she returned to the NEC for an appearance in *The Sixteenth Round** in 1980.

Credits: The Wayward Stork (1966); Junebug Graduates Tonight!; To Bury a Cousin (1967); Song of the Lusitanian Bogey*; Kong's Harvest*; Daddy Goodness* (1968); *God Is a (Guess What?)**; *Ceremonies in Dark Old Men**; *An Evening of One Acts**; *Man Better Man** (1969); *The Harangues**; *Day of Absence** (1970); *Charlie Was Here and Now He's Gone** (1971); *King Lear* (1973); *The Sixteenth Round* (1980).

Reference: "Rosalind Cash" File, PFL/TC.

**CHILDRESS, ALICE** (1920- ). Childress was born in Charleston, South Carolina, but Harlem was her real home. After two years of high school, she joined the American Negro Theatre* there in 1941, where she performed a variety of leading roles for eleven years. Essentially a self-educated woman without academic degrees, Childress won a Harvard appointment as playwright and scholar to the Radcliffe Institute for Independent Study (1966-1968).

Her first play, *Florence* (1949), dramatizes in one act a casual conversation between a black woman and a white woman across the little fence separating them in a Jim Crow railroad station in the Deep South. Mama tells the white woman that she plans to bring her daughter Florence home from New York where the girl is struggling with little success to become a dramatic actress. With insensitivity and condescension, the white woman offers to find Florence a domestic position. Angered, Mama sells back her ticket and wires the money to her daughter with the message: "Keep trying." The play delighted audiences in a Harlem loft that barely seated twenty-five people.

The following year, Childress adapted the popular novel by Langston Hughes,* *Simple Speaks His Mind*, into a one-act play, *Just a Little Simple.* Two years later she presented *Gold Through the Trees*, the first play by a black woman professionally produced on the New York stage. During this time, Childress initiated Harlem's first all-union contracts recognizing both the Actors Equity Association and Harlem Stage Hand Local Union.

*Trouble in Mind** (1955), Childress's first full-length play, dramatizes the struggles of black actors confronted with subtle racism from white directors. In the play veteran actress Wiletta Mayer protests the verisimilitude of motivation of the character she has been cast to play. She tells the self-consciously liberal white director Manners that no real mother would send her son out to face a lynch mob. When she asks Manners if he would send his son out to be killed, the suddenly unmasked racist snaps back: "Don't compare yourself to me." Wiletta leads a cast walkout, knowing that her heroism on a matter of principle may be professional suicide. *Trouble in Mind* ran ninety-one performances at the Greenwich Mews Theatre and won the Obie award as the best original Off-Broadway play of the season.

*Wedding Band** offers Childress's ironic commentary on anti-miscegenation laws and what she calls "anti-woman" laws in the South after Reconstruction. The play features a tragic interracial love affair set in Charleston, South Carolina, in summer 1918. Although *Wedding Band* was given a successful rehearsed reading in 1963, the first professional production was not until 1966 at the University of Michigan. Finally, in 1972 it was presented at the New York Public Theatre.

In *Mojo: A Black Love Story*, presented at the New Heritage Theatre in 1970, Irene visits former husband Teddy before entering the hospital for serious cancer surgery. She tells him that she always loved him despite her difficulty in expressing her feelings. She reveals that she married him so that she could have a child by him. The daughter she bore in secret, however, became such an obsession that she had to give the baby up for adoption. Now she must share with Teddy her newly developed black pride and her need for blackness as she faces the whiteness of surgery.

Childress began writing for the theatre because she loved it, and black theatre in the 1940s and 1950s needed good material. Furthermore, Childress has always been an advocate of social justice and the rights of all oppressed people. In both her fiction and her drama, she features portraits of the genteel or intellectual poor. Her characters may lack formal education and social sophistication, but they value ideas and beautiful things. Childress characterizes lowly folk bursting with vitality, using earthy dialogue and crude figurative language. Although her characters exhibit passion, wit, and righteous rage, Childress never glorifies hatred or hostility. She portrays even fascist oppressors with compassion. As a feminist and black liberation playwright, Childress focuses primarily on the rights of black women, and she has supplied American theatre with delightful realistic portraits of brave female protagonists.

Credits: *Florence* (1949); *Just a Little Simple* (1950); *Gold Through the Trees* (1952); *Trouble in Mind* (1955); *Wedding Band* (1966/1972); *Wine in the Wilderness* (Teleplay, 1969); *String—An Evening of One Acts* (1969); *Mojo: A Black Love Story* (1970); *Sea Island Song* (South Carolina, 1979).

Reference: Abramson, Doris E., *Negro Playwrights in the American Theatre, 1925-1959*. New York: Columbia University Press, 1969.

ROSEMARY CURB

**COLE, BOB (ROBERT)** (1868-1911). Cole was one of the earliest black performers to gain success and recognition in the theatre. He was born in Athens, Georgia, attended Atlanta University, went to New York, and began a career of great variety and merit. He toured in the popular *Creole Show* in 1890 and met Stella Wiley, a comedienne who was performing in it. They formed a team and were later married for a few years. Cole performed a memorable singles "tramp act" in vaudeville, and wrote songs for himself and other performers. At the age of twenty-six he became a playwright and stage manager for Worth's Museum All-Star Stock Company. There he worked with twelve to fifteen performers presenting sketches and plays in "the first place where a group of coloured performers were able to gain anything approaching dramatic training and experience on the strictly professional stage" (Johnson, *Black Manhattan*, pp. 97-98). In 1896, two white producers, Voelckel and Nolan, commissioned him to write songs for Sissieretta Jones* to perform in her show *Black Patti's Troubadours*. The production was a major success, particularly in the South, but after a dispute about his salary, Cole took his music and left the theatre. He was arrested and taken to court where he vainly protested the unfair treatment he had received. Following this incident, he determined to write and produce his own musicals, and, forming a partnership with Billy Johnson, he presented *A Trip to Coontown** in the 1898-1899 season.

In 1901, Cole joined with James Weldon Johnson and J. Rosamond Johnson* in writing songs for Cole and J. Rosamond Johnson's vaudeville act as well as for white performers including Anna Held, Lillian Russell, and Marie Cahill. Among these popular songs were "Under the Bamboo Tree," "The Congo Love Song," and "The Maiden with the Dreamy Eyes." In 1905, Cole and Johnson performed as headliners in vaudeville at the Palace Theatre in London with a return engagement the next year. The last work written by the Johnson Brothers and Cole was the popular musical *The Shoo-Fly Regiment** which they began touring in 1906 with a cast of sixty, ending the tour at the Bijou Theatre on Broadway in 1907. The expenses of so large a production led to financial problems, but Cole and J. Rosamond Johnson went on to write *The Red Moon** in 1908. During this period, they continued to write songs, and Cole staged *The Supper Club* at the Winter Garden in New York, trained dancers, and performed as a singer and dancer. With his earnings he supported his mother and four sisters, and after *The Red Moon* he purchased a home in Harlem. Increasing ill health halted Cole's career, and in 1911 he died in New York.

Cole was innovative and courageous in the work he did for the stage. *A Trip to Coontown* was the first true black musical comedy. It made a clear break with the minstrel pattern and utilized a fully developed plot. It was also the first black musical to be organized, produced, and managed by blacks themselves. Even Cole's productions which were not financially successful, such as *The Red Moon*, were important because they made a break with the traditional crude and often obscene songs and acts, and they sought to present blacks in productions with elegance, wit, and a fresh bright style.

Credits (Acting): *Black Patti's Troubadours* (1896); *A Trip to Coontown* (1898); *The Shoo-Fly Regiment* (1907); *The Red Moon* (1909).

References: Johnson, James Weldon, *Black Manhattan*, New York: Knopf, 1930; Sampson, Henry T., *Blacks in Blackface*, Metuchen, N.J.: Scarecrow Press, 1980.

YVONNE SHAFER

**COMATHIERE, A.B.** (?- ). Comathiere began his acting career with the Lafayette Stock Company. He made his Broadway debut in a 1927 revival of *Goat Alley*,* and he attracted critical attention the same year in *Porgy*.*

Credits: *Goat Alley*; *Porgy* (1927); *Make Me Know It** (1929); *The Second Comin'** (1931); *Ol' Man Satan** (1932); *Louisiana** (1933); *Brain Sweat** (1934); *Too Many Boats* (1935).

Reference: "A. B. Comathiere" File, NYPL/TC.

**COOK, WILL MARION** (1869-1944). Although trained as a classical composer and violinist, Cook turned his attention to Broadway at an early age. With his friend Paul Laurence Dunbar (1872-1906), the noted poet, Cook composed the music for a Broadway musical entitled *Clorindy, the Origin of the Cakewalk*. After several delays, the musical premiered (minus most of the libretto) at the Casino Roof Garden in June 1898, with Ernest Hogan* in the leading role. Cook received raves for his score, and he collaborated again with Dunbar on *Jes' Lak White Fo'ks* (1899), which also opened at the Roof Garden.

By 1899, Cook began supplying songs to such Broadway musicals as *The Policy Players** (1899), *The Casino Girl* (1900), and *Wild Rose* (1902). Thereafter, he became the resident composer for the Williams* and Walker* entertainments: *In Dahomey** (1903), *Abyssinia** (1906), and *Bandana Land** (1908). He also composed the score for Broadway's first interracial musical, *The Southerners*,* in 1904.

Reference: Cook, Will Marion, "Clorindy, the Origin of the Cakewalk," *Theatre Arts* 31 (September 1947), 61-65.

**CREAMER, HENRY** (1879-1930). Lyricist Henry Creamer wrote several song hits with his collaborator Turner Layton ("After You've Gone" [1918] and "Way Down Yonder in New Orleans" [1922]). He also supplied lyrics for *The Oyster Man** (1907), *Three Showers* (1920), which was written by blacks but performed by whites, *Strut Miss Lizzie** (1922), *How Come?* (1923), Keep Shufflin'** (1928) and *Deep Harlem** (1929). Creamer and Layton also performed their songs in nightclubs and for records.

Reference: Kinkle, Roger D., *The Complete Encyclopedia of Popular Music and Jazz, 1900-1950*, New Rochelle, N.Y.: Arlington House, 1974.

# D

**DAVIS, OSSIE** (1917- ). Davis was born in Georgia and attended Howard University before beginning his acting career. He studied with the Rose McClendon Players before making his Broadway debut in *Jeb** (1946). In addition to his acting talents, Davis is recognized for his writings. His *Purlie Victorious** (1961) appeared on Broadway and was favorably reviewed. He has also appeared in and directed films (*Gone Are the Days!* [1963] and *Cotton Comes to Harlem* [1969]) and prepared a Public Television series on the black cultural experience in America. Davis has written several plays since 1949, with many enjoying brief runs in Harlem and regional theatres. These include *Point Blank*; *The Mayor of Harlem*

(1949); *Clay's Rebellion* (1951); *Alice in Wonder*; *The Big Deal* (1953); *What Can You Say to Mississippi?* (1955); *Montgomery Footprints* (1956); *Curtain Call Mr. Aldridge, Sir* (1963); and *Alexis Is Fallen* (1974).

Credits (Acting): *Jeb* (1946); *Leading Lady* (1948); *The Smile of the World*; *Stevedore** (1949); *The Wisteria Trees* (1950/1955); *The Royal Family*; *The Green Pastures**; *Remains to Be Seen* (1951); *Touchstone** (1953); *Jamaica** (1957); *Purlie Victorious* (1961); *Ballad for Bimshire** (1963); *The Zulu and the Zayda* (1965); *Take It from the Top* (1979).

Reference: Bigsby, C.W.E., "Three Black Playwrights: Loften Mitchell, Ossie Davis, Douglas Turner Ward," in Bigsby, *The Black American Writer*, Vol. 2, Deland, Fla.: Everett/Edwards, Inc., 1969.

**DAVIS, SAMMY, JR.** (1925- ). Primarily a nightclub entertainer, Sammy Davis, Jr., has made three dramatic Broadway appearances. He introduced "Too Close for Comfort" in *Mr. Wonderful* (1956) and "I Want to Be with You" in *Golden Boy** (1964). He revived his recording hit, "What Kind of Fool Am I?" by Anthony Newley and Leslie Bricusse, in *Stop the World, I Want to Get Off* (1978). He also appeared in the film version of *Porgy and Bess** (1959) as "Sportin' Life."

Reference: Davis, Sammy, Jr., *Yes I Can*, New York: Farrar, Straus, & Giroux, 1965.

**DEAN, PHILLIP HAYES** (?- ). Dean was born in Chicago. He moved to Pontiac, Michigan, as a teenager and attended Wayne State University. He began his career as an actor in such plays as *Waiting for Godot* and *The Wisteria Trees* in 1955. The American Place Theatre produced his first play, *This Bird of Dawning Singeth All Night Long* in 1968. He won a Drama Desk Award for the Negro Ensemble Company* production of *The Sty of the Blind Pig** in 1971, and a Rockefeller Foundation Grant in 1973. His most recent Broadway show was the controversial *Paul Robeson** (1978) with James Earl Jones.*

Credits: *This Bird of Dawning Singeth All Night Long* (1968); *The Sty of the Blind Pig* (1971); *Freeman** (1973); *American Night Cry** (1974); *Every Night When the Sun Goes Down** (1976); *Paul Robeson*; *If You Can't Sing, They'll Make You Dance* (1978).

Reference: *The Philadelphia Tribune*, October 18, 1977.

**DEE, RUBY** (1923- ). Ruby Dee began her acting career with the American Negro Theatre* in Harlem. She replaced the lead in *Anna Lucasta*,* where she met husband-to-be Ossie Davis.* Her most acclaimed roles were "Lutiebelle" in *Purlie Victorious** (1961) and "Lena" in *Boesman and Lena** (1970). She has appeared in films and television, and recently wrote *Take It from the Top*, which played for twelve performances at the Harry De Jur Playhouse in 1979.

Credits: *Walk Hard** (1944); *Jeb** (1946); *A Long Way from Home* (1948);

*The Smile of the World* (1949); *The World of Sholom Aleichem* (1953); *A Raisin in the Sun** (1959); *Purlie Victorious* (1961); *The Taming of the Shrew*; *King Lear* (1965); *Oresteia*; *The Birds* (1966); *Boesman and Lena* (1970); *Wedding Band** (1972); *Hamlet* (1975); *Take It from the Top* (1979).

Reference: *The Philadelphia Bulletin*, January 12, 1969.

**DOWNING, DAVID** (1943- ). Downing was born in New York City. He first attempted acting while in high school with a small role in *The Cool World** (1960). He later studied acting with Maxwell Glanville,* before joining the Negro Ensemble Company* in its early years. His first film appearance was in Robert Downey's *Putney Swope* (1969).

Credits: *The Cool World* (1960); *Song of the Lusitanian Bogey**; *Kongi's Harvest**; *Daddy Goodness**; *God Is a (Guess What?)** (1968); *Ceremonies in Dark Old Men**; *Man Better Man** (1969); *The Harangues**; *Day of Absence** (1970); *Perry's Mission/Rosalee Pritchett**; *The Dream on Monkey Mountain**; *Ride a Black Horse** (1971); *A Ballet Behind the Bridge**; *Please Don't Cry and Say No* (1972); *My Sister, My Sister**; *The Great MacDaddy**; *Richard III* (1974); *Branches from the Same Tree* (1980).

Reference: "David Downing" File, NYPL/TC.

**DUDLEY, S[herman] H[ouston]** (1872–1940). Dudley began his career in a medicine show in Shreveport, Louisiana. After appearing in several touring The Smart Set productions, he launched a theatrical booking agency for black musical shows. Dudley, who mainly booked shows along the East Coast, joined with other investors in 1920 to form the nationwide Theatre Owners Booking Association (TOBA or "tough on black actors"). Because he was often at odds with the other owners, he helped form the Colored Actors Union in 1924, which challenged several TOBA practices.

Reference: *The Messenger*, Vol. 7 (1926), 50, 62.

**DUNBAR, PAUL LAURENCE.** See COOK, WILL MARION.

**DUNCAN, TODD** (1900- ). Duncan was born in Danville, Kentucky, and received a B.A. degree from Butler College in Indianapolis. He began teaching music at Simmons University. After postgraduate work at Columbia University, he became head of the Music Department at Howard University.

Abbie Mitchell* (who appeared in *Porgy and Bess** as "Clara") is credited with suggesting Duncan's name to George Gershwin for his new folk opera. Gershwin hired him on the spot, and Duncan took a leave from Howard to appear as "Porgy" (1935).

Duncan continued to divide his career between music and academe during the 1940s. He also appeared in *Cabin in the Sky** (1940), a revival of *Porgy and Bess* (1942), and Kurt Weill's *Lost in the Stars** (1949).

Reference: "Todd Duncan" File, PFL/TC.

**DUNHAM, KATHERINE** (1910- ). Known primarily as a choreographer, Dunham also appeared in several Broadway shows. She first attracted attention as "Georgia Brown" in *Cabin in the Sky** (1940). She returned to Broadway for *Carib Song** (1945), which she co-directed. The following season she produced, directed, and starred in *Bal Negre* (1946). She continued her career as the director of "Katherine Dunham and Her Company," which made occasional Broadway appearances.

Reference: Dunham, Katherine, *A Touch of Innocence*, New York: Harcourt, Brace & World, 1959.

# E

**EDWARDS, GUS** (1939- ). Young Gus Edwards met Sidney Poitier* in his native Antigua, and Poitier convinced him to come to the United States and become an actor. He obtained some minor film roles in *The Pawnbroker* (1965) and *Stilleto* (1969), but he soon turned to writing. The success of his 1973 production, *Harry*, by the New York Theatre Ensemble confirmed his choice of career. The Negro Ensemble Company* (NEC) produced two of his plays in one season (a first): *The Offering** (1977) and *Black Body Blues** (1978). He received a Rockefeller Foundation Grant in 1979, allowing him to complete his play *Old Phantoms*,* which was produced by the NEC. Mel Gussow of *The New York Times* observed that this play "offers additional proof of Mr. Edwards' dramatic talent." His most recent work, *Weep Not For Me** (1981), was also produced by the NEC.

Reference: "Gus Edwards" File, NYPL/TC.

**ELDER, LONNE, III** (1932- ). The acclaimed author of *Ceremonies in Dark Old Men** (1969), Lonne Elder III, was born in Americus, Georgia, and moved to Harlem at the age of nineteen. While in Harlem he served as an "assistant numbers runner" for his uncle, who later became the model for the character of Russell B. Parker in *Ceremonies*.

Encouraged by Douglas Turner Ward* and the Negro Ensemble Company* (NEC), Elder prepared for his playwrighting career. During the early years of the NEC, he served as the director of its Playwrights Unit.

*Ceremonies in Dark Old Men* received rave notices and won an Outer Critics Circle Award, a Drama Desk Award, and a Stella Holt Memorial Playwrights Award.

Elder has written for television (*NYPD* and *McCloud*) as well as for films. His screenplay for *Sounder* (1972) won an Oscar nomination for best screenplay, the first for a black writer.

Reference: *The New York Times*, February 8, 16, 1969.

**ELLINGTON, DUKE (Edward Kennedy)** (1899-1974). Duke Ellington never managed to achieve the same success on Broadway that he achieved elsewhere. His orchestra provided the music for the Gershwins' *Show Girl* in 1929, but he did not return to Broadway until 1946 when he supplied the music for *Beggar's Holiday*, with lyrics by John La Touche. This adaptation of *The Beggar's Opera* starred Alfred Drake, but it had only a brief run. "Brown Penny" became the sole hit of the score. A 1966 effort, *Pousse Café*, based on the film *The Blue Angel*, expired after three peformances. Ellington's greatness was celebrated on Broadway only after his death with *Bubbling Brown Sugar** (1976), which included several Ellington melodies, and *Sophisticated Ladies** (1981), an Ellington tribute that featured Gregory Hines* and Judith Jameson.

Ellington completed two other musical shows—*Jump for Joy* (Los Angeles) and *My People* (Chicago), but they never received a New York showing.

References: Dance, Stanley, *The World of Duke Ellington*, New York: Charles Scribner's Sons, 1970; Duke Ellington, *Music Is My Mistress*, New York: Doubleday & Co., 1973; Jewell, Derek, *Duke, A Portrait of Duke Ellington*, New York: W. W. Norton, Inc., 1977.

**ELLIS, EVELYN** (1894-1958). Ellis, a Boston native, made her theatrical debut in *Othello* at the Lafayette Theatre in 1919. Her most notable performance was as "Bess" in *Porgy** in 1927. In her later years, she assumed directorial chores with *Horse Play* in 1937 and an all-black version of *Tobacco Road*,* in 1950.

Credits (Acting): *Roseanne** (1924); *Goat Alley**; *Porgy* (1927); *Native Son** (1941); *Deep Are the Roots** (1945); *Tobacco Road* (1950); *The Royal Family* (1951); *Touchstone** (1953); *Salvation on a String* (1954).

Reference: *The New York Times*, July 6, 1958.

# F

**FEDERAL THEATRE PROJECT (FTP).** The Federal Theatre Project (1935-1939), an offshoot of the Works Progress Administration program, was the most ambitious theatre program ever attempted by any government. Because it was designed to reverse the aristocratic posture of earlier theatrical practices in this country, it was not surprising that the FTP reflected the revolutionary character of the early New Deal program. As Loften Mitchell* explained it, "With Roosevelt's election, the country gave up nostalgic dreams and decided to make a complete change. Roosevelt brought a surge of hope to all of America. This bold hope made its way into the theatre" (Mitchell, *Black Drama*, p. 96).

Within the sprawling framework of its national program, the FTP established special ethnic theatre projects so that these groups would be able to do plays of their own literatures and cultures. Negro units were, of course, among these specially designated theatre groups. Not by accident, the FTP sponsored Negro theatre in twenty-two American cities. Unquestionably, such dispersed exposure not only was important to its black participants but also marked the first time that blacks as a group were allowed to surface in the national culture.

Aside from having their own production units because the FTP's national leadership was determined to contribute to the development of black theatre, blacks also shared fully in other theatre activities. They participated in the dramatic productions staged by the nonethnic units. In addition, they were an integral part of such diverse theatre operations as workshops for playwrights and technical craftsmen, research bureau services to communities, and project publications including the *Federal Theatre Magazine*. That blacks would share center stage with other groups was portended even before the FTP officially began in 1935, since they were involved at all levels in the planning of this theatre venture.

Perhaps the FTP's greatest contribution to the growth of black drama was its "honest attempt to develop black playwrights who could express life in their own vernacular" (Gaffney, "Black Theatre," pp. 10-11). Limited to writing part-time because of the necessity of earning a living as a dishwasher, custodian, housepainter, pullman porter, redcap, or common laborer, the black writer's unseemly vocational fate was nicely underlined by Langston Hughes*: "The steam in hotel kitchens/And the smoke in hotel lobbies/And the slime in hotel spittoons/Part of my life" (Ottley, *Negro in New York*, p. 255). Government subsidy radically altered this employment pattern, however, by freeing black playwrights to learn and practice their craft on a full-time basis.

Theodore Ward,* Hughes Allison, Theodore Browne,* Laura Edwards, Abram Hill,* George Norford, Lew Payton, R. Washington Porter, John Silvera, J. Augustus Smith,* and Frank Wilson* all became resident dramatists with Negro units. Daily exposure to the total theatre environment was invaluable to these budding craftsmen, as was the lengthy rehearsal period for FTP productions which allowed them to make necessary alterations in their scripts. Theatre scholar Floyd Gaffney was not mistaken, therefore, when he wrote that the FTP afforded black writers "an entree into American mainstream theatre for the first time" (Gaffney, "Black Theatre," p. 10).

At last given a chance to assume center stage in the professional theatre in America, blacks compiled an outstanding record during their four years of participation in the FTP. In fact, Negro unit productions so dominated project headlines that an overwhelming preponderance of contemporary observers adjudged their work as the best done in the entire FTP. One such observer, Sterling Brown, wrote that the project "deserves credit . . . for presenting the largest number of serious, ambitious plays by Negro authors ever to be presented on the professional stage, and for giving the best productions that Negro playwrights have ever been afforded" (Brown, et al., *Negro Caravan*, p. 504). These plays included *Run, Little Chillun!,** *Big White Fog,** *Stevedore,** and the Negro *Macbeth*.

References: Brown, Sterling, Ulysses Lee, and Arthur Davis, eds., *The Negro Caravan: Writings by American Negroes*, New York: Arno Press, 1969; Gaffney, Floyd, "Black Theater: Commitment and Communication," *Black Scholar* (June 1970); Mitchell, Loften, *Black Drama: The Story of the American Negro in the Theatre*, New York: Hawthorn Books, 1967; Ottley, Roi, *The Negro in New York: An Informal Social History*, New York: New York Public Library, 1967; Patterson, Lindsay, ed., *Black Theater: A 20th Century Collection of the Work of Its Best Playwrights*, New York: Dodd, Mead, & Co., 1971; Ross, Ronald P., *Black Drama in the Federal Theatre, 1935-1939*, Ann Arbor, Mich.: University Microfilms, 1972.

RONALD P. ROSS

**FISHER, RUDOLPH** (1897–1934). Fisher was born in Washington, D.C., and spent his formative years in Rhode Island. Graduating from high school with honors, he enrolled at Brown University in Providence. By the time he had earned his A.B. degree in 1919, this son of a minister had also been chosen class day orator and elected to Phi Beta Kappa. He earned an M.A. in biology from Brown before returning to his birthplace to enroll in the Howard University School of Medicine in 1920, graduating with highest honors in 1924. Interested in the medical specialty of roentgenology, he entered Columbia University for advanced studies. By 1927, he had set up his own x-ray laboratory in Manhattan, a medical practice he would continue until his premature death in 1934. Soon after he established his lab, he turned to the writing of novels, publishing *The Walls of Jericho* in 1928 and *The Conjure Man Dies: A Mystery Tale of Dark Harlem* in 1932.

Although Fisher has been widely credited as the playwright of *Conjur Man Dies,** Arna Bontemps and Countee Cullen actually were responsible for crafting a drama out of his richly dramatic novel *The Conjure Man Dies* (Brown, et al., *Negro Caravan*, p. 503). Fisher, in fact, had been dead for over a year when the play opened in 1936 as a late substitute for the Federal Theatre Project's* scheduled production of *Macbeth*. Less sociological than previous FTP offerings, *Conjur Man Dies* combined the street culture and humor of Harlem with the element of mystery to fashion what turned out to be the most popular production of New York's Negro unit. Sterling Brown explained why this play was so well attended, attracting over eighty-three thousand patrons to thirty-six performances over a four-month span:

> *Conjur Man Dies* . . . was the most popular of all Federal Theatre productions to the Negroes of Harlem. Remaining dubious of the playwright's picture of working-class unity which they checked by a hard reality, rendered uncomfortable

by the shameful indignities of Southern life shown so powerfully in the social plays, they packed the house to hear a language they understood, to see something closer to the chief theatrical tradition they knew. (Patterson, *Anthology*, p. 105).

These same audiences were, of course, attracted by the play's reputation for witty dialogue, for which Fisher himself must be fully credited. As his friend Langston Hughes* remarked, "Fisher was the wittiest of these New Negroes of Harlem, whose tongue was favored with the sharpest and saltiest humor" (Abramson, *Negro Playwrights*, p. 60). Entertainment aside, the presentation also provided glimpses into the harsh realities of Harlem life which other literary depictions, including the agit-prop play and the purpose novel, often overlooked or failed to record.

References: Abramson, Doris, *Negro Playwrights in the American Theatre, 1925-1959*, New York: Columbia University Press, 1969; Brown, Sterling, Ulysses Lee, and Arthur Davis, eds., *The Negro Caravan: Writing by American Negroes*, New York: Arno Press, 1969; Patterson, Lindsay, ed., *Anthology of the American Negro in the Theatre*, New York: Publishers Co., 1967.

RONALD P. ROSS

**FOSTER, FRANCES** (1924- ). A native of Yonkers, Frances Foster made her professional debut in the role of Dolly May in *The Wisteria Trees* in 1955. She became an early member of the Negro Ensemble Company in 1967, and has appeared in several of its productions in the late 1960s and 1970s. She has also performed in television soap operas (*All My Children*) as well as in the mini-series *King*.

Credits: *The Wisteria Trees* (1955); *Take a Giant Step** (1956); *The Last Minstrel* (1963); *Day of Absence/Happy Ending** (1965/1970); *Summer of the Seventeenth Doll**; *Kongi's Harvest**; *God Is a (Guess What?)** (1968); *String**; *Malcochon**; *Song of the Lusitanian Bogey**; *Man Better Man** (1969); *Brotherhood**; *Akokawe**; *The Good Woman of Setzuan* (1970); *Behold! Cometh the Vanderkellans**; *Rosalee Pritchett**; *The Sty of the Blind Pig** (1971); *A Ballet Behind the Bridge**; *The River Niger** (1972); *Terraces** (director, 1974); *The First Breeze of Summer** (1975); *Livin' Fat** (1976); *Mahalia*; *Nevis Mountain Dew**; *Daughters of the Mock** (1978); *Plays from Africa** (1979); *Big City Blues** (1980); *Zooman and the Sign** (1981).

Reference: "Frances Foster" File, PFL/TC.

**FOSTER, GLORIA** (1936- ). Foster first appeared at the Goodman Theatre in her hometown of Chicago. She made her debut in the Off-Broadway production of *In White America** (1963) for which she won an Obie and a Drama Desk Award. Since then, she has performed in such classics as *Medea* (1965), for which she won a Theatre World Award, and Ntozake Shange's* recent adaptation of Brecht's *Mother Courage and Her Children* (1980).

Credits: *In White America* (1963); *Medea* (1965); *A Hand Is on the Gate**; *Yerma* (1966); *A Midsummer Night's Dream* (1967); *Black Visions** (1972); *The Cherry Orchard* (1973); *Agamemnon* (1977); *Julius Caesar*; *Coriolanus* (1979); *Mother Courage and Her Children* (1980); *Long Day's Journey into Night* (1981).

Reference: "Gloria Foster" File, NYPL/TC.

**FRANKLIN, J[ennie] E[lizabeth]** (1937- ). Franklin was born in Houston, Texas, on August 10, 1937, one of thirteen children in the family of Robert and Mathie (Randie) Franklin. While still a child, she began recording her impressions of life in writing. In 1964, she received a B.A. degree from the University of Texas and in the same year married Lawrence Siegel, now deceased.

Although primarily a writer, Franklin has had a varied career. In the summer of 1964, she was a primary school teacher in the Freedom School in Carthage, Mississippi. This stint was followed by her service as a youth director at the Neighborhood House Association in Buffalo, New York; as an analyst in the United States Office of Economic Opportunity in New York City; and as a lecturer in education at the Herbert N. Lehman College of the City University of New York (Bronx).

Franklin's playwrighting began before the 1970s when the success of *Black Girl** brought her to the attention of black theatregoers. Her first play to be performed, *First Step to Freedom* (1964), combined her interest in education and writing. This work was performed in Harmony, Mississippi, as part of a Congress of Racial Equality-Student Non-Violent Coordinating Committee program whose purpose was to interest students in reading.

In 1971, Woodie King, Jr.,* produced the play *Black Girl* at the New Federal Theatre before it was moved to the Theatre de Lys, where it ran for 234 performances. Franklin, the playwright, King, the producer, and Shauneille Perry,* the director, proved to be a powerful trio, for audiences filled the theatre and waited after each performance to congratulate members of the cast. For black theatregoers, *Black Girl* was the play to see. The play went on tour and, in addition, became a movie, with Ossie Davis* as director and Franklin as author of the screenplay.

In 1974, *The Prodigal Sister,** a musical with book and lyrics by Franklin and music and lyrics by Micki Grant,* opened at the Theatre de Lys. This work was Franklin's second major New York production. The director was again Shauneille Perry and the producer, Woodie King, Jr. *The Prodigal Sister* concentrates on the experiences of a black girl, an unwed mother-to-be, who leaves home to avoid her father's stern disapproval. Alone in the city, she has several bad incidents before returning home, this time to an understanding father. The scenes in the musical are divided into "beats," with a "Do Wah" musical group as an important ingredient in this theatre piece.

In addition to these dramatic works, Franklin has written other plays, including *The In-Crowd* (1965), *Mau Mau Room* (circa 1972), and *Cut Out the Lights and Call the Law* (1972). In 1977, *The In-Crowd* was produced as a musical at the New Federal Theatre.

Franklin has brought a fresh, strong feminine voice to black theatre. In her two major productions, she won the approval of audiences as well as many critics. Focusing her creative eye on black women, she has presented major characters who, in overcoming seemingly insurmountable difficulties, give hints of continued progress.

References: Beauford, Fred, "A Conversation with *Black Girl*'s J. E. Franklin," *Black Creation* 3 (Fall 1971), 38-40; Hunter, Charlayne, "Two Black Women Combine Lives and Talent in Play," *The New York Times*, July 13, 1971; Parks, Carole A., "J. E. Franklin, Playwright," *Black World* 21 (April 1972), 49-50.

JEANNE-MARIE A. MILLER

**FREEMAN, AL, JR.** (1934- ). Freeman, the son of a San Antonio, Texas, musician, first studied theatre in Los Angeles. He appeared at the Ebony Showcase in Los Angeles in 1954 and made his Broadway debut in 1960 in *The Long Dream.** He has displayed his singing talents in *Look to the Lilies* (1970), a musical adaptation of the film *Lilies of the Field*, and *The Great MacDaddy** (1974). He also received acclaim for his National Broadcasting Company television appearance in *My Sweet Charlie*.

Credits: *The Long Dream* (1960); *Tiger, Tiger Burning Bright** (1962); *The Living Premise*; *Trumpets of the Lord** (1963); *Blues for Mr. Charlie**; *Conversation at Midnight*; *The Slave** (1964); *Troilus and Cressida* (1965); *All's Well That Ends Well*; *Measure for Measure* (1966); *The Dozens* (1969); *Look to the Lilies* (1970); *Medea* (1973); *The Great MacDaddy* (1974); *One Crack Out* (1978); *Long Day's Journey into Night* (1981).

References: *Philadelphia Bulletin*, August 10, 1969; *The New York Times*, January 18, 1970.

**FREEMAN, MORGAN** (1937- ). Freeman pursued a variety of careers before turning to acting in an Off-Broadway play, *The Niggerlovers* (1967). He moved to Broadway later the same season for an appearance in the Pearl Bailey*-Cab Calloway version of *Hello Dolly!* He received his greatest acclaim for his performance as an aging wino in *The Mighty Gents** (1978). He is also a veteran of public television's *The Electric Company*.

Credits: *The Niggerlovers*; *Hello Dolly!* (1967); *The Dozens*; *Exhibition* (1969); *The Jungle of Cities*; *Purlie** (lead understudy, 1970); *Black Visions** (1972); *Cockfight** (1977); *The Mighty Gents*; *White Pelicans* (1978); *Julius Caesar*; *Coriolanus* (1979); *Mother Courage and Her Children* (1980); *The Connection* (1981).

Reference: *The New York Times*, April 21, 1978.

**FULLER, CHARLES** (1939- ). Although Philadelphian Charles Fuller has been writing plays since the late 1960s, he did not begin to attract notice until 1969 with *The Perfect Party.** *In the Deepest Part of Sleep** (1974) and *The Brownsville Raid** (1976) received additional praise, and *Zooman and the Sign** (1980) won an Obie. Fuller's most recent work, the Negro Ensemble Company's *A Soldier's Play** (1981), received the 1982 Pulitzer Prize for Drama. Fuller is thus the second black to receive this award in the playwrighting category. This play, which concerns the murder of a tyrannical black technical sergeant at a Louisiana army camp in 1944, has been optioned to Warner Brothers for a film version. Frank Rich of *The New York Times* called *A Soldier's Play* "a relentless investigation into the complex, sometimes cryptic pathology of hate."

Reference: *The New York Times*, April 13, 1982.

# G

**GAINES, J. E. (SONNY JIM)** (1928- ). Gaines displayed a variety of talents during the late 1960s and 1970s. As an actor (under the name Sonny Jim), he appeared in Ed Bullins's* *In the Wine Time** (1968) and *The Fabulous Miss Marie** (1971), which won him an Obie. As a director, he staged Bullins's *The Corner** (1972) at the Public Theatre. As a dramatist, he presented four well-received plays: *Don't Let It Go to Your Head,** *What If It Had Turned Up Heads?,** *Sometimes a Hard Head Makes a Soft Behind* (1972), and *Heaven and Hell's Agreement** (1974).

Reference: "J. E. Gaines" File, NYPL/TC.

**GILPIN, CHARLES S.** (1879–1930). After several tours with a Canadian minstrel show, Gilpin joined the Pekin Theatre in Chicago. He moved to New York's Lafayette Theatre, where he was "discovered" and booked for a run in *Abraham Lincoln* (1919). He portrayed William Curtis, an ex-slave, who represented a Frederick Douglass figure. This performance led to his triumph the following year in the title role of *The Emperor Jones.** Gilpin later appeared in *Roseanne** (1924) and *So That's That* (1925). His health began to fail during a road tour of *The Emperor Jones* in 1929, and he died the following year. He has often been compared to Paul Robeson* (who replaced him in *The Emperor Jones*), and is considered one of the best black actors of the 1920s.

Reference: "Charles Gilpin" File, PFL/TC.

**GLANVILLE, MAXWELL** (1918- ). Noted actor Maxwell Glanville has a lengthy list of Broadway and Off-Broadway credits. He is also a staunch supporter of Harlem theatre. His American Community Theatre introduced such talents as Clarence Williams III, David Downing,* and Arthur French. During the 1950s, Glanville co-produced *Alice in Wonder* (by Ossie Davis*), *The Other Foot*, and *A World Full of Men* (by Julian Mayfield); he directed the first two plays. He is also the author of a novel, *The Bonus.*

Credits: *Natural Man** (1941); *Home Is the Hunter** (1942); *Walk Hard** (1946); *Rain* (1948); *How Long Till Summer** (1949); *Freight*; *The Son* (1950); *The Autumn Garden* (1951); *In Splendid Error** (1954); *Cat on a Hot Tin Roof* (1955); *The Cool World** (1960); *Golden Boy** (1964); *Zelda* (1969); *Lady Day: A Musical Tragedy* (1972); *Anna Lucasta** (1978); *Branches from the Same Tree* (1980).

Reference: "Maxwell Glanville" File, NYPL/TC.

**GORDONE, CHARLES** (1925- ). Gordone was the first black to win the Pulitzer Prize for Drama for *No Place to Be Somebody** (1969). Gordone was born in Cleveland and majored in drama at Los Angeles State College, graduating in 1952. He came to New York and managed to get small acting roles in *The Climate of Eden* (1952), *Mrs. Patterson** (1955), *Fortunato* (1956), and *The Blacks** (1961). Gordone began writing the first draft of *No Place to Be Somebody* in 1960. The Negro Ensemble Company* initially turned the play down; Joseph Papp finally agreed to produce it. Gordone's other plays include *Gordone Is a Muthah* (1973) and *The Last Chord* (1976).

References: *The New York Times*, June 8, 1969; January 25, 1970.

**GOSSETT, LOUIS, JR.** (1936– ). Gossett, an Emmy Award winner (for *Roots*), began his acting career while in high school in Brooklyn, New York. A leg injury forced him to sit out the basketball season, so he turned his attention elsewhere. He auditioned for a role in *Take a Giant Step** (1953) and won a lead over several hundred rivals. He won a Donaldson Award for Best Newcomer of the Year for that show.

After several Broadway and Off-Broadway appearances in the 1950s and 1960s, Gossett moved to Hollywood where he has appeared in many film and television roles. He recently won an Oscar for his performance as a feisty drill instructor in Paramount's *An Officer and a Gentleman* (1982).

Credits: *Take a Giant Step* (1953); *The Desk Set* (1955); *A Raisin in the Sun** (1959); *The Blacks** (1961); *Tambourines to Glory** (1963); *Golden Boy** (1964); *The Zulu and the Zayda* (1965); *My Sweet Charlie* (1966); *Tartuffe* (1967); *Carry Me Back to Morningside Heights** (1968); *Murderous Angels* (1971).

Reference: *The New York Times*, August 30, 1970.

**GRANT, MICKI** (1941– ). Grant was born in Chicago and attended the University of Illinois. She moved to Los Angeles, where she appeared in a production of *Fly Blackbird.** She came with the show to New York and began her acting career. Grant appeared in several shows during the 1960s and revealed new talents in the 1970s as a songwriter for *Don't Bother Me, I Can't Cope** (1972), *The Prodigal Sister** (1974), *Your Arms Too Short to Box with God** (1976), *Working* (1978), and *It's So Nice to Be Civilized** (1981). She also participated in the formation of Vinnette Carroll's* Urban Arts Corps.

Credits (Acting): *Fly Blackbird* (1962); *Tambourines to Glory** (1963); *The Cradle Will Rock* (1964); *Leonard Bernstein's Theatre Songs* (1965); *Don't Bother Me, I Can't Cope* (1972).

Reference: *The New York Times*, May 7, 1972.

**GREEN, EDDIE** (1901–1950). Green appeared in several black musicals of the 1930s, but he received his greatest praise for his portrayal of "Ko-Ko" in *The Hot Mikado** (1939). Green was also a songwriter ("A Good Man Is Hard to Find"), a playwright (*Blackberries of 1932**), and a radio comedian (*Duffy's Tavern* and *The Rudy Vallee Show*). He organized the Sepia Art Picture Company which made several film shorts for black audiences.

Credits: *Hot Chocolates** (1929); *Blackberries of 1932*; *A Woman's a Fool to Be Clever* (1938); *The Hot Mikado* (1939).
Reference: "Eddie Green" File, NYPL/TC.

**GUILLAUME, ROBERT** (1927- ). The star of the American Broadcasting Company's television show, "Benson," was first known as a theatrical performer and musical comedy star. Born Robert Williams in Saint Louis, Guillaume first had dreams of an operatic career but later changed his goals. He made his Broadway debut in *Kwamina** in 1961. His most recent Broadway role was "Nathan Detroit" in an all-black version of *Guys and Dolls** in 1976.

Credits: *Kwamina* (1961); *Fly Blackbird** (1962); *Tambourines to Glory** (1963); *Porgy and Bess** (1964); *The Life and Times of J. Walter Smintheus** (1970); *Charlie Was Here and Now He's Gone**; *Purlie** (replacement lead) (1971); *Music! Music!* (1974); *Apple Pie*; *Guys and Dolls* (1976).
Reference: *The New York Times*, December 18, 1977.

**GUNN, BILL** (1934- ). Although he is known primarily as a playwright (*Black Picture Show** [1975] and *Marcus in the High Grass* [1960]), Philadelphian Gunn began his career as an actor. A novelist (*All the Rest Have Died*) and a screenwriter as well, he has also turned to directing, including his *Black Picture Show*.

Credits (Acting): *The Immoralist* (1954); *Take a Giant Step** (1956); *Sign of Winter* (1958); *Moon on a Rainbow Shawl** (1962); *Antony and Cleopatra* (1963); *Troilus and Cressida* (1965).
Reference: *The New York Times*, November 26, 1969.

**GUNN, MOSES** (1929- ). Gunn, originally from Saint Louis, began performing while at college in Tennessee. He gained his first job as an understudy in *The Blacks** in 1962, and later filled the role of "The Governor." He has appeared in a wide variety of roles, from Shakespeare to contemporary black theatre with the Negro Ensemble Company.* He has also been in several films (*Shaft*, *The Great White Hope*, and *Rollerball*) and television. He directed Ted Shine's *Contributions** in 1970.

Credits: *In White America** (1963); *The Lonesome Train*; *Hard Travelin'*; *Day of Absence** (1965); *Bohikee Creek**; *Measure for Measure*; *A Hand Is on the Gate** (1966); *Junebug Graduates Tonight!*; *Titus Andronicus* (1967); *Song of the Lusitanian Bogey**; *Summer of the Seventeenth Doll**; *Kongi's Harvest**; *Daddy Goodness**; *Romeo and Juliet* (1968); *Cities in Bezique**; *The Perfect Party** (1969); *Othello* (1970); *The Sty of the Blind Pig** (1971); *Twelfth Night* (1972); *The First Breeze of Summer** (1975); *The Poison Tree* (1976).
Reference: *The New York Times*, June 16, 1968.

# H

**HALL, ADELAIDE** (1910- ). Hall was one of the many 1920s musical stars who appeared in *Shuffle Along** (1921). She first attracted notice in *Runnin' Wild** (1923), and later appeared with Bill Robinson* in *Blackbirds of 1928*.* She traveled to Europe and continued her nightclub and theatrical career abroad in the 1930s and 1940s. She returned to America for *Brown Buddies** (1930) with Bill Robinson, *Jamaica** (1957), and *Black Broadway** (1980).

Reference: "Adelaide Hall" File, PFL/TC.

**HALL, JUANITA** (1901-1968). Tony Award winner Juanita Hall is best remembered for introducing "Bali Ha'i" and "Happy Talk" in *South Pacific* (1949). Her career embraced both musical and dramatic roles.

Credits: *Sailor, Beware!* (1935); *Conjur* (1938); *The Pirate* (1942); *The Secret Room* (1945); *St. Louis Woman**; *Mr. Peebles and Mr. Hooker* (1946); *S. S. Glencairn/Moon of the Caribees* (1948); *South Pacific* (1949); *The Ponder Heart* (1956); *South Pacific* (1957); *Flower Drum Song* (1958); *Mardi Gras!* (1965); *A Woman and the Blues* (1966).

Reference: "Juanita Hall" File, PFL/TC.

**HANSBERRY, LORRAINE** (1930-1965). Playwright and civil rights activist, Lorraine Hansberry was the first black woman to write a successful Broadway play. She was also a woman who believed that "the acceptance of our condition is the only form of extremism which discredits us before our children" [Nemiroff, p. 214]. Hansberry's life and writing revolved around these two axes: the desire to produce good dramatic art, and the need to address the condition of black people.

Born May 19, 1930, in Chicago, the youngest of four children of Carl A. Hansberry and Nannie (Perry) Hansberry, Lorraine Hansberry spent her childhood in a secure middle-class household. Yet the comfortable quality of her family life, made possible by the success of her father as a real estate broker, could not shut out the surrounding poverty in the South Side ghetto, nor the impact of racism. When she was eight the family moved to a white neighborhood. Carl Hansberry hoped that this would lead to a general movement of blacks out of the ghetto. While the family withstood the violence of the white community, Carl Hansberry and the NAACP fought a successful battle to have restrictive covenants declared illegal (Hansberry v. Lee 311 U.S. 32 [1940]). The legal victory, however, did not lead to widespread migration out of the South Side, and finally despairing of change, Carl Hansberry went to Mexico. In 1945 he died there, at the age of 51, while making plans to have the family join him in exile. Lorraine

Hansberry always felt that racism had hastened his death. [*New York Times*, January 13, 1965]

Educated at inadequate and segregated "Jim Crow" schools in the South Side, Lorraine Hansberry graduated from Englewood High School in 1948 and went to the University of Wisconsin. Unable to find anything to hold her interest, she left two years later for New York. While living on the Lower East Side and sharing an apartment with three other women, she soon found both intellectual stimulation and a place to earn a meager living when she joined the staff of Paul Robeson's* radical newspaper, *Freedom* (Cruse, *Crisis of the Negro Intellectual*, pp. 267-284; Nemiroff, *To Be Young, Gifted and Black*, pp. 77-79). This involvement shaped her growing social conscience and intensified her desire to write. Under the tutelage of W. E. B. DuBois, Louis E. Burnham, and the black intellectuals who congregated at the Harlem headquarters of the newspaper, she became an active civil rights advocate, "obsessed with a rather desperate desire for a new world" (Nemiroff, *To Be Young*, p. 83).

Hansberry met Robert Nemiroff on a picket line at New York University, and they married in June 1953. Nemiroff, a music publisher and songwriter, supported Hansberry's desire to write, and the eventual outcome was her first play, *A Raisin in the Sun*,* which opened on Broadway on March 11, 1959. This play became an immediate hit, receiving the New York Drama Circle Critics Award for 1959. She was the first black playwright to receive such an award, and her success was reinforced when the film version of the play won a Cannes Film Festival award in 1961.

Hansberry's second play, *The Sign in Sidney Brustein's Window** (1964), has been judged to be less artistically coherent than her first, but the major criticisms initially lay with the subject matter. Set in Greenwich Village, with an all-white cast (the sole exception of a "passing" black), the play attacked political apathy among the nation's intellectuals.

Increasingly incapacitated by terminal cancer, Hansberry saw much of the production of *Sidney Brustein* from a wheelchair and was an onlooker in the battle to keep the play alive. She died after some months of hospitalization, on January 12, 1965, at the age of thirty-four. *The Sign in Sidney Brustein's Window* closed that day and did not open again.

Hansberry and Nemiroff had been divorced some ten months before her death, a fact that was kept from the public. They continued their working relationship, however, and Nemiroff helped to produce *Sidney Brustein*. After her death, he edited Hansberry's remaining manuscripts and in 1967 created an "autobiography" from her papers which was taped for radio and then successfully produced Off-Broadway in January 1969 as *To Be Young, Gifted, and Black*.* *Les Blancs*,* a play Hansberry left unfinished, was completed by Nemiroff and appeared on Broadway on November 15, 1970, with James Earl Jones* playing the leading character.

Hansberry possessed a prescient vision and substantial creative abilities.

Her work was suffused by the continuing tension between the Afro-American heritage and the mainstream white culture which surrounds and impinges upon the black world. Creating characters with depth and solidity, and achieving critical and financial success, Hansberry succeeded on Broadway as few black playwrights, and no other black women, had. Hansberry revealed something of what it was to be black and American, the dreams deferred, the frustrations of the world between despair and joy, which for her was the realm of human drama.

References: Cruse, Harold, *The Crisis of the Negro Intellectual: From Its Origin to the Present*, New York: William Morrow, Inc., 1967; Kaiser, Ernest, and Robert Nemiroff, "A Lorraine Hansberry Bibliography," *Freedomways* 19 (1979), 285-304; Nemiroff, Robert, *To Be Young, Gifted, and Black: Lorraine Hansberry in Her Own Words*, Englewood Cliffs, N.J.: Prentice-Hall, 1969; Riley, Clayton, "Lorraine Hansberry: A Melody in a Different Key," *Freedomways* 19 (1979), 205-212.

MARION ROYDHOUSE

**HARRISON, RICHARD B[erry]** (1864–1935). Harrison, the son of fugitive slaves, was born in London, Ontario. While a bellhop in nearby Detroit, Harrison briefly attended dramatic school. He later earned a living by reciting Shakespeare to black audiences in Canada. He taught drama in several southern schools, but achieved fame as "De Lawd" in *The Green Pastures** (1930). He remained with the show for five years (giving 1,658 performances); he missed his first performance only after suffering a heart attack which led to his death.

Reference: *Time*, March 4, 1935.

**HARVEY, GEORGETTE** (1883–1952). Ernest Hogan* first noticed Georgette Harvey in her native Saint Louis and invited her to join his troupe. After a tour in *Rufus Rastus*,* she traveled throughout Europe and lived in Russia until the 1917 revolution. She returned to Broadway in *Runnin' Wild** (1923). She gradually expanded her talents to include acting and enjoyed a lengthy Broadway career.

Credits: *Runnin' Wild* (1923); *Porgy** (1927); *Solid South*; *Five Star Final* (1930); *Ol' Man Satan** (1932); *The Party's Over* (1933); *Stevedore**; *Dance with Your Gods* (1934); *Lady of Letters*; *The Hook-Up*; *Porgy and Bess** (1935); *Pre-Honeymoon* (1936); *Brown Sugar** (1937); *Mamba's Daughters**; *Pastoral* (1939); *Morning Star* (1940); *Porgy and Bess* (1942); *The Power of Darkness* (1948); *Stevedore**; *Lost in the Stars** (1949).

Reference: *The New York Times*, February 18, 1952.

**HERNANDEZ, JUANO (JUAN)** (1896–1970). Hernandez came from San Juan, Puerto Rico, and made his first stage appearance in Rio de Janeiro as an acrobat. He later became a professional boxer and finally a member of a minstrel company before turning to the theatre. His most notable Broadway performances include *Strange Fruit* (1945) and *Set My People Free** (1948). He turned to films in 1949, giving an impressive performance as "Lucas Beauchamp" in William Faulkner's *Intruder in the Dust*. He also appeared in *Trial* (1955), *St. Louis Blues* (1958), *Sergeant Rutledge* (1960), and *The Pawnbroker* (1965).

Credits: *Savage Rhythm**; *Marriage of Cana*; *Black Souls** (1932); *Sailor, Beware!* (1935); *Sweet River* (1936); *Brown Sugar** (1937); *Swingin' the Dream** (1939); *The Patriots* (1943); *Strange Fruit* (1945); *Set My People Free* (1948).

Reference: *The New York Times*, July 20, 1970.

**HEYWOOD, DONALD** (1901-1951). Composer, lyricist, and playwright Heywood left his Venezuela home to study black American music at Fisk University. While he wrote songs for several revues, he also attempted to write plays and operas concerning black life. None of his serious efforts, such as *Ol' Man Satan** (1932) and *Africana** (1934), had a successful Broadway run.

Credits: *Africana** (1927); *Veils* (1928); *Ginger Snaps**; *Hot Rhythm** (1930); *Blackberries of 1932**; *Ol' Man Satan* (1932); *Africana* (1934); *Black Rhythm** (1936); *How Come, Lawd?** (1937).

Reference: *The Messenger* 7 (1925), 47.

**HILL, ABRAM** (1911- ). Hill attended the City College of New York and Lincoln University in Pennsylvania with the intention of becoming a doctor, but he was sidelined by his love of theatre. He later joined the Federal Theatre Project,* where he wrote *Liberty Deferred* (unproduced, 1936) and *Hell's Half Acre* (1937). During this period, Hill also completed his social satire of Harlem life, *On Striver's Row*,* which was later produced by the Rose McClendon Players in Harlem.

After the Federal Theatre Project was dissolved, Hill was instrumental in organizing the American Negro Theatre* (ANT) in June 1940. The first production was Hill's *On Striver's Row*, which ran for 101 performances. Hill also adapted plays for the new theatre group, such as Phoebe and Henry Ephron's *Three's a Family* (1943) and the ANT hit, Philip Yordan's *Anna Lucasta** (1944). Hill also contributed *Walk Hard** (1944) to the ANT troupe.

Hill's later plays include *Power of Darkness* (1948), *Miss Mabel* (1951), and *Split Down the Middle* (1970).

Reference: *New York Post Magazine*, December 29, 1943.

**HINES, GREGORY** (1946- ). Hines and his brother Maurice have made tap-dancing respectable on Broadway once again. After a debut in *The Girl in Pink Tights* (1954), Hines did not return to Broadway until 1979 with *Eubie!** for which he won a Theatre World Award. He has also appeared in *Comin' Uptown** (1979), *Black Broadway** (1980), and *Sophisticated Ladies** (1981). He has also been featured in such films as *Wolfen* and *A History of the World—Part I* (1980). Maurice Hines recently assumed Gregory's role in the Broadway company of *Sophisticated Ladies*.

Reference: "Gregory Hines" File, NYPL/TC.

**HOGAN, ERNEST** (1865–1913?). Although acclaimed throughout America during the 1890s and 1900s as an actor, singer, and songwriter, Hogan lived much of his life in comparative obscurity. All that is generally and definitely known is that Hogan began performing in New York during the middle 1890s and that he quickly achieved such success as a comedian that he earned the nickname "the unwashed American." In 1895, Hogan launched his career as a songwriter with "La Pas Ma La," a dance tune popularized in *By the Sad Sea Waves*, a Broadway musical comedy. In 1896, Hogan apparently wrote both music and lyrics for "All Coons Look Alike to Me," the song that began a ten-year-long coon-song craze in Europe and America. (Some doubt exists, however, as to how much Hogan actually had to do with the actual composition of this or many of the other songs attributed to him by publishers during the next eleven years.) By 1899, Hogan's reputation had grown enormously; he performed with Black Patti's Troubadours and toured the eastern United States in anticipation of future European jaunts. In the same year, he took a leading part in the successful premiere performance of *Clorindy, or The Origin of the Cakewalk*, Will Marion Cook's* all-black musical comedy. Hogan met and went to work for producer Gus Hill in 1902, shortly after publishing "Roll On! Mr. Moon," another coon-song which achieved some success. From 1905 to 1907, Hogan starred in the hit musical comedy *Rufus Rastus*,* for which he may have helped write both the songs and lyrics. In any event, he is identified as composer and lyricist on sheet-music covers of songs taken from that show. Only a few reports of Hogan's activities as a performer are available after 1908. He may have died in Harlem in 1913.

Hogan is best known today in histories of black American music for the song "All Coons Look Alike to Me" and for his participation in early all-black musical comedies and revues. In his account of the first performance of *Clorindy*, Will Marion Cook describes Hogan as a genial, optimistic, and generous man who volunteered to learn his part for *Clorindy* at the last minute. Hogan sang with such aplomb that his performance of "Who Dat Say Chicken in Dis Crowd?" had to be repeated ten times before he could leave the stage. Hogan's contributions to all-black musical theatre and to American popular song helped bridge the gap between "colored entertainments" and the legitimate Broadway stage.

Credits (Acting): *Sit Down, Brophy!* (1897?); *Clorindy, or the Origin of the Cakewalk* (1898); *Black Patti's Troubadours* (1899-1901?); *Rufus Rastus* (1905-1907); *The Oyster Man** (1907).

MICHAEL SAFFLE

**HOLDER, GEOFFREY** (1930– ). Holder, a native of Trinidad, has been a director, actor, choreographer, dancer, singer, composer, and costume designer during his many years in the theatre. He made his debut in *House of Flowers** (1954), and his career bloomed after he received two Tony

Awards for directing and designing *The Wiz** (1975). His similar attempt to update *Kismet* into *Timbuktu!** met with less success in 1978. His film roles include *Doctor Doolittle* (1967), *Live and Let Die* (1973), and *Annie* (1982).

Credits (Acting): *House of Flowers* (1954); *Show Boat* (1956); *Waiting for Godot* (1957); *Twelfth Night* (1959); *Josephine Baker and Her Company* (1964); *The Masque of St. George and the Dragon* (1973).

Reference: *The New York Times*, May 25, 1975.

**HOOKS, ROBERT** (1937- ). Bobbie Dean Hooks made his debut in a touring company of *A Raisin in the Sun** in 1960. He continued using his given name for his first New York appearances in *Tiger, Tiger Burning Bright** (1962), *Ballad for Bimshire** (1963), and *The Milk Train Doesn't Stop Here Anymore* (1964). In 1964, he was forced to choose between a small role in *Blues for Mr. Charlie** at $200 per week and the lead in *Dutchman** at $65. He made the right choice (he chose *Dutchman*) and his career skyrocketed under the name Robert Hooks. He has appeared in several plays, films (*Hurry Sundown*), and television. He won a Theatre World Award for his performance in *Where's Daddy?* in 1966. He was a co-founder of the Negro Ensemble Company* in 1968 and a founder of the Washington D.C. Black Repertory Company in 1973.

Credits: *Dutchman* (1964); *Henry V*; *Happy Ending/Day of Absence** (1965); *Where's Daddy?* (1966); *Hallelujah, Baby!** (1967); *Kongi's Harvest** (1968); *The Harangues** (1970); *The Great MacDaddy** (replacement) (1974).

Reference: *The New York Times*, April 9, 1967.

**HOPKINS, LINDA** (1925- ). Mahalia Jackson discovered Linda Hopkins in a church choir. Hopkins sang with the Southern Harp Spiritual Singers for eleven years and made her Broadway debut in *Purlie** (1970), in a small but memorable role. She won a Tony for her supporting role in *Inner City** in 1971, but she is best remembered for her striking tribute to Bessie Smith, *Me and Bessie** (1975).

Reference: *The New York Times*, March 19, 1976.

**HORNE, LENA** (1917- ). Lena Horne received a special Tony Award for *Lena Horne—The Lady and Her Music* (1981), a retrospective of her show business career from the Cotton Club to Broadway and Hollywood. Lew Leslie first featured her in the short-lived *Blackbirds of 1939.** She returned to Broadway in *Jamaica** in 1957. In the interim she appeared in several films, mostly at Metro-Goldwyn-Mayer. Both *Cabin in the Sky** and *Stormy Weather* (1943) revealed her talents in starring roles. Unfortunately, in most of her films she appeared only briefly in specialty numbers. Her most recent triumph was her portrayal of Glinda the Good Witch in the film version of *The Wiz** (1978).

Reference: Horne, Lena, and Richard Schickel, *Lena*, London: Andre Deutsch, 1966.

**HUGHES, LANGSTON** (1902–1967). Hughes was born in Joplin, Missouri, in 1902, and grew up under the care of first his grandmother, and then his mother, in many midwestern towns, primarily Lawrence, Kansas City, and Topeka, Kansas; Lincoln, Illinois; and Cleveland, Ohio. His well-educated parents separated early in his life, but he gained a love for literature from his grandmother and attended theatre and opera performances with his mother. In his late teens, he spent a difficult year with his father, who had become a prosperous landowner in Toluca, Mexico. His father decided he should study engineering and sent him to Columbia University. Hughes loved New York but hated engineering and, after a year, he left his studies to go to sea. He visited Africa and Europe, left his ship to work at menial jobs in Paris and Italy, and returned to New York to work as a busboy. All this time he was writing, and occasionally publishing, poetry. Vachel Lindsay "discovered" him in the early 1920s, and his literary reputation began. Lindsay's enthusiasm for his work may have led to literary awards from *Opportunity* magazine in 1925 and from *Crisis* in 1926, and his subsequent scholarship at Lincoln University in Pennsylvania.

This same year, 1926, he published his first volume of poetry, *The Weary Blues*; was being published by *Vanity Fair*, *New Republic*, and *Bookman*; and was recognized as a leader in the "Negro Renaissance." He had published his first play, *The Gold Piece*, in *Brownie's Book* in July 1921; this early interest in dramatic writing continued throughout his career. In the early 1930s, he worked with Jasper Deeter of the Hedgerow Theatre, an outstanding regional theatre in Moylan, Pennsylvania. This experience gave him encouragement and knowledge for his considerable success in his dramatic endeavors. From his commercial success with *Mulatto*,* in 1935, to his death, he was vitally concerned with writing for and producing his plays in the theatre. In the late 1930s and 1940s, he founded three black theatres: the Suitcase Theatre, in Harlem; the Negro Art Theatre, in Los Angeles; and the Skyloft Players, in Chicago. *Simply Heavenly** (1957) and *Tambourines to Glory** (1963) had substantial New York runs and were performed throughout the United States and Europe. His best known plays appear in *Five Plays by Langston Hughes* (1963).

Although Hughes will be remembered primarily for his poetry, stories, and the autobiographical *The Big Sea* and *I Wonder as I Wander*, he is a crucially important figure in the development of black drama and theatre. In addition to the plays mentioned above, he wrote six other plays that had professional productions. There were also two outstanding short plays, *Soul Gone Home* and *Don't You Want to Be Free?*, librettos for four produced operas, lyrics for the musicals *Just Around the Corner* (1951), which did not reach Broadway, and for the Kurt Weill-Elmer Rice *Street Scene* (1947), which did.

In his last years Hughes sought to make the black religious experience theatrically available to wide audiences with the productions of his four

"Gospel Song-Plays." The most successful of them, *Black Nativity*,* enjoyed runs in New York, England, and on the European continent from its opening in 1961 through 1964.

Hughes's plays, like his poetry and stories, dealt with Negro life, particularly urban Negro life. His home—physically and spiritually—was in Harlem, where he lived from the mid-1930s until his death. By the time he died in 1967, other black playwrights had become important, probably more important, in the American theatre. However, from the production of *Mulatto*, in 1935, until the success of Lorraine Hansberry's* *A Raisin in the Sun*,* Hughes set an example of professionalism as a dramatist, unmatched by any other black playwright to that time. In spite of his limitations as a playwright, and they are many, his example for those playwrights who have followed him served as a major contribution to the black theatre of America—and it is a contribution of considerable dimension.

Credits (Plays): *Mulatto*; *Little Ham*; *Troubled Island* (1935); *When the Jack Hollers*; *Don't You Want to Be Free?* (1936); *Soul Gone Home*; *Joy to My Soul* (1937); *Front Porch* (1938); *The Sun Do Move* (1942); *Simply Heavenly* (1957); *Shakespeare in Harlem** (1960); *Tambourines to Glory* (1963).

(Gospel Song Plays): *Black Nativity* (1961); *Gospel Glow* (1962); *Jerico-Jim Crow** (1963); *The Prodigal Son** (1965).

(Lyrics for Musicals): *Street Scene* (1947); *Just Around the Corner* (1951).

(Opera Librettos): *Troubled Island* (1949); *The Barrier** (1950); *Esther* (1957); *Port Town* (1960).

References: Dickinson, Donald C., *A Bio-bibliography of Langston Hughes*, Hamden, Conn.: Archon Books, 1967; O'Daniel, Therman B., *Langston Hughes, Black Genius*, New York: William Morrow, 1971.

WEBSTER SMALLEY

**HUNTER, EDDIE** (1888- ). Black comedian and vaudevillian Eddie Hunter claimed that Enrico Caruso inspired him to write for the theatre. Caruso read Hunter's sketches when Hunter worked as an elevator operator in Caruso's hotel. Hunter's first opportunity came with *How Come?** (1923) in which he co-starred and co-wrote. He followed this show with burlesque appearances and a British revue, *Good Gracious*. He returned to Broadway for *My Magnolia** (1926) and *Blackbirds of 1933*.*

Reference: Mitchell, Loften, *Voices of the Black Theatre*, Clifton, N.J.: James T. White, 1975.

**HYMAN, EARLE** (1926- ). Hyman attended school in Brooklyn, where his North Carolina family felt there would be greater opportunities. Canada Lee* witnessed his first audition and hired him for radio work. Hyman later joined the American Negro Theatre* and appeared in *Anna Lucasta** as "Rudolph." He played the role for almost 1,500 performances, including a two-year stint in London. When he returned to New York, he faced a long period of joblessness and worked as a messenger. His career revived in the mid-1950s when he attracted considerable attention in *Mister Johnson** (1956).

Credits: *Three's a Family*; *Run, Little Chillun!** (1943); *Anna Lucasta* (1944); *Sister Oakes* (1949); *Hamlet* (1951); *The Climate of Eden* (1952); *The Merchant of Venice*; *Othello* (1953); *No Time for Sergeants* (1955); *Mister Johnson*; *Saint Joan* (1956); *Waiting for Godot*; *Hamlet*; *The Duchess of Malfi*; *Othello* (1957); *Everyman Today* (1958); *A Raisin in the Sun** (1959); *Mr. Roberts* (1962); *The Worlds of Shakespeare* (1963); *The White Rose and the Red* (1964); *Jonah!* (1966); *Saint Joan* (1968); *Les Blancs**; *The Life and Times of J. Walter Smintheus** (1970); *Orrin**; *House Party** (1973); *Carnival Dreams* (1975); *Agamemnon* (1977); *Othello* (1978); *Julius Caesar*; *Coriolanus*; *Remembrance* (1979); *The Lady from Dubuque* (1980); *Long Day's Journey into Night* (1981).

Reference: *The New York Times*, March 25, 1956.

# I

**INGRAM, REX** (1896–1969). Ingram claimed to have studied medicine at Northwestern University and went to Los Angeles to set up practice. A talent scout suggested he play a native in an early Tarzan film, and, shortly, Ingram abandoned his medical career. He made his theatrical debut in *Lulu Belle* in 1929 and continually traveled between Broadway and Hollywood for the rest of his career. His best remembered film role was "De Lawd" in *The Green Pastures** (1936). After that film he resolved to "take no roles that showed Negroes in a demeaning light" (*The New York Times*, September 20, 1969), and, as a result, his job offers disappeared. He returned to acting via the Federal Theatre Project* production of *Haiti** (1938), which garnered rave reviews.

Credits: *Theodora the Queen*; *Stevedore**; *Dance with Your Gods* (1934); *Caesar and Cleopatra*; *Stick-in-the-Mud* (1935); *The Emperor Jones** (1936); *Marching Song*; *How Come, Lawd?** (1937); *Haiti*; *Sing Out the News* (1938); *Cabin in the Sky** (1940); *St. Louis Woman**; *Lysistrata* (1946); *Waiting for Godot* (1957); *Kwamina** (1961).

Reference: *The New York Times*, September 20, 1969.

# J

**JOHNSON, HALL** (1888–1970). Born in Athens, Georgia, Johnson spent his formative years in the American South. Before arriving in New York City in 1914, he had attended the Knox Institute in Athens, Allen University in Columbia, South Carolina, Atlanta University, the Hahn School of Music in Philadelphia, and the University of Pennsylvania, where he received a B.A. degree in 1910. Johnson later studied at the New York Institute of Musical Art, the Juilliard School of Music, and the Philadelphia Music Academy, from which he earned a Doctor of Music degree in 1934.

By the time Johnson decided to organize the Hall Johnson Choir in 1925, he had already been an instrumentalist in several New York orchestras, had participated in numerous musical reviews, including *Shuffle Along** in 1922, and had begun his composing career. The Choir was an immediate hit, being besieged with requests to appear on radio and in various musical stage productions, including the commercially popular *The Green Pastures*.* In fact, Johnson's ensemble enjoyed a five-year tenure with this production before departing for Hollywood in 1935 to do a filmed version of the play. Johnson himself was the musical arranger and director for both the stage and film renditions of *Pastures*. Once in the Los Angeles area, Johnson stayed on to write the music for a number of movies, including *Lost Horizon* (1937) and *Meet John Doe* (1941). Such contributions won Johnson a place in the Black Filmmakers Hall of Fame, voted posthumously to him in 1975.

At the time Johnson turned his attention to playwrighting in 1933, he was already recognized nationally as an outstanding musical talent. Not particularly anxious to change creative direction, he nevertheless sensed the rewards awaiting the writer who skillfully blended both musical and dramatic elements. The result was that Johnson wrote *Run, Little Chillun!**, a folk drama heavily indebted to black artist Zora Neale Hurston. In rehearsal for a full nine months before it opened on Broadway in 1933, it played to packed audiences for four months during the midst of the nation's worst depression. The production repeated its Broadway success in the Federal Theatre Project* (FTP) minus the presence of its creator, who never participated in the FTP. Johnson's play was the only black drama revived by the FTP that was transferred intact to government stages.

In the opinion of several observers, *Run, Little Chillun!* was the most brilliant play by a black author to reach Broadway before 1940. On the strength of this one play, therefore, Johnson richly deserves a significant place in black theatre history.

Reference: Johnson, Hall, *Run, Little Chillun!*, New York: New York Public Library, Schomburg Collection, 1933.

RONALD P. ROSS

**JOHNSON, J. C.** (1896- ). J. C. ("Jimmy") Johnson was from Chicago and began his career as a pianist and bandleader. He later turned to composing and wrote songs with Fats Waller,* Andy Razaf,* and George Whiting. He contributed songs to *Keep Shufflin'** (1928) and *Brown Buddies** (1930) and wrote the entire score for *Change Your Luck** (1930).

Reference: Kinkle, Roger D., *The Complete Encyclopedia of Popular Music and Jazz, 1900-1950*, New Rochelle, N.Y.: Arlington House, 1974.

**JOHNSON, JAMES P[rice]** (1891-1955). Born in New Brunswick, New Jersey, Johnson started out as a ragtime pianist. He turned to songwriting in 1914 (with Will Farrell) and contributed songs to J. Leubrie Hill's Harlem entertainment, *The Darktown Follies. Runnin' Wild** (1923), his first Broadway show, brought forth the 1920s classic "The Charleston" and "Old Fashioned Love." He also wrote the score for *Messin' Around** (1929) *Sugar Hill** (1931), and a revised version of the latter show produced in California in 1949. In addition to his popular music career, Johnson composed ballets, operettas, and symphonies.

Reference: Davin, Tom, "Conversations with James P. Johnson," *Jazz Review*, July-August 1959.

**JOHNSON, JAMES WELDON.** See JOHNSON, J[ohn] ROSAMOND.

**JOHNSON, J[ohn] ROSAMOND** (1873-1954). Johnson, the son of a Baptist minister and the brother of James Weldon Johnson, grew up in Jacksonville, Florida. His early interest in music led him to the New England Conservatory of Music in Boston. After completing his studies, he toured in the highly successful musical *Oriental America* in 1896. He returned to Jacksonville where he taught music and was a choir master and organist at the Baptist church. He began composing music for the poems his brother had written, and the two composed an opera. In the summer of 1899, they went to New York to try to sell their work. Collaborating with Bob Cole,* who had already established a reputation in the theatre, they wrote the love song "Louisiana Lize" and, following its sale, formed a partnership with Cole. J. Rosamond Johnson performed a vaudeville act with Cole, wrote music with his brother and Cole, and became a notable figure in the American theatre. Some of his successful songs (written for such performers as Anna Held, Lillian Russell, and Marie Cahill) were "The Maiden with the Dreamy Eyes," "Nobody's Lookin' but the Owl and the Moon," and "Oh, Didn't He Ramble." At the end of 1901, James Weldon Johnson temporarily left the partnership to return to Jacksonville, but J. Rosamond Johnson and Bob Cole remained in New York and went on to great success in vaudeville in America and in England, appearing twice as headliners at the Palace in London.

Johnson and Cole toured in *The Shoo-Fly Regiment** (the last work by the two Johnsons and Cole) with a company of sixty performers, ending their tour at the Bijou Theatre in New York. Financial losses put a strain on Johnson, and at this time he nearly lost his voice. He and Cole continued their performances and writing, presenting *The Red Moon** in 1908. Despite the financial failure of the play, it was important in the development of black musicals and contained several successful songs.

After Bob Cole died in 1911, Johnson performed in vaudeville with Charles Hart. He composed music for many plays in New York, and for the production of *Hello Paris* in 1911, he trained the company, wrote the music, and was the first black conductor for a white musical with a white orchestra. In 1913, he became supervisor of music at Oscar Hammerstein's London Opera House. His fiancee Nora Floyd came from Jacksonville for an elegant wedding in London. Johnson then became director of music at the Music School in New York, and for several years he gave music lessons and composed. He joked about the small salary on which he supported his wife. Financial considerations may have forced him to return to vaudeville where he toured with the Rosamond Johnson Quintet on the Orpheum and Keith circuits. He later appeared in plays including *Mamba's Daughters** and *Porgy and Bess** when he was in his sixties. He died in New York in 1954.

Credits (Composing): *Sleeping Beauty and the Beast* (1902); *In Newport*; *Humpty Dumpty* (1904); *The Shoo-Fly Regiment* (1907); *The Red Moon* (1909); *Mr. Lode of Koal** (1909); *Hello Paris* (1911); *Brown Buddies** (1930); *Blackbirds of 1939.**

(Acting): *The Shoo-Fly Regiment* (1907); *The Red Moon* (1909); *Americana* (1928); *Porgy and Bess* (1935); *Blackbirds of 1939* (with choir); *Mamba's Daughters* (1939); *Cabin in the Sky** (1940); *Porgy and Bess* (1942).

References: Burton, Jack, *The Blue Book of Tin Pan Alley*, New York: Century House, 1950; Johnson, James Weldon, *Along This Way*, New York: Viking Press, 1945; Johnson, James Weldon, *Black Manhattan*, New York: Knopf, 1930.

YVONNE SHAFER

**JONES, JAMES EARL** (1931- ). Jones, son of actor Robert Earl Jones, studied acting at the University of Michigan where he made his stage debut as "Brett" in *Deep Are the Roots** in 1949. He has portrayed a great variety of roles from Shakespeare to Brecht to Fugard. He received his greatest acclaim for his portrayal of "Jack Jefferson" in *The Great White Hope** (1968), which won him a Tony Award and an Oscar nomination for the film version. His recent performance in *Othello* (1982) was greeted with critical raves.

Credits: *Wedding in Japan* (1957); *Sunrise at Campobello* (1958); *The Pretender*; *Henry V* (1960); *Romeo and Juliet*; *The Blacks**; *A Midsummer Night's Dream*; *Richard II*; *Clandestine on the Morning Line*; *The Apple* (1961); *Moon on a Rainbow Shawl**; *The Merchant of Venice*; *The Tempest*; *P. S. 193* (1962); *The Love Nest*; *The Winter's Tale*; *Next Time I'll Sing to You* (1963); *The Blood Knot**; *Othello*: *The Emperor Jones** (1964); *Baal*; *Coriolanus*; *Troilus and Cressida*;

*Danton's Death* (1965); *Bohikee Creek**; *Macbeth*; *A Hand Is on the Gate** (1966); *The Great White Hope* (1968); *Boesman and Lena**; *Les Blancs** (1970); *Hamlet* (1972); *The Cherry Orchard*; *King Lear*; *The Iceman Cometh* (1973); *Of Mice and Men* (1974); *Paul Robeson** (1978); *A Lesson from the Aloes* (1980); *Othello* (1982).
Reference: *The New York Times*, August 2, 1981.

**JONES, LEROI (BARAKA, AMIRI)** (1934- ). The son of a postal supervisor and a social worker, Baraka grew up in his native Newark, New Jersey, where he enrolled in Rutgers University on a science fellowship. In 1952, he transferred to Howard University where he studied with Sterling Brown and E. Franklin Frazier before dropping out of college and joining the air force.

Upon his return to civilian life, Baraka moved to the Lower East Side of Manhattan and joined a loose circle of Village artists, musicians, and writers. In 1958, he married Hettie Cohen with whom he co-edited the avant-garde magazine *Yugen*, which also published Baraka's first poetry and prose. In 1960, Baraka went to Cuba and described his visit in the famous essay "Cuba Libre." At the same time, his interest in dramatic work grew, resulting in the production of his play "The Eighth Ditch Is Drama" under the title *Dante* at the Off Bowery Theatre in 1961. The controversial play attacked sexual and racial taboos. When it appeared in print, Baraka was arrested and tried for sending obscenities through the mail. In the course of the 1960s, Baraka wrote much poetry and prose but made his impression on the decade as a playwright.

In *The Baptism** (1961), he reviewed the territory of James Baldwin's* *Go Tell It On the Mountain* with a surrealist imagination. A minister and his complete congregation are denounced as hypocrites, whereas the playwright's sympathies are with a boy who is saved from his fate as a sacrificial lamb by a homosexual, who plays something of an attractive devil figure. *The Toilet** (1962) again focuses on homosexuality and dramatizes the trauma of adolescence as a quest for love in the socially enforced guise of toughness, as the conflict between self-realization and racial loyalty sharpens.

Baraka's reputation as a playwright was established with the production of *Dutchman** at the Cherry Lane Theatre in New York in 1964. In the manner of the absurd one-act play, *Dutchman* shows the encounter of Lula, a white Village bohemienne, with Clay, a young black intellectual, in a New York subway setting. Lula, the flirtatious social allegory representing everything Clay has repressed, succeeds in prompting the black man to deliver an anti-white tirade, whereupon she stabs him and discards him on the subway tracks, and then approaches a new victim. Clay's speech became a key text of the 1960s. Baraka won an Obie award for the play, and Anthony Harvey made a film of *Dutchman* in England. In *The Slave** (1962), Baraka continued the theme of the confrontation of a black poet/revolutionary with a white woman friend/antagonist.

At the height of his Off-Broadway fame, Baraka turned his back on his previous life and career. His marriage broke up, and he moved to Harlem and Newark where he married Amina (Sylvia Robinson). He dropped his Western name LeRoi Jones and adopted the name Amiri Baraka. In 1965, he founded the Black Arts Repertory Theatre/School in Harlem, where he showed his older as well as his new, often explicitly anti-white, but always rather complex, agit-prop plays (among them *Experimental Death Unit #1* and *Jello*) to all-black audiences. Continuing his black theatre work in his native Newark, he founded the Spirit House players as well as cultural and political organizations. Among the Newark premieres was *A Black Mass* (1966), based on the myth of Yacoub, which Baraka phrases as a black Frankenstein/white monster show. *Police* and *Arm Yourself and Harm Yourself* (1967) were two agit-prop plays against police brutality; *Home on the Range* was performed at a benefit for the Black Panther party at the Fillmore East in New York in 1968. *Great Goodness of Life** became part of the successful *A Black Quartet** show Off-Broadway in 1969. *Slave Ship** was produced in the same year under the direction of Gilbert Moses,* was widely reviewed, and had a successful run at the Brooklyn Academy of Music. This play portrays black history as suffering on a two-tier stage, where black people are always in the steerage, on the slave market, in the quarters—always on the lower tier.

At the end of the 1960s, Baraka was more prominent in politics (such as in the city government of Kenneth Gibson's first Newark administration and in the organization of the Black Congress in Gary, Indiana, in 1972) and in academics (he has taught at the New School, Columbia, Yale, and is currently on the faculty at Stony Brook) than in Off-Broadway. New Baraka plays were indeed shown at various stages throughout the 1970s—*Junkies Are Full of (SHHH . . . )*, *Sidnee Poet Heroical or If in Danger of Suit*, *The Kid Poet Heroical*, *The New Ark's a moverin*, *The Motion of History*, *S-1*, and *What Was the Relationship of the Lone Ranger to the Means of Production?*—and older plays were revived at repertory and college theatres. But Baraka elicited much less public attention as a playwright in the 1970s than he had in the 1960s.

Baraka's contribution to the theatre is in the combination of fearless outspokenness and modernist strategy, which made his best one-act plays so intriguing and upsetting to American audiences. Steeped in Genet and Ionesco, immersed in popular culture from radio drama to comics and horror movies, yet articulating real American voices and dramatizing pressing social questions, Baraka's plays could powerfully evoke a vision of the deep sexual, social, psychological, and artistic implications of "race" in the United States. Wedding the "populist" social concerns of many earlier black playwrights with an uncompromisingly "modernist" sensibility, Baraka's drama ended the predominance of naturalism and one-issue pleading that had reached its peak in the period of Lorraine Hansberry.* There are few contemporary black dramatists for whom the production of

*Dutchman* and Baraka's work in black community theatre did not provide a negative foil, if not a positive model. The works of Ed Bullins,* Richard Wesley,* Marvin X, Ben Caldwell,* Robert Macbeth,* and Barbara Ann Teer* have widened the road which Baraka's theatre opened for contemporary writers.

Reference: Sollors, Werner, *Amiri Baraka/LeRoi Jones. The Quest for Populist Modernism*, New York: Columbia University Press, 1978.

WERNER SOLLORS

**JONES, SISSIERETTA (BLACK PATTI)** (1869–1933). Sissieretta Jones, known as "Black Patti," was the most publicized and outstanding black artist of the late nineteenth and early twentieth century. She began her singing career in the Pond Street Baptist Church at the age of fifteen, and she studied at the Providence (Rhode Island) Academy of Music. At eighteen, she continued at the New England Conservatory of Music and later went to New York City where she studied with Louise Cappiani. The *New York Clipper* gave her the sobriquet "Black Patti" after Adelina Patti, the great soprano of the nineteenth century.

Jones interrupted a concert career for the formation of *Black Patti's Troubadours*, where she sang her operatic repertory amidst an assemblage of comedians, dancers, and tumblers. Ernest Hogan,* J. Rosamond Johnson,* Bob Cole,* Billy Johnson, and Ada Overton Walker* were among the troupe's early performers. They gave the theatrical stage qualified black performers, upgrading the music with standard popular and serious repertory. *Black Patti's Troubadours* afforded new opportunities and a widened perspective for black performers on the American stage near the turn of the century.

References: *Record Research* (June 1980-October 1981).

HENRY HENRIKSEN

**JOPLIN, SCOTT** (1868–1917). Joplin, the "king of ragtime," experimented with opera throughout his career. *A Guest of Honor* (1903) vanished without a trace, but *Treemonisha* was saved from a similar fate because Joplin published the score himself in 1911. A 1913 production (proposed for the Lafayette Theatre) came to naught, and a 1915 run-through failed to interest backers. Joplin died without seeing a production of his masterwork. The Houston Grand Opera revived the production in 1975 and moved it to Broadway's Leon Uris Theatre where it enjoyed a sixty-four performance run. This highly praised production featured Carmen Balthrop, Betty Allen, Curtis Rayam, and Willard White, and was directed by Frank Corsaro.

Reference: Southern, Eileen, *The Music of Black Americans*, New York: Norton, 1971.

**JORDAN, JOE** (1882- ). Jordan studied music in St. Louis where he played ragtime piano in cafes. He became director of music at Chicago's Pekin Theatre in 1906 and later moved to New York City. He provided both songs and complete scores for a variety of shows, including *Bandana Land** (1908), *Bottomland** (1927), *Deep Harlem** (1929), *Brown Buddies** (1930), and *Fast and Furious** (1931).

Reference: Blesh, Rudi, and Harriet Janis, *They All Played Ragtime*, New York: Oak Publications, 1971.

# K

**KENNEDY, ADRIENNE** (1931- ). Kennedy was born Adrienne Lita Hawkins on September 13, 1931. When she was four, the Hawkins family moved from Georgia to Cleveland, Ohio. Adrienne's mother, who was a teacher, encouraged her daughter to compete in the predominantly white neighborhood where they lived. Adrienne later attended Ohio State University, where social life was dominated by sororities and football, and she recalls black students were subjected to blatant racial prejudice, ridicule, and humiliation.

Two weeks after graduation with a degree in education, Adrienne married Joseph C. Kennedy on May 15, 1953. When the army sent her husband to Korea six months after their marriage, Adrienne returned home to live with her parents. There she wrote her first play based on Elmer Rice's *Street Scene* to distract her from being alone at night. After Joseph returned to the United States to continue his graduate studies at Columbia, the Kennedys moved to New York City. Adrienne studied creative writing at Columbia from 1954 to 1956. In 1957, 1958, and 1962, she studied playwrighting at the New School, the American Theatre Wing, and Circle in the Square. Two years after her first attempt at playwrighting, she wrote a play patterned after Tennessee Williams's *The Glass Menagerie* titled *Pale Blue Flowers*, which has not been published or produced.

Adrienne Kennedy began writing *Funnyhouse of a Negro*,* her most celebrated work, in 1961 in Africa. When she completed it, she submitted it to Edward Albee's workshop at Circle in the Square, where it was produced with Diana Sands* in the central role. The play portrays the personality fragmentation of Sarah the Negro, an English major, into four identities: Queen Victoria, the Duchess of Hapsburg, Jesus, and Patrice Lumumba. Sarah experiences the conflict within her own soul between the cool whiteness and submissive femininity of her mother and the rebellious blackness and aggressive masculinity of her father. Kennedy received an Obie Award for the production of *Funnyhouse of a Negro*.

As a member of the playwrighting unit of Actors Studio from 1962 to 1965, Kennedy wrote the other plays for which she is best known. In 1965, Joseph Papp produced *Cities in Bezique: The Owl Answers* and *A Beast's Story.** *The Owl Answers* portrays the fragmentation of a young black schoolteacher called "She who is Clara Passmore who is the Virgin Mary who is the Bastard who is the Owl." Unlike the multiple character portrayal of Sarah the Negro, Clara is played by a single performer who keeps the same costume, gestures, and personality throughout the short play. External action exposes not only the protagonist's confusion about herself but also her shifting and distorted perceptions of her parents, who change costumes, wigs, and mannerisms to represent different persons with various shades of black and white skin. Kennedy has stated that most of her material for this play comes from autobiography, family history, and her own dreams.

In *A Beast's Story*, Beast Girl's parents, Beast Man and Beast Woman, prevent their daughter from growing into happy young womanhood by forcing her to act out their own anger and terror. The girl rejects her husband, Dead Human, by fleeing from bed on their wedding night and later by smothering him with a pillow. While her mother looks on, Beast Girl splits her father's skull with an ax in the final moments of the play. Two 1966 plays (*A Rat's Mass* and *A Lesson in a Dead Language*) explore similar themes as *Cities in Bezique.*

While living in London in the late 1960s, Kennedy collaborated with Victor Spinetti and John Lennon on a play entitled *The Lennon Play: In His Own Write.* The work was first presented by the National Theatre Company in London in 1967 and in expanded form in 1968. Kennedy's most recent work, a poem play entitled *SUN*, based on the death of Malcolm X, was produced by Ellen Stewart at Cafe La Mama in 1970.

Kennedy has received numerous awards, grants, and academic appointments. She received a Guggenheim Fellowship (1968), a Rockefeller Fellowship (1967-1969), a National Endowment for the Arts Grant (1973), a Rockefeller Grant (1974), the Creative Artists Public Service Grant (1974), and a Yale Fellowship (1974-1975). In the 1980s, Kennedy continues to teach playwrighting.

Reference: *The New York Times*, May 20, 1977.

ROSEMARY CURB

**KING, WOODIE, JR.** (1937- ). After graduation from Wayne State University in Detroit in 1961, Woodie King, Jr., came to New York City. He first appeared as an actor in such Off-Broadway plays as *A Study in Color* (1964), *The Displaced Person* (1966), *The Perfect Party** (1969) and Broadway's *The Great White Hope** (1968). Yet, he made his most enduring contribution to the history of the black theatre as the director of the New Federal Theatre. He has supported such playwrights as Ed Bullins,* Amiri Baraka,* J. E. Gaines,* and Ron Milner.* Several New Federal Theatre projects have moved on to Broadway productions. These include *The First Breeze of Summer** (1975), a Negro Ensemble Company* co-production, and *For Colored Girls Who Have Considered Suicide/ When the Rainbow Is Enuf** (1976), which King spotted in a performance in a Lower East Side bar.

Credits (Producing): *Slave Ship** (1969); *In New England Winter**; *Behold! Cometh the Vanderkellans**; *Black Girl** (1971); *Jamimma**; *Don't Let It Go to Your Head** (1972); *A Recent Killing** (1973); *What the Wine-Sellers Buy**; *The Prodigal Sister** (1974); *The First Breeze of Summer*; *The Taking of Miss Janie** (1975); *The Medal of Honor Rag*; *For Colored Girls Who Have Considered Suicide/When the Rainbow Is Enuf* (1976); *Cockfight** (Director, 1977); *Reggae** (1980).

Reference: *The New York Times*, October 31, 1976.

**KIRKSEY, KIRK** (?- ). Kirksey was born on Chicago's South Side. At seventeen his family moved to California, where he studied acting at Los Angeles City College. He followed *Big Time Buck White** (1968) on its move to New York City. He received an Obie in the 1970-1971 season for "general excellence."

Credits: *Big Time Buck White* (1968); *Five on the Black Hand Side** (1970); *The Duplex** (1972); *What the Wine-Sellers Buy**; *The Prodigal Sister** (1974); *The Taking of Miss Janie** (1975); *Unfinished Women* (1977).

Reference: "Kirk Kirksey" File, NYPL/TC.

**KITT, EARTHA** (1928- ). Eartha Kitt began her career with the Katherine Dunham Dancers and later sang in European nightclubs. Her rendition of "Monotonous" in *New Faces of 1952* attracted critical acclaim. She appeared in three more Broadway shows during the 1950s: *Mrs. Patterson** (1954), *Shinbone Alley* (1957), and *Jolly's Progress** (1959). When she criticized the Johnson Administration at a much publicized luncheon, she suddenly found her career options blocked. She did not return to Broadway until the late 1970s when she appeared as "Sahleem-La-Lume" in Geoffrey Holder's* reworking of *Kismet*, *Timbuktu!** (1978).

Reference: Kitt, Eartha, *Alone with Me*, Chicago: Henry Regnery Co., 1976.

# L

**LEE, CANADA** (1907-1952). Lionel Canagata, the son of West Indian parents, was born in New York. He first became a jockey and then a boxer before turning to acting. The fight game found his name too difficult, and it was changed to Canada Lee. He began his acting career with the Federal Theatre Project* and gave notable performances in *Stevedore** (1934) and

Orson Welles's *Macbeth* (1936). Richard Wright's* *Native Son** provided him with his most notable stage role in 1941. He also appeared in such films as *Lifeboat* (1944), *Body and Soul* (1947), *Lost Boundaries* (1949), and *Cry, the Beloved Country* (1952).

Credits: *Stevedore* (1934); *Sailor, Beware!* (1935); *Macbeth* (1936); *One-Act Plays from the Sea*; *Brown Sugar** (1937); *Haiti** (1938); *Mamba's Daughters** (1939); *Big White Fog** (1940); *Native Son* (1941); *Across the Board on Tomorrow Morning*; *Talking to You* (1942); *South Pacific*; *Anna Lucasta** (1944); *The Tempest* (1945); *On Whitman Avenue** (1946); *The Duchess of Malfi* (1947); *Set My People Free** (1948).

Reference: "Canada Lee" File, PFL/TC.

**LITTLE, CLEAVON** (1939– ). Born in Chickasha, Oklahoma, Little received his theatrical training at San Diego State University. His most notable Broadway role to date has been his Tony Award-winning performance in *Purlie** (1970). He also made a promising film debut in Mel Brooks's *Blazing Saddles* (1974).

Credits: *MacBird!*; *Scuba Duba* (1967); *Hamlet*; *Jimmy Shine* (1968); *Someone's Comin' Hungry**; *The Ofay Watcher* (1969); *Purlie (1970); Narrow Road to the Deep North* (1972); *The Great MacDaddy** (replacement); *All Over Town* (1974); *The Poison Tree*; *Joseph and the Amazing Technicolor Dreamcoat* (1976).

Reference: *The New York Times*, October 5, 1969.

**LONG, AVON** (1910– ). Singer and actor Avon Long made his debut at the Cotton Club in 1931. The Baltimore-born performer then initiated a fifty-year career, specializing in musical theatre. His latest triumph, *Bubbling Brown Sugar** (1976), provided a musical catalogue of his years in show business.

Credits: *Black Rhythm** (1936); *La Belle Helene* (1941); *Porgy and Bess** (1942); *Memphis Bound!**; *Carib Song** (1945); *Beggar's Holiday* (1946); *The Green Pastures** (1951); *Shuffle Along of 1952**; *Mrs. Patterson** (1954); *The Ballad of Jazz Street* (1959); *Fly Blackbird** (1962); *Porgy and Bess** (1965); *Don't Play Us Cheap!** (1972); *Bubbling Brown Sugar* (1976).

Reference: "Avon Long" File, PFL/TC.

**LYLES, AUBREY.** See MILLER, FLOURNOY E., and AUBREY LYLES.

# M

**MACBETH, ROBERT** (?– ). Macbeth first studied theatre at Morehouse College in Atlanta and later appeared on Broadway in *The Merchant of Venice* and *Tiger, Tiger Burning Bright** (1962). He was the founder and director of the New Lafayette Theatre, which was established with grants from the Ford and Rockefeller Foundations and the New York Council of the Arts in 1967. The New Lafayette (which opened on the site of the "Old Lafayette" at 132nd Street and 7th Avenue) presented Ron Milner's* *Who's Got His Own?** and Athol Fugard's *The Blood Knot** during its first season. A fire destroyed the theatre in January 1968, but the company relocated by the end of the year to 137th Street and 7th Avenue. The New Lafayette produced a variety of new plays, including several by Ed Bullins,* but the company dissolved in 1973. Macbeth also is recognized as an outstanding director (*The Electronic Nigger and Others**) as well as a filmmaker (*In the Streets of Harlem*).

Credits (Directing): *Who's Got His Own?* (1967); *The Electronic Nigger and Others* (1968); *In the Wine Time** (1968/1976); *The Fabulous Miss Marie** (1971); *On-the-Lock-in* (1977).

Reference: *The New York Times*, August 20, 1967.

**MACK, CECIL** (1883–1944). Songwriter Cecil Mack (Richard C. McPherson) contributed special material for the Williams* and Walker* shows, and later provided lyrics for *Runnin' Wild** (1923) and *Swing It** (1937). His choir also appeared in *Rhapsody in Black** (1931) which starred Ethel Waters.* Mack founded the Gotham-Attucks Music Publishing Company which encouraged black songwriters.

Reference: Kinkle, Roger D., *The Complete Encyclopedia of Popular Music and Jazz, 1900-1950*, New Rochelle, N.Y.: Arlington House, 1974.

**MACKEY, WILLIAM WELLINGTON** (?– ). Mackey was born in Louisiana and earned his Master's degree at the University of Minnesota. While a student, he began work on *Behold! Cometh the Vanderkellans*,* which later received an Off-Broadway production in 1971. Mackey also wrote a musical, *Billy Noname*,* which opened Off-Broadway in 1970. Other works, such as *Requiem for Brother X* and *Family Meeting*, have been performed throughout the country. His most recent New York production has been *Love Me, Love Me Daddy, or I Swear I'm Gonna Kill You*, presented in 1980 at the Theatre at Holy Name House.

Reference: Couch, William, Jr., *New Black Playwrights*, Baton Rouge, La.: Louisiana State University Press, 1970.

**McCLENDON, ROSE** (1885–1936). McClendon is a native of New York City. She appeared in several of the black-cast dramas of the 1920s. She had a small role in *Deep River** (1924), which only involved a slow descent of a spiral staircase, a walk through a patio, and then an exit. Her performance riveted audience attention to her and helped to establish her on Broadway. In 1935, she began to organize the Negro People's Theatre in order to develop black acting talent. She became ill with pneumonia while performing in *Mulatto** (1935) and died soon after. The Rose McClendon Players in Harlem continued her goals and dreams after her death.

Credits: *Roseanne** (1924); *Deep River*; *In Abraham's Bosom** (1926); *Porgy** (1927); *The House of Connelly* (1931); *Never No More**; *Black Souls** (1932); *Brain Sweat**; *Roll, Sweet Chariot** (1934); *Panic*; *Mulatto* (1935).

Reference: "Rose McClendon" File, PFL/TC.

**McKAYLE, DONALD** (1930- ). Harlem-born Donald McKayle first attracted attention as the choreographer of his modern dance troupe. He brought his skills to Broadway, choreographing such musicals as *Golden Boy** (1964) and *A Time for Singing* (1966). He extended his skills to direction with *Trumpets of the Lord** in 1963. His greatest success, however, was *Raisin** (1973), written by childhood friend Lorraine Hansberry.* He also choreographed (with Michael Smuin) and provided the "concept" for *Sophisticated Ladies** (1981), the recent tribute to Duke Ellington.*

Credits (Directing): *Trumpets of the Lord* (1963); *I'm Solomon* (1968); *Raisin* (1973); *Dr. Jazz* (1975).

References: *Philadelphia Inquirer*, September 9, 1973; *The New York Times*, November 4, 1973.

**McNEIL, CLAUDIA** (1917- ). A native of Baltimore, McNeil sang in nightclubs and vaudeville theatres before coming to Broadway as a replacement in *The Crucible* in 1953. Best known for her role of "Lena Younger" in *A Raisin in the Sun** (1959), she recently reprised her classic role in a revival of the musical comedy *Raisin** in 1981.

Credits: *Simply Heavenly** (1957); *Winesburg, Ohio* (1958); *A Raisin in the Sun* (1959); *Tiger, Tiger Burning Bright** (1962); *The Amen Corner** (1965); *Something Different* (1967); *Her First Roman* (1968); *The Wrong Way Light Bulb* (1969); *Contributions** (1970); *Raisin* (1981).

Reference: "Claudia McNeil" File, PFL/TC.

**MILLER, FLOURNOY E.** (1886–1971), **and AUBREY LYLES** (1884–1932). The premier black comedians of the Jazz Age, Miller and Lyles began their partnership as young Fisk University students shortly after the turn of the century. Both were Tennesseans—Miller from Columbia and Nashville, and Lyles from Jackson. In their initial campus theatricals emerged the distinctive character pairing and the mixture of slapstick and topical satire that became their comic trademarks. After graduation, the team began professionally with Robert Mott's Negro stock company at Chicago's Pekin Theater, where their sketch, "The Mayor of Dixie," was successful in 1907. Attracting the fancy of the city's white elite, they moved to the downtown Majestic Theater. In 1907, they wrote *The Oyster Man*,* which was later staged at the Pekin with Ernest Hogan* in the title role. Their vaudeville debut came in Columbus, Ohio, on August 28, 1910, and their first Broadway appearance was with Blossom Seeley in the short 1912 run of George Lederer's *The Charity Girl*. In 1915, they unsuccessfully attempted their own all-black show, *Darkydom*, at Harlem's Lafayette Theater and also toured England with a Charlot revue, but for most of the 1910s they starred in bigtime vaudeville on the Keith and Orpheum circuits.

They met Noble Sissle* and Eubie Blake* at a National Association for the Advancement of Colored People benefit in Philadelphia in 1920, and the four struck up plans that resulted in the landmark all-black production *Shuffle Along*,* which made its Broadway opening on May 21, 1921. Miller and Lyles's book for the show took its main plot from "The Mayor of Dixie," incorporating other bits from their vaudeville act, along with Sissle and Blake's musical numbers and exhilarating dance sequences. Despite a shaky start—rehearsals and the trial road tour were financed largely by the two teams themselves—*Shuffle Along* met with rave reviews and ran for over five hundred performances, reviving the black musical comedy form and setting the pattern for numerous productions to come.

In the next few years, Miller and Lyles enjoyed unequaled popularity, keeping an active stage schedule and contracting with Okeh records, which issued eleven of their comedy routines by 1925. In 1923, they collaborated with composer James P. Johnson* to repeat their Broadway success with *Runnin' Wild*.* Although still quite popular, they lost preeminence after mid-decade to two white black-face teams—Correll and Gosden, ("Amos 'n' Andy") and Moran and Mack ("Two Black Crows"). Miller and Lyles did remain in demand in vaudeville and made two more notable all-black Broadway ventures, *Rang Tang** and *Keep Shufflin'*,* but neither reversed his declining career.

After the failure of *Great Day!* in late 1929, the partnership dissolved as the disenchanted Aubrey Lyles departed for Africa with the Marcus Garvey movement. In his absence, Miller collaborated with Andy Razaf* to write the script for Lew Leslie's *Blackbirds of 1930*,* and his starring role in the revue included dialogues with Mantan Moreland.* Lyles returned in 1931 and rejoined Miller for *Sugar Hill*,* a parody of life in a prosperous Harlem neighborhood which was canceled shortly after its Christmas night opening. In hopes of resurrecting their 1921 triumph, the team planned a reunion with Sissle and Blake the next year, but Lyles died of tuberculosis on July 28 before rehearsals had even begun. The ill-fated production was eventually staged, with Moreland replacing Lyles, as *Shuffle Along of 1933*,* but a dismal response to the show attested that continual repetition had made the black musical comedy formula outdated.

In later life, Miller remained an active comedy writer and performer. He was involved in numerous all-black films, including appearances with Mantan Moreland in *Harlem on the Prairie* (1939) and *Mr. Washington Goes to Town* (1940). In *Stormy Weather* (1943), Miller teamed with Johnny Lee to reenact dialogue bits from his earlier partnership. In an ironic turn, he became principal scriptwriter for the "Amos 'n' Andy" radio show, and in 1948 he oversaw the casting of black actors for the controversial television version of the series. In 1955 and 1956, he participated in the Palace Theatre's programs by old-time vaudevillians. He lived in retirement in Hollywood until his death on June 6, 1971.

Credits: *The Charity Girl* (1912); *Darkydom* (1915); *Shuffle Along* (1921); *Runnin' Wild* (1923); *George White's Scandals of 1925* (1925); *Great Temptations* (1926); *Rang Tang* (1927); *Keep Shufflin'* (1928); *Great Day!* (1929); *Sugar Hill* (1931).

Credits to Miller alone: *Blackbirds of 1930* (1930); *Shuffle Along of 1933*; *Shuffle Along of 1952*.

Reference: Kimball, Robert, and William Bolcom, *Reminiscing with Sissle and Blake*, New York: Viking Press, 1973.

ROBERT COGSWELL

**MILLS, FLORENCE** (1895–1927). Mills died at the age of thirty-two after an appendix operation. Since she left no recordings or films, her reputation rests on the rhapsodic reviews she received during the 1920s. She first appeared as a replacement for Gertrude Saunders in the long-run hit *Shuffle Along** (1921), where she sang "I'm Cravin' for That Kind of Love." Lew Leslie (of *Blackbirds* fame) helped her career in the United States and Europe. She appeared in *Plantation Revue** in 1922, and by 1924 she was declared a major star in *Dixie to Broadway*,* where she sang her theme song "I'm a Little Blackbird Looking for a Bluebird." After the show closed, she continued to perform in Europe. Her sudden death shocked New Yorkers, and thousands attended her Harlem funeral.

Reference: Johnson, James W., *Black Manhattan*, New York: Knopf, 1930.

**MILNER, RON** (1938– ). Milner was born in Detroit on May 29, 1938. After graduating from Northeastern High School and attending area colleges, he participated in Harvey Swados's Writing Workshop at Columbia University during the early 1960s. He later received a Rockefeller Grant and a John Hay Whitney Fellowship. With the American Place Theatre's production of *Who's Got His Own?** in 1966, Milner gained attention as a promising playwright. The play was chosen as the opening production for the New Lafayette Theatre in Harlem during the fall of 1967. While his play was running in New York, Milner served an appointment as writer-in-residence at Lincoln University in Pennsylvania. Despite several productions in the New York and Los Angeles areas, Milner has remained active in the Detroit community and has followed his own dictum that black theatre must remain close to the black community. In 1970, he founded and served as director of the Spirit of Shango Theatre Company in Detroit. He has also taught at Michigan State University and at Wayne State University.

Milner's most commercially successful drama has been *What the Wine-Sellers Buy*,* produced by the New Federal Theatre in 1973 and later presented at Lincoln Center by the New York Shakespeare Festival. Set in Detroit, the play is a rather old-fashioned melodrama in which a teenage boy is faced with a choice between good and evil: should he choose the path of honest struggle advocated by his churchgoing, ailing mother or that of easy money as proffered by a neighboring pimp? Virtue does triumph at the end, but during the course of the play, Milner raises some serious questions concerning the images of success that tempt ghetto youths. While such questions may be of little importance to Broadway critics, they are of intense concern to the community Milner addresses in the play.

In 1976, Milner collaborated with Charles Mason for a musical, *Season's Reasons: Just a Natural Change*, which opened at the Langston Hughes Theatre in Detroit and was presented at the New Federal Theatre a year later. Based upon a Rip Van Winkle concept, the musical presents a panorama of the changes black people have undergone during the period that one of the main characters, R. B., has been in jail. The shift to a musical form is not surprising considering Milner's claim that even in *Who's Got His Own?* he tried to capture the rhythms of different styles of black music to individualize the speech of the main characters (Smitherman, "We Are the Music," p. 11). In his last major play of the 1970s, *Jazz Set*, presented at the Mark Taper Forum in 1979, Milner presents characters whose speech patterns are very clearly modeled after the rhythm and sound of jazz.

Often described as "the people's playwright," Milner is a gifted writer with a fine sense of detail that gives a rich texture of authenticity to his dramas of the black experience. He is a playwright who speaks to his people in order that they might better understand themselves and their unique experience.

References: King, Woodie, Jr., "Directing 'Winesellers'," *Black World* (April 1976), 20-26; Milner, Ron, "Black Magic, Black Art," *Negro Digest* (April 1967), 8-12, 93-94; Saddler, Jeanne E., "On the Aisle: Ron Milner: The People's Playwright," *Essence* (November 1974), 20; Smitherman, Geneva, " 'We Are the Music': Ron Milner, People's Playwright," *Black World* (April 1976), 4-19.

GERALD T. GOODMAN

**MITCHELL, ABBIE** (1884–1960). Mitchell began her career with the Williams* and Walker* company in *In Dahomey** (1903). She appeared at two British command performances with that troupe. A throat ailment curtailed her singing career in 1912, and she turned to drama as a featured player with the Lafayette Theatre. Broadway soon saw her performances in the mid-1920s in such shows as *In Abraham's Bosom** (1926). She sang once again ("Summertime") in *Porgy and Bess** (1935).

Credits: *In Dahomey* (1903); *The Southerners** (1904); *Bandana Land** (1908); *The Red Moon** (1909); *In Abraham's Bosom* (1926); *The House of Shadows*; *Coquette* (1927); *Stevedore** (1934); *Porgy and Bess* (1935); *The Little Foxes* (1939); *On Whitman Avenue** (1946).

Reference: "Abbie Mitchell" File, PFL/TC.

**MITCHELL, LOFTEN** (1919- ). Mitchell, a native of Columbus, North Carolina, is known both as a dramatist and as an historian of the black theatre. After an acting career in the 1930s in New York City, Mitchell turned to playwrighting. His early efforts include *Blood in the Night* (1946), *The Bancroft Dynasty* (1948), and *The Cellar* (1952). He first attracted critical attention with his dramatization of the life of Reverend Dr. Joseph DeLaine and his efforts to provide equal education to the black children of South Carolina in *A Land Beyond the River** (1957). His musical, *Ballad for Bimshire** (1963), written with Irving Burgie, also received high praise.

Mitchell's *Black Drama: The Story of the American Negro in the Theatre* (New York: Hawthorn, 1967) has become a major reference source for black theatre history. Mitchell drew on this knowledge when he wrote *Star of the Morning*, an unproduced historical drama of the life of entertainer Bert Williams,* as well as the smash musical cavalcade, *Bubbling Brown Sugar** (1976).

Reference: Bigsby, C.W.E., "Three Black Playwrights: Loften Mitchell, Ossie Davis, Douglas Turner Ward," in Bigsby, *The Black American Writer*, Vol. 2, Deland, Fla.: Everett/Edwards, Inc., 1969.

**MONAGAS, LIONEL** (1903-1945). Monagas (var.: Monagus) was born in Caracas, Venezuela, and began his theatrical career with the Lafayette Players in Harlem. During the 1920s, he moved to Broadway and appeared in several black dramas (*Appearances** [1925]) and musicals (*Runnin' Wild** [1923]). He performed with the Federal Theatre Project* in the late 1930s before moving to Hollywood to appear in films. He returned to New York for *Peepshow* (1944) and became fatally ill while appearing in his last show, *Anna Lucasta** (1944).

Credits: *The Chip Woman's Fortune**; *Runnin' Wild* (1923); *Appearances* (1925); *My Magnolia** (1926); *Ol' Man Satan** (1932); *Louisiana**; *Humming Sam**; *Blackbirds of 1933** (1933); *Walk Together Chillun**; *Conjur Man Dies** (1936); *One-Act Plays from the Sea* (1937); *Big White Fog** (1940); *Peepshow*; *Anna Lucasta* (1944).

Reference: "Lionel Monagas" File, NYLP/TC.

**MONTGOMERY, BARBARA** (?- ). Montgomery came to New York City from East Orange, New Jersey, in 1957. She studied acting with Vinnette Carroll* and also appeared in Harlem nightclubs. She later joined the Negro Ensemble Company* and appeared in several of its major productions.

Credits: *Ubu Roi*; *Street Sounds* (1970); *Black Visions** (1972); *Thoughts** (1973); *My Sister, My Sister**; *Les Femmes Noires**; *A Song for Now* (1974); *The First Breeze of Summer**; *Waiting for Mongo**; *Kennedy's Children* (1975); *Eden** (1976); *The Great MacDaddy** (1977); *Nevis Mountain Dew** (1978); *A Season to Unravel**; *Old Phantoms** (1979); *Lagrima del Diablo**; *Companions of the Fire** (1980); *Inacent Black** (1981).

Reference: "Barbara Montgomery" File, NYPL/TC.

**MOORE, MELBA** (1945- ). Moore began her career as a music teacher and became a backup singer for Aretha Franklin, Frank Sinatra, and others. She moved to Broadway for a role in *Hair* in 1968, leaving for a leading role in *Purlie** (1970), which won her a Tony and a Theatre World Award. She returned to Broadway for *Timbuktu!** (1978), Geoffrey Holder's* black version of *Kismet*, and *Inacent Black** in 1981.

Reference: "Melba Moore" Files, PFL/TC.

**MOORE, TIM** (1888-1958). Moore was born in Rock Island, Illinois, and appeared in vaudeville (with Cora Mitchell and Her Gold Dust Twins) and in the boxing ring before turning to the stage. A major comic presence in the black musicals of the 1920s, he appeared in *Lucky Sambo** (1925), *Blackbirds of 1928,** *Fast and Furious** (1931), *Blackberries of 1932,** *Blackbirds of 1939,** and *Harlem Cavalcade** (1942). He also appeared on television's *Ed Sullivan Show* and *Amos 'n' Andy.*

Reference: "Tim Moore" File, PFL/TC.

**MORELAND, MANTAN** (1902-1973). Wide-eyed comic Mantan Moreland graced several of the black musicals of the 1920s as well as appearing in numerous motion pictures. He ran away from his Monroe, Louisiana, home to join the circus, and he later appeared in vaudeville. He made his Broadway debut in *Blackbirds of 1928** and later moved to Hollywood, where he appeared in several of the Charlie Chan mystery films. Although a comedian, his final Broadway role in *Waiting for Godot* (1957) revealed his strong dramatic talents.

Credits: *Blackbirds of 1928*; *Blackbirds of 1930**; *Singin' the Blues** (1931); *Blackberries of 1932**; *Yeah Man** (1932); *Shuffle Along of 1933**; *Waiting for Godot* (1957).

Reference: 'Mantan Moreland" File, PFL/TC.

**MOSES, GILBERT** (1942- ). Moses began his theatrical apprenticeship at Cleveland's Karamu Theatre and later at the Free Southern Theatre. He made his directorial debut Off-Broadway with Baraka's* *Slave Ship** (1969), which won him an Obie, and on Broadway with *Ain't Supposed to Die a Natural Death** (1971). Since then, he has also devoted considerable time to such regional theatre groups as the American Conservatory Theatre and the Boston Theatre Company.

Credits: *Slave Ship* (1969); *Ain't Supposed to Die a Natural Death*; *Charlie Was Here and Now He's Gone** (1971); *The Duplex** (1972); *The Taking of Miss Janie** (1975); *1600 Pennsylvania Avenue*; *Every Night When the Sun Goes Down** (1976).

Reference: *The New York Times*, March 5, 1972.

**NEGRO ENSEMBLE COMPANY.** After Douglas Turner Ward* wrote an article in *The New York Times* in 1966 which called for the establishment of a black theatre group, the Ford Foundation asked him to develop a proposal. Ford supplied initial funding for the new organization, the Negro Ensemble Company* (NEC), headed by Ward, Gerald S. Krone, and actor Robert Hooks.* The goal of the new company was to develop black actors, playwrights, technicians, and managers.

The NEC began operations in 1968 at the St. Marks Playhouse to laudatory reviews for *Song of the Lusitanian Bogey.** Initial presentations emphasized black American playwrights (Lonne Elder III,* Alice Childress,* Ted Shine, Douglas Turner Ward, and Joseph Walker*) but playwrights from Africa and the Caribbean (Wole Soyinka, Afolabi Ajayi, Derek Wolcott, and Errol Hill) were represented as well.

While the critics from the major newspapers heartily praised the NEC, some black critics argued that it was too "establishment" and "safe." An emphasis on "Themes of Black Struggle" in the fourth season attempted to answer these criticisms.

The success of the NEC may be measured in a variety of ways. Several of its productions have moved on to Broadway showings (*The River Niger,** *The First Breeze of Summer,** and *Home**), and several of its actors have launched promising careers. Among the most renowned actors that have performed with the NEC are Roscoe Lee Browne,* Adolph Caesar,* Rosalind Cash,* Bill Cobbs, Frances Foster,* Al Freeman, Jr.,* Moses Gunn,* Robert Hooks,* Ron O'Neal,* Esther Rolle,* Roxie Roker, and Hattie Winston.* Joseph Walker's *The River Niger* won a Tony for Best Play, and the recent *A Soldier's Play** won a Pulitzer Prize for author Charles Fuller* in 1982. The NEC also won a special Tony Award in 1969 for its initial efforts.

After some years of financial hard times in the late 1970s, the NEC moved from its original home to the larger Theatre Four. The success of *A Soldier's Play* and other recent productions has eased the company's financial burdens and has allowed it to continue to foster new productions of black theatre artists.

Negro Ensemble Company productions: *Song of the Lusitanian Bogey*; *Summer of the Seventeenth Doll**; *Kongi's Harvest**; *Daddy Goodness**; *God Is a (Guess What?)** (1968); *Ceremonies in Dark Old Men**; *An Evening of One Acts**; *The Reckoning**; *Man Better Man** (1969); *The Harangues**; *Brotherhood*/Day of Absence**; *Akokawe**; *Ododo** (1971); *Perry's Mission*/Rosalee Pritchett**; *The Dream on Monkey Mountain**; *Ride a Black Horse**; *The Sty of the Blind Pig** (1971); *A Ballet Behind the Bridge**; *Frederick Douglass . . . Through His Own*

*Words**; *The River Niger* (1972); *The Great MacDaddy**; *Black Sunlight**; *Nowhere to Run, Nowhere to Hide**; *Terraces**; *Heaven and Hell's Agreement**; *In the Deepest Part of Sleep** (1974); *The First Breeze of Summer*; *Liberty Call**; *Orrin*/Sugar-Mouth Sam Don't Dance No More**; *The Moonlight Arms*/The Dark Tower**; *Waiting for Mongo**; *Welcome to Black River** (1975); *Eden**; *Livin' Fat** (1976); *The Square Root of Soul**; *Survival* (co-production); *The Offering** (1977); *Black Body Blues**; *The Twilight Dinner**; *Nevis Mountain Dew** (1978); *A Season to Unravel**; *Old Phantoms**; *The Michigan**; *Home* (1979); *Lagrima del Diablo**; *Companions of the Fire*/Big City Blues**; *The Sixteenth Round**; *Zooman and the Sign** (1980); *Weep Not for Me**; *In an Upstate Motel**; *A Soldier's Play* (1981).

Reference: Foreman, Ellen, "The Negro Ensemble Company, A Transcendent Vision," in Errol Hill, ed., *The Theater of Black Americans*, Vol. 2, Englewood Cliffs, N.J.: Prentice-Hall, Inc., 1980.

**NEGRO PLAYWRIGHTS COMPANY.** The Negro Playwrights Company was founded in 1940 to "supply America with vital, interesting, and colorful theatre reflecting the reality of the Negro people, free from the inane stereotyped distortions of Hollywood" (group prospectus). Richard Wright* and Paul Robeson* spoke at the opening forum, and its initial members included Theodore Ward,* Langston Hughes,* and Theodore Browne. Despite lofty intentions, the Negro Playwrights Company produced only *Big White Fog** (1940) before disbanding. Several of its adherents moved to the American Negro Theatre.*

Reference: Ward, Theodore, "The Negro Playwrights Company," in Karen M. Taylor, ed., *People's Theatre in America*, New York: Drama Book Specialists (DBS), 1972.

**NELSON, NOVELLA** (1939- ). Nelson combines a variety of talents as an actress, singer, producer, and director. She first attracted attention as Pearl Bailey's* understudy in *Hello Dolly!* and later in *Purlie** (1970). Her directorial credits include *Nigger Nightmare* (1971), *Black Visions** (1972), *Les Femmes Noires** (1974), and *Sweet Talk* (1974).

Credits (Acting): *House of Flowers** (1968); *Unto Thee a Garden* (1968); *Horseman, Pass By* (1969); *Purlie* (1970); *Caesar and Cleopatra*; *The Passing Game* (1977); *The Little Foxes* (1981).

Reference: "Novella Nelson" File, PFL/TC.

**NEW FEDERAL THEATRE.** See KING, WOODIE, JR.

**NEW LAFAYETTE THEATRE.** See MACBETH, ROBERT.

# O

**O'NEAL, FREDERICK** (1905– ). O'Neal, one of the founders of the American Negro Theatre,* hails from Saint Louis. After several appearances with this group, he moved to Broadway in a supporting role (Frank) in *Anna Lucasta** (1944), for which he received a Clarence Derwent Award and the New York Critics Circle Award. After additional appearances throughout the world, he appeared in such Hollywood films as *Pinky* (1949), *Something of Value* (1957), *Anna Lucasta* (1959), *Take a Giant Step** (1961), and *The Sins of Rachel Cade* (1961).

Credits: *Natural Man** (1941); *Three's a Family* (1943); *Anna Lucasta* (1944); *Henri Christophe* (1945); *Take a Giant Step* (1953); *The Winner*; *Salvation on a String*; *House of Flowers** (1954); *The Man with the Golden Arm* (1956); *Twelfth Night* (1959); *God's Trombones** (1960); *Ballad For Bimshire** (1963); *The Iceman Cometh* (1968); *The Madwoman of Chaillot* (1970).

Reference: "Frederick O'Neal" File, NYPL/TC.

**O'NEAL, RON** (1937– ). O'Neal received instant fame as "Super Fly" in the 1972 film, but he had begun his acting career years earlier on the stage. Trained at the Karamu Theatre in Cleveland, he made his Off-Broadway debut in *American Pastoral* in 1968. He turned down a role in *Ceremonies in Dark Old Men** for *No Place to Be Somebody** (1969), which won him four major acting awards (Drama Desk, Theatre World, Clarence Derwent, and Obie).

Credits: *American Pastoral* (1968); *No Place to Be Somebody* (1969); *The Dream on Monkey Mountain** (1971); *All Over Town* (1974); *Agamemnon* (1977).

Reference: *The New York Times*, September 17, 1972.

# P

**PERRY, SHAUNEILLE** (1930– ). Perry attended Howard University and the Goodman Theatre in Chicago for her dramatic training. After a brief acting career (*The Goose* [1960] and *Clandestine on the Morning Line* [1961]), she turned to directing with *Rosalee Pritchett** (1971). She also co-wrote the book for *Daddy Goodness*,* a 1979 musical that closed before reaching Broadway. Her latest work, *Things of the Heart: Marian Anderson's Story*, was produced by the New Federal Theatre in January 1981.

Credits (Directing): *Rosalee Pritchett*; *Black Girl**; *Jamimma**; *The Sty of the Blind Pig** (1971); *The Prodigal Sister** (1974); *Bayou Legend* (1975); *Trouble in Mind** (1979).

Reference: *The Village Voice*, April 27, 1972.

**PETERS, BROCK** (1927- ). Peters, a native of Harlem, originally studied psychology and physical education at City College but was unable to cure his love of acting. He received a small role in the 1943 revival of *Porgy and Bess** and then moved to Chicago for a run in *Anna Lucasta.** He later returned to Broadway for a role in *Mister Johnson** (1956). He has also appeared in several critically acclaimed films, such as *Porgy and Bess* (1959), *To Kill a Mockingbird*, *Heavens Above!*, *The L-Shaped Room* (1963), and *The Pawnbroker* (1965). He appeared in the road company of *The Great White Hope** and won a Tony nomination for his performance in *Lost in the Stars** (1972).

Credits: *Mister Johnson* (1956); *King of the Dark Chamber*; *Kwamina** (1961); *The Caucasian Chalk Circle* (1966); *Lost in the Stars* (1972).

Reference: "Brock Peters" File, PFL/TC.

**PETERSON, LOUIS** (1922- ). Peterson moved from his native Hartford, Connecticut, to New York to launch an acting career. After appearances in *A Young American* (1946) and *Our Lan'** (1947), he turned to playwrighting with the autobiographical *Take a Giant Step** (1953). Despite good reviews, the production languished, but an Off-Broadway revival with Beah Richards* and Bill Gunn* survived for 264 performances in 1956. Peterson has also written *Entertain a Ghost* (1962), a mystery thriller, for Off-Broadway.

Reference: "Louis Peterson" File, NYPL/TC.

**POITIER, SIDNEY** (1927- ). Although known primarily as a film actor and director, Poitier began his career in the theatre. After a stint in the army, he joined the American Negro Theatre* in 1945. During this period, he appeared in such diverse productions as *Days of Our Youth* (debut), *On Striver's Row,** *Rain*, *Freight*, *You Can't Take It with You*, *The Fisherman*, *Hidden Horizon*, *Riders to the Sea*, and *Sepia Cinderella*.

Poitier made his Broadway debut in *Lysistrata* (1946) and then played "Lester" in a revival of *Anna Lucasta** (1947) at the Barrymore Theatre. He attracted attention in the role of "Walter Lee Younger" in *A Raisin in the Sun** (1959). Poitier also directed the short-lived *Carry Me Back to Morningside Heights** (1968). His film roles include *No Way Out* (1950), *Cry the Beloved Country* (1952), *The Blackboard Jungle* (1955), *Porgy and Bess* (1959), and his Oscar-winning performance in *Lilies of the Field* (1963).

Reference: Poitier, Sidney, *This Life*, New York: Knopf, 1980.

**PREER, EVELYN** (1896–1932). Preer, a native of Vicksburg, Mississippi, joined the Lafayette Stock Company when she moved to New York City. She later distinguished herself in the Ethiopian Art Company's *The Chip Woman's Fortune*,* *Salome*, and *A Comedy of Errors* in 1917. Still later, she moved to Hollywood and appeared in several silent films, including *The Devil's Disciple* (1926). She returned to Broadway for a brief run in *Rang Tang** in 1927.

Reference: "Evelyn Preer" File, PFL/TC.

**PRICE, GILBERT** (1942– ). Price began his career in *Fly Blackbird** in 1962 and has since graced the stage of several musical comedies. His clear, strong voice often stops the show whenever he appears. After winning a Theatre World Award for *Jerico-Jim Crow** (1964), he moved to Anthony Newley and Leslie Bricusse's *The Roar of Greasepaint, the Smell of the Crowd* (1965), where he sang "Feeling Good." He also won Tony Award nominations for *Lost in the Stars** (1972) and *The Night That Made America Famous* (1975).

Credits: *Fly Blackbird* (1962); *Jerico-Jim Crow*; *A Midsummer Night's Dream* (1964); *The Roar of Greasepaint, the Smell of the Crowd* (1965); *Promenade* (1969); *Slow Dance on the Killing Ground* (1970); *Six* (1971); *Lost in the Stars* (1972); *The Night That Made America Famous* (1975); *1600 Pennsylvania Avenue* (1976); *Timbuktu!** (1978).

Reference: "Gilbert Price" File, PFL/TC.

# R

**RAZAF, ANDY** (1896–1973). Razaf, noted for his classic *double-entendre* lyrics, was born in Madagascar as Andreamenentania Paul Razafinkeriefo. His collaborators included both Eubie Blake* and Fats Waller.* Razaf contributed lyrics to *Keep Shufflin'** (1928), *Hot Chocolates** (1929), and *Blackbirds of 1930.** His lyrics were revisited in such recent hits as *Bubbling Brown Sugar** (1976), *Ain't Misbehavin'** (1978), and *Eubie!** (1979). Among his hits are "Memories of You" and "My Handyman Ain't Handy No More."

Reference: Kimball, Robert, and William Bolcom, *Reminiscing with Sissle and Blake*, New York: Viking Press, 1973.

**RICHARDS, BEAH** (?– ). Richards of Vicksburg, Mississippi, first studied drama at Dillard University in New Orleans. Her parents, encouraged by her talent, sent her to study at the Globe Theatre in San

Diego, where she appeared in *The Little Foxes* and *Another Part of the Forest*. After three years at the Globe, Richards left for New York for a role in *Take a Giant Step** (1956). She repeated her performance in the film version of the play.

Richards later received major praise for her portrayal of "Sister Margaret" in James Baldwin's* *The Amen Corner** (1965). She has also appeared in such films as *Gone Are the Days!* (1963), *Guess Who's Coming to Dinner?* (which brought her an Oscar nomination), and *In the Heat of the Night* (1967). In recent years, she has been a guest artist at the Inner City Repertory Company in Los Angeles.

Credits: *Take a Giant Step* (1956); *The Miracle Worker* (1959); *Purlie Victorious** (1961); *The Amen Corner* (1965); *The Little Foxes* (1967).

Reference: "Beah Richards" File, PFL/TC.

**RICHARDS, LLOYD** (1923- ). Richards studied social work at Wayne State University in Detroit, but he soon became interested in theatre. He started as an actor in such plays as *Stevedore** (1949), *Trouble in July* (1949), *Freight* (1950), and *The Egghead* (1957), where James Earl Jones* was his understudy. His first directorial chore, *A Raisin in the Sun** (1959), won critical praise and began a new facet of his career. He is currently artistic director of the Yale Repertory Theatre.

Credits (Directing): *A Raisin in the Sun* (1959); *The Long Dream** (1960); *The Moon Besieged* (1962); *I Had a Ball* (1964); *The Amen Corner**; *The Yearling* (1965); *Who's Got His Own?**; *The Ox Cart* (1966); *Freeman**; *Two Plays by Richard Wesley* (*The Past Is Past/Going Through Changes*) (1973); *Paul Robeson** (1978).

Reference: *The New York Times*, January 11, 1981.

**RICHARDSON, WILLIS** (1889-1977). Born in Wilmington, North Carolina, Richardson was raised in Washington, D.C., and spent his life there, working as a government clerk until his retirement in 1954. He began writing plays in response to a 1916 production of Angela Grimké's *Rachel*, for while he valued the "propaganda play," as he termed it, he preferred plays that revealed "the soul of a people" (Richardson, *The Chip Woman's Fortune*, pp. 338-339) and set out to provide them. He was encouraged by such figures as Alain Locke, Mary Burrill, and especially W.E.B. DuBois, who published several of his plays in *The Crisis* and *The Brownies' Book* and whose magazine's annual literary competition twice awarded him first prize. In 1923, the Ethiopian Art Players of Chicago took Richardson's *The Chip Woman's Fortune** to Broadway, the first serious play by a black writer to receive a Broadway production.

Richardson's plays were also the first by a black writer produced by the Howard University Players (*Mortgaged*, 1924) and the Gilpin Players of Karamu House, Cleveland (*Compromise*, 1926). During the 1920s and 1930s, his works received countless productions by black school, university, and community groups all over the country.

The author of forty-two plays, Richardson satisfied the needs of the many early black theatrical groups seeking material by black writers. His best plays are his folk plays: *Flight of the Natives*, *The Chip Woman's Fortune*, *The Broken Banjo*, *The Idle Head*, and *Compromise*, which present ordinary black people facing situations caused or exacerbated by racism and to which they seek moral and honorable solutions.

References: Peterson, Bernard, "Willis Richardson/Pioneer Playwright," *Black World* (April 1975), 4-48, 86-88; Richardson, Willis, *The Chip Woman's Fortune*, in Darwin Turner, ed., *Black Drama in America: An Anthology*, Greenwich, Conn.: Fawcett, 1971.

LESLIE SANDERS

**ROBERTS, CHARLES "LUCKEY"** (1895–1968). Charles Luckeyeth (Luckyeth) Roberts, noted ragtime pianist, claimed to have written the scores of fifteen musical comedies. His first two Broadway productions, *Go-Go* and *Sharlee* (1923), were composed for white casts, a rarity in the early 1920s. *My Magnolia** (1926) had only a brief run, but Roberts earned praise for his score.

Reference: Blesh, Rudi, and Harriet Janis, *They All Played Ragtime*, New York: Oak Publications, 1971.

**ROBESON, PAUL** (1898–1976). All-American Paul Robeson made his stage debut while still attending law school. He first appeared with the "Four Harmony Kings" in *Shuffle Along** (1921). His wife then urged him to audition for a Harlem YMCA revival of *Simon the Cyrenian*, and he landed the lead. She also invited several members of the Provincetown Playhouse to witness Robeson's performance.

Robeson swiftly moved to the lead in *Taboo** (1922), which later toured England with Mrs. Patrick Campbell in the lead. Robeson's fame continued to grow after his Provincetown Players debut in the controversial Eugene O'Neill play, *All God's Chillun Got Wings** (1924), which he performed in repertory with *The Emperor Jones.**

After a run in *Black Boy** (1926), and as a replacement in *Porgy** (1928), Robeson traveled again to London to appear in *Show Boat* (1928). He had been offered the lead in New York, but previous commitments made it impossible. In this production, Robeson made the classic "Ol' Man River" his trademark. After the *Show Boat* run, he appeared in his first Shakespearean play, *Othello*, in 1930.

Films soon beckoned, and Robeson appeared in a variety of British and American productions, including *The Emperor Jones* (1933), *Sanders of the River* (1935), *Show Boat* (1936), *King Solomon's Mines* (1937), *Dark Sands* (1938), *Proud Valley* (1941), *Native Land*, and *Tales of Manhattan* (1942).

Robeson returned to Shakespeare in 1942 in a performance of *Othello* at Cambridge. This production with Jose Ferrer and Uta Hagen later came to Broadway under the sponsorship of the Theatre Guild. The show toured until 1945, and it remains Robeson's greatest triumph.

Angered by the treatment of blacks in the United States, Robeson preferred performing and living in Europe. During the 1930s, he became attracted to communism and the Soviet Union, and he eventually supported leftist movements in the United States. These activities were questioned in the Cold War era, especially when Robeson refused to state whether he was a communist before the House Committee on Un-American Activities.

Robeson found new job opportunities increasingly limited in the McCarthy Era, and his income plummeted. He retreated from public life after becoming ill in the late 1960s. He died in Philadelphia in 1976.

Robeson's life was dramatized in a 1978 play, *Paul Robeson*,* by Phillip Hayes Dean.* Many claimed it sentimentalized Robeson, while others found it important to commemorate the life of one of America's greatest actors and to expose his reactions to America's racism.

Credits: *Shuffle Along* (1921); *Taboo* (1922); *The Emperor Jones/All God's Chillun Got Wings* (1924); *Black Boy* (1926); *Show Boat* (London, 1928); *Othello* (London, 1930/United States, 1942-1945); *The Hairy Ape* (1931); *Basalik*; *Stevedore** (1935); *Toussaint L'Ouverture* (1936); *John Henry** (1939).

References: Gilliam, Dorothy Butler, *Paul Robeson, All-American*, Washington, D.C.: New Republic Book Co., 1976; Hamilton, Virginia, *Paul Robeson*, New York: Harper and Row, 1974; Robeson, Susan, *The Whole World in His Hands*, Secaucus, N.J.: Citadel Press, 1981.

**ROBINSON, BILL** (1878–1949). Bill "Bojangles" Robinson, the king of the tap-dancers, claimed to have begun dancing at age eight. He displayed his talents in a series of four Shirley Temple films (*The Littlest Rebel*, *The Little Colonel*, *Rebecca of Sunnybrook Farm*, and *Just Around the Corner*) in the 1930s, but he dazzled the critics on Broadway as well. He moved from vaudeville to *Blackbirds of 1928** and helped to make it a long-run hit with his rendition of "Doin' the New Low Down." Robinson remained fit throughout his entire life, whether dancing with Lena Horne* in the film *Stormy Weather* (1943) at age sixty-five or in the Broadway musical *Memphis Bound!** (1945) at age sixty-seven.

Credits: *Blackbirds of 1928*; *Brown Buddies** (1930); *Blackbirds of 1933**; *The Hot Mikado** (1939); *All in Fun* (1940); *Memphis Bound!* (1945).

Reference: Stearns, Marshall and Jean, *Jazz Dance*, New York: Schirmer Books, 1979.

**ROGERS, ALEXANDER** (1876-1930). Rogers left his Nashville, Tennessee, home to travel with a minstrel show. His writings for a Philadelphia newspaper attracted the attention of Bert Williams* and George Walker.* He joined their company as a librettist, lyricist, and actor for *In Dahomey** (1903), *Abyssinia** (1906), *Bandana Land** (1908), and *Mr. Lode of Koal** (1909). His most famous contribution of this period was the verse for Williams's classic "Nobody."

After Williams left for the *Ziegfeld Follies*, Rogers teamed with Charles "Luckey" Roberts* to write popular songs for Norah Bayes and the shows of John Cort. He wrote the books for *This and That* and *Baby Blues* (1919), two black shows, as well as the lyrics for *Go-Go* and *Sharlee* (1923), performed by whites. His final Broadway contribution was *My Magnolia** (1926) which he wrote and directed.

Reference: "Alexander Rogers" File, PFL/TC.

**ROLLE, ESTHER** (1922- ). Rolle, television's "Florida" from *Maude* and *Good Times* (Columbia Broadcasting System) first appeared Off-Broadway as a replacement in *The Blacks** in 1962. Her first major role, "Miss Maybelle" in *Don't Play Us Cheap!** (1972), attracted the attention of Norman Lear, and she was lured to Hollywood. She also participated in several plays of the early years of the Negro Ensemble Company.*

Credits: *Happy Ending*/Day of Absence** (1965); *Summer of the Seventeenth Doll**; *God Is a (Guess What?)** (1968); *An Evening of One Acts**; *Song of the Lusitanian Bogey**; *Man Better Man** (1969); *Day of Absence*; *Akokawe** (1970); *Rosalee Pritchett**; *The Dream on Monkey Mountain**; *Ride a Black Horse** (1971); *A Ballet Behind the Bridge**; *Don't Play Us Cheap!* (1972); *Horowitz and Mrs. Washington* (1980).

Reference: "Esther Rolle" File, PFL/TC.

# S

**SANCHEZ, SONIA** (1934- ). Sanchez was perhaps the most significant woman playwright in the Black Revolutionary Theatre Movement of the late 1960s and early 1970s in the United States. She was born on September 9, 1934, in Birmingham, Alabama, to Wilson and Lena (Jones) Driver. She started writing poetry as a child. Sanchez received her B.A. degree from Hunter College in 1955 and did further study in 1957 at New York University. In 1972, she was awarded an honorary doctorate from Wilberforce University. The mother of three children, Sanchez has combined a busy career as a teacher, lecturer, editor, writer, and poet.

Sanchez turned to plays as a form of expression because they permitted the expansion of ideas beyond the confines of a poem. Most of her plays are short and range from the starkly realistic to those that employ symbolism and poetry. She has experimented with abbreviated, slashed, and fused words as well as with irregular capitalization and punctuation. Her language is that of the people whom she is portraying: often men and women who, from their spiritually impoverished lives shaped by an environment of oppression, are struggling to create new and improved existences that will be informed by a high level of black consciousness.

Because of the destructive effects of the overcrowded and underkept urban ghettoes into which many blacks have been forced to live, environments that have even killed some of their inhabitants, Sanchez, in a planned trilogy, proposes that blacks leave these conditions and return to the land where they will be reborn—where they will become human beings once again. *The Bronx Is Next*, published in a special Black Theatre Issue of *The Drama Review* (Summer 1968), is the first play in the trilogy and the only one completed to date. In this work, black revolutionaries use the strategy of burning all the tenements in Harlem, after leading the tenants to safety. A black woman and a white policeman involved in a sexually intimate but loveless relationship are left to perish in the fire. Surfacing in this play are the problems faced by black women and their relationships with their men. Theatre Black produced *The Bronx Is Next* in New York City in October 1970.

In 1969, *Sister Son/ji*,* a single-character play, was published in *New Plays from the Black Theatre*, edited by Ed Bullins.* In 1972, Sanchez's play was produced, along with the works of two other playwrights, at the New York Shakespeare Festival Public Theatre in New York City. In *Sister Son/ji*, through the method of flashbacks, a fiftyish black woman recalls major incidents in her past. As a young college student, she walked out of a class because of a white teacher's disrespectful attitude toward blacks. Her transformation into a black woman who realizes her identity is attributed to the persuasive teachings of Malcolm X. At a Black Power Conference, she was further impressed by a woman who preached love and respect between black men and women. But as the Black Revolutionary Movement heightened, she experienced loneliness and rejection as her husband's activities excluded her. In an actual war between the races, she suffered the loss of her young son. She then protested the presence of a white woman in the camp, for she felt that this woman's place was among their own people, working to change their attitudes. At the end of the play, the central character is as she was at the beginning, but with good memories and without bitterness for her losses, for blacks were active in seeking to change their lives. She challenges the audience to follow a similar pattern—to perform the work needed for blacks to realize their ideal. To date, *Sister Son/ji* is Sanchez's most important play.

Sanchez's major contribution to black theatre has been the exploration in dramatic terms of the problems blacks face in a society where they have been less than free—problems of their identity, of how to overcome and rectify centuries of oppression and injustice, and of how to deal sensitively and understandably with each other. In her plays Sanchez deals courageously with these topics and offers viable solutions.

References: Clarke, Sebastian, "Sonia Sanchez and Her Work," *Black World* 2 (June 1971), 44-48, 96-98; Miller, Jeanne-Marie A., "Images of Black Women in Plays by Black Playwrights," *CLA Journal* 20 (June 1977), 494-507; Palmer, R.

Roderick, "The Poetry of Three Revolutionists: Don L. Lee, Sonia Sanchez, and Nikki Giovanni," *CLA Journal* 15 (September 1971), 25-36; Sanchez, Sonia, "The Bronx Is Next," *The Drama Review* 12 (Summer 1968), 78-83; and Walker, Barbara, "Sonia Sanchez Creates Poetry for the Stage," *Black Creation* 5 (Fall 1973), 12-14.

JEANNE-MARIE A. MILLER

**SANDS, DIANA** (1934–1973). Sands began acting in Off-Broadway productions while still a student at the High School of Performing Arts, making her debut in *Major Barbara* in 1954. She became an "overnight" success with her portrayal of "Beneatha Younger" in *A Raisin in the Sun*,* winning an Outer Circle Critics Award for best supporting actress. She was never typecast during her brief career, playing comedy, drama, Shakespeare, and Shaw. She died of cancer at thirty-nine years of age.

Credits: *Major Barbara* (1954); *Fortunato*; *Mary and the Fairy* (1956); *A Land Beyond the River** (1957); *The Egg and I* (1958); *A Raisin in the Sun* (1959); *Another Evening with Harry Stoones* (1961); *Black Monday*; *Tiger, Tiger Burning Bright** (1962); *The Living Premise* (1963); *Blues for Mr. Charlie**; *The Owl and the Pussycat* (1964); *Phaedra* (1967); *Saint Joan*; *Tiger at the Gates*; *We Bombed in New Haven* (1968); *The Gingham Dog* (1969).

Reference: *Evening Bulletin* (Philadelphia, Pa.), April 23, 1967.

**SCHULTZ, MICHAEL [A.]** (1938- ). Schultz directed his first play, *Waiting for Godot*, at Princeton's McCarter Theatre in 1966. He soon became associated with the Negro Ensemble Company,* with *Song of the Lusitanian Bogey*,* his first production in 1968. He turned to Hollywood in the 1970s, directing such films as *To Be Young, Gifted, and Black** (1971) and several Richard Pryor films.

Credits: *Song of the Lusitanian Bogey*; *Kongi's Harvest**; *God Is a (Guess What?)** (1968); *Does a Tiger Wear a Necktie?*; *Every Night When the Sun Goes Down**; *The Reckoning** (1969); *Operation Sidewinder*; *Sambo** (1970); *The Dream on Monkey Mountain** (1971); *Thoughts**; *The Cherry Orchard* (1973); *What the Wine-Sellers Buy** (1974).

Reference: "Michael Schultz" File, NYPL/TC.

**SHANGE, NTOZAKE** (1948- ). Ntozake Shange, an outstanding poet and playwright, was born Paulette Williams on October 18, 1948, in Trenton, New Jersey. She is the eldest daughter of a surgeon and a psychiatric social worker. Her assumed Zulu names mean "she who comes with her own thing" and "one who walks like a lion." In 1970, Shange, who became a poet while in college, received a B.A. degree with honors in American Studies from Barnard College and in 1973, an M.A. degree from the University of Southern California. Although best known as an author, she has studied music and dance, performed in jazz and music collaborations, and directed productions.

Shange, who uses free-form in her theatre pieces, has definite views about the path black playwrights should travel. She has advocated that they forsake European models for their plays and move their theatre into the drama of their lives. She urges that the dicta of straight theatre be forgotten for a decade or so and that playwrights work with dancers and musicians. As a poet in the American theatre, Shange is "interested solely in the poetry of a moment/the emotional & aesthetic impact of a character or line." [*Three Pieces*, p. ix]

*For Colored Girls Who Have Considered Suicide/When the Rainbow Is Enuf*,* the theatre piece that catapulted Shange to fame in 1976, actually began its life in California a few years earlier. In 1974, *For Colored Girls* was presented for the first time at the Bacchanal, a women's bar near Berkeley, California. The poems that comprise the work were designed to explore the realities of seven different types of women. As Shange and Paula Moss developed *For Colored Girls*, it was presented in women's studies departments, bars, cafes, and poetry centers, culminating in an unusually successful engagement at Minnie's Can-Do Club in Haight-Ashbury. Just two years later, it began a successful Broadway run.

In 1977, *Where the Mississippi Meets the Amazon*, orchestrated in the fashion of a musical composition, was produced at the Public Theatre Cabaret. In this piece, Shange, Jessica Hagedorn, and Thulani Nkabinde, called The Satin Sisters, performed their own poetry, danced, and sang alone or in ensemble, while a band, Teddy and His Sizzling Romancers, played jazz.

Also, in 1977, *A Photograph: A Study of Cruelty*,* produced at the Public Theatre, became Shange's second major production in New York. Described as a poem-play, this work approaches a more conventional form of drama than the playwright's previous offerings.

In *Spell #7*,* Shange returned to the choreopoem and expanded it. A two-act theatre piece, *Spell #7* is composed of song, dance, poetry, and prose. Unlike *For Colored Girls*, this work, which opened in 1978 at the Public Theatre, uses both male and female characters who interact with one another. In the beginning, the characters wear grotesque black minstrel show masks, which they shed when revealing the truths about their lives. A narrator, an interlocutor, is instrumental in binding the vignettes together.

In 1980, Shange's adaptation of Bertolt Brecht's *Mother Courage and Her Children* was produced at the Public Theatre. In this version, the time and place were changed from seventeenth-century Sweden, Poland, and Germany to post-Civil War America, with Mother Courage as an emancipated slave.

*Boogie Woogie Landscapes* was first presented as a one-woman performance in the New York Shakespeare Festival's Poetry at the Public Series and then in play form at the Symphony Space Theatre as a fundraiser for the Frank Silvera's Writer's Workshop. It opened in 1980 at the Kennedy Center for the Performing Arts in Washington, D.C.

In all of her theatre pieces, Shange has explored the black American experience, using the black idiom and experimenting with form, often with brilliant results. Her special focus has been the joy and pain of being a black woman; her special vision is to conjoin poetry and theatre on her terms. Her works often tremble with memorable lines of intense beauty and pain. In the space of approximately five years, the stage literature of Ntozake Shange has earned her a respected position not only in black theatre but in world theatre as well.

References: Early, James, "Interview with Ntozake Shange," in Juliette Bowles, ed., *In Memory and Spirit of Frances, Zora, and Lorraine: Essays and Interviews on Black Women and Writing*, Washington, D.C.: Institute for the Arts and the Humanities, Howard University, 1979, 23-26; Jordon, June, "Shange Talks the Real Stuff," *The Dial* (February 1982), 11-13; Miller, E. Ethelbert, "For Zake—Who Dances the Bomba," *New Directions: The Howard University Magazine* (April 1980), 29-31; Miller, Jeanne-Marie A., "Black Women Playwrights from Grimké to Shange," in Gloria T. Hull, Patricia Bell Scott, and Barbara Smith, eds., *But Some of Us Are Brave*, Old Westbury, N.Y.: Feminist Press, 1982, 280-296; Shange, Ntozake, *Three Pieces*, New York: St. Martin's Press, 1981.

JEANNE-MARIE A. MILLER

**SISSLE, NOBLE.** See BLAKE, EUBIE, and NOBLE SISSLE.

**SMITH, J. AUGUSTUS** (1891-1950). Smith combines as many names as talents. Known alternately as Gus Smith, J. A. Smith, and Augustus Smith, this actor-playwright-director played a major role in the Federal Theatre Project* during the 1930s. This Florida-born actor toured with the Rabbit's Foot Minstrels and later appeared in a silent film version of *Uncle Tom's Cabin*. He wrote and directed two plays during the 1930s, *Louisiana** (1933) and *Turpentine** (1936). He also directed *The Case of Philip Lawrence** (1937) and *Conjur Man Dies** (1936, with Joseph Losey).

Credits (Acting): *Walk Together Chillun** (1936); *On Whitman Avenue** (1946); *A Long Way from Home*; *Grandma's Diary* (1948).

Reference: "J. Augustus Smith" File, NYPL/TC.

# T

**TAYLOR, CLARICE** (1927- ). Taylor moved from her Virginia home to New York City where she became an early member of the American Negro Theatre.* She made her acting debut with the group as "Sophie Slow" in *On Striver's Row** in 1942. After several years on Broadway, she joined the Negro Ensemble Company.* She later won Broadway audiences as "Addaperle" in *The Wiz** in 1975.

Credits: *On Striver's Row* (1942); *Home Is the Hunter** (1945); *The Peacemakers* (1946); *Rain* (1948); *A Medal for Willie** (1951); *In Splendid Error** (1954); *Trouble in Mind** (1955); *The Twisting Road* (1957); *The Egg and I* (1958); *Summer of the Seventeenth Doll**; *Kongi's Harvest**; *Daddy Goodness**; *God Is a (Guess What?)** (1968); *An Evening of One Acts**; *Man Better Man** (1969); *Five on the Black Hand Side**; *Day of Absence**; *Akokawe** (1970); *Rosalee Pritchett**; *The Sty of the Blind Pig** (1971); *The Duplex**; *Wedding Band** (1972); *The Wiz* (1975).

Reference: "Clarice Taylor" File, NYPL/TC.

**TEER, BARBARA ANN** (1937- ). Teer (Roho Taji Taifu) began her career as an actress in such plays as *Raisin' Hell in the Son* (1962), *Home Movies* (1964), *Day of Absence** (1965), *Where's Daddy?*, *Who's Got His Own?** (1966), *Does a Tiger Wear a Necktie?*, and *The Experiment* (1967). She founded the National Black Theatre in 1968. She has also received attention as a director for such plays as *The Believers** (1968), *Five on the Black Hand Side** (1970), and *A Revival* (1972), written with Charlie Russell. She is also the "creator" of *The Ritual* and *Sojourney into Truth* (1977).

Reference: Harris, Jessica B., "The National Black Theatre. The Sun People of 125th Street," *The Drama Review* 16 (December 1972), 39-45.

**THEATRE OWNERS BOOKING ASSOCIATION (TOBA).** See DUDLEY, S[herman] H[ouston].

**THURMAN, WALLACE** (1902-1934). Thurman died of tuberculosis at the age of thirty-two, cutting short the career of a talented novelist (*The Blacker the Berry* [1929]), playwright (*Harlem** [1929]), and literary editor and critic. A native of Salt Lake City, Utah, Thurman drifted to New York City after his graduation from the University of Southern California. He wrote articles and appeared as an extra in *Porgy** (1927) in order to support himself. *Harlem*, written with William Jourdan Rapp, was one of the two dramas by black authors to appear on Broadway during the 1920s. Before his death, Thurman completed the manuscript for another play, *Jeremiah the Magnificent*, in 1930.

Reference: Abramson, Doris E., *Negro Playwrights in the American Theatre, 1922-1959*, New York: Columbia University Press, 1969.

**TURNER, DOUGLAS.** See WARD, DOUGLAS TURNER.

**TUTT, J. HOMER.** See WHITNEY, SALEM TUTT, and J. HOMER TUTT.

**TYSON, CICELY** (1939- ). George C. Scott viewed a fledgling actress, Cicely Tyson, in *The Blacks** (1961), and she was soon invited to Hollywood to appear in the short-lived, but critically acclaimed, television series,

*East Side, West Side*. The series attracted considerable attention, and Tyson began a career that bridged theatre, film, and television. In addition to her Broadway roles, she received an Emmy for *The Autobiography of Miss Jane Pittman* in 1974 and raves for her role in *Sounder* in 1972.

Credits: *The Cool World** (1960); *The Blacks* (1961); *Tiger, Tiger Burning Bright** (1962); *The Blue Boy in Black**; *Trumpets of the Lord** (1963); *A Hand Is on the Gate** (1966); *Carry Me Back to Morningside Heights** (1968); *To Be Young, Gifted, and Black**; *Trumpets of the Lord* (1969).

Reference: *The New York Times*, October 1, 1972.

# V

**VAN PEEBLES, MELVIN** (1932- ). Van Peebles began his career as a film-maker in France with *The Story of a Three-Day Pass* (1968). He brought the film to the San Francisco Film Festival where it attracted considerable attention. After his return to America, Columbia Pictures signed him to direct *Watermelon Man* (1970), a comedy with Godfrey Cambridge. He next turned to Broadway during the 1971-1972 season, where he wrote the book, music, and lyrics for *Ain't Supposed to Die a Natural Death** and *Don't Play Us Cheap!** He also produced and directed the latter show. In addition, he wrote, composed, produced, and directed *Sweet Sweetback's Baadasssss Song* (1971), a highly successful film that demonstrated to Hollywood producers the "existence" of a massive black audience. Van Peebles recently returned to Broadway with another musical, *Waltz of the Stork* (1982).

Reference: *Philadelphia Inquirer*, May 11, 1975.

**VEREEN, BEN** (1946- ). Multi-talented Ben Vereen first appeared Off-Broadway in *The Prodigal Son** in 1965. His singing and dancing talents came to the fore in his role as "Judas" in *Jesus Christ Superstar* (1971), for which he won a Theatre World Award. He received a Tony Award for *Pippin* in 1973.

Reference: "Ben Vereen" File, NYPL/TC.

# W

**WALKER, ADA (AIDA) OVERTON** (1880–1914). Ada Overton, a former chorus member of the Black Patti and Oriental America Company, married George Walker* (of Williams* and Walker) in 1899. She appeared in her husband's shows until *Bandana Land*,* when George became ill. During the latter part of the run, she impersonated her husband when he could not perform. She then appeared with the Cole* and Johnson company and "The Smart Set" troupe. She died at the young age of thirty-four.

Credits: *The Policy Players**(1900); *Sons of Ham** (1902); *In Dahomey** (1903); *Abyssinia** (1906); *Bandana Land* (1908); *The Red Moon** (1909); *His Honor the Barber** (1911).

Reference: Charters, Ann, *Nobody: The Story of Bert Williams*, New York: Macmillan, 1970.

**WALKER, GEORGE.** See WILLIAMS, BERT, and GEORGE WALKER.

**WALKER, JOSEPH A.** (1935– ). Walker was born in Washington, D.C., on February 24, 1935. He grew up in Washington, attending the then segregated schools of the city and going on to Howard University.

It was at Howard that Walker's interest in drama was strengthened. Although his major field of study was philosophy, he minored in drama and spent most of his out-of-class time working with dramatic productions as a member of the Howard Players. It was in one of their productions that Walker played a key role in a work by another black playwright who was to become famous; Joe played Luke, the returned husband, in James Baldwin's* *The Amen Corner*,* a play that premiered at Howard University in May 1955. Walker received his B.A. from Howard in 1956 and his Master's of Fine Arts in drama from Catholic University in 1964.

Although actively engaged in teaching at Howard University, Walker's first love remained the theatre. In addition to his playwrighting, Walker had extensive professional experience as an actor. He appeared in such productions as *Once in a Lifetime* at Washington, D.C.'s Arena Stage; *A Raisin in the Sun** at Maryland's Olney Theater; and in Off-Broadway musicals, such as *The Believers*,* which he also co-authored and which was made into an RCA record album.

In 1970, Walker and his second wife, Dorothy Dinroe-Walker, founded the Demi-Gods, a professional music-dance theatre repertory company. Walker also had contact with the Negro Ensemble Company* which produced several of his works, including *The Harangues*,* *Ododo*,* and the award-winning drama, *The River Niger*.*

*The River Niger*, more than any other of his works, established Walker's place in contemporary American theatre. Although, as in all his works, the theme is black oriented, it is a universal play. The characters, situations, and conflicts are drawn from Walker's own life but find relevance in the lives of all Americans, black and white. The play is not a washed-out capitulation to whites, however; it is in its adherence to the truth of the black situation that its universality is felt, for human situations transcend color.

The universality of Walker's depiction and its relevance to the lives of others are demonstrated in a letter to *The New York Times* which said, "I'm still chuckling to myself about episodes that I swear took place in my own childhood, while . . . I can only marvel at the total honesty achieved by the entire production" (LeNoire, Letter to the Editor, 1973). The critic Clive Barnes stated, "This play is not simply a black play, although black it is . . . this strong drama eludes simple labels such as black . . . black, white or skyblue pink will assuredly react to the strength of its melodrama and the pulse of its language" (Barnes, "Stage," p. 35). Walker, then, has given a strong expression of the realities of the black experience, while, perhaps more important, by giving the still negative feelings held by many non-blacks about blacks, he has shown the universality of the black experience. Like Shakespeare's Shylock, the black man is seen to have the same traits, needs, and desires that all humans have.

In 1974, *The River Niger* received the Tony Award for the best play of the 1973-1974 season. It also received numerous other awards, which attest to the importance of the play to American drama, and not just to the black aesthetic.

Credits: *The Believers: The Black Experience in Song** (with Josephine Johnson) (1968); *The Harangues*; *Ododo*; *Theme of the Black Struggle* (1970); *Yin Yang*; *The River Niger* (1972); *The Lion Is a Soul Brother* (1976).

References: "Amen Corner," Program of the May 11-14, 1955, production directed by Owen Dodson at Howard University, Washington, D.C.; Barnes, Clive, "Stage: Walker's Strong River Niger," *The New York Times*, March 28, 1973, 35; Cooper, Theodore G., "Development of the Black Theatre Through the Black Playwright," *Onstage* 1 (1973), 3-5+; LeNoire, Rosetta, Letter to the editor of *The New York Times*, April 22, 1973, II, 16; Peterson, Maurice, "Taking Off with Joseph Walker," *Essence* 4 (April 1974), 55; Taylor, Clarke, "In the Theatre of Soul," *Essence* 5 (April 1975), 48-49; Walker, Joseph, "Broadway's Vitality Is Black Vitality," *The New York Times*, August 5, 1973, II, 1.

GRACE COOPER

**WALLER, THOMAS "FATS"** (1904-1943). The recent musical hit, *Ain't Misbehavin'** (1976), celebrated the considerable talents of Fats Waller, composer of such hits as "Squeeze Me," "Honeysuckle Rose," "Black and Blue," as well as the classic title tune. Waller began studying the keyboard at an early age, displaying an interest in religious, classical, and jazz music.

He also studied with ragtime masters James P. Johnson* and Willie "the Lion" Smith.

Waller began to write for Broadway in the heyday of the black musicals of the 1920s. *Keep Shufflin'** (1928), written with Andy Razaf,* brought favorable reviews for his musical skills, while *Hot Chocolates** (1929) firmed his growing reputation.

Waller abandoned Broadway during the 1930s, continuing his live performances with his band throughout the nation. He also recorded for RCA Victor and appeared in both film shorts and full-length features. His most notable film appearances were *King of Burlesque* (1936) with Alice Faye and *Stormy Weather* (1943) with Lena Horne and Bill Robinson.

Fats Waller completed his final Broadway show, *Early to Bed* (1943), shortly before his death. This musical with lyrics by George Marion, Jr., concerned life in a New Orleans bordello. Unlike Waller's musicals of the 1920s, *Early to Bed* was performed by white performers. Its 380 performance run marked another Waller success.

Waller fell ill with pneumonia during the run of *Early to Bed* and died in 1943. He left a legacy of excellent songs which some suggest underestimates his real output. Waller, like many black composers of the 1920s, often sold the rights to his songs to white producers and songwriters for a flat fee. As a result, the full extent of his musical talents may never be known.

References: Vance, Joel. *Fats Waller. His Life and Times.* New York: Berkley Medallion Books, 1979; Kirkeby, Ed. *Ain't Misbehavin'. The Story of Fats Waller.* New York: Dodd, Mead, & Company, 1966.

**WARD, DOUGLAS TURNER** (1930- ). Ward left his Burnside, Louisiana, home for colleges in Ohio and Michigan. He arrived in New York City at age nineteen and became involved in political activities. He soon decided to become a playwright and studied at the Paul Mann Workshop. He began his Broadway career as an actor in a small role in *A Raisin in the Sun** (1959), and as an understudy to Sidney Poitier* and Lonne Elder III.* After several acting jobs (as Douglas Turner), he made his debut as a playwright with two one-act plays *Happy Ending** and *Day of Absence** in 1965. In 1968, Ward, Robert Hooks,* and Gerald S. Krone founded the Negro Ensemble Company*; Ward continues to serve as its artistic director. He has also written the following plays: *The Reckoning** (1969) and *Brotherhood** (1970).

Credits (Acting): *A Raisin in the Sun* (1959); *The Blacks** (1961); *A Porter in a Pullman Car Hiawatha* (1962); *Coriolanus*; *Happy Ending/Day of Absence* (1965); *Kongi's Harvest**; *Daddy Goodness** (1968); *Ceremonies in Dark Old Men**; *The Reckoning* (1969); *The Harangues** (1970); *Frederick Douglass . . . Through His Own Words*; *The River Niger** (1972); *The First Breeze of Summer** (1975); *The Brownsville Raid** (1976); *The Offering** (1978); *Old Phantoms**; *The Michigan** (1979).

Credits (Directing): *Daddy Goodness* (1968); *An Evening of One Acts**; *Man*

*Better Man** (1969); *Brotherhood/Day of Absence* (1970); *Perry's Mission**; *Ride a Black Horse** (1971); *A Ballet Behind the Bridge**; *The River Niger* (1972); *The Great MacDaddy** (1974); *The First Breeze of Summer*; *Waiting for Mongo** (1975); *Livin' Fat** (1976); *The Great MacDaddy* (1977); *The Offering*; *Black Body Blues**; *The Twilight Dinner** (1978); *Home**; *Zooman and the Sign** (1980); *Weep Not for Me** (1981).

Reference: Bigsby, C.W.E., "Three Black Playwrights: Loften Mitchell, Ossie Davis, Douglas Turner Ward," in Bigsby, *The Black American Writer*, Vol. 2, Deland, Fla.: Everett/Edwards, Inc., 1969.

**WARD, THEODORE** (1903–1983). Ward was born in Thibodaux, Louisiana, in 1902. At thirteen he began his travels, working at a variety of jobs that led him out of the south to St. Louis, Chicago, Portland, and other big cities where he made a marginal living during the 1920s, usually as a bootblack. With only a grammar school education behind him, he educated himself through voracious reading. Living on the fringes of the University of Utah in Salt Lake City, he joined a playwrighting workshop and taught himself the fine points of writing skills by pouring over an English grammar book. In 1931, he won a Zona Gale Scholarship to study creative writing for a year at the University of Wisconsin. It was renewed for a second year when Zona Gale herself took a personal interest in his development (Gobbins, "Story of Theo. Ward," March 8, 1950). In Madison, Ward had his own radio show on which he read poems and extracts from plays.

In 1935, Ward moved to Chicago, where for a time he was recreational director at Abraham Lincoln Center on the South Side. In 1937, he wrote his first play, a one-act work entitled *Sick and Tiahd*. His first full-length play, *Big White Fog*,* was produced by the Chicago unit of the Federal Theatre Project* (FTP) in 1938 and again by the short-lived Negro Playwrights Company* in Harlem in 1940. A play about a black family's struggles in the 1920s, *Big White Fog* "embodied the major life options open to Black Americans today: nationalism, communism, and 'party-time' " (Hatch, "Theodore Ward," p. 39). In both Chicago and New York, the play's critics made more of it as left-wing propaganda than as drama, while audiences seem to have responded with enthusiasm to its honesty.

Ward moved to New York in 1940, arriving as a member of the Federal Theatre Project's *The Swing Mikado** cast and staying on after the project's demise. He lived in Brooklyn for the next twenty-four years, and New York saw the production of his best play, *Our Lan'*,* in 1947. During the war years, he served on the Writers' War Board (1942) and the Office of War Information (1945) in Washington, D.C. He wrote scripts for overseas broadcasts but had little success in introducing material related to black experience. In 1945, on the basis of a draft of *Our Lan'*, he received a Theater Guild scholarship and membership in a playwrighting seminar conducted by Kenneth Rowe.

In 1946, *Our Lan'* ran for one week at the Henry Street Playhouse, and in

1947 Eddie Dowling produced it on Broadway, where it ran for five weeks. On a National Theatre Conference Award for 1947 and 1948, Ward wrote *Shout Hallelujah!*, a slice-of-life drama about black and white construction workers dying of silicosis, a "ravaging industrial disease." A 1947 Guggenheim Fellowship allowed him to begin to write a play about John Brown. Later called *Of Human Grandeur*, as *John Brown* it failed Off-Broadway in 1950. It was a work-in-progress then and remains so to this day.

Ward has lived in Chicago since 1964 and served as general manager of the South Side Center of the Performing Arts from 1966 to 1969. *Our Lan'* was revived there in 1967. *Candle in the Wind*, a play about an early Negro state senator from Mississippi, which opened that same year, had a production by the Free Southern Theatre of New Orleans in 1978 under a grant from the Rockefeller Foundation.

Ward continues to work on revisions of his plays, many of which have not been published. His most recent work is *Charity*, a play with music based on the life of Blind Tom, the early black pianist (Ward, Letter to Author, January 31, 1981).

Theodore Ward is a most distinguished black American playwright, and he has been praised by both black and white critics.

Credits: *Sick and Tiahd* (1937); *Big White Fog* (1938); *Our Lan'* (1947); *Shout Hallelujah!* (1948); *John Brown* (1950); *Candle in the Wind* (1967); *The Daubers* (1974).

References: "Black Drama of the Federal Theatre Project," *Federal One*, I (May 1976), 1 (this is an irregular publication of the Research Center for the FTP, George Mason University); Gobbins, Dennis, "Story of Theo. Ward, Leading Negro Playwright," *Daily Worker*, March 8, 1950; Hatch, James V., "Theodore Ward Black American Playwright," *Freedomways* 15 (First Quarter 1975), 37-41; Ward, Theodore, *Letter to Author*, January 31, 1981; Ward, Theodore, *Shout Hallelujah!* in *Masses and Mainstream* (May 1948) (copy in Theodore Ward folder, Schomburg Collection, New York Public Library).

DORIS E. ABRAMSON

**WARREN, EDITH.** See WASHINGTON, FREDI.

**WASHINGTON, FREDI** (1903- ). Washington began her career in the chorus of the Boston production of *Shuffle Along*,* even though she did not know how to dance when she got the job. She soon appeared (under the name Edith Warren) in *Black Boy** (1926) in the role of a black woman who passes for white. Playing opposite Paul Robeson,* Washington revealed herself to be a major talent. After a European tour as a dancer (Moiret and Fredi), she returned to Broadway in a series of dramas. She appeared with her sister Isabel (Isabell) in *Singin' The Blues** in 1931. She also received recognition in films for her portrayal of "Peola" in *Imitation of Life* (1934).

Credits: *Black Boy* (1926); *Sweet Chariot** (1930); *Singin' The Blues* (1931); *Run,*

*Little Chillun!** (1933); *Mamba's Daughters** (1939); *Lysistrata* (1946); *A Long Way from Home* (1948); *How Long Till Summer** (1949).

Reference: Bogle, Donald, *Brown Sugar*, New York: Harmony Books, 1980.

**WATERS, ETHEL** (1900–1977). Ethel Waters of Chester, Pennsylvania, began her career at age seventeen as a vaudeville singer. She introduced "Dinah" at the Plantation Club in 1925, and soon afterwards she appeared in her first Broadway show, *Africana** (1927). After a brief stint with Warner Brothers for *On with the Show* (1929), she returned to Broadway for *Blackbirds of 1930.** Irving Berlin spotted her at the Cotton Club, where she introduced "Stormy Weather," and he featured her in his new revue, *As Thousands Cheer* (1933). She stopped the show with "Supper Time," a song about a woman who is preparing dinner for a man who will never arrive because he has been lynched. She received raves for her performance, and by this date she was the highest paid woman on Broadway.

Waters expanded her talents to include dramatic roles as well, receiving critical raves for *Mamba's Daughters** (1939) and *The Member of the Wedding* (1950). She also appeared in the motion picture version of the latter play and won an Academy Award nomination. Her most notable film roles include *Cabin in the Sky** (1943), in which she again repeated her Broadway role, *Pinky* (1949), and *The Sound and the Fury* (1959).

Credits: *Africana* (1927); *Blackbirds of 1930*; *Rhapsody in Black** (1931); *As Thousands Cheer* (1933); *At Home Abroad* (1935); *Mamba's Daughters* (1939); *Cabin in the Sky* (1940); *Laugh Time* (1943); *Blue Holiday** (1945); *The Member of the Wedding* (1950); *At Home with Ethel Waters** (1953); *An Evening with Ethel Waters* (1959).

Reference: Waters, Ethel, *His Eye Is on the Sparrow*. New York: Doubleday & Co., 1950.

**WELCH, ELISABETH** (1908– ). Often credited as the originator of the Charleston in *Runnin' Wild** (1923), Elisabeth Welch (also Elizabeth Welsh) has established a career on two continents. After her run in *Blackbirds of 1928*,* she moved to London. She appeared in a variety of British musicals, including Cole Porter's *Nymph Errant* (1933), Ivor Novello's *Arc de Triomphe* (1943), and *Pippin* (1973). She recently returned to New York for *Black Broadway** (1980), a tribute to the black musicals of the 1920s and 1930s.

Credits: *Runnin' Wild* (1923); *The Chocolate Dandies** (1924); *Blackbirds of 1928*; *Black Broadway* (1980).

Reference: *The New York Times*, May 16, 1980.

**WESLEY, RICHARD** (1945– ). Wesley was born in Newark, New Jersey, and attended Howard University. At age nineteen his first play won an honorable mention in the National Collegiate Playwrighting Contest. In 1968, he attended a playwrighting workshop at the New Lafayette Theatre, where he was tutored by Ed Bullins.* His first major production, *The Black Terror** (1971), won him an Obie Award, and a Rockefeller Foundation Grant followed soon after. After devoting his efforts to writing screenplays (*Uptown Saturday Night* [1974] and *Let's Do It Again* [1975]), Wesley returned to Broadway with the highly acclaimed *The Mighty Gents** (1978).

Credits: *The Black Terror* (1971); *Gettin' It Together**; *Strike Heaven in the Face* (1972); *Two Plays by Richard Wesley* (*The Past Is Past/Going Through Changes*); *The Sirens* (1974); *The Last Street Gang* (1977); *The Mighty Gents* (1978).

Reference: "Richard Wesley" File, NYPL/TC.

**WHIPPER, LEIGH** (1877-1975). Whipper, the first black member of Actors Equity and the founder of the Negro Actors Guild, originally studied to be a lawyer at Howard University. Instead of practicing law, he took to the road with the Georgia Minstrels. He made his Broadway debut in *Porgy** (1927), where he played the "Crabman," and continued his career until 1952 with *The Shrike*. His films include *Of Mice and Men* (1940), *Mission to Moscow* (1943), where he played Haile Selassie, and *The Ox-Bow Incident* (1943).

Credits: *Porgy* (1927); *Change Your Luck** (1930); *Never No More**; *Yeah Man** (1932); *Stevedore** (1934); *White Man* (1936); *How Come, Lawd?**; *Of Mice and Men* (1937); *Medicine Show* (1940); *Lysistrata* (1946); *Volpone*; *Set My People Free** (1948); *How Long Till Summer** (1949); *Child of the Morning* (1951); *The Shrike* (1952).

Reference: *The New York Times*, July 27, 1975.

**WHITE, JOSH** (1908-1969). White was known primarily as a folk singer in the 1960s, popularizing such songs as "One Meatball," "Jim Crow Train," "Strange Fruit," and "Hard Time Blues." While he used his singing talents on Broadway in *John Henry** (1939) and *Blue Holiday** (1945), he also displayed a flair for drama in such plays as *How Long Till Summer** (1949) and *Touchstone** (1953).

Credits: *John Henry* (1939); *Blue Holiday* (1945); *A Long Way from Home* (1948); *How Long Till Summer* (1949); *The Man* (1950); *Touchstone* (1953); *Only in America* (1959); *The Long Dream** (1960).

Reference: "Josh White" File, PFL/TC.

**WHITNEY, SALEM TUTT** (1869-1934), **and J. HOMER TUTT** (?- ). Whitney and Tutt, brothers despite their different names, began their careers with S. H. Dudley's* Smart Set Company (1904-1906) and then moved to *Black Patti's Troubadours* (1906-1908). They eventually organized a second Smart Set Company in 1908 and assumed complete control of a third company, The Smarter Set, in 1916.

Whitney and Tutt wrote several musicals for their company including *His Excellency, the President*, *The Mayor of Newton*, *George Washington Bullion Abroad*, *My People*, *Darkest Americans*, *Children of the Sun*, *Up and Down*, and *North and South. Oh Joy!** (1922) managed a brief run at the Bamboo Isle Theatre, and *Deep Harlem** (1929) exhibited a book by the prolific team. Tutt also contributed songs to the short-lived *Ginger Snaps** (1929). Both Whitney and Tutt made occasional stage appearances during the 1920s and early 1930s, with each appearing in various companies of *The Green Pastures.**

Reference: *The Messenger*, Vol. 7 (1926), 46.

**WILLIAMS, BERT** (1874–1922), **and GEORGE WALKER** (1873–1911). Egbert Austin (Bert) Williams and George Walker became one of the foremost musical comedy teams of the first decade of this century. After touring in vaudeville, the team was hired to perk up Victor Herbert's faltering musical, *The Gold Bug* (1896). The show failed, but Broadway had its favorable impressions of Williams and Walker.

After a vaudeville stand, the team returned to Broadway with *The Policy Players** (1899) and *Sons of Ham** (1900). By this time, their comic personae had evolved, with Walker as a fast-talking dandy and Williams as a shuffling "Jonah Man" who waited for disasters to happen to him.

By the time *In Dahomey** opened on Broadway in 1903, Williams and Walker had formed their own theatrical troupe. *In Dahomey* enjoyed a successful run and then moved to London for a brief engagement, where Williams and Walker performed before the King.

*Abyssinia** (1906) and *Bandana Land** (1908) continued the team's success, but Walker became ill during the run of *Bandana Land*, and his wife (Ada Overton Walker*) was forced to substitute for him. Walker died in 1911, and Williams was forced to perform solo in *Mr. Lode of Koal** in 1909.

Flo Ziegfeld offered Williams a major role in the new "Follies," and he found a new career. He appeared in the *Follies* of 1910, 1911, 1912, 1914, 1915, 1917, and 1919. He emerged as a major star during this period and became identified with his theme song, "Nobody."

Reference: Charters, Ann, *Nobody: The Story of Bert Williams*, New York: Macmillan, 1970.

**WILLIAMS, BILLY DEE** (1937– ). Williams, a later addition to the *Star Wars* saga as Lando Calrissian in *The Empire Strikes Back* (1980), first appeared on stage at age seven in *The Firebrand of Florence* (1945). As a teenager, he appeared on Broadway in *The Cool World** and *A Taste of Honey* (1960). Roles dried up for the young Williams, but soon films offered new opportunities. He made his motion picture debut in *The Last Angry Man* (1959) and received great acclaim co-starring with Diana Ross in *Lady Sings the Blues* (1972). Williams returned to Broadway in 1976 as the Reverend Martin Luther King, Jr., in *I Have a Dream.**

Credits: *The Cool World*; *A Taste of Honey* (1960); *The Blue Boy in Black** (1963); *The Firebugs* (1968); *Ceremonies in Dark Old Men** (1969); *Slow Dance on the Killing Ground* (1970); *I Have a Dream* (1976).
Reference: *The New York Times*, September 19, 1976.

**WILLIAMS, DICK ANTHONY** (1938- ). Chicago-born Dick Williams first achieved attention as the director of the Watts Writers Workshop which was formed in the aftermath of the riots. He appeared as "Buck White" in *Big Time Buck White** in California, and he later moved to New York with the show to favorable reviews. Williams has continued his career as an actor, but has also directed such plays as *The Pig Pen** (1970) and *In New England Winter** (1971). He co-produced (with Woodie King, Jr.*) *Black Girl** (1971) and *A Recent Killing** (1973).
Credits (Acting): *Big Time Buck White* (1968); *Nigger Nightmare*; *Ain't Supposed To Die a Natural Death** (1971); *Jamimma** (1972); *What the Wine-Sellers Buy** (1974); *Black Picture Show**; *We Interrupt This Program* (1975); *The Poison Tree* (1976).
Reference: *The New York Times*, November 24, 1968.

**WILLIAMS, SAMM-ART** (1946- ). Although Samm-Art (Samuel Arthur) Williams is known primarily as a playwright, he has also received attention as an actor in several Negro Ensemble Company* (NEC) productions. The NEC has produced five of his plays ( *Welcome to Black River** [1975], *The Coming, A Love Play* [1976], *The Frost of Renaissance*, and *Brass Birds Don't Sing* [1978]) in workshop and showcase productions, but his play *Home** (1979) received the greatest critical praise and merited a Broadway production. His most recent work is *The Sixteenth Round** (1980).
Credits (Acting): *Nowhere to Run, Nowhere to Hide** (1974); *Liberty Call**; *Waiting for Mongo**; *The First Breeze of Summer** (1975); *Eden**; *The Brownsville Raid** (1976); *Night Shift* (1977); *Black Body Blues**; *Nevis Mountain Dew** (1978); *Old Phantoms**; *Plays from Africa** (1979); *Big City Blues** (1980).
Reference: *The New York Times*, February 24, 1980.

**WILSON, DOOLEY** (1894-1953). Arthur (Dooley) Wilson of Tyler, Texas, graduated from minstrel shows to legitimate theatre and motion pictures. He is best known for his rendition of "As Time Goes By" in the Warner Brothers classic *Casablanca* (1942), but he also received notice on Broadway in such plays as *Conjur Man Dies** (1936), *The Strangler Fig*, *Cabin in the Sky** (1940), and *Bloomer Girl* (1944).
Reference: "Dooley Wilson" File, NYPL/TC.

**WILSON, EDITH** (1897-1981). Wilson made her singing debut at the Park Theatre in Louisville in 1919. She made her New York City debut at the Town Hall in *Put and Take** in 1921. Columbia signed her to a recording contract soon afterwards, making her one of the first black artists to record for a major company.

Wilson appeared in several of the black musical revues of the 1920s on both sides of the Atlantic. Her London appearances included *Dover Street to Dixie* (1923) and *Blackbirds of 1933*.* She later toured with Duke Ellington's* band and played nightclubs throughout Europe. In the 1940s, she moved to Hollywood where she became a regular on such radio shows as *Amos 'n' Andy* and *The Great Gildersleeve*.

Shortly before her death in 1981, she returned to Town Hall for an appearance in *Black Broadway** (1980).

Credits: *Plantation Revue** (1922); *Hot Chocolates** (1929); *Hot Rhythm** (1930); *Shuffle Along of 1933*; *Blackbirds of 1933*; *Humming Sam** (1933); *Memphis Bound** (1945); *Black Broadway* (1980).

Reference: *The New York Times*, April 1, 1981.

**WILSON, FRANK** (1886–1956). A native of Manhattan, Wilson labored there full-time as a postal clerk and part-time as a performer in vaudeville and the legitimate theatre during the early years of his checkered career. In 1914, he hooked up with the Lafayette Players in Harlem, an apprenticeship that gave him the opportunity to develop abiding interests in playwrighting and acting. He did not squander this chance, writing a new one-act play every six weeks that he would direct and act in and the Lincoln or Lafayette Theatres would present. Several of these early efforts at playwrighting, *Colored Americans*, *Confidence*, and *Race Pride*, focused on the common denominator of race.

Wilson also studied acting at the American Academy of Dramatic Arts in New York, attending evening classes for 3½ years, beginning in 1917. His acting career kept him busy during the period 1917-1925, including leading parts in *All God's Chillun Got Wings** and *The Emperor Jones*,* but it was his performance as a replacement for Julius Bledsoe* in the title role of *In Abraham's Bosom** that catapulted him to stardom in 1926. Thereafter, he played prominent roles in most of the significant stage productions of the late 1920s, 1930s, and 1940s that featured black themes and black actors: *Porgy** (1927), *We the People* (1933), *Roll, Sweet Chariot*,* *They Shall Not Die* (1934), *The Green Pastures** (1935), and *Memphis Bound** (1945). His last stage appearance was in the 1953 production of Louis Peterson's *Take a Giant Step*.* More than one student of black theatre has remarked that Wilson was the most versatile black actor of his generation; certainly, he was one of the most consistently employed black actors.

In addition to his stage career, Wilson enjoyed a fifteen-year tenure enacting parts in radio serials, acted in and wrote movie scripts, and made several television appearances during the 1940s.

Wilson was forty years of age and starring on Broadway in *In Abraham's Bosom* when he won an Urban League contest for unpublished black playwrights in 1926 with his submission of a one-act play, *Sugar Cane*. The work was an awkward attempt to dramatize the social mores that have always separated the races in Georgia. At the time Wilson's first full-length play, *Meek Mose*,* opened on Broadway in 1928, he himself was once again acting in a Broadway production, this time performing the title role in *Porgy*.

Wilson's dual career continued to overlap until 1935, when he took up residence as a contributing playwright with the Federal Theatre Project* (FTP)'s Harlem unit. Government employment allowed him to concentrate solely on writing, something he had been unable to do previously. The result of this opportunity was *Walk Together Chillun*,* a 1936 FTP production that possessed a realism and significance that his earlier plays utterly lacked. This three-act social drama focused on the tensions that developed when a group of black migrant workers were brought north by white politicians interested in lowering the cost of existing cheap labor supplied by the town's black work force.

Both as actor and playwright, Wilson deserves an important place in black theatre history. Although not as prodigiously gifted an actor as an Ira Aldridge or Paul Robeson,* Wilson must be given a prominent niche in the annals of the American stage on the basis of his many Broadway and Off-Broadway portrayals in title roles of black drama. And although he never attained any lofty status as a playwright, the undeniable fact is that he had two plays produced on Broadway and two others produced by FTP's black units. No other black has had such a distinguished dual acting-playwrighting career.

Credits (Acting): *All God's Chillun Got Wings* (1924); *In Abraham's Bosom*; *Porgy* (1927); *Sweet Chariot** (1930); *Singin' the Blues** (1931); *Bloodstream* (1932); *We the People* (1933); *They Shall Not Die*; *Roll, Sweet Chariot* (1934); *The Green Pastures*; *Sailor, Beware!* (1935); *The Emperor Jones* (1936); *Journeyman*; *All the Living*; *Kiss the Boys Goodbye* (1938); *Watch on the Rhine* (1941); *South Pacific* (1943); *Memphis Bound* (1945); *Set My People Free** (1948); *The Big Knife*; *How Long Till Summer** (1949); *Take a Giant Step* (1953).

References: Gold, Michael, "At Last, a Negro Theatre?" *New Masses* (March 10, 1936), 18; Ross, Ronald P., *Black Drama in the Federal Theatre, 1935-1939*, Ann Arbor, Mich. University Microfilms, 1972.

RONALD P. ROSS

**WINSTON, HATTIE** (1945- ). Winston attended Howard University before making her Off-Broadway debut in *The Prodigal Son** in 1965. She joined the Negro Ensemble Company* in 1968 with an appearance in *Song of the Lusitanian Bogey*.* She has also appeared on Public Television's *The Electric Company* and in films (*Sweet Love, Bitter* [1968]).

Credits: *The Prodigal Son* (1965); *Song of the Lusitanian Bogey*; *Summer of the Seventeenth Doll**; *Kongi's Harvest**; *God Is a (Guess What?)** (1968); *Man Better Man**; *Sambo** (1969); *The Me Nobody Knows**; *Billy Noname** (1970); *The Great MacDaddy** (1974); *A Photograph** (1977); *The Michigan** (1979); *Mother Courage and Her Children* (1980).

Reference: "Hattie Winston" File, NYPL/TC.

**WRIGHT, RICHARD** (1908–1960). Richard Wright's early life contains the key that unlocks almost all his work, because nearly everything he wrote proves that he never recovered from his childhood experiences in the racial hell of the Deep South. Wright was born to Ella and Nathan Wright on September 4, 1908, on a farm near Natchez, Mississippi. In 1914, his father, Nathan, deserted the family, leaving Ella Wright to care for Richard and his younger brother, Leon. The desertion left the family poorer than ever, a condition intensified by Ella's illness, which caused Wright to drop out of school in order to care for her. Nevertheless, there were books in the young Wright's home, and he did receive some formal education, although only sporadically, because of his mother's almost constant moving from one southern town to another.

Resolving to leave the South forever, Wright fled to Memphis in the fall of 1925, not realizing that his experiences in Dixie had permanently shaped his outlook as well as his literary imagination. In Memphis, he began reading such writers as Mencken, Sinclair Lewis, and Dreiser; they saved him from incomprehending rage by demonstrating that he was not the first to notice the frequent contradictions between America's official ideals and her reality. In 1927, when he left Memphis for Chicago, he faced major obstacles to his literary ambitions; these handicaps have been divided into four categories—racial, educational, familial, and economic (Kinnamon, *Emergence of Richard Wright*, passim). The last three would have been enough to destroy the hopes of most beginning writers, but when Wright's being black in a profoundly bigoted society is added, his literary accomplishments loom even larger.

Wright spent the next decade in Chicago, where he quickly learned that the South extends beyond the Mason-Dixon line. He passed his nights as a postal clerk, his days as a reader and writer. After the Great Depression eliminated his job at the post office, he was given public assistance. The relief office sent him to the South Side Boys' Club; there he met many prototypes for Bigger Thomas the protagonist of his best-known novel, *Native Son.** In 1932 he became involved with communism. He attended meetings of the John Reed Club, a communist literary organization, and became a party member the following year. He also published poems and short fiction in leftist journals such as *New Masses* and *International Literature.* Chicago also saw the beginning of his activity in the black theatre, for in 1936 he was given a job on the Federal Theatre Project,* "to act as literary adviser and press agent for the Negro Federal Theatre of Chicago." Also during his decade in Chicago, he may have written his two unpublished plays (Fabre, *Unfinished Quest*, pp. 131-32).

In New York City, where Wright lived for about ten years beginning in 1937, he became more prominent in Afro-American drama as well as a central figure on the American literary scene. He published his first book,

*Uncle Tom's Children* (1938), a collection of short stories that rejected stereotypical notions about black life; the next year he finished *Native Son*. He later collaborated with Paul Green on the stage version of that classic work. In 1945, he published one of the finest American biographies ever written, *Black Boy*.

After visiting France in 1946, Wright moved there in 1947 and made it his home base for extensive traveling, particularly in the Third World. In France, he continued to write profusely, but most critics agree that his work in Europe does not compare favorably with the writing he did in America. In 1949, Wright began to make the arrangements for a film version of *Native Son* in which he starred.

In 1956, Wright adapted a play that recalls Father Divine, Louis Sapin's *Papa Bon Dieu*, which was performed Off-Broadway in 1969 under Wright's title of *Daddy Goodness** (Fabre, *Unfinished Quest*, p. 611, n. 11). Following the publication of a collection of lectures, *White Man, Listen!* (1957), *The Long Dream** (1958), a novel concerned with corrupt black life in a small southern town, appeared. It was later adapted by Ketti Frings for a Broadway production that closed to poor reviews after five performances (Fabre, *Unfinished Quest*, p. 500).

Although Wright's major accomplishments are found in his fiction and in his autobiography, his place in the history of the black American theatre is assured by virtue of his premier position in Afro-American literature of this century, and by the stage version of *Native Son*, as well as by his two radio plays. Not as powerful or compelling as the novel, which relates the thoughts and actions of a murderous black youth who is the inevitable product of the ghetto, the dramatized version of *Native Son* nevertheless is part of the transition between minstrel shows and the cakewalk, on the one hand, and the aggressively black drama of the 1960s, on the other. The stage version was also relatively successful, while still managing to show audiences, particularly white ones, what their prejudices had produced, instead of pandering to their racist expectations, as so much earlier black drama had done.

Credits: *Native Son** (1941); *The Long Dream** (1960); *Daddy Goodness** (1969).

References: Abcarian, Richard, ed. *Richard Wright's "Native Son": A Critical Handbook*. Belmont, California: Wadsworth Publishing Co., 1970; Bone, Robert A. *Richard Wright*. Minneapolis: University of Minnesota Press, 1969; Fabre, Michel. *The Unfinished Quest of Richard Wright*. Trans. Isabel Barzun. New York: William Morrow, 1973; Felgar, Robert. *Richard Wright*. Boston: Twayne Publishers, 1980; Gayle, Addison. *Richard Wright: Ordeal of a Native Son*. Garden City, N.Y.: Doubleday, 1980; Kinnamon, Kenneth. *The Emergence of Richard Wright*. Urbana: University of Illinois Press, 1972; Wright, Richard. *American Hunger*. New York: Harper & Row, 1972.

ROBERT FELGAR

# Appendix I: A CHRONOLOGY OF THE BLACK THEATRE

**1898–1919**

*A Trip to Coontown*, 1898
*The Policy Players*, 1899
*Sons of Ham*, 1900
*In Dahomey*, 1903
*The Southerners*, 1904
*Abyssinia*, 1906
*Rufus Rastus*, 1906
*The Oyster Man*, 1907
*The Shoo-Fly Regiment*, 1907
*Bandana Land*, 1908
*Mr. Lode of Koal*, 1909
*The Red Moon*, 1909
*His Honor the Barber*, 1911
*The Rider of Dreams*, 1917

**1920–1921**

*The Emperor Jones*, November 1, 1920
*Shuffle Along*, May 23, 1921

**1921–1922**

*Goat Alley*, June 20, 1921
*Put and Take*, August 23, 1921
*Taboo*, April 4, 1922

**1922–1923**

*Strut Miss Lizzie*, June 19, 1922
*Plantation Revue*, July 17, 1922
*Oh Joy!*, August 3, 1922
*Liza*, November 27, 1922
*How Come?*, April 16, 1923
*The Chip Woman's Fortune*, May 7, 1923

**1923–1924**

*Runnin' Wild*, October 29, 1923
*Roseanne*, December 29, 1923
*All God's Chillun Got Wings*, May 15, 1924

**1924–1925**

*The Chocolate Dandies*, September 1, 1924
*Dixie to Broadway*, October 29, 1924

**1925–1926**

*Lucky Sambo*, June 6, 1925
*Appearances*, October 13, 1925

**1926–1927**

*My Magnolia*, July 8, 1926
*Deep River*, October 4, 1926
*Black Boy*, October 6, 1926
*In Abraham's Bosom*, December 30, 1926
*Earth*, March 9, 1927

**1927–1928**

*Bottomland*, June 27, 1927
*Africana*, July 11, 1927
*Rang Tang*, July 12, 1927
*Porgy*, October 10, 1927
*Meek Mose*, February 1, 1928
*Keep Shufflin'*, February 27, 1928
*Blackbirds of 1928*, May 1, 1928

**1928–1929**

*Deep Harlem*, January 7, 1929
*Harlem*, February 20, 1929
*Messin' Around*, April 22, 1929
*Pansy*, May 14, 1929

**1929–1930**

*Hot Chocolates*, June 20, 1929
*Bamboola*, June 26, 1929
*Make Me Know It*, November 4, 1929
*Ginger Snaps*, December 31, 1929
*The Green Pastures*, February 26, 1930

## 1930–1931

*Change Your Luck*, June 6, 1930
*Hot Rhythm*, August 21, 1930
*Brown Buddies*, October 7, 1930
*Blackbirds of 1930*, October 22, 1930
*Sweet Chariot*, October 23, 1930
*Rhapsody in Black*, May 4, 1931

## 1931–1932

*Fast and Furious*, September 15, 1931
*Singin' The Blues*, September 16, 1931
*Second Comin'*, December 8, 1931
*Sugar Hill*, December 25, 1931
*Savage Rhythm*, December 31, 1931
*Never No More*, Janury 7, 1932
*Black Souls*, March 3, 1932
*Blackberries of 1932*, April 4, 1932
*Yeah Man*, May 26, 1932

## 1932–1933

*Ol' Man Satan*, October 3, 1932
*Shuffle Along of 1933*, December 26, 1932
*Louisiana*, February 27, 1933
*Run, Little Chillun!*, March 1, 1933
*Humming Sam*, April 8, 1933

## 1933–1934

*Blackbirds of 1933*, December 2, 1933
*Four Saints in Three Acts*, February 20, 1934
*Brain Sweat*, April 4, 1934
*Stevedore*, April 18, 1934

## 1934–1935

*Roll, Sweet Chariot*, October 2, 1934
*Africana*, November 26, 1934

## 1935–1936

*Porgy and Bess*, October 10, 1935
*Mulatto*, October 24, 1935
*Walk Together Chillun*, February 2, 1936
*Conjur Man Dies*, March 11, 1936

### 1936–1937

*Turpentine*, June 27, 1936
*Black Rhythm*, December 19, 1936

### 1937–1938

*The Case of Philip Lawrence*, June 7, 1937
*Swing It*, July 22, 1937
*The Trial of Dr. Beck*, August 10, 1937
*How Come, Lawd?*, September 30, 1937
*Brown Sugar*, December 2, 1937
*Haiti*, March 2, 1938

### 1938–1939

*Mamba's Daughters*, January 3, 1939
*Blackbirds of 1939*, February 11, 1939
*The Hot Mikado*, March 23, 1939
*Swing Mikado*, May 1, 1939

### 1939–1940

*Swingin' the Dream*, November 29, 1939
*John Henry*, January 10, 1940

### 1940–1941

*Big White Fog*, October 22, 1940
*Cabin in the Sky*, October 25, 1940
*Native Son*, March 24, 1941
*Natural Man*, May 8, 1941

### 1941–1942

*Harlem Cavalcade*, May 1, 1942

### 1942–1943

(No shows)

### 1943–1944

*Carmen Jones*, December 2, 1943

### 1944–1945

*Anna Lucasta*, August 30, 1944

*Blue Holiday*, May 21, 1945
*Memphis Bound*, May 24, 1945

**1945–1946**

*Deep Are the Roots*, September 26, 1945
*Carib Song*, September 27, 1945
*Home Is the Hunter*, December 20, 1945
*Jeb*, February 21, 1946
*On Striver's Row*, February 28, 1946
*Walk Hard*, March 27, 1946
*St. Louis Woman*, March 30, 1946
*On Whitman Avenue*, May 8, 1946

**1946–1947**
(No shows)

**1947–1948**

*Our Lan'*, September 27, 1947
*Caribbean Carnival*, December 5, 1947

**1948–1949**

*Set My People Free*, November 3, 1948

**1949–1950**

*Lost in the Stars*, October 30, 1949
*How Long Till Summer*, December 27, 1949

**1950–1951**

*The Barrier*, November 2, 1950

**1951–1952**

*Shuffle Along of 1952*, May 8, 1952

**1952–1953**

*Touchstone*, February 3, 1953

**1953–1954**

*At Home with Ethel Waters*, September 22, 1953
*Take a Giant Step*, September 24, 1953

**1954–1955**

*In Splendid Error*, October 26, 1954
*Mrs. Patterson*, December 1, 1954
*House of Flowers*, December 30, 1954

**1955–1956**

*Trouble in Mind*, November 4, 1955
*Mister Johnson*, March 29, 1956

**1956–1957**

*A Land Beyond the River*, March 28, 1957

**1957–1958**

*Simply Heavenly*, August 20, 1957
*Jamaica*, October 31, 1957

**1958–1959**

*A Raisin in the Sun*, March 11, 1959

**1959–1960**

*Jolly's Progress*, December 5, 1959
*The Long Dream*, February 17, 1960
*The Cool World*, February 22, 1960

**1960–1961**

*The Blacks*, May 4, 1961

**1961–1962**

*Purlie Victorious*, September 28, 1961
*Kwamina*, October 23, 1961
*Black Nativity*, December 11, 1961
*Moon on a Rainbow Shawl*, January 15, 1962
*Fly Blackbird*, February 5, 1962

**1962–1963**

*Tiger, Tiger Burning Bright*, December 22, 1962
*The Blue Boy in Black*, April 30, 1963

**1963–1964**

*Ballad for Bimshire*, October 15, 1963
*In White America*, October 31, 1963
*Tambourines to Glory*, November 2, 1963
*Trumpets of the Lord*, December 21, 1963
*Jerico-Jim Crow*, January 12, 1964
*Funnyhouse of a Negro*, January 14, 1964
*The Blood Knot*, March 1, 1964
*Dutchman*, March 23, 1964
*Blues for Mr. Charlie*, April 23, 1964
*The Baptism*, May 1, 1964

**1964–1965**

*The Sign in Sidney Brustein's Window*, October 15, 1964
*Golden Boy*, October 20, 1964
*The Toilet/The Slave*, December 16, 1964
*The Amen Corner*, April 15, 1965
*The Prodigal Son*, May 20, 1965

**1965–1966**

*Happy Ending/Day of Absence*, November 15, 1965
*Bohikee Creek*, April 28, 1966

**1966–1967**

*A Hand Is on the Gate*, September 21, 1966
*Who's Got His Own?*, October 12, 1966
*Hallelujah, Baby!*, April 26, 1967

**1967–1968**

*The Trials of Brother Jero/The Strong Breed*, November 9, 1967
*Song of the Lusitanian Bogey*, January 2, 1968
*Summer of the Seventeenth Doll*, February 20, 1968
*Carry Me Back to Morningside Heights*, March 2, 1968
*The Electronic Nigger and Others*, March 6, 1968
*Kongi's Harvest*, April 14, 1968
*The Believers*, May 1, 1968

**1968–1969**

*Daddy Goodness*, June 4, 1968
*The Great White Hope*, October 3, 1968

*Big Time Buck White*, December 8, 1968
*In the Wine Time*, December 10, 1968
*God Is a (Guess What?)*, December 17, 1968
*To Be Young, Gifted, and Black*, January 2, 1969
*Cities in Bezique*, January 4, 1969
*Ceremonies in Dark Old Men*, February 4, 1969
*The Perfect Party*, March 20, 1969
*An Evening of One Acts*, March 25, 1969
*Someone's Comin' Hungry*, April 13, 1969
*No Place to Be Somebody*, May 4, 1969

**1969–1970**

*Man Better Man*, July 2, 1969
*A Black Quartet*, July 30, 1969
*The Reckoning*, September 4, 1969
*Buck White*, December 2, 1969
*Five on the Black Hand Side*, December 10, 1969
*Sambo*, December 12, 1969
*The Harangues*, January 13, 1970
*Slave Ship*, January 13, 1970
*Billy Noname*, March 2, 1970
*Contributions*, March 9, 1970
*Purlie*, March 15, 1970
*Brotherhood*, March 17, 1970
*The Pig Pen*, April 29, 1970
*The Me Nobody Knows*, May 18, 1970
*Akokawe*, May 27, 1970

**1970–1971**

*Boesman and Lena*, June 22, 1970
*Les Blancs*, November 15, 1970
*Ododo*, November 17, 1970
*Perry's Mission/Rosalee Pritchett*, January 21, 1971
*In New England Winter*, January 26, 1971
*The Fabulous Miss Marie*, March 9, 1971
*The Dream on Monkey Mountain*, March 14, 1971
*Behold! Cometh the Vanderkellans*, March 31, 1971
*Underground*, April 18, 1971
*Ride a Black Horse*, May 25, 1971

**1971–1972**

*Charlie Was Here and Now He's Gone*, June 6, 1971
*Black Girl*, June 16, 1971
*Ain't Supposed to Die a Natural Death*, October 20, 1971
*The Black Terror*, November 10, 1971

*The Sty of the Blind Pig*, November 23, 1971
*El Hajj Malik*, November 29, 1971
*Inner City*, December 19, 1971
*Don't Let It Go to Your Head*, January 20, 1972
*Black Visions*, February 29, 1972
*The Duplex*, March 9, 1972
*A Ballet Behind the Bridge*, March 15, 1972
*Don't Bother Me, I Can't Cope*, April 19, 1972
*Frederick Douglass . . . Through His Own Words*, May 9, 1972
*Jamimma*, May 15, 1972
*Don't Play Us Cheap!*, May 16, 1972

**1972–1973**

*The Corner*, June 22, 1972
*Safari 300*, July 12, 1972
*Wedding Band*, September 26, 1972
*What If It Had Turned Up Heads?*, October 13, 1972
*A Recent Killing*, January 26, 1973
*Freeman*, February 5, 1973
*The River Niger*, March 27, 1973

**1973–1974**

*House Party*, October 16, 1973
*Raisin*, October 18, 1973
*The Great MacDaddy*, February 12, 1974
*What the Wine-Sellers Buy*, February 14, 1974
*Les Femmes Noires*, February 21, 1974
*American Night Cry*, March 7, 1974
*Black Sunlight*, March 19, 1974
*Nowhere to Run, Nowhere to Hide*, March 26, 1974
*Terraces*, April 2, 1974
*Heaven and Hell's Agreement*, April 9, 1974
*My Sister, My Sister*, April 30, 1974

**1974–1975**

*In the Deepest Part of Sleep*, June 4, 1974
*The Prodigal Sister*, November 25, 1974
*The Wiz*, January 5, 1975
*Black Picture Show*, January 6, 1975
*Liberty Call*, April 28, 1975
*The Taking of Miss Janie*, May 4, 1975
*Sugar-Mouth Sam Don't Dance No More/Orrin*, May 6, 1975
*The Moonlight Arms/The Dark Tower*, May 13, 1975
*Waiting for Mongo*, May 18, 1975
*Welcome to Hard Times*, May 20, 1975

**1975–1976**

*The First Breeze of Summer*, June 10, 1975
*Me and Bessie*, October 22, 1975
*So Nice They Named It Twice*, December 26, 1975
*Every Night When the Sun Goes Down*, February 15, 1976
*Bubbling Brown Sugar*, March 2, 1976
*Eden*, May 3, 1976
*For Colored Girls Who Have Considered Suicide/When the Rainbow Is Enuf*, May 17, 1976

**1976–1977**

*Livin' Fat*, June 1, 1976
*Guys and Dolls*, July 21, 1976
*I Have a Dream*, September 20, 1976
*The Brownsville Raid*, December 5, 1976
*Your Arms Too Short to Box with God*, December 22, 1976

**1977–1978**

*The Square Root of Soul*, June 14, 1977
*Cockfight*, October 7, 1977
*The Offering*, November 26, 1977
*A Photograph*, December 1, 1977
*Black Body Blues*, January 19, 1978
*Paul Robeson*, January 19, 1978
*Timbuktu!*, March 1, 1978
*The Twilight Dinner*, April 14, 1978
*The Mighty Gents*, April 16, 1978
*Ain't Misbehavin'*, May 9, 1978

**1978–1979**

*Eubie!*, September 20, 1978
*Nevis Mountain Dew*, December 7, 1978
*Daughters of the Mock*, December 20, 1978
*Plays from Africa*, January 10, 1979
*A Season to Unravel*, January 24, 1979
*Old Phantoms*, February 7, 1979

**1979–1980**

*Spell #7*, July 15, 1979
*But Never Jam Today*, July 31, 1979
*One Mo' Time*, October 22, 1979
*The Michigan*, November 16, 1979

*Comin' Uptown*, December 20, 1979
*Lagrima del Diablo*, January 10, 1980
*Companions of the Fire/Big City Blues*, February 7, 1980
*Reggae*, March 27, 1980
*Black Broadway*, May 4, 1980
*Home*, May 7, 1980

**1980–1981**

*It's So Nice to Be Civilized*, June 3, 1980
*Jazzbo Brown*, June 24, 1980
*The Sixteenth Round*, September 30, 1980
*Zooman and the Sign*, November 25, 1980
*Weep Not for Me*, January 27, 1981
*Sophisticated Ladies*, March 1, 1981
*In an Upstate Motel*, April 4, 1981
*Inacent Black*, May 6, 1981
*The First*, November 17, 1981
*A Soldier's Play*, November 28, 1981
*Dreamgirls*, December 20, 1981

Appendix II:

# A DISCOGRAPHY OF THE BLACK THEATRE

*Ain't Misbehavin'*, RCA Victor CBL-2-2966
*Ain't Supposed to Die a Natural Death*, A & M SP-3510
*At Home with Ethel Waters*, Monmouth-Evergreen MES-6812
*Ballad for Bimshire*, London AMS 78002
*Believers, The*, RCA Victor LSO-1151
*Billy Noname*, Roulette SROC-11
*Black Nativity*, Vee Jay VJS-8503
*Blackbirds of 1928*, Columbia OL-6770
*Bubbling Brown Sugar*, H & L Records, HL-69011
*Cabin in the Sky* (1940), Columbia CSP CCL 2792; (1964 revival), Capitol SW-2703
*Carib Song*, International Records B-401-6
*Carmen Jones*, Decca DL-8014/MCA 2054e
*Don't Bother Me, I Can't Cope*, Polydor PD-6013
*Don't Play Us Cheap!*, Stax STS 2-3006
*Eubie!*, Warner Bros. HS-3267
*Fly Blackbird*, Mercury OCS-6206
*For Colored Girls Who Have Considered Suicide/When the Rainbow Is Enuf*, Buddah BDS-95007OC
*Four Saints in Three Acts*, RCA LM-2756
*Guys and Dolls*, Motown M6-876S1
*Hallelujah, Baby!*, Columbia KOS-3090
*Hand Is on the Gate, A*, Verve FVS-9040-2
*Hello Dolly!* (Pearl Bailey), RCA Victor LSO-1147
*Hot Chocolates*, Smithsonian P 14587
*House of Flowers* (1954), Columbia CSP-COS-2320; (1968 revival), United Artists UAS-5180
*In White America*, Columbia OS-6030
*Inner City*, RCA Victor LSO-1171
*Jamaica*, RCA LSO-1103
*Jerico—Jim Crow*, Folkways FL-9671
*Kwamina*, Capitol SW-1645
*Lost in the Stars*, Decca 9120/MCA 2071e
*Me Nobody Knows, The*, Atlantic SD-1566
*Mrs. Patterson*, RCA Victor LOC-1017

*My People*, Contact CS-1
*One Mo' Time*, Warner Bros. HS-3454
*Porgy and Bess* (1940), MCA 2035e; (1953), RCA Victor LSC 2679; (1976, complete), RCA Victor ARL 3-2109.
*Purlie*, Ampex A-40101
*Raisin*, Columbia KS-32754
*St. Louis Woman*, Capitol DW-2742
*Shuffle Along*, New World NW-260
*Shuffle Along of 1952*, RCA Victor LPM-3154
*Simply Heavenly*, Columbia OL-5240
*Sophisticated Ladies*, RCA CBL-2-4053
*Tambourines to Glory*, Folkways FG-3538
*Wiz, The*, Atlantic SD-18137
*Your Arms Too Short to Box with God*, ABC AB-1004

# SELECTED BIBLIOGRAPHY

## PUBLISHED PLAYS

Several of the plays discussed in Part I of this work are included in the following anthologies:

Brasmer, William, and Dominick Consolo. *Black Drama. An Anthology.* Columbus, Ohio: Charles E. Merrill, 1970.
Bullins, Ed, ed. *The New Lafayette Theatre Presents.* New York: Anchor Press, 1974.
Hatch, James V., and Ted Shine, eds. *Black Theater, USA. Forty-five Plays by Black Americans, 1847-1974.* New York: The Free Press, 1974.
King, Woodie, and Ron Milner, eds. *Black Drama Anthology.* New York: New American Library, 1971.
Patterson, Lindsay. *Black Theater.* New York: New American Library, 1971.
Turner, Darwin T. *Black Drama in America.* Greenwich, Conn.: Fawcett, 1971.

The plays discussed in Part I are listed below by title with publication information following. References to the anthologies listed above will be in abbreviated form.

*Ain't Supposed To Die a Natural Death.* New York: Bantam Books, 1973.
*All God's Chillun Got Wings.* In O'Neill, Eugene, *Nine Plays by Eugene O'Neill.* New York: Modern Library, 1932.
*Amen Corner, The.* In Patterson, *Black Theater.*
*American Night Cry.* Indianapolis: Bobbs-Merrill Co., 1973.
*Andrew.* In Goss, Clay, *Homecookin'; Five Plays.* Washington, D.C.: Howard University Press, 1974.
*Anna Lucasta.* In Mantle, Burns, ed., *The Best Plays of 1944-1945.* New York: Dodd, Mead & Co., 1945.
*Appearances.* In Hatch and Shine, *Black Theater, USA.*
*Baptism, The.* New York: Grove Press, 1966.
*Big Time Buck White.* New York: Grove Press, 1969.
*Big White Fog.* In Hatch and Shine, *Black Theater, USA.*
*Black Girl.* New York: Dramatists Play Service, 1971.
*Black Picture Show.* Berkeley, Calif.: Reed, Cannon, Johnson Co., 1975.
*Black Quartet, A.* New York: New American Library, 1970.
*Black Terror, The.* In Bullins, *The New Lafayette Theatre Presents.*

*Blacks, The*. London: Faber & Faber, 1967.
*Blancs, Les*. New York: Samuel French, 1972.
*Blood Knot, The*. In Wellwarth, George E., *Themes of Drama: An Anthology*. New York: Thomas Crowell, 1973.
*Blues for Mr. Charlie*. New York: Dial Press, 1964.
*Boesman and Lena*. In Guernsey, Otis L., *The Best Plays of 1970-1971*. New York: Dodd, Mead & Co., 1971.
*Brotherhood*. In King and Milner, *Black Drama Anthology*.
*Carmen Jones*. New York: Knopf, 1945.
*Ceremonies in Dark Old Men*. New York: Farrar, Straus & Giroux, 1969.
*Chip Woman's Fortune, The*. In Turner, *Black Drama in America*.
*Cities in Bezique*. In Harrison, Paul Carter, ed., *Kuntu Drama; Plays of the African Continuum*. New York: Grove Press, 1974.
*Clara's Ole Man*. In Bullins, Ed, *Five Plays by Ed Bullins*. Indianapolis: Bobbs-Merrill Co., 1969.
*Companions of the Fire*. New York: Dramatists Play Service, 1980.
*Contributions*. In Brasmer and Consolo, *Black Drama. An Anthology*.
*Corner, The*. In King and Milner, *Black Drama Anthology*.
*Day of Absence*. In Hatch and Shine, *Black Theater, USA*.
*Don't Bother Me, I Can't Cope*. New York: Samuel French, 1972.
*Don't Play Us Cheap!* New York: Bantam Books, 1973.
*Dream on Monkey Mountain, The*. In Walcott, Derek, *The Dream on Monkey Mountain and Other Plays*. New York: Farrar, Straus & Giroux, 1971.
*Duplex, The*. New York: William Morrow and Co., 1971.
*Dutchman*. In Patterson, *Black Theater*.
*Eden*. New York: Samuel French, 1976.
*El Hajj Malik*. In Bullins, Ed, ed. *New Plays from the Black Theatre*. New York: Bantam Books, 1969.
*Electronic Nigger, The*. In Bullins, Ed. *Five Plays by Ed Bullins*. Indianapolis: Bobbs-Merrill Co., 1969.
*Emperor Jones, The*. In O'Neill, Eugene, *Nine Plays by Eugene O'Neill*. New York: Modern Library, 1932.
*Fabulous Miss Marie, The*. In Bullins, *The New Lafayette Theatre Presents*.
*First Breeze of Summer, The*. New York: Samuel French, 1973.
*Five on the Black Hand Side*. In Schotter, Richard, *The American Place Theatre*. New York: Delta, 1973.
*Fly Blackbird*. In Hatch and Shine, *Black Theater, USA*.
*For Colored Girls Who Have Considered Suicide/When the Rainbow Is Enuf*. New York: Macmillan, 1977.
*Freeman*. New York: Dramatists Play Service, 1973.
*Funnyhouse of a Negro*. In Brasmer and Consolo, *Black Drama. An Anthology*.
*Gentleman Caller, The*. See *Black Quartet, A*.
*Gettin' It Together*. New York: Dramatists Play Service, 1979.
*Goat Alley*. Cincinnati: Stewart Kidd Co., 1922.
*Golden Boy*. New York: Atheneum, 1965.
*Granny Maumee*. See *Rider of Dreams, The*.
*Great Goodness of Life*. In Harrison, Paul Carter, ed., *Kuntu Drama; Plays of the African Continuum*. New York: Grove Press, 1974.

*Great MacDaddy, The.* In Harrison, Paul Carter, ed., *Kuntu Drama; Plays of the African Continuum.* New York: Grove Press, 1974.
*Great White Hope, The.* New York: Dial Press, 1968.
*Green Pastures, The.* In Gassner, John, ed., *Twenty Best Plays of the Modern American Theatre.* New York: Crown, 1939.
*Happy Ending.* In Brasmer and Consolo, *Black Drama. An Anthology.*
*Harangues, The* (*Tribal Harangue Two*). In Richards, Stanley, *The Best Short Plays, 1971.* New York: Chilton, 1971.
*His First Step.* In Bullins, *The New Lafayette Theatre Presents.*
*Home.* New York: Dramatists Play Service, 1981.
*House of Flowers.* New York: Random House, 1968.
*In Abraham's Bosom.* In Green, Paul, *Five Plays of the South.* New York: Hill & Wang, 1963.
*In New England Winter.* In Bullins, Ed, ed., *New Plays from the Black Theatre.* New York: Bantam Books, 1969.
*In Splendid Error.* In Patterson, *Black Theater.*
*In the Wine Time.* In Patterson, *Black Theater.*
*In White America.* In Gassner, John, and Clive Barnes, eds., *Best American Plays, 6th Series.* New York: Crown, 1971.
*Jeb.* In Ardrey, Robert, *Plays of Three Decades.* London: Collins, 1968.
*John Henry.* New York: Harper & Row, 1939.
*Land Beyond the River, A.* Cody, Wyoming: Pioneer Drama Service, 1963.
*Life and Times of J. Walter Smintheus, The.* In White, Edgar, *The Crucificado.* New York: William Morrow, 1973.
*Lost in the Stars.* In Hewes, Henry, ed., *Famous American Plays of the 1940s.* New York: Dell, 1960.
*Malcochon.* See *Dream on Monkey Mountain, The.*
*Mamba's Daughters.* New York: Farrar, Straus & Giroux, 1939.
*Man Better Man.* In Gassner, John, ed., *The Yale School of Drama Presents.* New York: Dutton, 1964.
*Medal for Willie, A.* In King and Milner, *Black Drama Anthology.*
*Mighty Gents, The.* New York: Dramatists Play Service, 1980.
*Mister Johnson.* In Chapman, John, ed., *Theatre 1955.* New York: Random House, 1955.
*Moon on a Rainbow Shawl.* In Tynan, Kenneth, ed., *The Observer Plays.* London: Faber & Faber, 1958.
*Mulatto.* In Brasmer and Consolo, *Black Drama. An Anthology.*
*My Sister, My Sister.* New York: Samuel French, 1973.
*Native Son.* In Hatch and Shine, *Black Theater, USA.*
*Natural Man.* In Hatch and Shine, *Black Theater, USA.*
*Nevis Mountain Dew.* New York: Dramatists Play Service, 1980.
*No Place to Be Somebody.* In Patterson, *Black Theater.*
*Ododo.* In King and Milner, *Black Drama Anthology.*
*Old Phantoms.* New York: Dramatists Play Service, 1980.
*On Whitman Avenue.* New York: Dramatists Play Service, n.d.
*Orrin.* In Evans, Don, *The Prodigals.* New York: Dramatists Play Service, 1977.
*Our Lan'.* In Turner, *Black Drama in America.*
*Owl Answers, The.* In Hatch and Shine, *Black Theater, USA.*

*Paul Robeson*. Garden City, N.Y.: Doubleday, 1978.
*Photograph, A*. In Shange, Ntozake, *Three Pieces*. New York: Penguin Books, 1982.
*Pig Pen, The*. In Bullins, Ed, *Four Dynamite Plays*. New York: William Morrow, 1972.
*Porgy*. In Gassner, John, and Clive Barnes, eds., *Fifty Best Plays of the American Theatre*. New York: Crown, 1969.
*Porgy and Bess*. In Richards, Stanley, ed., *Ten Great Musicals of the American Theatre*. Philadelphia: Chilton Book Co., 1973.
*Prayer Meeting*. See *Black Quartet, A*.
*Prodigal Sister, The*. New York: Samuel French, 1974.
*Purlie*. New York: Samuel French, 1971.
*Purlie Victorious*. In Patterson, *Black Theater*.
*Raisin in the Sun, A*. In Patterson, *Black Theater*.
*Reckoning, The*. New York: Dramatists Play Service, 1980.
*Rider of Dreams, The*. In Locke, Alain, and Gregory Montgomery, eds., *Plays of Negro Life*. New York: Harper & Row, 1927.
*River Niger, The*. New York: Samuel French, 1973.
*Rosalee Pritchett*. New York: Dramatists Play Service, 1972.
*St. Louis Woman*. In Patterson, *Black Theater*.
*Shoes*. New York: Dramatists Play Service, 1972.
*Sign in Sidney Brustein's Window, The*. In Gassner, John, and Clive Barnes, eds., *Best American Plays, 6th Series*. New York: Crown, 1971.
*Simply Heavenly*. In Patterson, *Black Theater*.
*Sister Son/ji*. In Bullins, Ed, ed., *New Plays from the Black Theatre*. New York: Bantam Books, 1969.
*Slave, The*. In Hatch and Shine, *Black Theater, USA*.
*Slave Ship*. Newark, N.J.: Jihad Productions, 1977.
*Son Come Home, A*. In Bullins, Ed, *Five Plays by Ed Bullins*. Indianapolis: Bobbs-Merrill Co., 1969.
*Soldier's Play, A*. New York: Hill & Wang, 1981.
*Song of the Lusitanian Bogey*. In Weiss, Peter, *Two Plays*. New York: Atheneum, 1970.
*Spell #7*. In Shange, Ntozake, *Three Pieces*. New York: Penguin Books, 1982.
*String*. New York: Dramatists Play Service, 1971.
*Sty of the Blind Pig, The*. Indianapolis: Bobbs-Merrill, 1973.
*Sugar Mouth Sam Don't Dance No More*. In Evans, Don, *The Prodigals*. New York: Dramatists Play Service, 1977.
*Take a Giant Step*. In Patterson, *Black Theater*.
*Taking of Miss Janie, The*. In Hoffman, Ted, ed., *Famous American Plays of the 1970s*. New York: Dell, 1981.
*Tambourines to Glory*. In Smalley, Webster, ed., *Five Plays by Langston Hughes*. Bloomington: Indiana University Press, 1963.
*Tiger, Tiger Burning Bright*. Cleveland: World Publishing Co., 1963.
*To Be Young, Gifted, and Black*. New York: Samuel French, 1971.
*Toilet, The*. In Turner, *Black Drama in America*.
*Trials of Brother Jero, The*. Nairobi: Oxford University Press, 1969.
*Trouble in Mind*. In Patterson, *Black Theater*.
*Walk Hard*. In Hatch and Shine, *Black Theater, USA*.

*Warning, The—A Theme for Linda.* See *Black Quartet, A.*
*Wedding Band.* New York: Samuel French, 1972.
*What If It Had Turned Up Heads?* In Bullins, *The New Lafayette Theatre Presents.*
*What the Wine-Sellers Buy.* New York: Samuel French, 1974.
*Who's Got His Own?.* In King and Milner, *Black Drama Anthology.*

## BOOKS, ARTICLES, AND DISSERTATIONS

Abramson, Doris E. *Negro Playwrights in the American Theatre, 1925-1959.* New York: Columbia University Press, 1969.

Alkire, Stephen Robert. "The Development and Treatment of the Negro Character as Presented in American Musical Theatre, 1927-1968." Ph.D. diss., Michigan State University, 1972.

Arata, Esther Spring. *More Black American Playwrights.* Metuchen, N.J.: Scarecrow Press, 1978.

______, and Nicholas John Rotoli. *Black American Playwrights, 1800 to the Present.* Metuchen, N.J.: Scarecrow Press, 1976.

Belcher, Fannin S. *The Place of the Negro in the Evolution of the American Theatre, 1767-1940.* Ann Arbor, Mich.: University Microfilms, 1945.

Bigsby, C.W.E. "Black Drama in the Seventies." *Kansas Quarterly* 3 (2), 1971, pp. 10-20.

Blesh, Rudi, and Harriet Janis. *They All Played Ragtime.* New York: Oak Publications, 1971.

Bogle, Donald. *Brown Sugar.* New York: Harmony Books, 1980.

Bond, Frederick W. *The Negro and the Drama.* Washington, D.C.: McGrath, 1969.

Brawley, Benjamin. *The Negro Genius: A New Appraisal of the Achievement of the American Negro in Literature and the Fine Arts.* New York: Dodd, Mead & Co., 1937.

Brown, Elizabeth. "Six Female Black Playwrights. Images of Blacks in Plays by Lorraine Hansberry, Alice Childress, Sonia Sanchez, Barbara Molette, Martie Charles, and Ntozake Shange." Ph.D. diss., Florida State University, 1980.

Brown, Lorraine. "A Story Yet to Be Told." *Black Scholar* (July-August 1979), 70-78.

Brown, Sterling, Ulysses Lee, and Arthur Davis, eds. *The Negro Caravan: Writings by American Negroes.* New York: Arno Press, 1969.

Bumsted, J. M. "Ridgely Torrence's Negro Plays: A Noble Beginning." *South Atlantic Quarterly* 68 (1), 1969, pp. 96-108.

Burton, Jack. *The Blue Book of Tin Pan Alley.* New York: Century House, 1950.

Busacca, Basil. "Checklist of Black Playwrights: 1823-1970." *Black Scholar* (September 1973), pp. 48-54.

Chapman, Abraham, ed. *Black Voices: An Anthology of Afro-American Literature.* New York: New American Library, 1968.

Charters, Ann. *Nobody: The Story of Bert Williams.* New York: Macmillan, 1970.

Clark, V. A. "Archaeology of Black Theatre." *Black Scholar* 10 (1979), pp. 43-56.

Craig, E. Quita. *Black Drama of the Federal Theatre Era.* Amherst: University of Massachusetts Press, 1980.

Cruse, Harold. *The Crisis of the Negro Intellectual: From Its Origin to the Present.* New York: William Morrow, Inc., 1967.

Cuney-Hare, Maud. *Negro Musicians and Their Music.* New York: Da Capo Press, 1974.

Emanuel, James. *Langston Hughes.* New York: Twayne, 1967.

Fabre, Geneviève E. *Afro-American Poetry and Drama, 1760-1975.* Detroit: Gale Research Co., 1969.

Fisher, Rudolph. *The Conjur Man Dies: A Mystery Tale of Dark Harlem.* New York: Corvici-Friede, 1932.

Funke, Lewis. *The Curtain Rises: The Story of Ossie Davis.* New York: Grosset, 1971.

Goodman, Gerald Thomas. "The Black Theatre Movement." Ph.D. diss., University of Pennsylvania, 1974.

Haley, Elsie Galbreath. "The Black Revolutionary Theatre: LeRoi Jones, Ed Bullins, and Minor Playwrights." Ph.D. diss., University of Denver, 1971.

Hall, Frederick Douglass, Jr. "The Black Theatre in New York from 1960-1969." Ph.D. diss., Columbia University, 1973.

Hansberry, Lorraine. *The Movement: Documentary of a Struggle for Equality.* New York: Simon and Schuster, 1964.

Harrison, Paul Carter. *The Drama of Nommo.* New York: Grove, 1972.

Hatch, James V. *Black Image on the American Stage: A Bibliography of Plays and Musicals, 1770-1970.* New York: DBS Publications, 1970.

______. "Theodore Ward, Black American Playwright." *Freedomways* 15 (First Quarter 1975), p. 39.

______, and Omanii Abdullah. *Black Playwrights, 1823-1977: An Annotated Bibliography of Plays.* New York: R. R. Bowker, 1977.

Hicklin, Fannie. *The American Negro Playwright, 1920-1964.* Ann Arbor, Mich.: University Microfilms, 1965.

Hill, Edward Steven. "A Thematic Study of Selected Plays Produced by the Negro Ensemble Company." Ph.D. diss., Bowling Green State University, 1975.

Hill, Errol, ed. *The Theater of Black Americans.* 2 vols. Englewood Cliffs, N.J.: Prentice-Hall, 1980.

Houseman, John. *Run-Through.* New York: Simon and Schuster, 1972.

Huggins, Nathan. *Harlem Renaissance.* New York: Oxford University Press, 1971.

Hughes, Langston, and Milton Meltzer. *Black Magic: A Pictorial History of the Negro in American Entertainment.* Englewood Cliffs, N.J.: Prentice-Hall, 1967.

Isaacs, Edith. *The Negro in the American Theatre.* New York: Theatre Arts, 1947.

Johnson, Helen Armstead. "Playwrights, Audiences, and Critics." *Negro Digest* 19 (April 1970), p. 18.

Johnson, James Weldon. *Along This Way.* New York: Viking Press, 1945.

______. *Black Manhattan.* New York: Knopf, 1930.

Kaiser, Ernest, and Robert Nemiroff. "A Lorraine Hansberry Bibliography." *Freedomways* 19 (1979).

Kimball, Robert, and William Bolcom. *Reminiscing with Sissle and Blake.* New York: Viking Press, 1973.

Kornweibel, Theodore, Jr. "Theophilus Lewis and the Theater of the Harlem Renaissance." In Arna Bontemps, ed., *The Harlem Renaissance Remembered.* New York: Dodd, Mead & Co., 1972.

Locke, Alain, and Montgomery Gregory, eds. *Plays of Negro Life.* New York: Harper and Brothers, 1927.

Lovell, John, Jr. *Black Song: The Forge and the Flame.* New York: Macmillan, 1972.
Miller, Jeanne-Marie A. "Black Women Playwrights from Grimké to Shange." In Gloria T. Hull, Patricia Bell Scott, and Barbara Smith, eds., *But Some of Us Are Free.* Old Westbury, N.Y.: Feminist Press, 1982, pp. 280-296.
______. "Dramas by Black American Playwrights Produced on the New York Professional Stage (From 'The Chip Woman's Fortune' to 'Five on the Black Hand Side')." Ph.D. diss., Howard University, 1976.
______. "Images of Black Women in Plays by Black Playwrights." *CLA Journal* 20 (June 1977), pp. 494-507.
______. "Successful Federal Theatre Dramas by Black Playwrights." *Black Scholar* (July-August 1979), 79-85.
Mitchell, Loften. *Black Drama: The Story of the American Negro in the Theatre.* New York: Hawthorn Books, 1967.
______. "The Negro Theatre and the Harlem Community." *Freedomways* 3 (Summer 1963), p. 392.
Monroe, John Gilbert. "A Record of the Black Theatre in New York City." Ph.D. diss., University of Texas, 1980.
O'Connor, John, and Lorraine Brown. *Free, Adult, Uncensored: The Living History of the Federal Theatre Project.* Washington, D.C.: New Republic Books, 1978.
Ogunbiyi, Yemi. "New Black Playwrights in America (1960-1975): Essays in Theatrical Criticism." Ph.D. diss., New York University, 1976.
Oliver, Clinton F. *Contemporary Black Drama.* New York: Scribner, 1971.
Over, William. "New York's African Theatre: The Vicissitudes of the Black Actor." *Afro-Americans in New York Life and History* 3 (1979), pp. 7-13.
Paris, Arthur. "Cruse and the Crisis in Black Culture: The Case of Theater, 1900-1930." *Journal of Ethnic Studies* 5 (1979), pp. 51-68.
Patterson, Lindsay, ed. *Anthology of the American Negro in the Theatre.* New York: Publishers Co., 1967.
Riley, Clayton. "Lorraine Hansberry: A Melody in a Different Key." *Freedomways* 19 (1979), pp. 205-212.
Roach, Hildred. *Black American Music.* Boston: Crescendo Publishing Co., 1973.
Rose, Al. *Eubie Blake.* New York: Schirmer Books, 1979.
Ross, Ronald P. *Black Drama in the Federal Theatre, 1935-1939.* Ann Arbor, Mich.: University Microfilms, 1972.
______. "The Role of Blacks in the Federal Theatre Project, 1935-1939." *Journal of Negro History* (January 1974), pp. 38-50.
Sampson, Henry T. *Blacks in Blackface.* Metuchen, N.J.: Scarecrow Press, 1980.
Sanders, Leslie Catherine. "From Shadows to Selves: Developing the Black Theatre in America." Ph.D. diss., University of Toronto, 1978.
Sherr, Paul C. "*Change Your Luck*: A Negro Satirizes White America." *Phylon* 32 (1971), pp. 281-289.
Shockley, Ann Allen, and Sue P. Chandler. *Living Black American Authors.* New York: R. R. Bowker, 1973.
Southern, Eileen. *The Music of Black Americans.* New York: Norton, 1971.
Stearns, Marshall and Jean. *Jazz Dance.* New York: Schirmer Books, 1979.
Toll, Robert C. *Blacking Up: The Minstrel Show in Nineteenth-Century America.* New York: Oxford University Press, 1974.

Turner, Darwin. "The Negro Dramatist's Image of the Universe, 1920-1960." *CLA Journal* 5 (December 1961), pp. 106-120.

———, and Jean Brights, eds. *Images of the Negro in America.* Boston: D. C. Heath and Co., 1965.

Vacha, J. E. "Black Man on the Great Way." *Journal of Popular Culture* 7 (1973), pp. 283-301.

Vance, Joel. *Ain't Misbehavin'. Fats Waller: His Life and Times.* New York: Berkley Medallion Books, 1979.

Walker, Ethel Pitts. "The American Negro Theatre: 1940-1949." Ph.D. diss., University of Missouri, Columbia, 1975.

Waters, Ethel, with Charles Samuels. *His Eye Is on the Sparrow.* New York: Doubleday & Co., 1950.

Wilson, Robert Jerome. "The Black Theatre Alliance: A History of Its Founding Members." Ph.D. diss., New York University, 1974.

Young, Artee Felicita. "Lester Walton: Black Theatre Critic." Ph.D. diss., University of Michigan, 1980.

# NAME INDEX

Page numbers in italic type indicate the location of the main entry.

# PLAY AND FILM INDEX

Page numbers in *italic* type indicate the location of the main entry.

# SONG INDEX

# NOTES ON CONTRIBUTORS

DORIS E. ABRAMSON is a professor in the Department of Theatre at the University of Massachusetts. She is the author of *Negro Playwrights in the American Theatre, 1925-1959* (1969).

ROBERT COGSWELL, a folklorist, studied at Vanderbilt and Indiana universities and now teaches at the University of Louisville. Among his interests are traditional humor, the relationships between Afro-American and Anglo-American folklore, and early phonograph recordings. His current research focuses on black-face comedy in the twentieth century.

GRACE COOPER is associate professor of English Studies at the University of the District of Columbia. She has been active in community theatre since the age of five when she joined the Children's Theater of Washington as an actress. She has continued acting. She is also a playwright, her most notable work being a children's play, *Kojo and the Leopard*, which has played at university, school, and community theatres across the United States. She holds the doctoral degree in psycholinguistics from Howard University.

ROSEMARY CURB is associate professor of English at Rollins College. Dr. Curb's articles have recently appeared in *Chrysalis*, *Kentucky Folklore Record*, *Theatre Journal*, *MELUS Journal*, and the book *Women in the American Theatre*. Her book *Decade of Revolution: Afro-American Drama in the 1960s* is being published by Columbia University Press.

ROBERT FELGAR is associate professor of English at Jacksonville State University. In addition to his book, *Richard Wright* (1980) (Twayne), he has published articles in *College Language Association Journal*, *Black American Literature Forum*, and *Studies in Black Literature*. His work has also appeared in *Browning Newsletter*, *Browning Society Notes*, and *Studies in Browning and His Circle*.

GERALD T. GOODMAN is an associate professor of English at Delaware State College. He received a Ph.D. in British and American Drama from the University of Pennsylvania. He serves as a film critic for the *Delaware State News* and is the co-producer for "In Perspective," a radio series dealing with the humanities.

HENRY HENRIKSEN, of Minneapolis, Minnesota, has done research on phonograph companies, and has written articles on Gennet, Black Patti, Autograph, and Herschel Gold Seal.

SANDRA MAYO is writing her Ph.D. dissertation at Syracuse University. She is a developing scholar in black theatre history, literature, and performance. She has taught black theatre at several universities and has directed numerous black plays.

JEANNE-MARIE A. MILLER is an administrator and an associate professor of English at Howard University. She has published numerous articles on black playwrights and their works and is currently the editor of the *Black Theatre Bulletin*. She was formerly an associate editor of *Theatre Journal*, a publication of the American Theatre Association. In 1972, she received an award for her articles on black theatre in *Black World* magazine.

LOUIS H. PRATT is chairman of the Department of Languages and Literature at Florida A & M University. He is the recipient of the first J. Russell Reaver Award for the best creative scholarship in American literature or folklore at Florida State University. His recent publications include the Twayne critical study, *James Baldwin* (1978), and an article on Frank Yerby in *The Critical Survey of Short Fiction* (1981), edited by Frank N. Magill.

RONALD P. ROSS teaches history and literature at various universities in southern California. He received a Ph.D. in history from the University of Southern California in 1972 and has contributed articles to scholarly journals, including the *Journal of Negro History*, and to such collections of black theatre criticism as the recently published *Twentieth Century Views* series. Ross's primary research focus has been on the role of blacks during the Federal Theatre period.

MARION ROYDHOUSE, a Ph.D. recipient from Duke University, is an assistant professor of history at the University of Delaware. She is currently researching women and labor reform in the twentieth century.

MICHAEL SAFFLE, assistant professor of music and humanities at Virginia Polytechnic Institute & State University, completed his doctoral studies at Stanford University and the University of Bonn, West Germany.

His articles and reviews on musical subjects have appeared in *The Musical Quarterly*, the *Journal of the American Liszt Society*, and the *Bulletin of the Council for Research in Music Education.*

LESLIE SANDERS received her Ph.D. from the University of Toronto in 1978. She currently teaches humanities and English at Atkinson College, York University, in Downsview, Ontario. Her main interests are in Afro-American and Caribbean literature, particularly drama, and related critical questions.

YVONNE SHAFER was educated at the University of California at Santa Barbara, Stanford, and the University of Iowa. Her articles have appeared in *Women in the American Theatre*, *Theatre Journal*, *Theatre Design and Technology*, *CLA*, and other journals. She has frequently taught courses on black drama and black theatre history.

WEBSTER SMALLEY is professor of drama and former chairman of the Department of Drama at the University of Texas at Austin. He has edited *Five Plays by Langston Hughes* (1963) and has written a number of plays (including *The Man with the Oboe* and *The Boy Who Talked to Whales*). In addition, he has produced many plays by new playwrights. Smalley is a member of the American Theatre Association, the National Theatre Conference, and The Players.

WERNER SOLLORS teaches in the Department of English and Comparative Literature of Columbia University. A graduate of the Freie Universität Berlin, he is the author of *Amiri Baraka/LeRoi Jones: The Quest for a "Populist Modernism"* (1978) and of articles on docudrama, the melting pot, and ethnicity in the United States.

**About the Author**

ALLEN WOLL is Associate Professor of History at Rutgers University, Camden, New Jersey. He is the author of *A Functional Past: The Uses of History in Nineteenth-Century Chile*, *The Latin Image in American Film*, *Puerto Rican Historiography*, *The Hollywood Musical Goes to War*, and *Songs from Hollywood Musical Comedies* and articles in *History and Theory*, *Journal of Latin American Studies*, *Journal of the History of Ideas*, *Journal of Popular Film*, and *Journal of Popular Culture*.